Draculas, Vampires, and Other Undead Forms

Essays on Gender, Race, and Culture

Edited by
John Edgar Browning
Caroline Joan (Kay) Picart

The Scarecrow Press, Inc.
Lanham, Maryland • Toronto • New York • Plymouth, UK
2009

SCARECROW PRESS, INC.

Published in the United States of America
by Scarecrow Press, Inc.
A wholly owned subsidiary of
The Rowman & Littlefield Publishing Group, Inc.
4501 Forbes Boulevard, Suite 200, Lanham, Maryland 20706
www.scarecrowpress.com

Estover Road
Plymouth PL6 7PY
United Kingdom

British Library Cataloguing in Publication Information Available

Library of Congress Cataloging-in-Publication Data

Draculas, vampires, and other undead forms : essays on gender, race, and culture
/ edited by John Edgar Browning, Caroline Joan (Kay) Picart.
    p. cm.
  Includes bibliographical references and index.
  ISBN 978-0-8108-6696-6 (hardback : alk. paper) — ISBN 978-0-8108-6923-3
(e-book)
  1. Dracula films—History and criticism. 2. Vampire films—History and
criticism. 3. Sex role in motion pictures. 4. Racism in motion pictures. 5.
Culture in motion pictures. I. Browning, John (John Edgar) II. Picart, Caroline
Joan, 1966–
  PN1995.9.D64D735 2009
  791.43'675—dc22
                    2008054143

∞™ The paper used in this publication meets the minimum requirements of
American National Standard for Information Sciences—Permanence of Paper
for Printed Library Materials, ANSI/NISO Z39.48-1992.
Manufactured in the United States of America.

Contents

Foreword

David J. Skal

$\mathcal{T}$he word *vampire* has almost become synonymous with *Dracula* in the 111 years since Bram Stoker wrote his indestructible novel, one of the best-selling books of all time. But Stoker's conception of the vampire has shape-shifted and fragmented throughout the world in ways he would barely comprehend, and probably not even recognize.

"Dracula" broke radically with an earlier, romantic conception of the vampire that had been popularized in literature, theatre, and opera, but itself was preceded by an animalistic, zombie-like creature of European folklore. However, as this eclectic anthology amply demonstrates, the vampire mythos was never confined to Europe, nor to Hollywood. Every culture in recorded time has had its own legends of hungry ghosts who feed on the energy of the living, in one way or another. And very few of them bear much resemblance to Bela Lugosi descending a staircase, holding a solitary, flickering candle that improbably lights the entire cavernous great hall of his castle for the legendary cinematographer Karl Freund.

It would actually take a thousand points of light (black light?) to really do the job, and this book adds considerably more illumination to the shadows of Dracula's abode by exploring "Draculas" rather than the vampire king in isolation. Dwight Frye's Renfield is hardly Dracula's solitary guest in Tod Browning's landmark film, which, however flawed cinematically, galvanized centuries of world folklore, literature, and the performing arts into an image so indelible that it has blocked our appreciation and understanding of the much larger context of ravenous revenants. That empty castle hall is, in essence, a reeling ballroom of the unseen undead.

It took a long time for horror as a category to be taken seriously by academics, and vampire studies in particular have exploded to the point that it is difficult to keep up with every book, essay, or documentary on this bottomless subject. *Draculas, Vampires, and Other Undead Forms* takes a useful step back from the standard obsession revolving around Bram Stoker and his maddeningly problematic text, however influential it is.

I hope you will enjoy this unique trans/cultural exploration of Transylvania as much as I have. *Transylvania*, of course, means "across the forest," and this volume does much to let us deeply examine the forest, not just a single tree.

Acknowledgments

We owe a considerable debt of gratitude to all contributors to this book for their infinite patience, willingness, and encouragement. We would also like to extend our gratitude to several dedicated people—particularly Stephen Ryan at Scarecrow Press for his editorial guidance, Jessica McCleary and others at Rowman & Littlefield Publishing Group for their editorial assistance, and our indexer, Jennifer Rushing-Schurr—without whom this collection could not have been brought to completion. Kay would like to thank her family, who has always been supportive of her numerous pursuits; John J. Stuhr, James Brummer, and Raymond Fleming, for their mentorship and collegiality across the years; and Jerry Rivera, for his love and faithful devotion. John would like to personally thank David J. Skal, for keeping an old dream alive; and Tim, for putting up with endless nights of editing. We would also like to thank and commend the following graduate students at Louisiana State University, whose copyediting skills and precision are matched only by their kindness (listed alphabetically): Andrew Banecker, Helana Brigman, Kevin Casper, Mel Coyle, Laura Keigan, Laura Marks, Kris Mecholsky, Anna Nelson, and Conor Picken. This collection has also benefited greatly from the generosity of the following (in no particular order): Boum Productions Ltd. and Andy Starke at Mondo Macabro; the Internet Movie Database (IMDb); PhotoFest; James Clatterbaugh at *Monsters from the Vault*; McFarland & Company, Inc., and Andrew Hock-Soon Ng and Jimmie E. Cain; Scarecrow Press and Donald Glut; the *Chicago Sun-Times* and Roger Ebert; Creaig A. Dunton at the *Journal of Criminal Justice and Popular Culture*; Fairleigh Dickinson University Press; and Julien Yoseloff at Associated University Presses. Copyright in the illustrations is the property of the production or distribution companies concerned.

Introduction: Documenting Dracula and Global Identities in Film, Literature, and Anime

John Edgar Browning and Caroline Joan (Kay) Picart

> We all know Dracula, or think we do, but . . . there are many Draculas—and still more vampires who refuse to be Dracula or to play him. . . . [V]ampires are easy to stereotype, but it is their variety that makes them survivors.[1]

*P*rompting this book are two things: First is the complex and highly porous framework that is *Dracula*'s, one that has accommodated an intricate web of interrelationships with historical, cultural, and literary counterparts since its inception. Most recognizable among *Dracula*'s offspring is a conventional body of cinematic works by studios like Universal (1930s–1940s, 1979, 2004) and Hammer (1950s–1970s), and more recently, Columbia (1992) and Dimension (2000). Partially illuminating, partially distorting, partly educating, partly stereotyping, this "mainstream" body of cinematic work includes horror/docudramas like *Bram Stoker's Dracula* (1992), for example, that blur the boundaries separating history from fiction. In addition are the earlier Hammer narratives like *Dracula A.D. 1972* (1972) and *Dracula* (1958, *Horror of Dracula* [US title]), whose use of color and overtly sexual overtones are juxtaposed with the social ills and hysterias of the time to project the new symbolic and psychological *other* embodied by Christopher Lee as the Count. And even earlier are the black and white narratives by, among others, Universal, with films like *Abbott and Costello Meet Frankenstein* (1948), *Dracula's Daughter* (1936), and *Dracula* (1931).

The prototypical use of symbolic fear, shadow (*mise-en-scène*), gender inversion, and genre hybridization inaugurated by these early black and white narratives, which help to found Dracula's parentage in cinema, is essential for building our earliest conceptualization of "Dracula/ness" and entrenching Dracula's popularity in global markets. But it's not until *Dracula* goes into the public domain in the early 1960s that we really begin to understand just how entrenched Dracula had become in cultures outside of England and America; it is also here that Dracula's transformation into a "cultural body" and performance space (wherein ideological tensions swell and contract) becomes realized. Foreign markets and nonmajor production studios begin to outproduce "mainstream" cinematic depictions of Dracula by a ratio of at least 3:1 over the next thirty years, literally affording him an almost ravenous multiplicity in markets outside of England and America, in venues besides film, and in genres beyond conventional horror.[2]

Second, it is this significantly larger, yet predominantly underappreciated (and less explored) body of cinematic work—again mainly fiction—that precipitates the bulk of the anthology proposed here. Little known, this body of cinematic work by mostly non-Universal, non-Hammer, and nonmajor American production companies is in dire need of discovery, cataloging, and critical commentary. These films remain mostly obscure as a result of their having little circulation and exposure in countries dominated by major production companies, and yet these films attest to Dracula's tendency to transcend cultural, historical, and geographical boundaries. Furthermore, an intersectional analysis of not only gender, media (i.e., TV products and anime), and ideological tensioning, but also race and nationality (i.e., East-West, Dracula's "cross-cultural fertilisation" [Ng's term]) is instructive in understanding the complexity Dracula embodies outside of the conventional strain of films and analyses with which the vampire is typically envisaged in Western imaginary. Clearly, there stands a greater need to address this gap in current scholarship on Dracula and vampire films than any other.

Questions about what it means to be Dracula, or a Dracula-type character, are increasingly germane to the dominant representations solidified by Universal and Hammer. Thus, the reach of this collection of essays is far ranging and varied, prompting us to examine the various theoretical frames and cultures that may be useful in analyzing Dracula's global impact. However, while this anthology seeks to investigate and explore the impulse by which global communities continue to reinvent predominantly Dracula figures in film, it is also concerned with non-Dracula (i.e., pseudo) figures, culturally specific vampires, and various other vampire-type creatures (or hybrid undead creatures) as well, who, at times, may be better suited than Dracula to confront oppression or repression, or to embody social ills and taboos, as Dracula has done in various parts of the world at various times. Thus, theoretical analyses of the trans/national generation of Dracula's cinematic offspring largely represent the focus of this collection of essays, but not completely. These essays examine Dracula films and the ways in which Dracula's movement across borders of nationality, sexuality, ethnicity, gender, and film genre since the 1920s has engendered conflicting conceptualizations about the formation of the "other," identity, and ideology that oscillate between conservative and liberal spheres of normalcy. Essays in this anthology utilize single-film, multifilm, literary, period-based, and geographically based analyses.

With the focus of this book targeting predominantly Dracula and Dracula-type characters, and to a somewhat lesser degree culturally specific vampires (or hybrid undead creatures), in film, anime, and literature from predominantly non-Anglo markets, this anthology offers perspectives that seek to ground, again, mainly Dracula depictions and experiences within a larger political, historical, and cultural framework. It seeks to identify how different ethnic groups and nationalities represent themselves and their distinct movements across borders in the Dracula cinema myth. Chapters may focus on isolating new developing tendencies toward trans/national modes of cultural production, or may instead excavate and trace past tendencies from older depictions.

Chapters dealing with various thematic threads about Dracula research (e.g., the continuum between "fact" and "fiction" in Dracula visualizations; how gender, class, race, and sexuality are integral parts of the process of documenting the evolution of Dracula through film and other visual media; the less discussed aspects of the subgenre, such as representations of homosexuality or lesbianism, and of gender-specific violence), along with selected topics that examine variations of the Dracula cinema myth and vampirism, are crucial to giving this anthology its comprehensiveness. In specific, we intentionally sought chapters from both established and burgeoning scholars, who reside not only in the United States, but also in England, Canada, Spain, Ireland, Malaysia, and Australia, and whose analyses extend beyond commonly anthologized national borders like England and the United States. In addition to these conventional areas, this body of work also includes—in larger part—Slovakia, Europe, Germany, China, Japan, Pakistan, and Malaysia.

TACKLING RACE, GENDER, AND MODES OF NARRATION IN AMERICA

In Mary Shelley's *Frankenstein* (1818), Victor recounts:

> It was on a dreary night of November, that I beheld the accomplishment of my toils. With an anxiety that almost amounted to agony, I collected the instruments of life around me, that I might infuse a spark of being into the lifeless thing that lay at my feet. It was already one in the morning; the rain

pattered dismally against the panes, and my candle was nearly burnt out, when, by the glimmer of the half-extinguished light, I saw the dull yellow eye of the creature open; it breathed hard, and a convulsive motion agitated its limbs.[3]

It is a peculiar thing that we should liken a collection of essays on global depictions of Dracula to Frankenstein's Monster. After all, Dracula is, or once was, human, whereas Frankenstein's Monster is merely the sum of many human parts, his birth having parthenogenic origins (i.e., "male self-birthing"). (Dracula, at least, had a mother and came from a biological womb, as opposed to an artificial womb.) The story of the birthing of Frankenstein's Monster, in many ways, is about our hopes and anxieties about the brave new worlds science can potentially make possible. In contrast, the narrative of Dracula seems its converse: it is about the primordial, dark matter that resists the rationalism of science—the "old magic" that science, as the "new magic," cannot completely counter, as the eternal resurrections of Dracula attest, despite Van Helsing's numerous stakings.

But are Frankenstein's Monster and Dracula's global progeny (examined holistically) really that different from one another? On the one hand, Frankenstein's Monster is an amalgam of many parts. But on the other hand, Dracula has engendered and is engendered by many subspecies and subparts of himself all over the world, and his flexibility has played host to an entourage of geographies, divergent beliefs and religions, and culturally specific vampire(-types), like the Malaysian *pontianak* (always female) or the Chinese *jiangshi* (also *chiang-shih*, *goeng si*, or *kiang shi*, Stein notes).

The following chapters engage the challenging ways in which global communities have accommodated Dracula and vampire configurations through their increasingly commercialized cultures. Individually, these chapters chronicle isolated moments in Dracula's and the vampire's filmography. However, the hybridization of these figures illuminates an ongoing cultural negotiation, wherein Dracula's body is transformed into a sort of global community. Our comparison between Frankenstein's Monster and Dracula's body as "global community" is consistent with Jeffrey Cohen's postulation that "The Monstrous body is pure culture."[4] Nevertheless, the stitching and assembling we do here with Dracula's body of films is ugly, bloody work that renders coherence only when all the pieces are together.

Like Europe and Asia, America too has seen no shortage of variations on Stoker's text or his infinitely porous aristocratic vampire. In part I, "Tackling Race, Gender, and Modes of Narration in America," six essays seek to address the ways in which issues of gender, race, and narration have converged, hybridized, and complicated one another in American *Dracula* and vampire narratives. Ambivalences surrounding narration and profit-driven serialization are particularly germane to Dracula's earliest conceptualization in American cinema. We therefore begin this section with an essay by Gary D. Rhodes, an established Bela Lugosi scholar. Rhodes's "Manly P. Hall, *Dracula* (1931), and the Complexities of the Classic Horror Film Sequel" explores a previously unmentioned film treatment for a *Dracula* (1931) sequel written in the late 1930s by Bela Lugosi's friend Manly P. Hall. Hall's "character names and actions," Rhodes points out, "are an obvious variation on those created by Bram Stoker, and initially they seem to be the expected conclusion to a Hollywood vampire movie." Instead, they describe the opening scene in Hall's treatment; thus, the familiar chapel sequence that concludes *Dracula* (1931) is, in effect, a beginning, rather than an ending. Hall's proposed sequel to Universal Studios's *Dracula*, with Hall's friend Lugosi in the title role, was a sort of "freelance effort," Rhodes exclaims, "intended to revive a popular character." However, by the time Hall had completed his somewhat belated *Sequel to Dracula* (working title), America's horror film industry of the sound era (then, still in its infancy) had begun to face problems of its own between "clear narrative resolution," as Rhodes puts it, that the three-act-structure Classical Hollywood Style demanded, and serialization, which resulting audience consensus and projected ticket sales necessitated. Ultimately, Rhodes brings into observation three distinct approaches to horror film serialization that Hollywood offered in the 1930s, while addressing Hall's treatment in detail.

If it is the narrative constraints of America's horror film industry of the sound era that frame the first chapter, then it is the political and cultural importance of narration-as-change that inhabits the second. Relying heavily on primary materials, and to some extent on secondary ones, Paul R. Lehman and John Edgar Browning's chapter, "The *Dracula* and *Blacula* (1972) Cultural Revolution," offers an interesting reappraisal of AIP's *Blacula* (1972) and *Scream, Blacula, Scream* (1973), arguing that, unlike the common variety of campy, self-parodying blaxploitation films by which scholars typically generalize films of this era, the *Blacula*s offer much more, in that they can be productively read against the backdrop of the 1970s cultural and civil rights movements, which "began to weigh in on the legitimacy of 'racial' division in America." In Lehman and Browning's view, these films function rhetorically to "alleviate and de-legitimize some of the ethnic biases ingrained in the 'white' and 'black' consciousness of the 1970s" by providing a model to the film industry from which to diminish African Americans' negative stereotyped images and attitudes about themselves.

In the next chapter, continuing the prior chapter's trajectory of mapping out how the "reel" and "real" worlds of "monstrosity" interact with each other, "The Compulsions of Real/Reel Serial Killers and Vampires: Toward a Gothic

Criminology," Picart and Greek demonstrate the overlap of vampiric themes in serial murder films. The most gripping and recurrent visualizations of the "monstrous" in the media and film lay bare the tensions that underlie the contemporary construction of the "monstrous," which ranges in the twilit realm where divisions separating fact, fiction, and myth are porous—a gothic mode. The constructions of two monstrous figures in contemporary popular culture—the serial killer and the vampire—blur into each other, and powerfully evoke not only our deepest fears and taboos, but also our most repressed fantasies and desires. Their presence shows how "primordial evil," using Paul Ricoeur's phenomenology, becomes recognizable as an essential narrative feature of the dread that "senseless murderers," like serial killers, seek to inspire, eliciting the same type of response as a vengeful deity. This chapter also tracks a significant change in the depiction of the vampire in more recent literary Gothic popular novels; for example, in Fred Saberhagen's *The Dracula Tape* (1975); Anne Rice's *Interview with the Vampire*; and Jody Scott's *I. Vampire* (1984)—novels wherein vampires acquire the authorial voice. In crafting their own narratives, such vampires become more sympathetic, more superhumanly human, and much less radically the "other."

However, where this move toward establishing the monstrous other as a site of identification becomes particularly disturbing is with the serial killer, the most compelling monster that dominates the last part of the twentieth century. While *sympathy* is not precisely the word to describe the response encouraged by serial killer narratives, as Picart and Greek point out in their analysis of fictional serial killer films, there is often nevertheless a certain ambivalence in the representations of modern monsters. In docudramas such as *Henry: Portrait of a Serial Killer* (1986) and *Ed Gein* (2000), the serial killer as an abused abuser emerges; in horror films such as *The Silence of the Lambs* (1991) and *Immortality* (1991), vampiric aristocraticism and Byronic sex appeal become key features of the mythic serial killer. The ongoing fascination with vampires and serial killers, both in the Hollywood film and criminological case studies, points to the emergence of a "Gothic criminology," with its focus on themes such as blood lust, compulsion, godlike vengeance, and power and domination. Rather than assuming that film is a medium that tells us little about the reality of criminological phenomena, Gothic criminology as envisaged here recognizes the complementarity of academic and aesthetic accounts of deviant behavior.

Continuing the examination of the complex ways in which behavior and identity converge (and diverge) in vampire narratives is Lisa Nystrom's chapter, which examines feminist and masculinist discourses in *Dracula*. Nystrom's "Blood, Lust, and the Fe/Male Narrative in *Bram Stoker's Dracula* (1992) and the Novel (1897)" draws parallels between what she terms "Female power" in

Francis Ford Coppola's film version of Stoker's *Dracula* and the novel itself. Nystrom problematizes the claim that Stoker's text is one of patriarchal dominance, arguing instead "that behind the testosterone-fueled exchanges between *Dracula*'s male protagonists lies a second narrative, which is driven by a presence that is most definitely female." Critics have argued, Nystrom aptly points out, that Coppola's film version fails at times to translate "much of Stoker's original vision from page to screen." However, Nystrom maintains that Coppola's film version does, at least, retain much of "Stoker's individual commentary relating to women and to Female power" and, in fact, reenvisages the novel's strong female presence, even extending the female subplot in the film. Thematically, Coppola's film version elevates Female power by "allowing for a more layered and detailed female presence than [the novel originally] permitted," but at the same time, this power is diluted, Nystrom notes, through the female characters' association in the film with Dracula; thus, the female presence in Coppola's film version is simultaneously liberating and restrictive.

Continuing the analysis of gender and vampires in relation to Gothic themes, Justin Everett's chapter, "The Borg as Vampire in *Star Trek: The Next Generation* (1987–1994) and *Star Trek: First Contact* (1996): An Uncanny Reflection," examines the reworking of vampire and Gothic motifs through the characters of the Borg and the Borg Queen. Developed over a series of *Star Trek: TNG* episodes and a feature-length film, the foreboding presence of the Borg, Everett points out, forever darkens the "optimistic future" creator Gene Roddenberry envisioned for *Star Trek*. Through the television incarnations, "the Borg are used to explore the relationship between humanity and machine intelligence, and particularly the themes of individuality, perfection, and the desirability or horror of human/machine interfacing." However, a largely unexplored aspect of the Borg becomes pronounced in *First Contact* through their "Gothic journey in the direction of vampirism," and through their ruler, the Borg Queen, whose "corpse-like pallor[,] 'royal' status," infectious "fang-like appendages," "endeavor to acquire (i.e., assimilate) property (i.e., worlds) to which she is a foreigner," and whose "role as a sensuous devourer" afford her Dracula-type qualities.

In line with this theme, sometimes vampiric and Dracula-type qualities infectiously propagate with unconventional sex (i.e., nonmale) and gender (i.e., nonmasculine), as in the opposing extreme of inversion when the *femme fatale* figure (like the Borg Queen) is replaced by the hypermasculinized (i.e., "butch") lesbian. Though the serial killer might seem to call for the most emphatic reassertion of social norms and the strongest reaffirmation of conservative values, this is, however, rarely the case in fictional narratives,[5] at least for male serial killers. As Picart and Greek point out in the next chapter,

"When Women Kill: Undead Imagery in the Cinematic Portrait of Aileen Wuornos," when serial killers are female and lesbian (and poor), it is not the glamorous vampire, but the ambivalently fearful and pitiful creature envisaged by Mary Shelley that becomes the monstrous metaphor, as shown in the fictional and documentary depictions of Aileen Wuornos. Male rogue serial murderers are typically construed as having vampiric qualities and embody the primordial evil that such murderers seek to inspire, assuming the status of a vengeful deity in relation to their victims. However, once a *female* rogue serial killer (and particularly a lesbian one) becomes the object of the narrative, it is less that of the vampire (which is aligned with the archetype of the male serial killer in popular film) than the Frankensteinian Monster, who becomes the main analogue. The topic of this chapter is focused specifically on depictions of Aileen Wuornos (and in particular Charlize Theron's interpretation of Wuornos) as a Frankensteinian Monster rather than a vampire or Dracula-type figure. Because vampires have a certain glamour about them, this aristocratic glamour is denied female serial killers, in terms of the teratologic mythic imagery given to them. In giving Wuornos the Frankensteinian creature image (an unloved creature in search of love, betrayed by the woman she loved), the film renders her worthy of pity, and not of the kind of "awe" that male serial killers have, in the popular imagination.

WORKING THROUGH CHANGE AND
XENOPHOBIA IN EUROPE

In part II, "Working through Change and Xenophobia in Europe," four essays address the European geographies with which Dracula and vampires have come to be associated; British fears about the arrival of foreigners; the "horrors" of modernity and decadence on conservative value systems; and the presence of universalism and global hegemony through *Dracula*. In the first chapter in part II, "Return Ticket to Transylvania: Relations between Historical Reality and Vampire Fiction," Santiago Lucendo investigates how the vampire is less of a "superstition imported from the 'East'" than it is "a series of fears and fancies projected over a territory badly or totally unknown." For many of us, Transylvania is neither a region of modern-day Romania, Lucendo points out, nor is it just Stoker's setting for the novel, but a location that years of images, literature, cinema, and television have (mis)constructed. Lucendo argues that the geographical settings represented in *Dracula* and vampire literature "are not themes secondary to the vampire but main ones, and they are the result of many versions and remakes of the same places." The significance of geographical setting in vampire literature "transcends mere location," Lucendo claims, because landscape, architecture, and maps "affect the image of the monster as much as its actions and its iconographic attributes." The vampire is a construction that is under continuous development, an assemblage of words, images, and places especially that almost resembles a Frankensteinian creature. From the beginning, Lucendo contends, "the vampire has been a culturally constructed body, reflecting the historical, political and social frameworks surrounding it, and it has served, both racially and geographically, as a space in which the fears and desires of a particular (i.e., dominant, 'ruling') culture can be played out."

In a convergent argument, Jimmie Cain's chapter, "Racism and the Vampire: The Anti-Slavic Premise of Bram Stoker's *Dracula* (1897)," posits that the fascination with foreign landscapes is overshadowed by Victorian anxieties about and contempt for the persons residing there, particularly Eastern European and Russian Jews. Their immigration to England, and the threat of disease and contaminants with which they were associated, "engender[s] a profusion of anti-Semitic literature." Stoker, according to Cain, incorporates in the villain of Dracula "such accounts of the immigrant Jews crowding the dilapidated and poorly drained slums of London's East End. The Count's residence at Carfax, in Purfleet, for instance, is well to the east of downtown London, near the Whitechapel district, the epicenter of the London immigrant community." It is obvious that Stoker appropriates attributes of the Jewish immigrant in his conception of Dracula, but Cain contends that Stoker's conceptualization equally "projects anxieties about a much more real and powerful threat to England and Victorian culture in the figure of the monstrous count: the Slavic menace posed by imperial Russia." In Stoker's research for *Dracula*, he consulted a number of works from that period about the geography, peoples, and customs of Eastern Europe that would have provided him with adequate materials for constructing a Slavic, Russian villain.

The next chapter, Paul Newland's "The Grateful Un-Dead: Count Dracula and the Transnational Counterculture in *Dracula A.D. 1972* (1972)," moves forward in time and ideals about race. Newland's chapter considers the ways in which Hammer's *Dracula A.D. 1972* (Christopher Lee's second to the last installment as Dracula for Hammer) represents "a contemporary world of moral and socio-cultural ambiguity in which the figure of Count Dracula effectively remains on the periphery of events." Despite the ensuing horror of Dracula's resurrection in the film through a ceremony held by a countercultural group of young thrill-seeking friends, who at once represent multiple races, classes, and genders but "who seem unable to decide whether to resurrect older un-dead hippy ideals of 'free love,' to embrace coeval interests in satanic practices, or to embrace the bourgeois lifestyle of their elders," Newland argues that the film's real horror "derives from a playing out of these concerns." *Dracula A.D. 1972* has received very little critical attention, Newland points out, despite the film's "resonat[ion] with the ruptures occurring across Western popular culture during the late 1960s and early 1970s." A reappraisal of the film, Newland hopes, may "facilitate a broader understanding of the ways in which a complex array of transnational cultural identities came into conflict during this period, and how and why, at the same time, underground cultural practices were effectively inculcated into mass cultural forms."

Concluding part II is Martina G. Lüke's chapter, "*Nosferatu the Vampyre* (1979) as a Legacy of Romanticism," which builds upon the Romantic literary and artistic traditions. Lüke surveys topics and motifs of Romanticism in this remake of F. W. Murnau's *magnum opus*, such as conflicts between the individual and society, sanity and insanity, love and death, dreams and reality, as well as the film's use of setting and music. Romanticism's fascination with and repulsion by the "exotic" visually intersects here with the "foreign" figure of Dracula, who is not only geographically but physically "other" (e.g., long fingernails, pale skin color, and rat-like fangs). Often, however, the Romantics saw the "savage" as "purer" in some ways, or more "genuine." A central feature of this adaptation by Werner Herzog can be seen in Dracula's unconventional stylization. Klaus Kinski's portrayal of Dracula in the film is neither the monster driven by bloodlust (e.g., in movies such as Stephen Norrington's *Blade* [1998] or Quentin Tarantino's *From Dusk Till Dawn* [1996]) nor the elegantly suave nobleman Lugosi and Lee personify, nor is Kinski's portrayal the phallic (i.e., "stiff"), "mechanical nightmare" of Murnau's post-WWI version. Instead, Herzog's remake reveals a deeply disturbed Dracula who "longs for redemption. He is the lonely outsider who would love to join the others" but who is instead damned to harm others and live forever (or as Dracula [Kinski] sees it, "to be unable to grow old [and die]"). Herzog's appropriation of Romantic themes foregrounds emotions and fantasies, Lüke writes, that unite global identities, thus highlighting the film's relevance in a globalized community of Draculas. Of course, over time there have been different strains of Romanticism, and many of them have had a national temper; some are lighter, and others, darker.

IMPERIALISM, HYBRIDITY, AND CROSS-CULTURAL FERTILIZATION IN ASIA

The final six essays in this anthology make up part III, "Imperialism, Hybridity, and Cross-Cultural Fertilization in Asia." Demons, ghosts, and culturally specific vampires more ancient than their American and European cousins have long haunted the literatures and folktales of Asia. Andrew Hock-Soon Ng's chapter, "'Death and the Maiden': The *Pontianak* as Excess in Malay Popular Culture," examines perhaps the most fearsome of Malay folkloric creatures, the *pontianak*, one of the vampire's more cryptic and less familiar in-laws. The *pontianak*, a strictly female vampiric creature, is characterized by "ear-piercing shrieks, overflowing hair, and a penchant for the blood of children." However, even though we attribute the term *vampire* to the *pontianak*, Ng exclaims, her Western nuances shy considerably in comparison to her roots in Malay folklore and popular culture, specifically through film. Various films during the 1950s–1960s in Malaysia (and again in 2004) helped to popularize the *pontianak* "as a hybrid creature that blends Eastern and Western vampiric characteristics." However, these cinematic representations have confusingly blurred and multiplied "the *pontianak*'s signifiers to the point that it is no longer clear where popular culture ends and traditional belief begins." Ng highlights, among other things, the *pontianak*'s ambiguous configuration, and how popular culture has reconstituted folklore for mass consumption. Ng also looks at the manner in which "cross-cultural fertilisation (East-West) has come to inform the construction of the *pontianak*," particularly in one of Malaysia's more recent films *Pontianak Harum Sundal Malam* (*Pontianak of the Tuber Rose* [2004]) by Shuhaimi Baba, which Ng examines in depth.

Continuing the examination of "local" vampires, Sean Moreland and Summer Pervez's chapter, "Becoming-Death: The Lollywood Gothic of Khwaja Sarfraz's *Zinda Laash* (*Dracula in Pakistan* [US title], 1967)," examines the interesting phenomenon of a culturally specific "Dracula," a rarity among films. Like Ng's *pontianak*, Moreland and Pervez's "local" vampire (i.e., Dracula) construction is obviously a transplantation of a Western model to Pakistan. However, instead of the "racially and linguistically coded outsider" we get with Dracula, the Dracula figure in *Zinda Laash*, Professor Tabani, "is recognizably a South Asian domestic, but one who bears stigma suggestive of a deleterious Western influence." Professor Tabani, Moreland and Pervez write, is "the product of an invasion which has already long since occurred." The actor who plays the professor stylistically mirrors (perhaps through a glass darkly) both Lugosi and Lee, a method that, combined with Tabani's attire (iconic of the Western Draculas) and his hunger for knowledge and power in place of the cultural and religious mores he has outright rejected, "renders him a striking embodiment of anxieties surrounding the long-term effects of British colonial control, Western cultural influence, and unchecked technological change." Moreland and Pervez assert that in decontextualizing Stoker's narrative away from Orientalist xenophobia, *Zinda Laash* simultaneously reterritorializes the *Dracula* text in a manner that foregrounds the film's "ambiguous status as an uneasy hybridization of Western cinematic influence and Pakistani cultural identity, which is often perceived as threatened not just by the encroachments of Western culture per se," but by Bollywood's thriving industry in nearby India.

The next chapter, Dale Hudson's "Modernity as Crisis: *Goeng Si* and Vampires in Hong Kong Cinema," also draws upon postcolonialism to examine its vampires. Ricky Lau Koon-wai's *Goeng si sin sang* (aka *Mr. Vampire* [Hong Kong: English title], 1985) inaugurated a profitable cycle of *goeng si* ("stiff corpse") films that relied on conventions from martial arts, comedy, and horror from major commercial film industries like Hong Kong, Hollywood, Japan, Britain, and others. Generally known in the Anglophone world as a "Chinese hopping vampire," the *goeng si*, Hudson notes, is a trans/cultural figure that ushered in a new attraction for Hong Kong cinema that translated well into a regionally, if not globally, exportable commodity. However, with the cycle's exhaustion by the late 1980s, a number of films emerged that placed the *goeng si* in dialogue, and sometimes in debate, Hudson exclaims, with European/Hollywood Dracula-type vampires. Hudson's chapter attempts to situate a selection of such films against both Hong Kong's ensuing crisis of modernity that followed its transition after 150 years as a Crown Colony to the future that awaited it as a Special Administrative Region of the People's Republic of China, and against post–Cold War globalization. Ripe with "'crisis emotions' of nostalgia, fear, and despair as discussion about the handover commenced, and 'crisis bodies'" gave to Hong Kong a "mutable cultural space that has been subjected to rapid transformations."

Also tapping into postwar(s) ambivalences about power, rule, and the impact of the West on the Far East is Wayne Stein's chapter, "Enter the Dracula: The Silent Screams and Cultural Crossroads of Japanese and Hong Kong Cinema." Stein problematizes the ability of very politicized Western narratives and figures, like Dracula and vampires, for example, to translate effectively in lands that share very different belief and value systems. More importantly, Stein adds, this mistranslation raises questions about these texts and figures that a purely Western politics, one that "defines normative behavior in terms of its own moral and religious conventions," cannot answer. In specific, "horror as a genre presents a strong case in point where cultural transparencies can fail." With only enough time to examine a short survey of Eastern films and animes that offer supporting examples of cultural mistranslation and failed attempts at relocating Westernized Dracula and vampire narratives onto Eastern shores, Stein discusses what, he terms, the lack of moral authenticity presents in Western-Eastern narratives. Such incommensurabilities emerge, for example, when Judeo-Christian religious underpinnings are pit-ted against the metaphysics of Buddhism and Confucianism, as well as the more local traditions of Taoism (Hong Kong) and Shintoism (Japanese).

As in the case of our next chapter, Nicholas Schlegel's "Identity Crisis: Imperialist Vampires in Japan?" Westernized Dracula and vampire narratives are sometimes less the product of cultural mistranslation and more projections of concerns about identity and modernity, and fears of foreign rule and occupation. Schlegel explores a trio of Japanese-financed, produced, directed, and distributed films commonly referred to as the Toho Dracula Trilogy: *Legacy of Dracula* (*Yûreiyashiki no kyôfu: Chi o suu ningyô* [Japanese title], 1970), *Lake of Dracula* (*Noroi no yakata: Chi o sû me* [Japanese title], 1971) and *Evil of Dracula* (*Chi o suu bara* [Japanese title], 1974). Directed by Michio Yamamoto and written by Ei Ogawa, Hiroshi Nagano, and Masaru Takesue, these three vampire films draw from a Western Gothic aesthetic that has incited the authors "to structure a formal inquiry into the *raison d'être* behind their inception and creation." These films uncover simultaneously a budding fascination with the West and a deep anxiety toward it, a dynamic that allows for Japanese national identity to manifest itself in the subtext of these films. However, key to locating this identity, Schlegel argues, is "defining what Japanese identity *is* and what it is *not*."

To close this corpus, Wayne Stein and John Edgar Browning's chapter, "The Western Eastern: Decoding Hybridity and Cyber*Zen* Goth(ic) in *Vampire Hunter D* (1985)," takes us to the mid-1980s using a hybrid text that amalgamates various genres like action, horror, fantasy, sci-fi, and Western. Conceived in the tradition of the American frontier Gothic, the Japanese anime *Vampire Hunter D* (*Bampaia hantâ D*, 1985) grapples with themes previously examined in this section: the cultural mistranslation of East-West that we saw in the Stein chapter, and the Japanese national identity and the ways in which it is manifested through Japan's fascination with and anxiety toward the West that we see in the Schlegel chapter. In this final chapter by Stein and Browning, we encounter a more effective juxtaposition of East-West cultural and religious identity, as *Vampire Hunter D* "uncovers or extends our understanding of a Gothic that is at once American frontier-defined and also uniquely Japanese" while at the same time "mak[ing] lucid the (inter-)complexities of what we call Japanicity." In doing so, Stein and Browning help to identify a new mode of spirituality that defines what they call "Cyber*Zen* Gothic," a construction that blends Eastern and Western Gothic/ness and transcends convention, identity, "as well as the forces of hybridity that surface from such a union."

The rich spectrum of these essays evoke how relationships connecting "fact" and "fiction," sex and gender, Eastern and Western cultural exchange, are not easily demarcated relations, and that the construction of Dracula/ness lies uneasily across apparently simplistic binaries—such as the binary between Frankenstein's Monster and Dracula. Ultimately, both are myths of origins (births) and immortality (death-rebirths). Both vampires and other undead creatures reveal and conceal our anxieties and hopes concerning possible utopic-dystopic new worlds, in their own culturally specific and historically grounded ways. These teratological accounts plot each culture's attempts to define what is "the same" or "normal" and what is "other" or "monstrous." Though rhetorical, literary, and film critics often cannot point to clear causal effects, the use of these various methodologies offers help in tracing the ways in which cultures and nationalities appropriate, mold, and reshape porous, malleable figures like Dracula and the vampire.

NOTES

1. Nina Auerbach, "Introduction," *Our Vampires, Ourselves* (Chicago: University of Chicago Press, 1995), 1.
2. John Edgar Browning and Caroline Joan (Kay) Picart, *The Dracula Film, Comic Book, and Game Sourcebook* (Jefferson, NC: McFarland and Company, forthcoming).
3. Mary Shelley, *Frankenstein: The 1818 Text, Contexts, Nineteenth-Century Responses, Modern Criticism*. A Norton Critical Edition, ed. J. Paul Hunter (New York: W. W. Norton and Company, 1996), 34.
4. Jeffrey Jerome Cohen, "Monster Culture (Seven Theses)," in *Monster Theory: Reading Culture*, ed. Jeffrey J. Cohen (London and Minneapolis: University of Minnesota Press), 4.
5. David Punter and Glennis Byron, *The Gothic* (Oxford, UK: Wiley-Blackwell Publishing, 2004), 265.

Part I

TACKLING RACE, GENDER, AND MODES OF NARRATION IN AMERICA

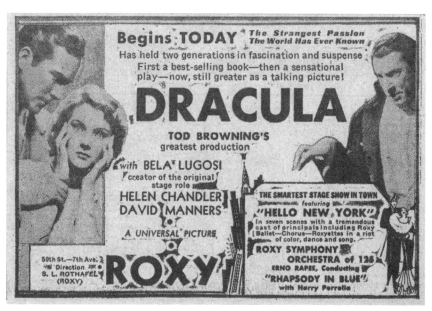

Newspaper ad for *Dracula* (1931). *Courtesy of John Edgar Browning*

Manly P. Hall, *Dracula* (1931), and the Complexities of the Classic Horror Film Sequel

Gary D. Rhodes

In the ruined chapel of Castle Dracula stands the ancient crumbling sarcophagus of the vampire. On the front is an armorial crest of Transylvanian nobility and the word DRACULA cut in great, deep letters.

Van Helsing and four other men are tugging frantically at the heavy stone lid. The last rays of the setting sun are filtering through broken casements and are shining upon the massive tomb. The vampire must be destroyed before the coming of the night. He is mortal only while sleeping through the daylight hours on the earth of his native land.

At last the heavy lid gives way and the five men gaze down upon the body of the vampire horrible in sleep. Van Helsing resolutely grasps the sharpened wooden stake. As he stands over the body of Dracula, the last ray of sunlight fades from the face of the vampire. Dracula awakes, leering hideously. It is now night and he is immortal.

Without a word Van Helsing drives the stake through Dracula's heart. The vampire howls with fiendish glee and shams death.

Their work done, the five depart.[1]

The quoted scene is a familiar one, with the specific words written by Manly P. Hall for a 1939 film treatment. The character names and actions are an obvious variation on those created by Bram Stoker, and initially they seem to be the expected conclusion to a Hollywood vampire movie. However, the text instead describes the opening scene in Hall's treatment: "When the last

---

This chapter originally appeared in *Monsters from the Vault*, vol. 13, issue 25 (June 2008).

sound of their footsteps has faded away, Dracula opens his eyes. 'Too late, you fools,' he hisses, 'the sun has set.'"

The chapel sequence is thus a beginning, not an ending. Hall's treatment was a proposed sequel to Universal Studios' *Dracula* (1931) with Bela Lugosi, a freelance effort intended to revive a popular character. That the vampire hunters have staked the Count after sunset means he does not die. Hall's opening scene concludes with the description: "Slowly the form of the vampire turns into a shimmering mist in which only the head remains visible. The weird plasma oozes over the side of the sarcophagus and vanishes into the dim corridors of the castle." Dracula lives, or—perhaps more accurately—lives again.

By the time Manly P. Hall crafted his *Sequel to Dracula* (working title), the US horror film of the sound era had already faced the conflict between—on the one hand—the clear narrative resolution demanded by the three-act structure of the Classical Hollywood Style, and—on the other hand—the continuation of storylines through sequels as necessitated by perceived audience interest and resulting ticket sales. For example, how can Dracula return if he was destroyed in a film witnessed by the very audiences who want to see him again? To provide answers to these questions, Hollywood offered three distinct approaches to creating horror film sequels in the 1930s.

HORROR FILM SEQUELS OF THE 1930s

One approach to sequels attempted to satisfy marketing demands, while completely avoiding the dilemma of continuing a resolved narrative. For example, when the Halperin Brothers made a sequel to their 1932 box-office hit *White Zombie*, they did not try to revive the lead villain (Murder Legendre, played by Bela Lugosi) or even return to the setting of Haiti. Their *Revolt of the Zombies* (1936) not only invented an entirely new cast of characters (and actors), but also used Cambodia as a setting. Advertising materials implied that *Revolt* was a sequel, even though it was not.

Warner Brothers proved even more adept at this approach with their film *The Return of Doctor X* (1939). The title suggests the return of the title character in *Doctor X* (1932), portrayed by Lionel Atwill. In addition to a completely different cast than its predecessor, *The Return of Doctor X* was about a *different* Dr. X, played by Humphrey Bogart. The word "Return" in the title, even if it intentionally implied a continuation of the 1932 storyline, was apparently justified by the fact that the new Dr. X had been brought back to life, returned from the dead.

Another approach of the 1930s horror film sequel was to attempt to continue the earlier storyline using the same setting and at least some of the original character names and cast members. In this approach, openings became endings, meaning that the scripts of sequels revisited the conclusions of the earlier films in an attempt at narrative continuity. The results manifested as the "further adventures" of the same characters and/or their family members.

The first example of this tactic came in Ernest B. Schoedsack's *The Son of Kong* (1933), released only eight months after its predecessor *King Kong* (1933), directed by Schoedsack and Merian C. Cooper. The film is set approximately one month after Kong wreaked havoc in New York City; the character Carl Denham, who captured Kong on Skull Island and presented him to high society in New York in the first film, hides from news reporters and an impending indictment. Once again, actor Robert Armstrong plays Denham. Similarly, the characters Englehorn and Charlie the Cook also return; they are once again portrayed by actors Frank Reicher and Victor Wong. Rather than revive the same ape who died in *King Kong*, the characters return to Skull Island and find his offspring.

Curiously, James Whale's *Bride of Frankenstein* (1935)—released nearly three and a half years after *Frankenstein* (1931)—goes to even greater lengths to force narrative coherence. The original film suggests that Frankenstein's Monster (Boris Karloff) is burned to death in a fire at a windmill. Whale begins *Bride* with a framing device where Mary Shelley (Elsa Lanchester), author of the novel *Frankenstein*, informs her onscreen friends—and thus the audience—that her story did not end at the windmill. The Shelley character attempts to add veracity to the fact the conclusion of the first film was not a conclusion and that she had intended for the tale to continue.

Bride's storyline (after the Shelley framing device) begins only moments after the first film ended. The windmill scene features the return of the Monster, who has survived the fire in an underground cellar full of water. As the film progresses, the audience sees and hears clips from the 1931 film as a further way of connecting the two films. Whale's tale somewhat logically explains the survival of the Monster, and the validity of the narrative connections is furthered by the reappearance of actors Colin Clive and Boris Karloff.

A third key example of this approach to horror film sequels is *Dracula's Daughter* (1936). Though directed by Lambert Hillyer instead of Tod Browning, *Dracula's Daughter* attempts to follow logically from its predecessor. Released five years and three months after *Dracula* (1931), the sequel begins by showing Renfield at the bottom of a staircase, dead at Dracula's hands, as shown in the earlier film. Then Van Helsing emerges from the catacombs having staked Dracula, only to encounter two policemen; as in the 1931 original, Edward Van Sloan portrays Van Helsing. Though Dwight Frye does not return as the deceased Renfield, the replacement hides his face with his arm to conceal the inconsistency. Vampirism then continues in England thanks to Countess Zaleska (Gloria Holden), who refers to herself as "Dracula's Daughter."

To be sure, all three of these examples do feature some (arguably minor) changes that may not have been desirable. The hillside set and Frankenstein lab in *Bride of Frankenstein* appear different than in *Frankenstein*; the same is true with Carfax Abbey in *Dracula's Daughter* versus Carfax Abbey in *Dracula*. In *Bride*, actress Valerie Hobson played Henry's wife, taking the place of Mae Clarke in the original. In *Dracula's Daughter*, Edward Van Sloan's character name changes slightly to "Von Helsing." And then there are a few characters who disappear without explanation. Ann Darrow (Fay Wray) doesn't return in *The Son of Kong*, nor do Mina (Helen Chandler), Jonathan Harker (David Manners), and Dr. Seward (Herbert Bunston) in *Dracula's Daughter*.

Despite these small discrepancies, *The Son of Kong*, *Bride of Frankenstein*, and *Dracula's Daughter* vigorously attempt to draw connections to prior films. Their shared goal is important enough that, for the sake of audience members who did not see the originals or might have forgotten elements of them, clear narrative exposition occurs. To this end, a young news reporter tells Denham information that he already knows in *The Son of Kong*, "You're the man who brought [Kong] here," a fact duplicated on a poster hanging in his tiny New York apartment. "I had no choice. Naturally, I destroyed him," Van/Von Helsing says in *Dracula's Daughter* to underscore his role in the earlier film. Making sense with the past, at least to the degree possible, seems to be the paramount concern.

By contrast, a third approach to the horror film sequel emerges in Rowland V. Lee's *Son of Frankenstein* (1939). *Bride* ended with the explosion of the Monster, the Bride, and Dr. Pretorius inside the laboratory. Rather than attempt to explain the discrepancy or cohere with the film's conclusion, *Son* chooses to ignore it. In fact, it chooses to ignore *Bride* entirely. For example, *Son* makes no mention of the Bride or Dr. Pretorius. The Monster no longer possesses the ability to talk as he did in *Bride*. How he has survived the explosion is not addressed either, outside of Ygor's vague mention that the Monster "Cannot be destroyed. Cannot die."

Lee does attempt to connect his film with the overall series, particularly with the casting of Boris Karloff as the Monster. But the attention to details is (perhaps intentionally) very loose. In *Son*, the Frankenstein family home is situated for the first time in a town called "Frankenstein." Henry has become Heinrich, a German equivalent, but a name never spoken in the earlier films. These changes seem all the more important when remembering the fact that the 1931 *Frankenstein* was in reissue during late 1938 and early 1939.

Rather than a marketing ploy like *Revolt of the Zombies* or a modernist attempt at narrative conformity like *Bride of Frankenstein, Son of Frankenstein* began to open the door to an increasingly postmodernist approach toward film sequels: pick and choose from the past, discard major characters, change important details, and ignore major discrepancies. The internal logic of the series was no longer the dominant factor.

Whether or not Manly P. Hall saw the films under discussion is unknown. Even if he did view them, he may not have perceived the typology under analysis here. But when he chose to pen what he called *Sequel to Dracula* (a working title) in 1939, Hall had to contend with the fact that Van Helsing killed Dracula in the 1931 film. That act was essentially re-created in *Dracula's Daughter* in 1936, a film in which Countess Zaleska (Gloria Holden) burns his corpse: "His body is in ashes," she declares. Bringing Dracula back to the screen would require some careful thought.

MANLY P. HALL, SCREENWRITER

Manly P. Hall was born in Canada and came to the United States with his parents at the age of two. By 1919, he had settled in Los Angeles, which he would use as his base until the time of his death.[2] During his lifetime, Hall gave over 7,000 lectures and wrote a large array of articles, essays, and books. His topics ranged from *The Lost Keys of Freemasonry* and *The Phoenix* to *Alchemy* and the *Holy Grail*. He also investigated all manner of occult subjects.

But Hall remains most famous for having founded in 1934 the Philosophical Research Foundation. In Hall's words, their goal was to "enable the individual to develop a mature philosophy of life, to recognize his proper responsibilities and opportunities, and to understand and appreciate his place in the unfolding universal pattern."[3] The foundation charged no membership dues and made available an enormous library of books and artifacts. The latter included Chinese oracle bones, Babylonian tablets, an Egyptian papyrus of *The Book of the Dead*, and a Japanese Buddhist Sutra written in blood.[4]

To help spread their word, Hall spoke on the radio several times in the 1930s.[5] Starting in 1941, he published the *PRS Journal*. He also spoke year after year on everything from Zen culture to space-age religion.[6] At the time of his death in 1990 at the age of eighty-nine, he was still giving biweekly talks at the foundation, which has continued to operate into the twenty-first century.

During his lengthy and productive life, Hall had various encounters with the Hollywood studios. For example, his story *When Were You Born?* became a William McGann film at Warner Brothers in 1938. The mystery tale of astrology and horoscopes starred Anna May Wong and Margaret Lindsay.[7] As it was being produced, Hall told the press:

> There is a ready-made audience of 10,000,000 for definitely metaphysical themes in the United States—in addition to the general public. It is the richest untouched field of entertainment that remains to be exploited, for nearly every human being has had an experience he cannot explain, yet cannot forget! And in such times as these, we turn eagerly toward that which may provide a clue, a key, to the Answer.

He added that he was aware of many different "obscure" subjects that could become the subjects of Hollywood films.[8]

In addition to *When Were You Born?* Hall penned at least two stories for Bela Lugosi, *The Emperor of Atlantis* and *The Mysterious Abbe.* In the latter, Lugosi would have played a French clergyman who solved crimes with arcane scientific knowledge. A surviving photograph shows Lugosi in test costume and makeup as the Abbe, apparently taken to help pitch the story to Warner Brothers sometime during the mid-to-late thirties.[9] In the end, the studio rejected both ideas.

Exactly how and when Hall and Lugosi became friends is difficult to determine, but they knew each other possibly as early as 1935. Abandoning formal education at an early age, Lugosi tried to compensate the rest of his life by voracious reading. He was likely drawn to Hall's intellectual abilities, as well as some of the specific topics Hall studied; he also must have appreciated the fact that Hall was a fellow stamp collector.

Later, Universal hired Hall to hypnotize Lugosi for the 1940 film *Black Friday.* According to the studio, Hall hypnotized Lugosi to add realism to his death scene in the film, though the event was little more than a publicity stunt. Years later, Lugosi enjoyed remembering that he and Hall had faked the entire episode.[10] Footage of Hall and Lugosi on the set appeared in a (now apparently lost) 1940 newsreel, as well as in the coming attraction trailer, which still survives.[11]

Their association continued until Lugosi's death in 1956, as the press repeatedly noted. In 1942, a syndicated column claimed that Hall had arranged for Lugosi to speak at an astrologer's convention in San Francisco, but that Lugosi declined because the stars declared he shouldn't travel.[12] In 1955, when Lugosi requested help in overcoming his drug addiction, newspapers mentioned that Hall had been bringing the broke actor groceries. Later that same year, after Lugosi was released from the hospital, Hall performed the marriage ceremony between Lugosi and his fifth wife, Hope Lininger. Hall also attended Lugosi's funeral in 1956.

As for his *Sequel to Dracula* in 1939, Hall's treatment might have stemmed from his friendship with Lugosi, but it might also have arisen out his own research. In *The Secret Teachings of All Ages*, his most famous book, Hall briefly addresses the topic of vampirism. Citing Paracelsus, Hall defines a vampire as being the

> astral body of a person either living or dead (usually the latter state). The vampire seeks to prolong existence upon the physical plane by robbing the living of their vital energies and misappropriating such energies to its own ends.[13]

The description of the astral body is none-too-different from his description of Dracula in the treatment as a "shimmering mist in which only the head remains visible."

Vampires had, of course, occupied much of Bela Lugosi's time since he first portrayed Dracula onstage in the Hamilton Deane–John L. Balderston play in 1927. After that came West Coast appearances in the role in 1928, 1929, and 1930, after which he played the role in the 1931 film at Universal Studios. During its production, he told one fan magazine: "When I am through with this picture, I hope to never hear of Dracula again. I cannot stand it."[14]

Lugosi's hope was futile, however. In 1932, he appeared in a production of *Dracula* onstage in Portland. In 1933, he appeared as a wax figure of himself as Dracula that comes to life in the short subject *Hollywood on Parade*. That same year, he appeared as Dracula in a vaudeville act, something he essentially repeated in 1936 at a Los Angeles production called *Night of 1000 Stars*. That was in addition to Universal Studios initially casting him in *Dracula's Daughter*, though studio writers could never work out a logical way to include the Lugosi character.

Shortly after *Dracula's Daughter* was released, Hollywood stopped producing horror films due to a British ban on the genre. But when US audiences embraced a reissue of *Dracula* (1931) and *Frankenstein* (1931) in 1938, Universal Studios quickly began work on *Son of Frankenstein* (1939). Horror returned, which meant that Hall (and a financially-strapped Lugosi) believed that Dracula should return as well.

SEQUEL TO DRACULA (1939)

In July 1939, Edwin Schallert of the *Los Angeles Times* wrote about Hall's treatment by announcing the new "Dracula Revival to Allow Series to Continue":

How to bring Dracula to life again, now that thrillers are enjoying their cycle of success anew, has been one of the problems debated at Universal. He was supposed to have been killed by having a stake driven through his body. Finis, of course, could only be written to his career while the sun was above the horizon.

It appears that a scenario has been devised, with Manly P. Hall, the occult expert, doing the treatment, which will go to show that the stake-driver missed disposing of Dracula by just one minute. In other words, the stake was driven through his body one minute after sundown.

Wherefore he will be probably brought to life once more with Bela Lugosi as the impersonator of the vampire. Locale of the plot will be Buenos Aires.[15]

As a surviving copy of the treatment mentions, Stanley Bergerman—formerly a Universal Studios producer for such films as *The Mummy* (1932), *WereWolf of London* (1935), and *The Raven* (1935, with Bela Lugosi)—acted as Hall's agent for the *Dracula* sequel.

Though he was convinced he had to explain Dracula's survival *vis-à-vis* Browning's film, Hall chose to ignore *Dracula's Daughter*, pretending that Countess Zaleska never existed and her burning of Dracula's corpse never occurred. At the same time, Hall began his treatment in a manner that echoes *Dracula's Daughter*; both stories attempt to rewrite the conclusion of Browning's *Dracula*. As previously mentioned, the changes in *Dracula's Daughter* are minor and the sequence occurs seemingly to remind audiences that Van Helsing has staked Dracula in the heart.

Hall takes far more liberties with Browning's ending. He recasts the action to Dracula's Transylvanian castle, rather than England's Carfax Abbey. He also adds four male characters to the imposing figure of Van Helsing. Perhaps one of the men is meant to be Jonathan Harker, but all are unnamed. The vampire hunters have apparently followed the Count to Transylvania; the treatment's opening sequence echoes the conclusion of Bram Stoker's novel, in which Van Helsing and company do chase the vampire from England to his Transylvanian castle. But Hall adds the curious touch of placing Dracula's coffin in a chapel.

Having thus addressed Dracula's survival, Hall's treatment explains that "for thirty years the vampire sleeps in his tomb, allowing old age and death to destroy his enemies one by one." Dracula hides to avoid another confrontation with Van Helsing, and then finally the important news arrives:

> In the ruined chapel, fallen into still further decay and spun with webs and filled deep with rubbish, a strange demented creature stands by the side of the sarcophagus and whispers into the crack under the lid: "Master, Van Helsing is dead. It is safe to come out now."

The Count emerges from his coffin at the behest of his servant, an unnamed character who takes on the persona of Renfield in *Dracula*. Indeed, the servant's whispering into Dracula's coffin smacks of Renfield doing the same aboard the Vesta in the Browning film.

Hall also offers another character who appeared in Browning's film, Mina. She now lives in Buenos Aires under an assumed name: "Señora Martinez is a cultured, sensitive woman approaching 60. She has spent the last several years of her life in a wheelchair." Hall does not mention Harker, her fiancée in Browning's film, but he does emphasize Dracula's ongoing interest in Mina. The treatment claims Dracula "has come to claim his bride according to the blood-pact made thirty years before."

Though Dracula's interest in Mina brings him to Argentina, his attention to her quickly wanes. After biting Mina, Dracula turns his attentions to Mercedes, a young woman soon to be Mina's daughter-in-law. In one curious and sexually-charged scene, "Mercedes drops her wraps and [unknowingly] seats herself in the very chair that Dracula is occupying." These problems quickly intensify, as Hall explains:

> In the days that follow, Mina slowly turns into a vampire. By day she is bound to her wheelchair, but with the setting of the sun she rises to obey the mental impulses of her infernal master. . . . Count Dracula leaves death and destruction in his way. He has descended as an evil blight upon the city.
> Mina turns upon Mercedes. But Dracula wishes the young girl for himself. The two vampires fight like beasts of the underworld.

Mina finally dies after a character drives a stake through her heart, thus freeing her from the vampire's curse. Her "face regains its beauty and dignity."

Though elements of Browning's 1931 version of *Dracula* are incorporated, Hall's sequel was constructed out of a number of sources. For example, he highlights the importance of Dracula's ring, which was not a key feature of the Browning film. But it was a central feature of Hillyer's *Dracula's Daughter*. Throughout that film, Countess Zaleska uses a "very old" and "beautiful" ring to hypnotize her victims.

Thanks to the setting of Argentina, the treatment recalls George Melford's Spanish-language *Dracula* (1931). Hall writes:

> Buenos Aires is the most beautiful city on the American continents, combining all that is new and modern with the grandeur of Spanish palaces and great flowered estates. The home of Senora Martinez is an imposing mansion in the midst of rose gardens. In spite of its beauty there is an air of mystery and fear about the entire establishment.

Hall also echoes Melford when he describes the "lid of the great [Dracula] sarcophagus [rising] by some mysterious mechanism," a device that also appears in the Spanish-language *Dracula*.

At the same time, key aspects of the treatment borrow from Bram Stoker. For example, Hall refers to the vampire as *Voivode Dracula*, a term that appears twice in Stoker. "Who was it but one of my own race who as Voivode crossed the Danube and beat the Turk on his own ground?" the Count asks Harker (Chapter Three, "Jonathan Harker's Journal Continued"). Later, Dr. Seward realizes the same when he writes, "He must, indeed, have been that Voivode Dracula who won his name against the Turk, over the great river on the very frontier of Turkeyland" (Chapter 18, "Dr. Seward's Diary"). By using *Voivode*—a Slavic term meaning "the governor of a province"—Hall drew not only on Stoker, but also by extension on Vlad the Impaler, Prince of Wallachia.

In the same way that Hall invoked Vlad by use of a term found twice in Stoker, he may have channeled Stoker in part through Browning. The 1931 *Dracula* is often regarded—even condemned—as being a "stagey" adaptation of Hamilton Deane and John Balderston's *Dracula—The Vampire Play*. But that description alone hardly encompasses Browning's film, which was heavily influenced by Stoker. After all, Browning (like Stoker) has a character travel to Transylvania to sell Dracula real estate, whereas the stage play takes place only in England. Browning also restored Mina as Harker's bride-to-be, with Lucy as Dracula's ill-fated victim, just as Stoker wrote it. By contrast, the Deane-Balderston play had switched those roles, with Mina already dead by the time the curtain first opens. Browning, and thus Hall, clearly utilized Stoker as a key resource.

In various ways, though, Hall's treatment borrows directly from the Stoker novel without the use of any intermediary. For example, Hall's description of the reawakened Dracula suggests: "He has had no blood for many years, therefore he is now a white-haired man, aged and bearded. His face is hollow with the sleep of years and his clothes are rotted about him." The connection between Dracula's appearance and hair color to his blood intake is nearly identical to Stoker, such as when Harker sees "gouts of fresh blood" at the corners of Dracula's mouth and notices that "his youth had been half restored. For the white hair and moustache were changed to iron-grey" (Chapter Four, "Jonathan Harker's Journal Continued").

Another element borrowed from Stoker is an emphasis on communication. The letters, telegrams, diaries, recordings, and newspaper clippings in Stoker's novel generally elucidate the unfolding events, which he claims do not "err, for all the records chosen are exactly contemporary, given from the standpoints and within the range of knowledge of those who made them." At the same time, Stoker reveals how communications can be falsified, as in the letters that Dracula forces Harker to sign. In his treatment, Hall offers the following scene:

> By the light of a single candle in a grotesque stand, Count Dracula wearing a long black robe is seated in his study writing a letter with an ancient quill pen. The envelope is addressed to Señora Martinez, 14 Plaza de la Republic, Buenos Aires, Argentina. The paper, aged and yellow, is emblazoned with the count's heraldic arms. The letter announces to the Señora that she is to prepare for his immediate arrival to renew a past acquaintance. It is signed with a medieval flourish, "Count Dracula."

Hall inverts Stoker here, however, by emphasizing the Count creating a communication; in the novel, the collected documents have been written by other characters. To the extent that Dracula's communications appear in Stoker (such as in his letter welcoming Harker to the Carpathians), they exist only in secondary form, as described by others (as in Chapter One, "Jonathan Harker's Journal, 3 May. Bistritz").

Similar to Stoker having Dracula move from Transylvania to England and back to Transylvania, Hall poses a situation where Dracula moves from Transylvania to Argentina and—at the end of the treatment—begins a return voyage to Transylvania. Indeed, Dracula's initial arrival in Argentina by boat is an event that Hall describes in great detail:

> Through this fog suddenly appears a magnificent black streamlined yacht bearing the name *Nemesis III.* The yacht enters the south basin slowly, approaching a dilapidated pier in the worst part of the city docks, which is called the *boca.*
>
> The harbormaster immediately announces the arrival of the strange ship. A group of detectives head for the dock. When they arrive they find the yacht moored to the dilapidated pier. Jumping aboard, they enter the captain's cabin and see that officer apparently studying his charts. When they shake him, however, he rolls out of the chair, dead. The second officer is dead also, roped to the wheel. The crew is dead. There apparently is nothing alive but a great black cat that hisses violently at them. In the storeroom are several great boxes.
>
> Leaving two men on guard, the others depart to make their various reports and to notify the quarantine officer. The two detectives standing beside the gangplank have not noticed the long black dray that has drawn up, nor do they see the shadowy figure that jumps from the under-piling of the pier to the deck of the yacht. This figure creeps along the deck and enters the door of the principal salon, a room of considerable size with an ornate flooring of inlaid wood. In the dim light, the central panel of the floor

slowly rises, and the hand of Dracula with its signet ring appears. The same half-crazed being that was seen at the tomb is crouched in the corner of the room. It whispers hoarsely: "Come, master, everything is in readiness."

The detectives on the dock are uneasy. The great black cat has walked across in front of them—an ill omen. Suddenly one of the detectives hears a slight sound and turns to see the demented creature that was on the yacht jump back to the under part of the pier. Cautioning the other to watch the gangplank, this officer crawls down under the pier, trying in vain to catch up to the elusive shadow.

The other detective who has been shivering slightly, turns up the collar of his coat as though the night had grown cold, and with a gesture of re-assurance lights a cigarette.

Suddenly two pale, gruesome hands encircle the inspector's throat.

The second officer has failed to catch the slinking figure under the pier. A powerful black automobile has just disappeared into the night. The detective sees a loading van containing several great boxes slowly pulling away.

The significance of the ship name *Nemesis III* is not addressed, but it reads like an oblique reference to the fact that Argentina was the third country (after England and Transylvania) that Dracula victimizes.

Also like Stoker, Hall gives Mina a son named Quincey. In Stoker, the child is named after Quincey Morris, the Texan whose Bowie knife plunges into Dracula's heart and causes the "miracle" of his body crumbling into dust (Chapter 27, "Mina Harker's Journal, 6 November"). In the treatment, Hall makes no reference to Quincey Morris, but describes Mina's son as, "an attractive young man approaching thirty who is hopelessly in love with Mercedes, one of the belles of the upper social set in which the family moves."

More unexpectedly, Hall includes a character named Lord Godalming. The treatment describes him as:

> [Mina's] alter ego; he is an aging Englishman with handlebar moustache and a monocle, a sort of perpetual guest most frequently found in slippers and jacket smoking a big meerschaum. For many years he has been silently and pathetically in love with Señora Martinez.

Nothing in the treatment suggests that Hall intends this character to be either of the two Lord Godalmings in Stoker's novel, meaning Arthur Holmwood's father or Holmwood himself, who inherits the title when his father dies.

In pitting Godalming and Quincey against Dracula, perhaps Hall remembered that Stoker's Lord Godalming and Quincey Morris work together in the novel: "'It is all right,' Godalming says. 'We found both places. Six boxes in each and we destroyed them all'" (Chapter 23, "Dr. Seward's Diary,

3 October"). However, it seems that Hall's major goal with his Godalming and Quincey is to re-create the Van Helsing–Harker relationship in Browning's film:

> Seeing the anguish in Lord Godalming's eyes, Quincey approaches and asks for an explanation. The Englishman tells the strange story of Dracula and finishes with the statement that the vampire is even now within the house. The young people are stunned. So this is the secret that his mother has kept all these years. Godalming lays out a program of defense. He appoints Quincey to watch his mother, and warning Mercedes of her danger, prepares in his own desperate but uncertain manner to fight the sinister force at work in their lives. Returning the diary to the locked chest, he prepares for an all-night vigil at the foot of the stairs that leads up to Mina's room. [. . .]
>
> Lord Godalming and Quincey use all of the skill and courage that they possess, and for a time succeed in disconcerting the vampire. During the day they still are searching for the body with the box in which it must rest.
>
> At last Dracula's hiding place is discovered. He had brought some of his earth, and destroying the records in the great chest, had taken up his abode right in the house.
>
> That night Lord Godalming leaves Quincey to protect Mercedes, and removing the earth from the chest pours it down a well on the property.

The treatment suggests that Godalming and Quincey are little more than names that Hall borrows from Stoker to use for his own narrative ends. Rather than creating a form-driven modernist sequel, Hall worked as postmodernist, incorporating ideas and character names from Stoker without any sense of fidelity to the novel.

Hall ventures further into a postmodernist terrain by having his characters directly reference the man Bram Stoker and his novel *Dracula*:

> Later Señora Martinez and Lord Godalming are seated in front of a great chest elaborately carved and painted in the Florentine manner. Lord Godalming opens the chest with an old massive key. The box is filled with books, bundles of papers, and old-fashioned tubular phonograph records. These documents are the diaries and stories concerning Count Dracula. They include Dr. Seward's notes, Jonathan Harker's journal, and Dr. Van Helsing's diary.
>
> From her wheelchair Señora Martinez asks for a book carefully wrapped and tied. There is a sad conversation in which she acknowledges that she had known all these years that Count Dracula was not dead. She has been a widow more than twenty years, but carefully has kept the story from her son lest it blast his life also. Knowing that the influence of a vampire cannot extend across water, she has put the Atlantic between herself and Dracula, but now he is going to come to her with his boxes of earth.

In the private offices of Justice Jose Gonzalez, Señora Martinez tells her whole story, pleading that the Argentine authorities will prevent the landing of the sinister count. She opens the carefully wrapped book and shows it to the Justice. It is Bram Stoker's *Dracula* and in the author's hand is the inscription on the flyleaf: "To Mina Harker with the sympathy and understanding of Bram Stoker."

Stoker's signed book (along with Dracula's letter to Mina) convinces Justice Gonzalez of the "gravity of the situation."

The tale grows increasingly dire as Dracula bites Mina, and she then has a stake driven through her heart. Hall describes the denouement as follows:

Notifying the authorities, [Lord Godalming] converges with them to the black yacht which still is moored to the dock. They find Mercedes in a sort of somnambulism, wandering towards the boat, stumbling over the broken planks and beams. On the black deck of *Nemesis III* stands Dracula. At his feet grovels his mad servant. The officers fire at him without result. Suddenly Lord Godalming stops and points towards the east. Dawn is breaking. Dracula also sees it and, with a howl of fury, rushes into the cabin. The black yacht moves out into the river with the madman at the wheel. Count Dracula lies in his box of earth underneath the floor.

Mercedes released by the dawn finds Quincey waiting for her; while Lord Godalming sadly but thankfully returns with them to the house of tragedy.

This conclusion, of course, posed a problem given the Production Code Authority of the 1930s; Dracula's escape meant the villain would go unpunished. At the same time, Hall provided an ending that easily allowed for yet another sequel, one that would not be burdened with the problem of bringing a dead monster back to life.

CONCLUSION

When Universal Studios decided not to shoot Hall's *Sequel to Dracula*, it became another addition to the vast Hollywood library of unproduced film treatments. Nonetheless, it still had an indirect influence on horror film history. For example, the fact it wasn't produced meant that Lugosi never appeared in a *Dracula* sequel. The lack of a major sequel in 1939, along with the box-office success of *Son of Frankenstein* (1939) and *The Wolf Man* (1941), thus relegated the character Dracula to a lesser status at Universal Studios in the 1940s.

Though the character did appear in films like *House of Frankenstein* (1944) and *House of Dracula* (1945), Universal only produced one more direct sequel to *Dracula.* Their *Son of Dracula* (1943, starring Lon Chaney Jr. instead of Lugosi) appeared seven years after *Dracula's Daughter* and twelve years after Browning's *Dracula.* Though Curt Siodmak (who wrote its story) and Eric Taylor (who wrote its script) may have never seen Hall's treatment, *Son of Dracula* echoes various elements of it. They too create a Dracula who is "invulnerable" at night and who travels to the Americas; they also incorporate Stoker as an overt plot device, as a page from his novel (taken from Chapter Three, "Jonathan Harker's Journal") appears onscreen.

Hall's treatment also appeared at the vanguard of that third approach to horror film sequels as inaugurated by *Son of Frankenstein* (1939). It represents exactly the kind of postmodern narrative methodology that guided many horror films of the forties. To be sure, Monogram did follow the first approach to horror sequels with *Return of the Ape Man* (1944); the use of the word *return* and the casting of Bela Lugosi gave the false impression that the film was a sequel to *The Ape Man* (1943). And as for the second approach to sequels, Universal did continue to produce sequels of the *Bride of Frankenstein* and *Dracula's Daughter* variety. For example, *The Mummy's Tomb* (1942) uses repeated characters, cast members, and recycled footage to so many numerous connections to *The Mummy's Hand* (1940) that it might well be the most faithful sequel of the era. And a few other efforts of the forties used the family member approach to sequels: Ludwig Frankenstein in *Ghost of Frankenstein* (1942), for example, and Dr. Frank Griffin in *The Invisible Man Returns* (1940).

But a number of Universal's wartime horror sequels don't feel the earlier need to justify their plots, opting instead for the path of *Son of Frankenstein* (1939) and Hall's *Sequel to Dracula.* The landscape changed to a postmodern play on characters and plotlines to the extent that, say, the time setting of *Frankenstein Meets the Wolf Man* (1943) takes place before *The Wolf Man* (1941), but for a variety of reasons it seems to be a loose sequel to it. *The Invisible Man's Revenge* (1944) pretends earlier films in the series don't exist. *The Mummy's Hand* (1940) ignores *The Mummy* (1932) completely; *The Mummy's Curse* (1944) makes no direct reference to *The Mummy's Tomb* (1942) and *The Mummy's Hand* (1940), and it inexplicably dislocates the northern college town geography of *The Mummy's Ghost* (1944) to the swamps of Louisiana. That Frankenstein's Monster, the Wolf Man, and Dracula are alive and appear together in *House of Frankenstein* (1944) and *House of Dracula* (1945) defies any sense of logical continuity to earlier films in their respective series, with the emphasis on combining their talents rather than making any larger narrative sense.

Though Bela Lugosi never managed to star in a *Dracula* sequel, he did reprise the role of Dracula in *Abbott and Costello Meet Frankenstein* (1948), a film that also includes the Wolf Man, Frankenstein's Monster, and the Invisible Man. Its plot discards any effort to connect logically with prior horror films. The bizarre convergence of monsters who have all been previously killed with Abbott and Costello results in a kind of wonderful nonsense. Among other changes, Lugosi's vampire casts a reflection in a mirror, though he hadn't seventeen years earlier in Browning's *Dracula*. Perhaps it was the appropriate end result of the kind of horror film sequel that Hall's treatment aimed to be.

NOTES

1. Manly P. Hall, *Sequel to Dracula* (1939), unproduced movie treatment. (Copyright and original reside with undisclosed owner.)

2. Alan Citron, "Research Center Pursues Ideas Most Won't Consider," *Los Angeles Times*, sec. B8, October 31, 1982.

3. Citron, "Research Center," B8.

4. Louis Sahagun, "Manly Palmer Hall Founded Philosophical Research Society," *Los Angeles Times*, sec. A34, September 3, 1990.

5. See, for example, the radio listings in *Los Angeles Times*, February 28, 1934, when it was announced that Hall would speak over station KTM.

6. Citron, "Research Center," B8.

7. "Novel Screen Feature Delves into Astrology," *Los Angeles Times*, June 16, 1938.

8. Philip K Scheuer, "Hollywood Goes Occult for New Film," *Los Angeles Times*, sec. C3, March 6, 1938.

9. These Hall story ideas are detailed in Gary D. Rhodes, *Lugosi: His Life in Films, on Stage, and in the Hearts of Horror Lovers* (Jefferson, NC: McFarland, 1997), 219–20.

10. Gary D. Rhodes, *Bela Lugosi: Dreams and Nightmares* (Narberth, PA: Collectibles, 2007).

11. Clips from this trailer appear in *Lugosi: Hollywood's Dracula*. Written and directed by Gary D. Rhodes, 55 min., Spinning Our Wheels Productions, 1997, DVD, www.lugosidvd.com.

12. "Movie Stars May Have to Predict Own Futures," *Hammond Times* (Hammond, IN), November 16, 1942.

13. Manly P. Hall, *The Secret Teachings of All Ages* (New York: Tarcher Penguin, 2003).

14. Lillian Shirley, "Afraid of Himself," *Modern Screen*, March 1931.

15. Edwin Schallert, "Lewis Stone to Play Chief Executive Role," *Los Angeles Times*, July 12, 1939.

The *Dracula* and the *Blacula* (1972) Cultural Revolution

Paul R. Lehman and John Edgar Browning

*W*hen director F. W. Murnau released the first "surviving"[1] film adaptation of *Dracula* (1897) with *Nosferatu: Eine Symphonie des Grauens* through Germany's Prana-Film company in 1922, director D. W. Griffin's *Birth of a Nation* (1915) had only been in theaters for seven years following its release through the D. W. Griffin Corporation. America, in 1922, was for African Americans a very segregated and biased society. Just one year earlier, the nation's worst ethnic riot had occurred in Tulsa, Oklahoma, and racially motivated lynching was still a common occurrence in various parts of the country. At the same time, this period also saw a budding movie industry, one of the few forms of entertainment that was available to the masses. For that reason, it held tremendous power over Anglo and African Americans, who afterward became subject to the sociopolitical conditioning ingrained in these early films. However, because society was segregated, viewing movies was not as readily available for African Americans. When the opportunity presented itself for "moviegoing," the places reserved for these viewers were either the balcony or a sectioned-off area away from Anglo Americans. Since society was separated, many African American communities had their own movie theaters. In some of them, movies by the pioneering African American filmmaker Oscar Micheaux were shown. Slavery had been over in the United States for roughly fifty years when movies became popular mass entertainment, but as a result of their power to influence the attitudes and behaviors of the viewing public, they provided an excellent vehicle for waging battle against ethnic biases. An example of this came fifty years after Murnau's *Nosferatu* with the release of director William Crane's *Blacula* (1972) through

We are greatly indebted to an outside reader for his insightful comments on earlier versions of this chapter.

From left to right: Charles Macaulay (as Dracula), William Marshall (as Mamuwalde/ Blacula), Vonetta McGee (as Luva/Tina). *Courtesy of American International Pictures/ PhotoFest*

American International Pictures (AIP), which provided other filmmakers with a model from which to launch an attack against the negatively stereotyped images and attitudes of African Americans.

What we attempt here—that is, within the thematic constraints of this chapter—is to examine *Blacula*'s reception within the context of the postsegregation, yet biased America of the 1970s. We propose to begin first with a brief examination of the "racial" construction that emerged in America during the colonial period, then move on to the social turmoil that occurred during the latter half of the twentieth century, when the strain caused by black activists in the Civil Rights movement and by artists in the Black Cultural Revolution began to weigh in on the legitimacy of "racial" division in America. With the help of primary materials like interviews and personal narratives, we then focus on William Marshall himself, the actor who played Blacula, whose artistic decisions during production, in addition to the film's socially liberating conception as a whole, helped to alleviate and delegitimize some of the ethnic biases ingrained in the "white" and "black" consciousness of the 1970s. We have also chosen to include a number of film reviews—particularly recent ones—in an effort to provide a balanced interpretative account of not only *Blacula*'s reception by the public but also the film's social ramifications, which continue to resonate in mainstream culture even thirty years after the film's release.

THE "(CINE)MYTH OF RACE" AND THE "ATTITUDE OF WHITE SUPERIORITY"[2]

According to Jacques Barzun, the term *race* was conceived to promote a sort of "We" versus "They" opposition between rivaling European peoples,[3] and later it was used by scientists to classify humans as one "race." Thus, the term has no scientific value outside of this usage. Nonetheless, the myth of the term *race* as a means to distinguish or divide within the "human race" (i.e., "white race," "black race," etc.) was, and still is, perpetuated. As a result, the inherent value placed upon the nonscientific use of the word *race*, and its perpetuation by the public, contributes to the extreme difficulty with which people try to divorce themselves from the illogical and irrational use of the word, particularly in America. Even though America is a multiethnic, multicultural society, and has been since its beginning, the biased social definition of white society created two so-called races, privileging the "white race" over those of the "negro race." When the socially defined "negro race" was made to see and accept itself as inferior, only time and (re)education would help to overcome the challenges created by this biased definition.

African Americans, like other Americans, attended the movies and identified with their heroes regardless of who they might be. Despite the social restrictions that were placed upon the "negro race" as a means of so-called self-preservation by the "white race," at the movies, a "suspension of disbelief" still had to prevail if entertainment was to take place. Therefore, "ethnicity,"[4] although lacking, in terms of diversity, in the characters generally portrayed on screen, was not a consideration of African American viewers because they accepted on screen that a hero was a hero and that a villain was a villain regardless of the genre or theme.

Social conditioning through highly politicized normative categorization was just as affective in early American society as it is today. In effect, all Anglo American people were viewed as "normal," while any person excluded from this category, in relation to his or her ethnic identity, was viewed as "other" or "different." Ethnic stereotypes had been created in society by every social institution, and the movies did nothing to discredit this practice. In the years before the World Wars and the Korean War, movies were often used as propagandistic tools to manipulate the minds of the American public. When heroes or villains were created on the big screen, our culture became saturated with their images, as did the public consciousness. A noteworthy example is *Dracula*, whose indoctrination into our cultural landscape and his resulting popularity need only be measured by the sheer quantity of films, TV series, TV spots, cartoons, documentaries, video games, and other productions that feature the famed vampire icon.[5] Cultural figures like Dracula transcend ethnic bias in general, and as society begins to become more sophisticated through education and socialization, then perceptions, preferences, and practices of the past can also change. Change came to the African American community in the late 1960s and early 1970s through the phenomena of the Black Cultural Revolution.

The winds of change for Afro-America came via the airwaves of African American civic leaders and entertainers. James Brown was one of the leaders in American society who advocated a change in the attitude of African Americans with songs such as "Say it Loud, I'm Black and Proud," and "I don't want you to give me nothing. Open up the door, I'll get it myself." In addition, groups like Curtis Mayfield and The Impressions had hit songs that helped to inspire pride in the "negro race." Songs like "Keep on Pushin'" and "People Get Ready" helped to prepare the American social and cultural landscape for greater inclusion of the African American community. African American moviegoers began to notice that they were not present in the majority of movies they frequented. And those films that did include them did so in token roles or gave them exaggerated characteristics that tended to underscore the negative qualities of African Americans. (Count Dracula, for example, never attacked African American people until 1972.)[6] Owing to the changes in society brought on by civil rights activities, one might understand the absence of ethnic people in the earlier films, but what of films produced after 1970? At the time, America was undergoing a cultural revolution as far as African Americans were concerned, and we begin to see this manifest in the new sense of (self-)worth evidenced by the "March on Washington Speech of Martin Luther King, Jr.," in "loud" Afro-hair styles, and in the clothing fashions that borrowed African themes. But what did this have to do with Dracula?

The plot and characters exhibited in *Blacula*, which were adapted from Bram Stoker's novel, allowed America to see (i.e., re-examine) Africans, African Americans, and a unified American society through Afrocentric entertainment. Stoker's vampiric character, a royal count, lived in a castle and exhibited the mannerisms of a refined gentleman. He lived and moved in an affluent level of society where the people were generally educated and socially well informed. The plot of the story is such that it keeps readers and viewers engaged in the action. What's more, the novel was easily adapted to film because it combines elements of horror, suspense, drama, murder, mystery, and the fantastic, all elements of a potential blockbuster. Thus, reworking the *Dracula* narrative for black cinema (i.e., relying heavily on elements of Afrocentric culture) for the purposes of entertainment, education, and enlightenment seemed the next likely (i.e., profitable) direction in Dracula's evolution. AIP responded with its highly profitable release of *Blacula* (1972), a film that would become not only AIP's highest-grossing film since the studio's inception in the mid-1950s,[7] but one of the most iconic films in Dracula's filmography.

"'BLACULA' STAR MARSHALL DIES"[8]

> Chained in the market-place he stood,
> A man of giant frame,
> Amid the gathering multitude
> That shrunk to hear his name.
>
> —"The African Chief" (1825),
> William Cullen Bryant[9]

Of William Marshall, the first African American to play a Dracula(-type) role, *Variety*'s Melissa Goldberg writes: "Actor William Marshall, known for bringing the horror genre into the blaxploitation era of the 1970s with 'Blacula' and 'Scream, Blacula, Scream,' died June 11[, 2003] in a Los Angeles rest

home after suffering from Alzheimer's. He was 78."[10] While the premise behind a *Dracula* film involving African American actors in an American setting may seem trivial to moviegoers in the 2000s, in the late 1960s and early
1970s the idea was quite simply fantastic (in the Gothic sense). Therefore, examining the various stages in the film's development, its contextuality, and the
importance placed on the film's lead, William Marshall, becomes crucial in
order to help us understand the film's transformation from script to financial
blockbuster to black cultural icon status.

With the increasing popularity of black performers in the early 1970s,
Dimension Productions and Meier-Murray announced their intention to film
Black Dracula, under the direction of Paul Nobert.[11] The film, was never produced, but eventually a studio named Power Productions did go on to film
and release *Blacula* with AIP. Originally, the title character in *Blacula*, Glut
points out, was to be, by all accounts, a quite unremarkable character (contrary
to Marshall's performance, which we shall discuss later) by the name of "Andrew Brown (named after Andrew H. Brown of radio and television's *Amos
'N' Andy)*" who, in a sort of Abbott and Costello fashion, accidentally stum-
bles upon Dracula's Gothic abode in Transylvania. According to Glut, Joseph
T. Naar, one of the film's producers, proceeded to interview a number of black
athletes to play the title role, but none could be found. Naar even approached
Raymond St. Jacques about the role, but with no success. In the end, the role
would fall to William Marshall, a fine Shakespearean actor for whom—at a
staggering six feet, five inches, sporting a brawny physique, and commanding
a baritone voice—the part seemed written.

A native of Gary, Indiana, Marshall worked as a waiter, a commercial
artist, even a soldier, and for a time, he had worked in the steel mills before
starting a career in acting. Schooled in both art and acting in New York City,
he had played a number of stage, television, and movie roles before ever being
offered the title role in *Blacula*. Choosing someone of Marshall's professional
stature, and at "a time in our history," Glut notes, "in which black actors playing black characters other than negro stereotypes was a rarity," profoundly af-
fected the film. Marshall carried with him the conviction of wanting something more for black Americans. Donald Bogle, film historian and author of
Blacks in American Film and Television (New York: Garland Publishing, 1988),
described Marshall: "Confident, polished, sophisticated, he projected an unusual mixture of physical strength and a sharp, discerning intelligence. He was
also sexual in a period when the lid was always kept on a black male's sexuality. Moreover, he was a good actor."[12] Marshall explains (June 1974):[13]

> How Prince Mamuwalde felt about his fate is what I tried to contribute to
> the movie, first by insisting on collaborating in the revision of the screen-

play and finally, of course, through the performance itself. The need for black input in making a movie meaningful to black audiences cannot be over-emphasized.[14]

After the shooting of *Blacula*, Marshall revealed to author Donald Glut that he (Marshall) had seen potential in the *Blacula* theme, "especially if [the film]," Glut (230) notes, "were not presented as merely another 'black exploitation' picture." Both Marshall and Glut (230) knew that "*Blacula* would probably be seen by almost as many white people as black"; thus, Marshall used the opportunity that *Blacula* presented. Glut (230) recounts:

> During a visit I made to the home of William Marshall, the actor revealed that he wanted to justify the presence of the eventual "Blacula" in nineteenth century Transylvania. Since slavery was still operative at the time, Marshall [himself] changed the character to Mamuwalde, an African prince, hoping to convince Count Dracula to use his influence in helping to place an embargo on the slave trade. Despite studio opposition, the slave issue was included in the script.
>
> Marshall also wrote in a scene in which Mamuwalde is drawn to a beautiful young woman, a reincarnation of his former love,[15] and the embodiment of all the virtues and riches that represented Africa to him. The scene established the human side of the vampire, made him someone with whom the audience could empathize. Though the scene was callously abbreviated by the studio editors, it does remain the most memorable part of the film.

Marshall's unrivaled performance and dedication to the role won him the first annual award of the Academy of Horror and Science Fiction Films, as well as the 1973 Cinema Award of the Count Dracula Society.[16] Of the years just prior to and after the shooting of *Blacula*, William Marshall recounts (June 1974):

> An effective vampire movie, I have discovered, must be flooded with urgent emotions of anguish, yearning, terror, and, ultimately, relief. This holds true, I believe, if to a lesser extent, for all horror and science fiction movies. I began to see the need, within the structure of our world, which is experienced so often and by so many as monstrous, for other worlds in which to dwell, if only for an occasional hour or two at the movies.
>
> For example, Americans didn't notice for a long time that the Vietnamese war was going on, but it's been impossible to shut it out or shut it off ever since. The destruction of fruitful land and fruitful people goes on and on, and no amount of turning the dial will blot the picture out. Or a fuel shortage suddenly disrupts millions of lives, whips the inflationary spiral higher ... [and] in the brief interval the profits of the oil companies rise more than 300%. Whales and sophisticated urban populations alike gasp

for air. Blacks look for space in which to stand up straight at last. Israelis and Arabs insist fiercely on their national pride. . . . [And for] the first time in history, doom is an immediate possibility in the minds of little children, [as] terrorist youth groups form to make guerrilla war on social inequality, sending tapes to announce their theory and tactics publicly. . . . [P]eople trying to make sense of the world tend to "look for scapegoats" such as the devil. Americans recently witnessed an illustration of this trend at the highest government level, when a Presidential advisor invoked "sinister forces" to explain the wiping out of a crucial 18 minutes in a subpoenaed White House tape.[17]

Receptive to Marshall's performance in *Blacula*, the public spurred the studio into approaching Marshall about doing a cameo appearance in *Blackenstein* (1973), but the actor declined. After the financial success of *Blacula*, however, Marshall did reprise his title role in the sequel that quickly followed from AIP with *Scream, Blacula, Scream* (1973). The plot in *Scream, Blacula, Scream* continues the story of the chief character while bringing in more information that focuses on the 1970s cultural setting. Troy Howarth, whose work on horror film pioneers like Mario Bava (*The Haunted World of Mario Bava* [FAB Press Ltd., 2002]) has brought him distinction, comments:

When Willis (Richard Lawson) is passed over as the new head of a voodoo sect, he swears revenge. To that end he obtains the bones and ashes of Prince Mamuwalde, a.k.a. Blacula (William Marshall), whom he brings back to (un)life. The vampire transforms Willis into his servant and then sets his eyes on Lisa (Pam Grier), a powerful voodoo priestess who possesses the power to release him from his suffering.[18]

Of the 1970s cultural dialogue we see in *Scream, Blacula, Scream*, another online reviewer, Bryan Theiss, asserts:

The afrocentric themes are better developed this time around. Mamuwalde admires African Americans who are interested in their heritage, and shares his knowledge with them. He dislikes ignorant young people who waste away their days partying, so he often chooses these people to transform into his vampire minions. In one memorable scene, Mamuwalde is enraged by two pimps who try to mug him. Before beating them to death, he lectures them from the point of view of an African prince who fought against slavery. He angrily accuses them of enslaving their sisters and imitating their slavemasters. William Marshall completely sells these lines, bringing to them an overwhelming righteousness.[19]

In large part, the success of these two films was due to the novelty they represented to the viewing public, who were conditioned to seeing a European actor playing the main character. The films were seen as humorous and farcical, and many of the film reviewers did not see any positive or artistic value in them. Even certain black critics and organizations—like the NAACP's Junius Griffin of the Hollywood chapter (who used the words "'cultural genocide'"[20]) and the Committee against Blaxploitation (CAB)—condemned the film, regarding it as demeaning and exploitative.[21] They were considered additions to a phenomenon that emerged out of the early-1970s called Blaxploitation, which Frances Gateward, professor of cinema and African American studies at the University of Illinois–Urbana Champaign, describes as

> one of American cinema's continually disparaged trends, that which is commonly referred to as Blaxploitation. The movie-viewing public often assumes incorrectly that all Black-themed films of the 1970s had Black talent in creative and/or financial control of the films—very few were written or directed by Blacks, financed and produced by Black production companies, or reached theaters through Black-owned distribution businesses. Many films are frequently misidentified, despite the fact that they are not ultra-low budget, campy violent films about pimps and drug dealers in stack shoes, bell bottoms and furs. *Blacula*, for example, is particularly unique for having a Black director, William Crain, and for linking the plight of its protagonist, Mamuwalde aka Blacula, to the destructive legacies of the slave trade.[22]

Despite the critics, "extratextual uses of the film," Benshoff adds (36), "became important to the struggle for racial advancement. For example, in both Los Angeles and San Francisco, gala premieres of *Blacula* were held in the black community[, and] *The Los Angeles Sentinel*, a weekly independent black newspaper, ran a two-page photo spread on the film's premiere."

The educational opportunity provided by *Blacula* through its socially liberating qualities was missed by many of the viewers. Nonetheless, a number of cultural elements were present in both *Blacula* films that not only challenged the stereotypical images of Africans, African Americans, and homosexuals in America but provided exposure for them as well (though one might argue that the homosexual images in *Blacula* encouraged stereotypes and bigotries more than they challenged them).

While the values and behavior of Prince Mamuwalde and his wife Luva were hardly acknowledged by reviewers, the fact is that the stereotypical treatment of Africans in American movies was in many instances negative. Often, the American public was presented with pictures of African tribes dressed in their cultural garb and living in some rural setting devoid of any of the modern conveniences common to the American public. On few occasions were

Africans of stature, education, and grace present in film. They were generally associated with jungle films featuring European males and females seen as normal people, while the Africans were viewed as savages, crude, ignorant, and silly. Their value was in doing the master's bidding. However, in *Blacula* we find quite the contrary: two well-dressed, intelligent Africans of stature— Mamuwalde and Luva (rulers of an African nation)—who travel to a foreign land to seek an audience with Count Dracula (a slave trader) in an effort to end the African slave trade.

This depiction of Africans, one which was unexpected and new for an American audience, represents an attempt by filmmakers to create a perspective that challenges the cultural stereotype. We are reminded that entertainment is the focus of the film when the two men of high degree result to physical force in an attempt to resolve their differences. We are also reminded of the history of American slavery when Dracula turns Mamuwalde into a vampire and (self-)names him Blacula in an attempt to further humiliate and transform him into something less than human, a practice paralleled by the loss of African identity in the American slave trade with the "devaluing [of] the African captive [by] calling him Negro; thus, little or no guilt would be associated with any kind of business transaction regarding the Negro."[23] For the Count, the word *black* still carried negative connotations.

Many of the viewers, including some film critics, believed that one of the best elements present in both *Blacula* films was the actors, especially William Marshall. Although the setting changes from the Count's castle to an African American neighborhood of the 1970s, the character of Blacula himself remains strong and dignified. After all, he was a prince in his former life. Online reviewer Bryan Theiss continues:

> In the book *What It Is . . . What It Was . . .* Marshall says that he wanted to remove the story "from the stereotype of ignorant, conniving stupidity that evolved in the United States to justify slavery." Instead, he suggested the "African hero who had never been subjected to slavery" who ultimately became the subject of the film. It is largely this challenging of stereotypes and respect for African heritage that makes the series so unique. Other blaxploitation films have presented strong African American heroes and heroines, but few have incorporated cultural issues so successfully into pulpy b-movie theatrics. These are movies that make you regret that you can't go out and rent more like them.[24]

Troy Howarth voices why he, too, believes that both *Blacula* films do not fit well into the so-called blaxploitation category. He states that:

> Key to their success is distinguished Shakespearean actor William Marshall (called "the best Othello of our time" by at least one critic. . . . Mar-

shall plays the potentially ludicrous role [in *Blacula* and *Scream, Blacula, Scream*] with such conviction and sincerity that he literally lifts them out of the blaxploitation gutter. Few elements in either film match his brilliance, but that they survive is a solid testimony to his indelible characterization. Marshall is one of the few screen vampires to elicit genuine pathos and scares—his transformation from cultured, dignified statesman to feral vampire being so utterly convincing and complete.[25]

In addition, *Blacula* treats the subject of homosexuality (still taboo by the early 1970s) and offers the American public a lesson on tolerance. This comes in the form of the two gay antique dealers who acquire the contents of Castle Dracula, including a coffin that, unbeknownst to them, contains Mamuwalde. The primary point here, however, is that the film portrays two American males, both gay, one Anglo American and the other African American, in business together. That they are present in the film and in a bi-"racial" relationship underscores the point that intolerances of the past, whether based on color or intelligence or sexuality, have no place in *Blacula*, which engages in the much greater dialogue of the 1970s cultural and sexual liberative movements. Adding to that point is the idea of these two men bringing symbols of the past, like Dracula's personal property, into the present of the 1970s and to America (Los Angeles).

In addition to providing opportunities for educating and entertaining American audiences, *Dracula* also presents itself as a model to enlighten them. The fact that Bram Stoker's character of Dracula comes from Europe gives him a degree of credibility[26] because Americans usually associate value and history with that continent; the fact that the story is based on the vampire mythos simply adds to its box-office appeal. Audiences are given the opportunity to enrich their knowledge of other peoples, considering questions of whether there was a real Count Dracula or a real Mamuwalde. Are vampires real? Is there really such a place as Castle Dracula, situated in the Carpathian Mountains on the border of Transylvania and Moldavia? These questions were particularly germane at that time since the early to mid-1970s saw some of the first flourishing Dracula scholarship.[27] The value of such inquiry, which testifies to the film's ability to arouse the viewer's curiosity, lies not in fixing answers, but in posing them, and exploring them, as they lead to new paths, and continue to evolve.

BLACULA'S LEGACY

The full impact of *Blacula* on the viewing public can never be known, but we can at least come to some understanding of the film's vitality over the last

El Pais, The Washington Post, Le Monde, Daily News (New York), *Daily Variety, Chicago Sun-Times, The Independent* (London), *The New York Times, CBS News On-line, USA Today, The Courier Mail/The Sunday Mail* (Australia), *The Boston Globe, McClatchy-Tribune News Service, St. Petersburg Times, The Sydney Morning Herald* (Australia), *Variety, The Washington Times, The Gazette* (Montreal), *The Globe and Mail* (Canada), *The Guardian* (London), *The Times* (London), *The Toronto Sun, The Philadelphia Inquirer, taz, die tageszeitung, The Toronto Star, Herald Sun/Sunday Herald Sun* (Melbourne, Australia), *Politiken & Politiken Weekly, Le Temps, The Herald* (Glasgow), *The Advertiser/Sunday Mail* (South Australia), *The Age* (Melbourne, Australia), *The Christian Science Monitor, Le Figaro, La Stampa, The Mirror* (*The Daily Mirror* and *The Sunday Mirror*), *The Observer, The Scotsman & Scotland on Sunday, The Australian, Birmingham Post, Daily Record & Sunday Mail, Les Echos, The Evening Standard* (London), *Evening Times* (Glasgow), *Frankfurter Rundschau, The Hollywood Reporter, The Irish Times, The Mercury/Sunday Tasmanian* (Australia), *The Press* (Christchurch, New Zealand), *The Sunday Times* (London), *The Washington Post Biographical Stories.*

Figure 2.1.   Newspaper Responses to *Blacula* and *Scream, Blacula, Scream* (Lexis-Nexis).

thirty-five years across print and virtual media by looking at some of the mixed responses to the film that we find in newspapers and in print and on-line reviews. The international variety of newspapers (see figure 2.1) speaks to the extensive popularity of *Blacula* that Marshall's performance instilled, as does the international variety of reviews (see figure 2.2).

In an effort to show the variety of attitudes and interests shared by many critics, we have provided selected excerpts from the works of two critics from the lists above. In 1973, Roger Ebert writes for the *Chicago Sun-Times*:

> "Scream, Blacula, Scream" is an adequate vampire movie, which is to say that a satisfactory number of vampires spring out of hiding and sink their teeth into helpless victims, and there are abundant shots of vampires with

Variety.com [Variety Staff], *New York Times, Horror Filmomanija* (Croatian), *Living-Corpse.com* [Ron Hogan], *TV Guide, 1000 Misspent Hours* [Scott Ashlin], *All Movie Guide* [Donald Guarisco], *3B Theater* [Chad Plambeck], *Danse Macabre* (Polish), *DVD Drive-In* [George R. Reis], *Doug Pratt's Laserdisc Review, DVD Talk* [G. Noel Gross], *Eccentric Cinema, FlickFilosopher.com* [MaryAnn Johanson], *Four Word Film Review, Video Graveyard, Guns, Girls & Ghouls, HorrorWatch*, review at metamovie.de, *Monsters at Play, The SF, Horror and Fantasy Film Review, Wooden Spoons, Oh, the Humanity!, Rotten Tomatoes—Reviews from the Nation's Top Critics, Cinema Laser, Time Out.*

Figure 2.2.   External Reviews for *Blacula* (LexisNexis).

blood drooling down their chins. But beyond those two prerequisites, the movie isn't exactly the best thing in its line since "Taste the Blood of Dracula."

Maybe that's because it's a Hollywood product. The best horror movies are turned out by the Hammer Film crowd in London, where an inexhaustible supply of overgrown cemeteries and crumbling churches is to be had. In Hollywood, a Gothic mansion is about all you can expect. Beyond that, "Scream, Blacula, Scream" shows some evidence of having been made in a hurry with limited funds.

The opening is so confusing that, in reading the movie's synopsis afterward, I couldn't recognize it. And the photography is consistently underlit and murky. Against these disadvantages there are a couple of reasons to see the movie anyway. William Marshall, who created the Blacula role, is back again with his terrifying dignity. . . . Marshall has the kind of pseudo-Shakespearean dialog and delivery that Vincent Price and others have been polishing at Hammer. . . . A really good black vampire movie remains to be made, however. The elements are there, and "Blacula" and this sequel have proven there's a market for the genre. But just hiring black actors, and giving them false fangs won't do; the Hammer Films people have encouraged us to expect lots of moody scenery, unsettling music and campy but sound performances, and a script that makes sense, incidentally. "Scream, Blacula, Scream" is just an interim exploitation effort, and a warm-up for the better vampires in Marshall's future.[28]

This final review demonstrates just how varied ideas and opinions about the film and Marshall's performance can be. Reprinted in *Time Out Film Guide* (2007), the review by film critic and horror and vampire film scholar David Pirie finds nothing of value in *Blacula*:

> Disappointing black movie which followed in the successful wake of *Shaft*. The script by Joan Torres and Raymond Koenig seems to be the real problem: apart from a garbled opening in which Blacula is vampirised while trying to liberate his people, the plot simply turns away from all the obvious political/social/sexual implications, even on the level of action. Instead, Blacula becomes a less than impressive lovesick vampire chasing his reincarnated wife through LA (one of the dullest plot mechanisms of all), and the film remains a lifeless reworking of heroes versus vampires with soul music and a couple of good gags.[29]

Pirie later writes in *The Vampire Cinema* (1977) that Stoker's incarnation "drew much of his power from the sexual guilt of Victorian England, so a black Dracula let loose in contemporary America might have effectively provided a focus for the guilt and neurosis of the dominant white culture."[30] Nevertheless, Pirie adds (138), "American International Pictures never once allowed this kind of suggestion to enter their film, except perhaps in its fee-ble prologue where a spokesman for the black nations fleetingly appears at Count Dracula's castle, hoping the Count will help him put an end to the slave trade." However, Pirie's negation fails to adequately address the very fea-tures that precisely extricate *Blacula* from other blaxploitation films, nor does it account for the film(s)'s economic success. (It is a wonder how, in review-ing *The Revenge of Frankenstein* [1958], an English film, Pirie is able to ma-neuver around the film's clumsy, pseudo-drunken Frankenstein's Monster and still produce a positive review.)[31]

CONCLUSION: [BL]ACULA LIVES![32]

Although *Blacula*'s public reception varied greatly over time, one thing is un-deniable: it has inspired a wealth of horror crossover films in the early-1970s, adding to the Black Cultural Revolution with such films as *The Thing with Two Heads* (1972), *Blackenstein, Ganja and Hess* (1973), *Abby* (1974), *The House on Skull Mountain* (1974), *Sugar Hill* (1974), *The House on Skull Moun-tain* (1974), *Dr. Black and Mr. Hyde* (1976), and *J.D.'s Revenge* (1976).[33] Some of the more recent films that share themes and sources with *Dracula* and *Blac-ula* include *The People Under the Stairs* (1991), the film *Candyman* (1992), and its sequels *Candyman: Farewell to the Flesh* (1995) and *Candyman: Day of the Dead* (1999), and *Tales from the Hood* (1995). More recent films dealing with this subject matter include *Street Tales of Terror, Hood of the Living Dead*, and *Vampiyaz*, all released in 2004; the films *Vampire Assassins* and *Zombiez* from 2005; and the *Blade* trilogy (1998, 2002, and 2004) and television series, *Blade: The Series* (2006). In no way an exhaustive listing, it serves to indicate something of the influence *Dracula* and *Blacula* have had on American cul-ture in general and on African American culture in particular, providing visi-bility to and negotiation for racial inequality. As noted by Harry M. Benshoff, "embracing the racialized monster and turning him or her into an agent of black pride and power, blaxploitation horror films created sympathetic mon-sters who helped shift audience identification away from the status quo 'nor-mality' of bourgeois white society. . . . expos[ing] white 'normality' . . . as *pro-ductive* of monsters [italics ours]."[34]

Commercially, *Dracula* and its influence will endure, because the qual-ities demonstrated by the novel's characters are, very simply, prone to en-tertainment, profitability, and above all, adaptability. Culturally, the frame-work we see in *Dracula* is a porous and malleable one, and it is probably inexhaustible in terms of future literary and filmic progeny. Commenting on Dracula's longevity, and the continuing viability of the subject of vampires, Marshall concludes a piece he wrote (June 1974) with the story of a young lady who approached him late one night during the shooting of *Blacula*:

> Late one night when we were shooting a street sequence for *Blacula* in Hollywood, a very beautiful woman wearing a long black cape approached me as I stood waiting on the sidewalk to be called for the next shot. I had not seen her before in the small shifting crowd of observers.
> "Are you the man?" she asked, looking at me intently.
> "If I understand your question," I said, "yes, I am."
> She smiled and confided eagerly, "I've always wanted to be a vampire."
> It occurred to me that she might be inviting me to do something on the spot about her dream, but my camera call came. Turning to leave, I paused to ask, "Why?"
> She answered without hesitation, her lovely face radiant, "Because vampires live forever! There's really no way to kill them. If you pull the stake out of their hearts, they revive. *They can't really be hurt, no matter what happens* [italics mine]."[35]

This simple yet powerful anecdote recognizes something intangible in Marshall's portrayal: that the enduring strength of Dracula can transcend the politics of ethnic and sexual categories—the trauma of "racial" and sexual divide. This is a testimony to all the underrepresented in America at that time. And, the question remains, to what extent have *Dracula* films continued to serve as performance spaces of trauma? While the answer fascinates us, it is clearly the subject of another essay. However, we think the outlines of the answer are something like this: There is power in the *Dracula* story, power in its transformation in the *Blacula* films, because of something in the fundamentally archetypical nature of the material. It appeals to filmmakers, actors, and audiences as mass entertainment, in and outside the United States, because it taps into issues central to our cultural identity and provides a forum in which attitudes and values that both divide and unite us can be explored and coped with in relative safety. There is health to be found in fantasy, in imagined violence, and in laughter, and William Marshall, in the *Blacula* films, is a good physician for the nation's ills.

NOTES

1. Aside from the Károly Lajthay film *Drakula halála* (aka *Dracula's Dream*), Hungary, circa 1921.

2. See chapters 1 and 2 in Paul R. Lehman, *The Making of the Negro in Early American Literature* (New York: Pearson, 2003), 3–16. For further discussion on the conceptualization of racial categories, see also Jacques Barzun, *Darwin, Marx, Wagner: Critique of a Heritage* (Garden City, NY: Doubleday Anchor Books, 1958) and Hugh A. MacDougall, *Racial Myth in English History: Trojans, Teutons, and Anglo-Saxons* (Hanover, NH: University Press of New England, 1982).

3. Jacques Barzun, *From Dawn to Decadence: 500 Years of Western Cultural Life 1500 to the Present* (New York: Harper Perennial, 2001), 108.

4. Here we apply Ashley Montagu's "conception of an 'ethnic group'" (quoted in Lehman, 4). For further discussion, see Ashley Montagu's *Man's Most Dangerous Myth: The Fallacy of Race* (New York: World, 1964); "'Ethnic Group' and 'Race,'" *Psychiatry* 8 (1945): 27–33; and "The Concept of Race in the Human Species in the Light of Genetics," *Journal of Heredity* 23 (1941): 243–47.

5. In *The Dracula Film, Comic Book, and Game Sourcebook* (Jefferson, NC: McFarland, forthcoming), John Edgar Browning and Caroline Joan (Kay) Picart estimate this figure to be in excess of 600 titles.

6. Browning, whose research examines Dracula's victimology in depth, first posited in "'Our Draculas tell us who we were': Shadows of Exotic, Ethnic, and Sexualized Self-Others" (*2004–2005 Film & History CD-ROM Annual*) that Dracula's attacks on both a "'non-white' [i.e., African] girl" and a male victim (though off-camera) in *Dracula A.D. 1972* (1972) gesture at miscegenation and homosexuality. Browning also postulates that previously, censorship and the symbology of Dracula's "bedroom visit" (i.e., his "penetrative" bite, the exchange of fluids, the "turning" [i.e., "birthing"] process), which almost always occurs in the victim's bedroom or in Dracula's (i.e., his crypt), incited studios to predominantly avoid these types of racially and sexually ambivalent attacks in *Dracula* films right up until the 1960s and 1970s.

7. Donald F. Glut, *The Dracula Book* (Metuchen, NJ: The Scarecrow Press, Inc., 1975), 232.

8. Stephen M. Silverman and Susan Mandel, "PASSAGES: Kate Beckinsale Betrothed," *People*, June 17, 2003, www.people.com/people/article/0,,626328,00.html. This headline is significant because it demonstrates the common variety of newspaper headlines we witnessed from newspapers and magazines all around the world at the time of Marshall's death. His wasn't *just* the death of an actor; his was the death of "Blacula." The role and the actor became nearly indistinguishable, which just further alludes to the cultural resonance with which we have come to endear Marshall and Blacula.

9. William Cullen Bryant, "The African Chief," in *Poetical Works of William Cullen Bryant* (Whitefish, MT: Kessinger Publishing, LLC, 2003), 232.

10. Melissa Goldberg, "William Marshall," in *Variety* (Obituaries): June 23, 2003–June 29, 2003, 56.

11. Glut, *The Dracula Book*, 227.

12. Quoted in Stephen Bourne, "Obituary: William Marshall," *The Independent* (London), July 3, 2003.

13. Extensive quotes from William Marshall, "Introduction (II)," *The Dracula Book*, by Donald F. Glut (Metuchen, NJ: The Scarecrow Press, Inc., 1975) and from

Donald F. Glut, *The Dracula Book* (Metuchen, NJ: The Scarecrow Press, Inc., 1975) reprinted by permission of the publisher.

14. Marshall, "Introduction(II)," xvii.

15. We observe the same "lost love/reincarnation" theme appear a year later in Dan Curtis's *Dracula* (1973) (*Bram Stoker's Dracula* [U.S. title]) and again twenty years later in Columbia's *Bram Stoker's Dracula* (1992).

16. Marshall, "Introduction(II)," xviii.

17. Marshall, "Introduction(II)," xviii.

18. Troy Howarth, "Scream, Blacula, Scream," guest rev. *Scream, Blacula, Scream* (Bob Kelljan, 1973), *Eccentric Cinema*, www.eccentriccinema.com/cult_movies/ scream_blacula_scream.htm (accessed 2006).

19. Bryan Theiss, "The Classics: Blacula and Scream Blacula Scream," rev. of *Blacula* (Dir. William Crain, 1972) and *Scream, Blacula, Scream* (Bob Kelljan, 1973), *Google Groups: rec.arts.movies.reviews*, http://groups.google.com/group/rec.arts.movies.reviews/ browse_thread/thread/b50bf718c250d3fb/13b4019d70173efa?lnk=gst&q=blacula #13b4019d70173efa (accessed July 30, 2008).

20. Quoted in Francis L. K. Hsu, "Intercultural Understanding: Genuine and Spurious," *Anthropology & Education Quarterly*, vol. 8, no. 4 (November 1977): 207.

21. Harry M. Benshoff, "Blaxploitation Horror Films: Generic Reappropriation or Reinscription?" *Cinema Journal* 39, no. 2 (Winter 2000): 34.

22. Frances Gateward, "Daywalkin' Night Stalkin' Bloodsuckas: Black Vampires in Contemporary Film," *Genders*, no. 40 (2004), www.genders.org/g40/g40_gateward.html.

23. Lehman, *Making of the Negro*, 20.

24. Theiss, "The Classics: Blacula and Scream Blacula Scream," http://groups .google.com/group/rec.arts.movies.reviews/browse_thread/thread/b50bf718c250d3f/ 13b4019d70173efa?lnk=gst&q=blacula#13b4019d70173efa.

25. Howarth, "Scream, Blacula, Scream," www.eccentriccinema.com/cult_movies/ scream_blacula_scream.htm.

26. In *The Vampire Cinema* (New York: Crescent Books, 1977), David Pirie asserts that this "credibility" stems from

> that peculiar affinity with the Gothic mode that had enabled England to produce all of the great literary archetypes of screen horror in the first place. Universal had always tried to give their work an English feel by employing many English actors and directors, but they could not hope to compete with the atmospheric tone that English landscape could lend these films. (70)

27. Selected readings include Donald F. Glut, *True Vampires of History* (Secaucus, NJ: HC Publishers, 1971); Raymond T. McNally and Radu Florescu, *In Search of Dracula* (New York: Warner, 1972); Leonard Wolf, *A Dream of Dracula* (New York: Popular Library, 1972); Gabriel Ronay, *The Truth about Dracula* (New York: Stein & Day, 1972); Anthony Masters, *The Natural History of the Vampire* (New York: G. P. Putnam's Sons, 1972), Florescu and McNally, *Dracula: A Biography of Vlad the Impaler* (New York: Hawthorn, 1973); McNally, *A Clutch of Vampires* (Connecticut: New York Graphic Society, 1974); Basil Copper, *The Vampire in Legend, Fact, and Art* (Secaucus, NJ: The Citadel Press, 1974); Wolf, *The Annotated Dracula*

(New York: Clarkson N. Potter, 1975), and Glut, *The Dracula Book* (Metuchen, NJ: The Scarecrow Press, 1975).

28. Roger Ebert, "Scream, Blacula, Scream," rev. of *Scream, Blacula, Scream* (1973), by American International Pictures, *Chicago Sun-Times* July 4, 1973. Reprinted in *rogerebert.com*, http://rogerebert.suntimes.com/apps/pbcs.dll/article?AID=/19730704/REVIEWS/307040302/1023 (accessed October, 14, 2008). (c) 1973 Chicago Sun-Times. Reprinted with Permission.

29. Pirie, "Blacula," in *Time Out Film Guide*, 15th ed., ed. John Pym (London: Time Out Guides Limited, 2006), 119.

30. Pirie, *Vampire Cinema*, 138.

31. Pirie, "Revenge of Frankenstein," in *Time Out Film Guide*, 15th ed., ed. John Pym (London: Time Out Guides Limited, 2006), 970.

32. Here, we make reference to a contemporary of the *Blacula* films: the popular comic magazine series *Dracula Lives!* (Marvel, 1973–1975): Issues 1–13. Also in 1973, the comic character Blade first appears in *Tomb of Dracula* (Marvel, vol. 1, 1972–1979): Issue 10. Blade, a vampire hunter and Dracula's archnemesis (second only to Van Helsing's offspring), is a *dhampir* (half-human, half-vampire) by birth. Neither fully human nor fully vampire, Blade (like Blacula/Mamuwalde) is torn between two worlds: the one he loathes and the one for which he yearns; yet both despise him.

33. Harry M. Benshoff assembles a more detailed list in "Blaxploitation Horror Films: Generic Reappropriation or Reinscription?" *Cinema Journal* 39, no. 2 (Winter 2000): 36–37.

34. Benshoff, "Blaxploitation Horror Films," 45.

35. Marshall, "Introduction (II)," xx.

• 3 •

The Compulsions of Real/Reel Serial Killers and Vampires: Toward a Gothic Criminology

Caroline Joan (Kay) Picart and Cecil Greek

There appear to be two monstrous figures in contemporary popular culture whose constructions blur into each other, and who most powerfully evoke not only our deepest fears and taboos, but also our most repressed fantasies and desires: the serial killer and the vampire as creatures compelled to kill. The social construction of these figures, in feature films that invoke the genre traditions of the documentary, melodrama, horror-psychological thriller, and romance, forms a crucial part of this chapter. This social construction will not only cover the cinematic depictions of these figures and their significance in terms of a critique of popular culture, but also in terms of contemporary criminological theories concerning serial killers' rationality and freedom of choice, or lack thereof, in committing these crimes.

Unnoted in previous literature except for Philip Simpson's *Psycho Paths: Tracking the Serial Killer through Contemporary American Film and Fiction* (Carbondale: Southern Illinois University Press, 2000) is a striking similarity between the mythic characterization of a vampire and the description of a serial killer: both kill out of an overpowering compulsion, and in similarly periodic and patterned ways. It is this interesting convergence between criminological theory and popular cultural representations that forms a significant section of this analysis. In other words, what enables the Gothicization of crime and in this particular case, serial killers, is a narrative mode that moves across fact (*verité*) and fiction (horror, melodrama). This movement across the

Condensed and adapted from *Monsters In and Among Us: Toward a Gothic Criminology* (2007). Edited by Caroline Joan (Kay) Picart and Cecil Greek by permission of Fairleigh Dickinson University Press, Mailstop M-GH2-01, 285 Madison Avenue, Madison, NJ 07940, fdupress@fdu.edu. This was originally published, in longer form, as Caroline J. S. Picart and Cecil Greek, "The Compulsions of Serial Killers as Vampires: Toward a Gothic Criminology," *Journal of Criminal Justice and Popular Culture* 10 (2003): 39–68, www.albany.edu/scj/jcjpc/vol10is1/picart.html.

narrative visual modes of the "authentic" documentary and the "fictional" is particularly evident in purported "true stories" of serial killers like Henry Lee Lucas and Ed Gein. In each of these accounts, the attempts to sketch the portraits of "real men" and to "explain" their supernatural compulsions to kill become reduced to Gothic tropes. These "real men," Gothicized into "reel archetypes" become either a monstrous cipher (*Henry*) or an offspring of *Psycho*'s Norman Bates, the conventional victim-monster (*Ed Gein*).

THE GOTHIC VAMPIRE

Prior to examining how contemporary cinematic characterizations of serial killers have appropriated Gothic vampire conventions, it is important to lay out a concise characterization of the relevant properties of the Gothic vampire.

The Gothic vampire is an undead entity that is compelled to drink human blood. Yet human blood represents more than just life, which this undead creature needs in order to rise. As David Pirie points out, quoting Ernest Jones's *On the Nightmare*, "blood is frequently an unconscious equivalent for semen and emphasizes the amount of sexual reference that abounds in even the oldest of vampire lore."[1]

The romantic image of the vampire as both satanic rake and alienated being seems derived from Lord Byron's own self-portraiture. Indeed, Byron was fascinated by the vampire, and was described by a contemporary, Blessington, as "taking the part of a fallen or exiled being . . . existing under a curse, pre-doomed to a fate . . . that he seemed determined to fulfill."[2] Pirie notes (20) that John Polidori, Byron's physician–drug provider during that fateful summer tryst with the Shelleys in 1816 that spawned the twin Gothic tales of *Frankenstein* and *The Vampyre*, is reputed to have stolen the idea from Byron. In an attempt to capitalize on his association with Byron, who by then had distanced himself from his former physician, Polidori developed the story, Pirie adds (23–24), and sent it in to the *New Monthly Magazine* under his name, but it was republished under Byron's name in 1819. Nevertheless, it is the Polidori-Byron version that first establishes the image of the vampire as an aristocratic, decadent, seductive, and charismatic antihero who feeds upon the blood of young girls. Bram Stoker's version immortalizes this same image, with its ambivalent tensions. Indeed, because of Stoker's influence, as filtered through numerous stage adaptations of *Dracula*, and even more Universal series horror movies of the 1930s and 1940s and Hammer films of the 1960s, "the vampire seems perpetually about to caress and violate the beautiful, reclining body of a mesmerized, and in some fashion, willing, virginal young woman."[3]

Despite *Nosferatu*'s (1922) deviation from Stoker's novelistic characterization of the vampire as a well-groomed, impeccably mannered demon, to a skeletal, contorted, and shuffling monster, *Nosferatu* maintains a central feature of the mythology of the Gothic vampire. This feature is simply that the landscape in which he operates must in some way correspond with his character. As Pirie notes: "The vampire may be the active agent of terror, but the passive agent is the landscape he inhabits."[4] To render the vampire an "authentic" or believable figure, one needs Gothic settings that render his wild work "natural"—whether they be wooded English hillsides, a lonely stretch of east European moorland, or even the urban jungle setting of New York, among others. These comprise the main relevant characterizations of the cinematic Gothic vampire; there are other more nuanced features that we take up later in our discussion of individual films.

THE EMERGENCE OF THE MODERN VAMPIRIC SERIAL KILLER

Though Alfred Hitchcock's *Psycho* (1960) is often credited with ushering in the age of the modern horror suspense film, Mike Hodges, in his documentary, *Murder by Numbers*, notes how serial killer movies emerged in the late 1980s as a defining genre in mass entertainment.[5] Similarly, though cinematic depictions of the vampire legend long predate the late 1980s where our discussion begins (e.g., most notably Murnau's *Nosferatu* in 1922, and Browning's *Dracula* in 1931), the vampire myth, as we will argue, has been given new impetus through its being integrated with the serial killer narrative. As we shall show, the most glamorous instance of this blurring of vampire and serial killer constructions is Anthony Hopkins's elegant portrayal of Hannibal Lecter—a figure of immense popularity, quite unlike the rat-like Graf (or Count) Orlock/Dracula in *Nosferatu*. It is important to note that the return to an ambivalent interpretation of the vampire–serial killer as an elegant and glamorous character, despite his odiousness, is actually more in keeping with Bram Stoker's novelistic interpretation of the character. As Pirie points out:

> . . . With brilliant ingenuity, Stoker disguises his anti-father and anti-Christ in smooth anglophile charm. In one of the very few biographical facts we have, Harry Ludlam quotes Stoker as often laughing to his friends about "how he made his vampire monster wait hand and foot on Jonathan Harker. . . at the castle." Even when Dracula is about to pitch Harker out

of the front door into a pack of wolves he speaks "with a sweet courtesy which made me rub my eyes it seemed so real."[6]

Though there have been precedents of the contemporary characterization of the serial killer–vampire figure, such as Lang's *M* (1931), Hitchcock's *Psycho* (1960), and Powell's *Peeping Tom* (1960), in the interests of clarity and compression, the focus of this chapter will remain on the period of the late 1980s onward and will concentrate on a collection of both well known and some more obscure American films like *Henry: Portrait of a Serial Killer* (produced in 1986 but not widely released until 1990); *Ed Gein: The True Story* (2001); *The Silence of the Lambs* (1991); *Immortality* or *The Wisdom of Crocodiles* (1998); and *Hannibal* (2001). The first two films purport to have some connection to "true" stories of how these serial killers became transformed into the monstrous figures they became, and are crucial to illustrating the contemporary popularity of cinematic serial killer narratives; furthermore, they illustrate how a Gothic criminology connects reel worlds with the look of the "real" world, while still mythologizing the serial killer as a Gothic construction. The last three films exploit the contemporary seductive glamour of the vampire myth to render the serial killer a charismatic and elegant *Übermensch*, transcending bourgeois distinctions of good and evil. Though there are other serial killer films that debut during this period (such as *Seven* [1995], *Copycat* [1995], *Summer of Sam* [1999], *The Cell* [2000]), none of these films have either the pseudodocumentary quality that *Henry* and *Ed Gein* are packaged to have (and thus their implicit claim to factuality, alongside their Gothic themes), or the overt references to the vampire legend that *Silence of the Lambs*, *Immortality*, and *Hannibal* utilize (and thus exploit the mythic power of the vampire narrative, with the contemporary twist that eroticizes him). We aim to show how a "natural" slippage from the realms of the natural/cinema verité to the supernatural/mythic is what enables the Gothicization of the serial killer as vampiric.

It is also important to note that all of the main characters in these specifically chosen films are white males—a rare area in which fact and fiction converge in so far as most serial killers who have been caught fit this raced and sexed demographic, with a very small majority being women, and African Americans constituting 10 percent (though their numbers appear to be on the rise), and Latino, Asian, and Native American groups comprising about 2 to 3 percent.[7] Naturally, being white and male are neither necessary nor sufficient to becoming a serial killer (trauma, such as physical and/or sexual abuse; alcoholism or addiction; low self-esteem; deep-seated hostility and a proneness to depression; and reading and viewing of violent pornographic materials all result in a powerful urge to indulge in compulsive and violent fantasies), but it is striking that in both the factual accounts and the popular imaginary, it is the white male who simultaneously occupies the dangerous and endangered positions of being the victimized Monster (the serial killer as abused son) and glamorous and superhuman predator (as vampiric seducer and genius).

In film, one of the rare exceptions to the white perpetrator (which still corresponds with the factual racial demographics of serial killers, with minorities not being typical) is Bernard Rose's *Candyman* (1992) and its sequels. Candyman is the revenge-seeking spirit of a post-antebellum black artist who made love to a young white female patron only to suffer revenge at the hands of the girl's father and an accompanying mob. Candyman had his arm hacked off, honey poured over his body to attract bees to sting him to death, and his body burned on a pyre. His spirit now resides in the Chicago projects of Cabrini Green and attacks both residents and visitors to the apartment complex. Rumored as a Gothic figure with Chicago depicted as a city beset by plague, Candyman seeks only to have the legacy of his fate remembered and continues to kill lest citizens forget what happened to him (and by implication the memory of all blacks who suffered at the hands of lynch mobs). He ultimately finds a white woman willing to be seduced by him in sacrificial exchange to save the life of a kidnapped black infant he holds hostage; she eventually becomes his bodily reincarnation after she, too, dies from burns, torched by a fearful and angry mob. Though subtle, this film also conflates and ambivalently glamorizes serial killing and vampirism. Candyman, like the vampire, possesses the capacity to hypnotize his prey, such that they appear to desire their victimizations. Candyman's kiss, which is marked by swarming bees emerging from decomposing flesh, underneath an elegant, fur-lined robe, parallels the bodily horror evoked by the vampire's physical Otherness clothed by his mythical wealth. The film's visual treatment of blood, which oozes as a rich, red fluid in copious amounts, is certainly symptomatic of both serial killer and vampiric cinematic narratives.

FACT AND FICTION IN PROFILING SERIAL KILLERS: *HENRY* AND *ED GEIN*, REAL OR REEL?

Both *Henry: Portrait of a Serial Killer* and *Ed Gein* purport in some way to connect with the "true stories" behind the myth of a particular "monster," such as Henry Lee Lucas or Ed Gein. In *Henry*'s case, the advertising rhetorical stress on "He's not Freddy, He's not Jason, He's *real* [italics ours]" shaped expectations of "authenticity" by making the claim that Henry Lee Lucas, the "real-life serial killer," was the basis of the film. Yet in both films, this implicit claim of laying bare "the truth" regarding how these monsters became what they were is problematic.

The attempt at simulating a "real-life" quality is particularly apparent in three sequences of *Henry*. The first is the opening sequence, which requires a detailed description of specific segments. This sequence uses a montage of scenes that seem to give the film a semidocumentary feel, which John Mc-Naughton, the director, prefers to describe as a "cinema verité" style, thus giving it a more "arty" trademark. This opening sequence juxtaposes the two sides of Henry's life: the violent and the mundane. It begins with an extreme close-up of a dead face; the camera then pulls back in a circular motion to reveal the naked body of a bruised woman with a bloody gash across her abdomen. Her body lies in a grassy field, which, in stark contrast, the background sound codes as idyllic through the use of the sounds of birds twittering and leaves rustling in the breeze. An unsettling musical score, Henry's leitmotif, overlays the sounds of nature. (This set of shots is interestingly coincident with the style of David Lynch's *Blue Velvet* [1986], which also styles itself as an independent and "arty" film, despite its use of "pulp" material for its subject matter.)

A cut moves into an extreme close-up of someone crushing a cigarette, and as the camera moves back gradually, we slowly see the figure of Henry (Michael Rooker), a soft-spoken young man, rise from yet another mundane meal at one of these ubiquitous "greasy spoon" diners. As he pays for his meal, he compliments the young waitress on her smile before he walks out to his car, as the camera looks up at his retreating back from a low angle.

The camera then pans across a liquor store counter to reveal the strewn bodies of a middle-aged couple whose faces are partially obscured by the crimson flow of blood that oozes from bullet holes in their heads. The same haunting leitmotif returns as an acoustic flashback occurs: the sounds of a gun firing, a woman screaming, and a man barking: "Shut up!" Sirens wail as the musical leitmotif wanes.

Another abrupt cut to Henry, this time showing his face in a close-up, as he listens to country music while he is driving down the highway.

The camera pans from the bloody sheets on a bed to a blood-spattered bathroom, where a woman who is provocatively seminude (wearing a garter belt, stockings, and high heels) is sitting on the toilet, her hands bound. Blood runs down her body, and a bottle is planted in the side of her face. The mundane sounds of a phone ringing and the water trickling mingle with the same leitmotif as an acoustic flashback occurs: a woman, aroused, coos "oooh baby"; a man shouts "shut up, bitch . . . die . . . die . . . die" with the sound of glass being broken intruding.

The opening sequence is particularly striking because it immediately breaks a standard feature of slasher/horror films: there is no lack of mutilated bodies on display, but instead of showing how the violence is actually done, it is almost a snapshot of the aftermath of the violence that we view. It is the acoustic flashback that *enacts* the scenes of violence for us, and yet because it is in the past, this enactment is muffled and jarringly dissonant with the sometimes peaceful and beautiful, and at other times, everyday surroundings within which these extraordinarily brutal crimes have occurred. What results is a rupture: the film appears to set up the audience expectation that this is going to be a movie about "the real" and that it will eventually explain how and why these murders occurred. But like the faded soundtrack, inevitably, all the film leaves the audience with is a standard Gothic trope: the image of monster as mysterious "lack" or absence. Henry's portrait as a serial killer remains consistently out of focus.

In the scene that is supposed to provide a clear reason for why Henry kills, Becky (Tracy Arnold), in a dialogue that resembles the later conversations between Clarice Starling (Jodie Foster) and Hannibal Lecter (Anthony Hopkins) in *The Silence of the Lambs*, tries to trade her vulnerabilities for intimate confessions from Henry. Becky offers her own confessions as an ill-fated go-go dancer who married a no-good husband who wound up in jail. She married hastily in order to escape from her abusive father, who would visit her bedroom at night, and hit her if she fought back. Using this as emotional capital, she asks why Henry killed his mother. The camera stays steadily in a close-up on Henry as he looks at her, though as if unseeingly, with dead eyes and barely concealed anger and disgust. He recounts that his father was a drunk, and that his mother, a whore, would make him wear a dress and watch her go about her business with her customers. Unlike the earlier sequences, there is no acoustic flashback; the camera stays unflinchingly steady and unabashed, relying on no external dramatic gimmicks, once again lending the scene a look of documentary "realism." The problem is that visual clarity is betrayed by the fuzziness and incoherence of Henry's "authentic" confession: he contradicts himself, and cannot seem to remember whether he shot, stabbed, or bludgeoned his mother to death.

The final scene of note is probably the scene that has generated the most controversy, which McNaughton labeled the "heart" of the movie: the "home invasion" scene. A *Rolling Stone* reviewer summarized this scene in the following way:

> In the film's most terrifying scene, the one that prompts the walkouts, Henry and Otis attack a suburban family and videotape the deed. "Take her blouse off," Henry tells Otis, who is grabbing a struggling housewife.

"Do it, Otis. You're a star." Cinematographer Charlie Lieberman . . . turned a camcorder over to Rooker to shoot this scene as Henry would. The footage—grainy, unfocused, crazily angled—makes the carnage joltingly immediate.[8]

What the review does not mention is that this three-minute scene, shot once again cinema verité style, without editing, and in a long shot produces an intense documentary realism that not only makes the audience believe it is a "real" thing going on in "real" time. That is, we believe we are peering through the camera's lens at something diegetically occurring at that time. Yet the camera pulls back to show the two killers, Henry and Otis (Tom Towles), sitting on a couch, thoroughly absorbed in watching the violence, reviewing their earlier exploits raptly. The implication is obvious: that we, exactly like the killers, have thus far been visually consuming the film in the same way the killers are, as entertainment that looks "real." Isabel Cristina Pinedo details some of the strongest reactions recorded by film critics:

> As Hal Hinson reports, "it's hard to know how to react . . . we feel as if we've been drawn into something we didn't expect; as if unwittingly, we've become accomplices in the making of a snuff film" . . . Similarly, Eleanor Ringel declares, "Then, we've pretty much let down our guard, the film-maker smacks us in the face with one of the most shocking sequences I've ever seen on film."[9]

What therefore emerges as a "real" depiction of Henry's and Otis's propensity for violence is revealed as something we, however ambivalently, share. The gaze of the camera is deflected from the "truth" about Henry and Otis, to the truth about us, the viewers. Once again, the "truth" regarding why Henry does what he does remains dim and obscure; despite the look of realism that characterizes his "portrait," nothing more than a Gothic cipher emerges.

In the final sequence, Henry gazes blankly at his image in a mirror at a hotel room; after his morning toilette, he leaves the hotel room that he is supposed to have shared with Becky the night before. But Becky is nowhere to be seen, and we are initially led to believe that he has perhaps abandoned her. The answer unfolds via a return to the narrative technique used at the beginning of the film: via an acoustic flashback. As Henry drives off, leaving behind him Becky's bulky and bloodstained suitcase, we hear a woman's screams. Henry's "portrait" remains a Gothic mask; the portrait that promises a close-up of the serial killer's soul remains a bland surface, mirroring back the audience's unsatisfied desire for "the truth" regarding how Henry became the soulless monster he became.

Similarly, *Ed Gein* begins (and ends) with bleak documentary footage of the well-known killer's arrest in his hometown of Plainfield, Wisconsin. Once again, the audience's expectations are primed to see "the truth" about why and how Ed Gein became the cannibalistic necrophiliac who created a "woman suit," and whose crimes provided the inspiration for *Psycho*'s Norman Bates, *The Texas Chainsaw Massacre*'s Leatherface, and *The Silence of the Lambs*' and *Hannibal*'s Hannibal Lecter. There is a clear "forensic" look to this film, which bears a certain resemblance to the look of "upmarket TV dramas, especially *Prime Suspect* whose first ever episode . . . dealt with a serial killer of prostitutes."[10]

Yet there are clear problems to taking the movie's claim to "authenticity" simplistically. In order to explain Ed's (Steve Railsback, who had played Charles Manson in an earlier film, *Helter Skelter*) actions, the movie resorts to creating the monster-behind-the-monster, popularized by Hitchcock's *Psycho*. Ed's mother, Augusta (Carrie Snodgress), whose misdirected and excessive religious zealotry, physical abuse, sexual repression, and "bedtime" stories of the more lurid sections of the Book of Revelation from the Bible, emerges as the reason why Ed becomes what he is. There is evidence to support the view that many of Ed's complexes arose from his tangled relationship with his mother, but the film, in deflecting the responsibility of monstrosity from the abused son to the abusive mother, simply falls back on stock representations of the mother-as-devouring-and-poisonous-figure, yet another standard Gothic fixture. In one scene, Ed prays to his mother's grave, asking that she be returned to him; a raven suddenly hovers in circles in the sky, breaking the stillness with its cries. Later, as Ed sets out to claim his first victim, Mary Hogan (Sally Champlin), a quick close-up of the raven implies that his mother's "ghost" (whether as a subjective delusion or an objective fact is immaterial in this characteristic blend of horror and psychological thriller) is present and urging him on to commit the crime. (The popular *Crow* films use a similar motif.) Unfortunately, this way of framing the story can be traced to the all-too-familiar Hitchcock rendition of Robert Bloch's novelistic rendition of Gein's life, in which it is the "monstrous mother," a product of pop psychology and Gothic cinematic representations, which constitutes the compulsive urge for why Gein commits the heinous acts that have granted him a certain mythic status.

Repeatedly, the movie makes allusions to Hitchcock's *Psycho*. When Ed reenters the general store to murder Colette Marshall (Carol Mansell), the camera is at an extreme high angle, looking down at the dwarfed characters, as if from the point of view of a bird of prey; this is a signature Hitchcockian move. The resemblance to Anthony Perkins's Norman Bates has been noted by film reviewers. For example, Carl Cortez remarks: "Steve Railsback stars as Gein and plays him as a maniacal little simpleton. In fact, Railsback seems to be resurrecting the ghost of Anthony Perkins (via Norman Bates) in this performance, but missing the humanity Perkins brought to his famous *Psycho* role."[11] Later, when Ed has been arrested and is committed to an asylum, the Hitchcockian flourishes are all over the place: the camera zooms into a close-up, with the shadows of the outline of a window in low key lighting at Ed's back, often signifying entrapment in the Hitchcockian universe. Like Hitchcock's Norman, Ed's monologues, shot in close-up or medium close-up, reveal a character steeped in self-delusion and madness, in contrast with his quiet and self-effacing veneer. The ending inserts the same documentary footage of Ed being arrested, but this time, zooms into the interior of the car where Ed sits, a diminutive figure who tries to cover his face with his gloved hands. The juxtaposition of the documentary footage once again is supposed to bolster the authenticity of the look we have at Ed Gein—but the style of the montage sequences built around the embedded documentary bear such a striking resemblance to *Psycho* that it is difficult not to collapse Hitchcock's Norman into Chuck Parello's Ed. As the closing credits begin, we are shown Ed uttering a prayer as he lights a match and asks that "this evil spirit [be stopped] from invading [his] body"; then he is shown exhuming his mother's body from a high angle shot in low key lighting; then he is shown in close-up fiercely enunciating his mother's views concerning whores; then placidly calling the mental institution that houses him a "good place" where people treat him "nice"[ly]—only to grin and say that one drawback to the place is that there are some people who are "really screwed up." The closing sequence ends with a black background that states matter-of-factly that he died at the asylum and was eventually buried beside his mother and brother. Yet the last image we see is of Ed, tearfully and vehemently proclaiming his mother "a saint"—a portrait not altogether different from Hitchcock's wild-eyed and tight-lipped Norman, whose thoughts, revealed through a voice-over, are those of his "mother" deciding to be "silent" just in case anyone is watching. Gein's mother, played by Carrie Snodgress, is a tall and thin woman with a low, husky voice, who repeatedly calls Ed "boy"—once again a derivation from *Psycho* rather than from "real life," because Gein's mother was obese (which explains why the women Ed killed were large—a fact that *The Silence of the Lambs* more accurately details in its graphic depiction of the skinned victims of "Buffalo Bill").

This brings us to the second feature film that *Ed Gein* references repeatedly in its Gothically styled "true" rendition of Gein's portrait: Jonathan Demme's *The Silence of the Lambs*. When Brian Hillman (Frank Worden) descends into the darkness of Ed's basement to find Colette Marshall's nude body hanging upside down from the ceiling, gutted like a deer, the scene is shot like Clarice Starling's (Jodie Foster) penetration of Jame Gumb's (Ted Levine) basement. In both, the subjective point of view is used, and the camera pans over the details of the contents of the underground, bringing to light its obscene contents. Later, as Sheriff Jim Stilwell (Pat Skipper) sits, dumbfounded at the discovery that the quiet man who used to babysit his young boys is someone who finds lurid descriptions of Nazi war crimes entertainment, the scene is shot in a manner again reminiscent of the ending of *The Silence of the Lambs*. A fast-paced montage, transitioning in keeping with the flashing of cameras taking shots (very like the ending of the film, after Clarice has shot Gumb and the contents of his basement are being documented), reveals the numerous items that abound in Ed's house of horror: a heart steeped in blood in a skillet on the stove, various body parts floating in a bottled solution, the "woman suit" and the belt of human nipples resting on a mannequin. Finally, the scene in which Ed emerges from his farmhouse, clad in his "woman suit" (from a dried facial mask and wig to labia strapped onto his pelvic area) is eerily reminiscent of the haunting scene in *The Silence of the Lambs* where Gumb cavorts and poses nude in front a camera, as he pulls his penis between his legs to make himself appear female. Yet the impact of both scenes is different: while Gumb's cavorting scene is terrifying, Gein's is oddly funny, particularly when he scurries back into his farmhouse, as if terrified that someone would see him, after he has spent the past two minutes beating his drum of human skin and carrying on loudly, like a stereotypic "savage." If Henry's portrait is dimly lit and out of focus, Ed's portrait is too well lit and obscured by prior renditions, resulting in the "real" Ed emerging as a caricature. The result, as one critic notes, is that "the original cannibal now seems like a pale imitation."[12] Nevertheless, both *Henry* and *Ed Gein* fall back upon Gothic tropes in order to "explain" the unnatural compulsions of these two well-known serial killers.

In the same way one could take issue with *Henry* for removing all traces of a homosexual liaison the real-life Otis claimed he and Henry had, one could take issue with *Ed Gein*'s implication that the murders of Mary Hogan and Bernice Worden (Colette Marshall in the film) took place within days or months, rather than three years. Nevertheless, one common "truth" that both portraits draw of these two serial killers is that they were abused sons— and as such, emerge as figures both imperiled and perilous; sympathetic and horrifying; all-too-human and unrecognizably monstrous. A key symptom and expression of this liminal space they occupy as simultaneously dangerous and endangered is that they suffer and are empowered by a compulsion to kill in a patterned, ritualistic way. The easy slippages between fact and fiction and the ambiguous positioning between the "documentary" look, the "arty" independent film look, and the splatter film look, are precisely what enable the Gothicization of these narratives of real serial killers, as enduring reel-life myths.

CONVERGING MYTHS: SERIAL KILLERS AND VAMPIRES

In *The Silence of the Lambs*, *Immortality*, and *Hannibal*, the figures of the vampire and the serial killer blur into each other. For example, the face of the monstrous in *The Silence of the Lambs* is initially visualized through Hannibal Lecter (Anthony Hopkins), a brilliant but institutionalized psychiatrist known as "Hannibal the Cannibal." Admittedly, there are technical differentiations between cannibals and vampires, but *The Silence of the Lambs* and *Hannibal* conflate these two, such that Hannibal's vampiric and hypnotic gaze (which is characteristic of vampires, not cannibals) becomes inextricable from his blood-soaked, man-eating teeth (which is ambiguously placed in between cannibalism, an atavistic "real-life" horror, and vampirism, a supernatural horror). More pertinently, in terms of the history of film (as opposed to literature), there is certainly precedent for the conflation of cannibalism with vampirism in zombie films like George Romero's *Night of the Living Dead* (1968), which spawned a host of derivatives, like *Horror Express* (1972), *Children Shouldn't Play with Dead Things* (1972), *The Living Dead at Manchester Morgue*, also released as *Don't Open the Window* (1974), *Fear No Evil* (1981), *One Dark Night* (1982), *Zombie* (1979), and *Dawn of the Dead* (1979). According to Waller, Romero's presentation of the living dead in *Night of the Living Dead* was derived from Richard Matheson's novel, *I Am Legend* (1954), which strips vampires of their ability to transform themselves in mists or bats, their legendary wealth, and of their need to be invited into a home in order to invade it.[13] *The Silence of the Lambs* and *Hannibal* continue this conflation of vampirism and cannibalism but restore to the serial killer–cannibal the vampire's aristocraticism, combined with a supernatural intelligence and the ever-present threat of his barely contained physical power, which "rationally" explain Hannibal's ability to terrorize and feed on others' terror.

In *The Silence of the Lambs*, Clarice Starling (Jodie Foster), a student at the FBI academy, probes Lecter for clues in an attempt to identify and apprehend a serial killer nicknamed Buffalo Bill (Ted Levine). Lecter, who feeds Clarice tidbits of information in return for details of her personal history, becomes one of the film's ambivalent figures of monstrosity: intriguing and horrifying at the same time. It is not difficult to catch the allusions to the myth of the vampire in the film's characterizations of Hannibal.

Dr. Chilton (Anthony Heald), the administrator of the asylum, in tones meant to frighten Clarice (and the audience), describes Lecter as "a monster. A pure psychopath."[14] Chilton, briefing Clarice on her way to visit Lecter for the first time, shows her a snapshot that proves that the madman is capable of extreme physical violence. The audience is spared from sharing Clarice's look at the photograph. Nevertheless, Chilton's graphic description of Hannibal's devouring of one of the woman's eyes and her tongue, while his blood pressure remained constant at eighty-five, leaves a powerful mental imprint precisely because of the absence of the specific image of the nurse's mutilation. Indeed, Lecter menaces not simply by assaulting, but by possessing a terrifying ability to insinuate himself into the minds of his patients/victims (and the audience). The other characters in the film recognize this subtle threat. "Believe me," FBI section chief Jack Crawford (Scott Glenn) warns Starling, "You don't want Hannibal Lecter inside your head." Craig McKay, the film's editor, describes Lecter as "leaning back, drinking it all in, vampirically" as he elicits personal information from Clarice.[15] One of the guards echoes this sentiment when he asks Clarice whether Lecter is "some kind of vampire." Traditional concepts of monstrosity clearly inform the film's portrayal of Lecter; nevertheless, he is tellingly characterized in terms of an attractive and fascinating monster—in keeping with contemporary (and original novelistic) characterizations of vampirism as a suave Count Dracula (rather than a clumsy and inarticulate Frankensteinian creature) who achieves penetration not so much by force as by the allure of his Otherness.

Alongside his apparent elegance, the film figures Lecter's monstrosity in terms of his ability to return the gaze—to echo, even in confinement, the voyeurism of Norman Bates. It is important to note that in *Silence of the Lambs*, Ed Gein's cannibalism was split apart from his gender uncertainties and fetishistic obsession on obese women's flesh. Cannibalism, conjoined with vampirism's ability to hypnotize and seduce, became a feature of the powerfully heterosexual, upper-class, and brilliant Dr. Lecter; and the desire to become a woman, conjoined with vampirism's gender uncertainties, became a feature of the gender-disturbed, blue-collar, and not-so-brilliant Jame Gumb.

The exchanges between Clarice and Lecter in the psychiatric ward reveal the complex interpenetrations of the vampiric gaze. His first appearance was carefully staged: Clarice finds the doctor, awaiting her approach, standing in the middle of his well-lit, glassed-in cell, staring out at her. Lecter's monstrous gaze, like Dracula's, is uncontained by his cell, penetrates, threatens, and controls the scene. The cell was carefully designed to promote this effect. Demme recalls in an interview that "Kristi Zea—the production designer—and I spent a tremendous amount of time trying to deal with the bars on Lecter's cage," eventually opting to dispose of the offending obstructions altogether.[16] Demme was concerned with showing each character's face clearly, transmitting an unobstructed gaze between Lecter and Clarice, his protégé and analysand (*The Silence of the Lambs* [2001]). Later, Lecter's wardens fit him with a mask, which, although it obscures his face almost entirely, leaves his eyes expressively visible. The specially constructed and eminently recognizable prop reveals the significance of his monstrous and hypnotic gaze.

As reviewers of the film and observers of pop culture have noted, Lecter became a wildly popular figure, enacting on a larger scale the dynamic of Clarice and her strange attraction to the "therapist." Novelist A. L. Kennedy observes "the nice folks in my cinema just cheered" at the triumphant ending where Hannibal Lecter announces his intentions for yet another cannibalistic dinner date.[17] Anthony Hopkins, celebrated for his performance of the character, explains that he wanted to defy the expectations of the audience when it came to the horror of Hannibal Lecter. "The thing is not to act in a frightening way," he explains. "I meant to play Lecter very friendly and very charming, very silky and seductive."[18] David Sundelson describes Lecter's ambivalence with the oxymoronic phrase "flashes of highbrow savagery."[19] As Hopkins implies, his character's monstrous power emerges not *despite* but precisely *because* of his genteel, cultured dignity.

While his propensity to create gourmet meals from his victims does indeed horrify, he stands in clear contrast to the simply offensive "Multiple" Miggs and the other inmates of his ward. Maintaining a calm, commanding presence in his cell, Lecter never physically threatens Clarice; instead, he plays an almost gallant role. Hopkins himself describes Lecter as the "prime dark angel" of the film's fairy-tale structure, emphasizing the grotesque attractiveness or elegant savagery of his character. He acknowledges that the story is "all very erotic."[20] Critics have observed the intimacy and implied attraction of Lecter's relationship with Clarice, and the film itself does nothing to dispel the notion. For example, upon Clarice's arrival in Memphis, Lecter remarks, since she had gone to all that trouble to interrogate him again, "people will think we're in love." His caress of Clarice's hand, shot in close-up at the conclusion of this scene, emphasizes that Clarice's interests on some level involve more than simple questioning. The allure of Lecter's monstrosity, the film reveals, brings Clarice back time and again.

Driving home the charisma, rather than the repulsiveness, of Lecter's monstrosity, the editing process cut out the most overt representations of his violence from the final version of the film. Chilton, for example, shows Clarice a photograph documenting Lecter's assault on a nurse, but the film does not treat the audience to the same view. The most violent scenes (Lecter's escape from the Shelby County courthouse) emphasize his power and brutality but at the same time deny the graphic details. At the conclusion of the attack, the camera switches from a low-angle shot to a high-angle view of the madman calmly surveying the domesticated cell, a phonograph, his drawings, and (ironically) a copy of *Bon Appétit* accessorizing the scene.[21] Ted Tally's discussion of the editing process reveals that shots of Lecter's escape elaborating upon the madman's brutal violence were cut, ostensibly in the interest of pacing.[22] The resulting rendering, however, not only moved the plot along but also produced the image of Lecter as a brilliant, refined, and dangerously sympathetic character.

Similarly, Po Chih Leong's *Immortality* centers principally on Steven Grlscz (Jude Law), a strikingly handsome London medical researcher, who seduces women before he kills them and drinks their blood. In the scene that reveals his modus operandi, after he has saved Maria Vaughn (Kerry Fox) from committing suicide by preventing her from throwing herself on the tracks of an oncoming train at a Tube station, he woos her and they become lovers. One night, Grlscz (pronounced "Grolsch") brings Maria flowers, and they commence a romantic evening together. The cinematic coding of Steven as a vampire grows particularly strong in this scene. He and Maria play a game in which they sit far apart, and he asks her whether she trusts him and commands her to close her eyes. She half-jokingly replies that she does not trust him, but obeys. The camera shoots from overhead, to reveal the top of Grlscz's head and the shadow it casts; gradually, the shadow of his head lengthens impossibly, and we cut to a close up of Steven gazing upon Maria's face, which is in shadow. The shadow disappears and Maria opens her eyes (a point of view the audience shares) to find Steven sitting at the far end of the room. She laughs in astonishment and delight, thinking that it is a magic trick meant to amuse her. Grlscz again commands her to close her eyes, and he repeats the same "trick," this time kissing her on the forehead and nose and withdraws from kissing her lips when she leans forward with her eyes closed. The third time, Grlscz places a thick silver band on her finger and commands her to open her eyes. To the audience familiar with the cinematic traditions of vampire lore, the signs are all there: the vampire's irresistible seductive charm; the expressionist shadows cast against a surface in order to signify the approach of the vampire; the use of the vampire's ring to claim a bride. The vampire's ring, signifying his authority, his supernatural powers, or heritage, is cinematic, rather than literary in origin, and seen in a multitude of movies such as *House of Frankenstein* (1944), *The Vampire's Ghost* (1945), *Blood of Dracula* (1957), where the ring is now a medallion, *Horror of Dracula* or *Dracula* (1958), *Taste the Blood of Dracula* (1970), and *Dracula Today* or *Dracula A.D. 1972* (1972).

A sharp cut ensues to reveal a steamy erotic scene in which the lovers kiss each other passionately on the stairs; in the bedroom, Steven holds Maria's hands behind her back as they fall on the bed. He climbs on top of her, running his hand along her face, as she responds, aroused. The low angle close up at his face, from her point of view, reveals him to be strangely detached. At the height of her passion, he suddenly covers her mouth, twists her face sideways, and bites her neck, as blood spurts on the wall. She struggles but he holds her down, continuing to sink his teeth into her neck. The camera moves further back to show that the blanket has becomes drenched with blood, and he sits up, his mouth ringed crimson. The deep brilliance of blood, introduced very early in the film (as blood drips from a car somehow suspended high up among some trees onto Steven's hand as he looks up), is also a hallmark of vampire films, and is a consistent feature as the plot unfolds. In addition, later shots of Grlscz also show him wearing a long black coat that swirls like a cape around him, reminiscent of the black cape that the archetypal vampire usually wears.

However, there is some difficulty with labeling Steven a vampire. If he is one, he is very different from the standard cinematic depiction. He does not have fangs, he can walk in broad daylight, he can touch crucifixes, and he is a medical researcher who reveals genuine compassion for his patients. Yet there are also clear hints that he is something other than human—perhaps even superhuman. For example, he moves faster than any ordinary human being can, as evidenced in the single fight sequence (reminiscent of Hong Kong martial arts films in which Leong specialized) in which Grlscz effortlessly overcomes an entire gang of thugs in order to save Anne from being raped. In addition, Grlscz almost unconsciously assimilates other peoples' attributes to become his own; it is as if he is a blank slate upon whom the imprint of those who grow close to him (and thus become marked as potential victims) are burnt in. Thus Maria's ability to write the opposing lines "I love you" and "I hate you" simultaneously later become transmuted into his ability to compose lines of poetry and to draw a portrait of Anne Levels (Elina Löwensohn), his final prey and love interest. Grlscz also possesses the ability to expel all the negative emotions his victims have felt toward him by coughing up a daggerlike crystal (a theme that has Cronenbergian resonances with its emphasis on the physical externalization of emotional tensions, such as in *The Brood*). His "unnaturalness" as a serial killer and Gothic creature is visualized in the scene where he squats at a beach, after he has disposed of Maria's body. The camera shoots him from a low angle as he sits, a dark, brooding figure with his hands clawlike and his body heaving strangely, like a bird of prey momentarily resting.

The title of the film was originally *The Wisdom of Crocodiles*, which illuminates one main theme of the film. During scenes of lovemaking with Anne, Steven, in a voice-over, tells his new lover that human beings have three brains: a human brain, which overlays a mammalian brain, which in turn overlays a reptile brain. Thus, Steven concludes his bizarre "bedtime story" with the words that every time the psychiatrist asks someone to lie on the couch, one is in effect being asked to lie down with a horse and a crocodile.

As the movie continues, we find out that Steven is more "crocodile" than human; though malice is not one of his flaws, like a vampire or a serial killer, he is compelled to kill, and to kill ritualistically in a patterned way. When he is ready to kill his victim, he lines his bed with a disposable silver sheet, which catches most of the blood and becomes his victim's shroud. Every month, he must feed upon a woman's blood, not for her blood itself, as popular vampire lore would have it, but in order to consume the love that resides in her blood so that he may continue to live. When he genuinely falls in love with Anne and fights the compulsion to kill her off, his body fails to heal, and in a haunting sequence that mimes the progression of AIDS, his body begins to degenerate.

Yet like the serial killers immortalized through film in both cinema verité and popular horror genres (of which psychological thrillers constitute a subgenre), Grlscz emerges as a figure both sympathetic and terrifying. It is clear that he detests his condition and is in search of that mythic woman who could love him "perfectly" and thus cure him of his affliction. Steven seems more like a victim driven to kill by his own nature, rather than a sadistic predator who enjoys his victims' suffering. In addition, Grlscz's friendship with Inspector Healey (Timothy Spall) may have been initially motivated by selfish motives (i.e., he saves the inspector, who was tailing him, from a gang of thugs, perhaps in order to throw suspicion off himself as a murderer), but the friendship between the two men later deepens and is cemented by mutual confessions. Grlscz also assimilates one characteristic feature of the inspector: the habit of crushing the very end of a burning cigarette with his fingertips. This acquisition of bodily "signatures" is a sign of intimacy usually reserved for one of his female victims. In the final moments of the film, which are slightly reminiscent of one of the concluding sequences of *Blade Runner* in which Rick Deckart (Harrison Ford) hangs from a ledge as Roy Batty (Rutger Hauer) hangs onto him, Anne hangs perilously from the side of a building as Steven hangs on to her. She has chosen to jump rather than to become his victim, and it appears that he is determined to claim his prize. After struggling in vain with him, she uses the ornamental chopstick she had used to prop up her hair (an Oriental family heirloom that signified that the owner of the chopsticks would always be safe and well fed) to stab Grlscz's hand repeatedly. He somehow manages to swap hands, and like Roy Batty (with his own hand impaled by a nail), who unexpectedly saves the blade runner who had come to kill him, Grlscz pulls Anne to safety and allows her to escape as he bleeds to death. The final sequence of the film shoots from high above, once again in a Hitchcock-like style, to reveal Grlscz, clad from head to toe in black, his bleeding hand punctured, as if by stigmata, and his body twitching in the final throes of fear and pain. Grlscz thus emerges as a stylish, charismatic, and even sacrificial vampire–serial killer figure, with whom the audience identifies despite his monstrosity.

Finally, Ridley Scott's *Hannibal* takes this process of identifying with a glamorously compelling and deadly vampiric character or "dark angel" even further. Whereas *The Silence of the Lambs* was peripherally about the relationship between Lecter and Starling, and particularly in Thomas Harris's original novel, more about Starling's determination to make it in an alpha-dominated male profession, the hinge upon which *Hannibal* turns is the cult worship of the seductive and malevolent doctor. As Todd R. Ramlow observes: "As the character's immense popularity suggests, there is something about Lecter that appeals to 'us,' there appears to be some level on which 'we' all wish we could be a little more like him, which is precisely what the filmmakers are banking on."[23] Charles Taylor puts his finger on the pulse of this hybrid of slick and arty cinematography with necro-thriller content when he declares: "Scott's 'Hannibal' is the apotheosis of serial-killer chic, the prestige movie version of a Manson T-shirt. No longer a villain, Lecter is now the hero, the superior being given the power of judgment over all the other characters—the serial killer as arbiter of taste."[24] One way in which this identification between monster and audience is forged in *Hannibal* is by creating an even more odious monster in Mason Verger (Gary Oldman), a former victim whom Hannibal had "hypnotized" to rip off his own face, as Hannibal fed the pieces to the dogs. Another way is to focus on the degree of corruption within the FBI, embodied particularly in the Justice Department ladder climber Paul Krendler (Ray Liotta), who accepts payments from Verger in order to disgrace Starling, and thus transform the distressed agent into unwitting bait to lure out Hannibal. As Ridley Scott remarks in the director's commentary on the film, Hannibal, like Clarice, is "pure in his own way"[25]—he seems to have a sense of honor and ethical responsibility to those who do not violate his sense of civility, such as Clarice and Nurse Barney Matthews (Frankie Faison). In fact Hannibal in this sequel, unlike *The Silence of the Lambs*, seems compelled to kill only if his sense of "good manners and taste" are assaulted. Thus, a narrative device that *Hannibal* uses in order to put the audience squarely on his side has been used in a prior film: Stanley Kubrick's *A Clockwork Orange*. In both films, what appears to be an omniscient or objective point of view is revealed to be the killer's point of view such that his murderous acts seem justified. In *Hannibal*, all of the doctor's victims are varieties of what he calls "free-range rude," including the avaricious, the lustful, and the pedophilic. Thus, it only seems poetic justice (tinged with very dark, sardonic humor) when he murders them, in a Dante-esque fashion, such that their deaths mirror their crimes. (*Seven* uses a similar approach, as each of the victims representing the seven deadly sins is murdered by getting their "just desserts.") For example, Inspector Francesco Pazzi (Giancarlo Giannini) is hanged and gutted, like his famous ancestor, for similar crimes of greed and treachery (to Hannibal). Mason Verger is condemned to being eaten by the man-eating hogs he had bred to make Hannibal suffer; the death he had dreamt of inflicting on Hannibal becomes his own. Paul Krendler is forced to eat delicately spiced and sautéed pieces of his own brain in front of the horrified and drugged Clarice, in atonement for his "rudeness" to Clarice. In all of these instances, it is Hannibal's point of view that justifies why these punishments are fitting and just. And in all of these instances, it is Hannibal's equanimity that renders the gore "entertaining" because we are drawn into sharing his point of view, without realizing it, in contrast with *Henry's* "home invasion" scene mentioned earlier.

The allusions to the vampire myth continue in *Hannibal*. Director Ridley Scott describes Hannibal's videotaped appearance during his murder of Pazzi (seen from the point of view of Clarice, who is viewing the footage) as reminiscent of *Nosferatu*, one of the most famous German expressionist depictions of the vampire legend.[26] As Hannibal walks through the streets of Florence, with his Borsali hat tipped at a rakish angle, his coat billows around him like Dracula's cape. Like the vampire, Hannibal seems to glide effortlessly through doors, and moves into and out of places with a speed and silence impossible to humans. Like the Count, Hannibal flirts suavely and successfully with women, such as the inspector's wife, Allegra Pazzi (Francesca Neri), and seems to be able to hypnotize his prey into inflicting pain upon themselves, like Mason Verger. Like the vampire, Hannibal possesses an uncanny command over animals; the man-eating hogs avoid him, and Krendler's guard dog is clearly intimidated by him. Like a vampire that "sleeps" until he is awakened, Hannibal is in "hibernation" and comes out of a "ten-year retirement" only when he hears of Starling's disgrace. (One movie review puns: "He's back . . . in all his gory"—drawing parallelisms between this contemporary vampire and an earlier, equally fashionable Frankensteinian monster: the Terminator.)[27] Artie Megibben once again renders explicit the Gothic appeal of *Hannibal*:

> Ever since the night Renfield met Dracula, moviegoers have had an appetite for blood-sucking villains with class. And not since Bela Lugosi has a villain had more class and style than Anthony Hopkins' Hannibal Lecter. He quotes the classics. He's a patron of the arts. And his fangs are

as acquainted with Bulugar caviar as with the soft, supple flesh of his victims. Hopkins' Lecter does not so much snarl as purr—whispering seductive innuendoes set to opera music—an approach matched only by Eden's subtle serpent.[28]

Thus, though both the serial killer and vampire movies we have surveyed end up with a similar conclusion regarding the nature of voyeurism in relation to the visual (i.e., that part of the visual pleasures of these films is that we share the killers' points of views at various points), it is interesting that our reactions to this realization is very different in *Henry*, as opposed to *Hannibal*. Perhaps it is because *Henry* seems too "real" with its rootedness in the blue-collar world and the gritty streets of Chicago, and its use of cinema verité, in contrast with *Hannibal*, which is an unabashed glorification of the serial killer as genius, vampire, and dark angel rolled into one, with its polished cinematography, Florentine locale, lush mise-en-scène, and beautiful musical score. It is clear that the issue of class creates a different type of identification in these two genres. Nevertheless, there is a clear sense in which the cinematic representations of serial killers and vampires, as "mythic" and "real" figures, blur into each other as simultaneously dangerous and endangered creatures who are driven to kill by compulsions as strong as the reflex to breathe. And it is the "authenticity" of easy slippage across the cinematic modes of "documentary" and "fiction" that enables the Gothicization of serial killers as vampiric.

DISCUSSION: THE COMPULSIONS OF "REAL" SERIAL KILLERS

Though it may now be impossible to separate real serial killers from their reel-life counterparts, as the two have been conflated over the last twenty years in the popular imaginary,[29] a summary of the prevailing behavioral science perspective as generated by the law enforcement community (and criminologists sympathetic to the law enforcement perspective) is in order to serve as a point of comparison with fictional, cinematic imagery. This perspective has come to the forefront within criminology as traditional psychological and sociological explanations cannot adequately explain the nature of sadistic serial murder.

Robert Ressler (n.d., Court TV), considered by some as the original "Profiler," coined the phrase *serial killer*, based on twenty years of tracking down killers for the FBI. Because he grew up in Chicago, Ressler first became fascinated with the criminal mind during the "Lipstick Murders" in 1946. He eventually studied psychology as a way to understand what motivates this type of criminal behavior and the "demon" that pushes a killer over the edge, as well as to establish a pattern that could have some predictive power in determining the killer's next violent act. While he worked with the FBI, Ressler perfected the art of the interview. There he worked closely with other agents, including Pierce Brooks, a former LAPD detective who helped found the FBI's Violent Criminal Apprehension Program in 1985.[30] Through numerous visits to prisons and scores of conversations with convicted killers, he was able to explore whether a killer is driven by an "irresistible compulsion or a compulsion that cannot be resisted." This "compulsion model" is important to delineate because it outlines how the imaging of the serial killer–vampire figure intersects with a theoretical model of what motivates serial killer behavior.

A serial killer, according to Ressler, is someone whose violent crimes must have claimed more than three victims, at different times, places, and events. This type of crime involves some premeditation or planning that is spurred by an overriding fantasy, formed early, which "drives" this type of killer to commit repetitive crimes. Dr. Helen Morrison, a forensic psychologist at the Evaluation Center at Chicago, adds the following characterization: that a serial killer, by the time he is an adolescent, is totally focused on sexual fantasies in an "experimental" sense. She cites a higher body count than Ressler; no less than ten homicides of a brutal, violent, and ritualistic nature (i.e., a "cookie cutter" format) are required in order to establish that the killer is indeed a "serial" killer.[31]

Robert Hazelwood, a former supervisory special agent of the FBI, forms a clear taxonomy that distinguishes between a "serial" killer, a "spree" killer, and a "mass" killer. A "serial" killer, like Gacy, commits murders with a certain "periodicity"; a "spree" killer, like Starkweather, may commit several murders separated by time and place, but all these murders are connected to one incident; a "mass" murderer, like Manson or Smith and Hickock (*In Cold Blood*), kills four or more people at one location at one time. Hazelwood also makes the provocative suggestion that serial killers have existed as long as humans have existed, and that myths concerning "werewolves" probably emerged because of the degree of mutilation wreaked on their victims by serial killers.[32] Lycanthropy remains an important Hollywood theme, as modern American tourists find themselves turned into werewolves in the primordial English countryside (*An American Werewolf in London* [1981]) or the primitive subterranean worlds of Paris (*An American Werewolf in Paris* [1997]).

What is common to all of these characterizations of serial killing is the powerful effect of violent fantasies, which serve as a compulsive force that impels these individuals to kill in a periodic or cyclical and ritualistic way. Much of what is meant when we talk about "cycles" of sexual fantasy is based on the vaguer notion of "biological or natural clocks." This is what enables the more or less accurate prediction of when the perpetrator needs to strike again. Although a basic understanding of sexual urges and needs is called for, we are concerned here with *abnormal* sexual urges and needs, particularly those that call for repeated or serial behaviors. In this sense, therefore, we can make comparisons to other addiction processes, such as the victimization cycle and the cycle of violence associated with domestic violence. With the addiction cycle, there's a distinctive "shame-pain" sequence, although with minor forms of dysfunction, the shame part may only be low self-esteem. The part that determines the addiction is when the person comes to associate continued use of the addictive agent with relief from pain (Lindesmith's theory of addiction). And the pain can be anything, even something as mild as the stress or hassles of living. There are a number of addictive agents. Here's a partial list: alcohol, drugs, work, money, control, power, food, sex, pornography, approval, relationships, physical illness (hypochondria), exercise, cosmetics, academics, intellectualism, religiosity, perfectionism, cleaning, organizing, materialism, and collecting things.

With the battering cycle, there's a relatively short battering incident in which the person is out of control, followed by a period of apology, gift giving, and a "honeymoon" phase in which the batterer is trying to be contrite with "hearts and flowers." Then the batterer starts finding fault and becoming verbally abusive. Jealousy develops, and the domestic partner can usually sense the tension building. This leads to a state of fear, helplessness, and inability to control the environment, which usually serves as ample ground for a precipitating or provocation incident (provocation if the partner "provokes" a scene to get it over with), which leads again to a battering incident.

Fantasy occurs well in advance of the crime, and for the serial killer, fantasy evolves into a compulsion. The subsequent behavior keeps true to the flavor of the original fantasy. For some, a symbol, such as a buck knife, represents the original fantasy, or more accurately, a link to the unrealized fantasy waiting in the mind for an opportunity. The crime itself is also the fantasy played out by the offender. The script is cast and well rehearsed in the mind. The victim is only inserted into a role that the offender needs for the fantasy to come true. Sometimes the victim will be called by a name that is of special importance to the offender. The fantasy becomes the motive and establishes the offender's signature.

Control refers to the way in which the offender keeps the world he creates with the victim true to his fantasy. Domination is the primary characteristic that is enhanced by sadistic sex, torture, mutilation, and murder. Some offenders feel they do not have control until the victim is dead, so they kill immediately and then turn to freely mastering the corpse. Others will take their time, engaging in repeated torture, escalation, and de-escalation of torment with the victim. Control is also expressed in the staging and ritual displays at the crime scene as well as in the location choice of the assault. Jack Katz,[33] in his discussion of monstrous, premeditated murder emphasizes the importance of time and place to the perpetrator's attempt to control every aspect of the event. Similarly, Kenneth Burke recognized the importance of "scene" as motivation for human behavior.[34] For example, standing at night on the edge of a precipice overlooking the sea might itself impel the onlooker to jump and commit suicide. Likewise, Katz's killers wait for the dead of night and imprison their victims in basements or other confined spaces prior to carrying out their murderous acts. The discussion of deeply rural areas, abandoned farmhouses, and dark cellars as places that serve as cliché-ic or "natural" backdrops for such murders or where bodies are dropped or buried resonates with the Gothic imagery that fills such descriptions.[35]

Katz goes on to note the godlike persona of the killer. The Gothic killer takes life away as a vindictive god does, without warning or remorse. Like a primordial god, the killer, in his total control of the victim, is an object of dread. In this sense the contemporary serial killer has replaced the mythical monsters of previous ages. According to Philip Jenkins, ". . . popular stereotypes of these threatening outsiders have come to assimilate most of the characteristics that in earlier societies were attributed to a variety of chiefly imaginary external enemies, including vampires, werewolves, and cannibals. All represent the threat of a reversion to primitive savagery, manifested most blatantly in acts of cannibalism and mutilation."[36]

Unlike Cesare Lombroso's 1911 atavistic evolutionary throwbacks,[37] the modern serial killer lives among us unrecognizable by outside physical features that might give away his primitivism. Monsters, as contemporary factual and fictional accounts tell us, are not "out there," completely discernible through an obvious physical aberration, but reside within ourselves and the enclave of the "normal."

Disassociation refers to how the offender successfully blends back into society, the thick superficial veneer of personality that is entirely disassociated from their violent criminal behavior. Serial killers carry their abilities at self-protective behavior to an extreme, although not to the point of multiple personality. They are intelligent to avoid detection, but they often "overtry" to avoid leakage to their true nature. Many are married or in a relationship, but they are disassociated. For example, New Jersey's "Ice Man" Richard Kuklinski left his wife and two daughters' home only to kill; otherwise he was the perfect house husband. The depth of the fantasy determines the depth or degree to which they disassociate. The offender knows fully well what behaviors are not acceptable to society, and to disassociate, they seek out "respectable" jobs, mates, and social activities that offer the best "front." In captivity, they often make model inmates. As a case study illustrating this point regarding serial killers, speaking of Jeffrey Dahmer, Richard Tithecott remarked:

> Dahmer is "the average-looking man," a "former tennis player, the son of middle-class parents," who has the appearance of being "a nice guy." But Dahmer, the boy next door, is also he who emitted "wolflike howling" and "demonic screams" when he was arrested, and when we read that "many witnesses quoted in the press have attested to his extraordinary Jekyll-and-Hyde transformations when drinking," we have little trouble in constructing Dahmer as the latest descendant of Stevenson's character(s). When we tell stories about our monsters, we like to imply that their monstrosity is everywhere, only hidden from view, concealed within.[38]

Reenactment is a behavioral aspect involving attempts to relive the fantasy. Reenactments are almost always sexual in nature, involving acts of masturbation, uses of pornography, or playing with souvenirs, trophies, or props. These things stimulate the offender, but they also reinforce the escalatory aspect of a serial killer's fantasy because the only thing they can control at this point is themselves. It is at this point also where the planning for future crimes occurs.

There's an additional way to think about the stages in this cycle, and that is to think of them as phases.[39] During Phase 1 (aura phase) twisted thoughts occur as the killer fantasizes about his next victim. Next, Phase 2 (trolling) begins as the killer goes out to look for the perfect victim. During Phase 3 (seduction) the trap is laid, often using "lures." Phase 4 (capture) occurs when the victim is at her/his most vulnerable moment, as there is no escape from her/his captor. This is followed by Phase 5 (the kill) in which the perpetrator's suppressed emotions are let loose. During Phase 6 (totem or trophy) the killer collects souvenirs or leaves props at the scene as reminders. Phase 7 (depression) follows the crime. This appears to be a withdrawal period, as the euphoria from the kill disappears, leading to a restarting of the cycle.

It is important to note, though, that the vampire (and addictive cycle) analogy is rhetorically effective only if the serial killer is implied to be white, male, and heterosexual. If the serial killer turns out female and lesbian (and from the lower classes) as in the case of Aileen Wuornos, the picture changes. It is now the lumbering, pitiful, and violent Frankensteinian creature who emerges in the implied discourse, which we examine more thoroughly in "When Women Kill: Undead Imagery in the Cinematic Portrait of Aileen Wuornos."

NOTES

1. David Pirie, *The Vampire Cinema* (New York: Crescent Books, 1977), 12.

2. Pirie, *The Vampire Cinema*, 18.

3. Gregory A. Waller, *The Living and the Undead: From Stoker's Dracula to Romero's Dawn of the Dead* (Urbana and Chicago: University of Illinois Press, 1986), 21.

4. Pirie, *The Vampire Cinema*, 41.

5. Mike Hodges, *Murder by Numbers* (Independent Film Channel, 2001).

6. Pirie, *The Vampire Cinema*, 26.

7. Charles Bahn et al., *Mind of a Serial Killer* (Cambrix Publishing [Kozel Multimedia], 1995), CD-ROM.

8. Peter Travers, "Henry: Portrait of a Serial Killer," *RollingStone.com* (1990): www.rollingstone.com/mv_reviews/review.asp?mid=73047&afl=imdb (accessed 2002).

9. Isabel Cristina Pinedo, *Recreational Terror: Women and the Pleasures of Horror Film Viewing* (Albany: State University of New York Press, 1997), 102–103.

10. John Atkinson, "Ed Gein," *kamera.co.uk*, www.kamera.co.uk/reviews_extra/edgein.php (accessed 2001).

11. Cortez, "Ed Gein," *iF Magazine Reviews* 27.1 (2001): www.ifmagazine.com/reviews/review.asp?reviewID=816 (accessed May 11, 2001).

12. "Ed Gein," *E!Online* (2001): www.eonline.com/Reviews/Facts/Movies/Reviews/0,1052,82655,00.html (accessed 2001).

13. Waller, *The Living and the Undead*, 275.

14. Ted Tally, "Script for *Silence of the Lambs*," www.godamongdirectors.com/scripts/lambs.shtmlm (accessed 1989).

15. Michael Bliss and Christina Banks, "Cutting It Right: An Interview with Craig McKay," in *What Goes Around Comes Around: The Films of Jonathan Demme* (Carbondale: Southern Illinois University Press, 1996).

16. Gavin Smith, "Identity Check: An Interview with Jonathan Demme, Director of *Silence of the Lambs*," *Film Comment* 27.1 (1991): 30, 33.

17. A. L. Kennedy, "He Knows about Crazy," *Sight and Sound* 5.6 (1995): 34.

18. R. Seidenberg, "*Silence of the Lambs*: Anthony Hopkins Creates a Monster," *American Film* 16.2 (1991): 49.

19. David Sundelson, "The Demon Therapist and Other Dangers," *Journal of Popular Film and Television* 21.1 (1993): 12–17.

20. Lawrence Grobel, "Anthony Hopkins Interview," *Playboy Magazine* (1994): 10 of online version.

21. *The Silence of the Lambs*, Special Edition, MGM, 2004, DVD.

22. Ted Tally, "Collaborations: Ted Tally on Jonathan Demme," *New Yorker* 70.5 (1994): 165.

23. Todd Ramlow, "Hannibal Lecter, C'est Moi," *PopMatters Film* (2001): www.popmatters.com/film/reviews/h/hannibal.html (accessed 2001).

24. Charles Taylor, "Hannibal," *Salon.com* (2001): www.salon.com/ent/movies/review/2001/02/09/hannibal (accessed 2001).

25. Ridley Scott, "Feature-Length Commentary," in *Hannibal*, Special Edition, MGM Home Entertainment, 2001, DVD.

26. Ridley Scott, "Feature-Length Commentary," in *Hannibal*, Special Edition, MGM Home Entertainment, 2001, DVD.

27. Michael Elliott, "A Movie Parable: Hannibal" (2001): www.christiancritic .com/movies/hannibal.htm (accessed 2001).

28. Artie Megibben, "Hannibal," rev. of *Hannibal* (2001), *Journal of Religion & Film* 5.1 (2001): http://cid.unomaha.edu/~wwwjrf/hann.htm (accessed 2001).

29. Philip Jenkins, *Using Murder: The Social Construction of Serial Homicide* (Piscataway, NJ: Aldine Transaction, 1994).

30. Robert K. Ressler and Tom Shachtman, *Whoever Fights Monsters* (New York: St. Martin's Press, 1992).

31. Bahn et al., *Mind of a Serial Killer*.

32. Bahn et al., *Mind of a Serial Killer*.

33. Jack Katz, *Seductions of Crime: Moral and Sensual Attractions in Doing Evil* (New York: Basic Books, 1990).

34. Kenneth Burke, "The Search for Motives," chapter in *Permanence and Change* (Indianapolis: Bobbs-Merrill, 1965): 216–36.

35. Philip Simpson, *Psycho Paths: Tracking the Serial Killer Through Contemporary American Film and Fiction* (Carbondale: Southern Illinois University Press, 2000), 33.

36. Jenkins, *Using Murder*, 16.

37. Cesare Lombroso, *Crime: Its Causes and Remedies* (Boston: Little, Brown, and Company, 1911).

38. Richard Tithecott, *Of Men and Monsters: Jeffrey Dahmer and the Construction of the Serial Killer* (Madison: University of Wisconsin Press, 1997), 18.

39. Joel Norris, *Serial Killers* (New York: Anchor Press, 1989), 23–35.

4

Blood, Lust, and the Fe/Male Narrative in *Bram Stoker's Dracula* (1992) and the Novel (1897)

Lisa Nystrom

$\mathcal{G}$othic literature is considered by some critics to be a genre "dominated by women—written by women; read by women; and choosing as its central figure a young girl, the Gothic heroine."[1] While this description may be apt in regard to a number of Gothic texts produced by writers such as Ann Radcliffe, author of *Mysteries of Udolpho* (1794), and also the Brontë sisters, Emily and Charlotte, who wrote *Wuthering Heights* (1847) and *Jane Eyre* (1847) respectively, it is far too limiting to encompass all Gothic works. For example, Bram Stoker's *Dracula* (1897), while undoubtedly read by women as well as men, was written by a man, and boasts a story line seemingly dominated by male characters. At first glance, one may claim that this story is indeed a fiction focused on a select group of men and their patriarchal dominance over women, such as the female lead, Mina Murray. However, it is possible to argue that behind the testosterone-fueled exchanges between *Dracula's* male protagonists, there lies a second narrative that is driven by a presence that is most definitely female.

The eponymous character of this piece is Count Dracula, a Transylvanian vampire who, since the publication of Stoker's novel, is world renowned thanks to various resurrections in both literature and film. One such resurrection is Francis Ford Coppola's 1992 film version, *Bram Stoker's Dracula*, starring Gary Oldman as the vampiric count. Though certain critics may argue that this version of *Dracula* at times fails to transfer much of Stoker's original vision from page to screen, Coppola's film does in fact retain a great deal of Stoker's individual commentary relating to women and to Female power. This adaptation of *Dracula* highlights the strong female presence felt within the story by centering much of its action around the women of the narrative. While Stoker himself took a similar approach by relating much of his tale through the eyes (or more accurately, journal entries) of his female protagonist, the film takes this approach one step further by creating an extended subplot for its heroine, focusing more fully on other women in the text, and allowing for a more layered and detailed female presence than its original permitted. Female power is a major theme throughout the film. However, as with Stoker's novel, much of this power is highlighted by the association the female characters share with the figure of the Count.

The character of Dracula as presented in both Stoker's text and Coppola's film is, from the very beginning, a transgressive character. As Barbara Creed notes, he not only crosses the "boundary between the living and dead, the human and animal,"[2] but he also manages to violate gender stereotypes, becoming "strangely feminised"[3] in the process. His feminization can be seen in a number of scenes throughout Coppola's film, most notably those that take place directly after the arrival of Jonathan Harker at Castle Dracula, with Harker being portrayed by Keanu Reeves. From the moment Harker steps foot inside Dracula's home, he finds his host catering to his every need in a manner that is more commonly attributed to the female sex. Dracula prepares a mouthwatering meal for his travel-weary guest before showing him to a room that he has also taken it upon himself to put in order. By taking on these menial tasks rather than foisting them off onto the nearest servant girl, it becomes clear that Dracula is no ordinary Count. Despite this, much of the uncertainty surrounding the sexuality of the vampires of Stoker's novel seems to be written out of the film, which in turn finds its footing as a love story between the characters Dracula and Mina. Stoker's original vision, however, possesses a morally disturbing subtext used to unnerve Victorian-era readers. Throughout his novel, Stoker makes much of the sexual ambiguity of his title villain, a ploy that serves to increase the feeling of apprehension Dracula inspires in those around him. This is illustrated in the scene in which the Count comes across three female vampires, commonly known as the Brides of Dracula, toying with Harker in a manner that is overtly sexual. Dracula is immediately overcome with rage and displays a fury that serves to terrify Harker, as he describes in his journal: "Never did I imagine such wrath and fury. . . . His eyes were positively blazing."[4] This ferocity is not directed at his male captive, however, but rather at the Brides, who have dared to touch the man whom Dracula had claimed as his own: "How dare you touch him, any of you? How dare you cast eyes on him when I had forbidden it?"[5] When accused by the Brides of being unable to love, the Count turns from Harker "after having looked at [his] face attentively, and said in a soft whisper: 'Yes, I too can love.'"[6]

Much of the horror sensed throughout the novel, and at times even in Coppola's film, is, as Fred Botting puts it, based on "the dangerous doubleness of sexuality"[7] displayed by Dracula. One of the most fearsome representations of Dracula comes from a scene that presents him at the height of his femininity. After Harker's wife, Mina (played by Winona Ryder in the film), finds herself succumbing to Dracula's will, the Count compels her to drink blood from a wound on his chest, and by doing so essentially re-creates the act of breast-feeding. This scene is described in detail in Stoker's novel: "His right hand gripped her by the back of the neck, forcing her face down on his bosom. Her white nightdress was smeared with blood, and a thin stream trickled down the man's bare breast."[8]

Dracula is seen as a figure of dread, not only because of his ambiguous sexuality, but also due to his ability to demonstrate and evoke "the existence of female passion"[9] within the innocent female leads. He both embodies, and is the cause of, a sexual deviance that cannot be tolerated within Victorian society, thus making him dangerous. Dracula is, indeed, a "seducer *par excellence*";[10] he possesses the ability to bring out in women a personality that is both self-assured and highly sexual. Stoker clearly sees this unleashing of female sexuality as the main threat to the patriarchal society in which both novel and film are based. Indeed, the terror inspired by the character of this sexually rapacious, feminized vampire is not half as horrific as the danger he presents as a corruptor of the otherwise well-behaved, passive women presented in Stoker's story. Once subject to Dracula's thrall, these women become passionate and powerful, making them harsh and ugly in comparison to their former, more docile and beautiful selves. This transformation is personified in the character of Lucy Westenra (played by Sadie Frost), who, once bitten by Dracula, transforms into a vampire before the eyes of her fiancé, Arthur Holmwood (Cary Elwes). As described in Stoker's novel, and brought to life on screen, Arthur's first impression of Lucy is a happy one, "with all the soft lines matching the angelic beauty of her eyes."[11] Soon after, as Lucy becomes possessed by the demon inside her, a seductive voluptuousness that is presented as antithetical to her feminine nature begins to take hold. This transformation sparks a reversal of gender roles that the male characters of the novel find at once both repulsive and intriguing.

By characterizing his lead villain as both effeminate and highly dangerous, Stoker has created a world in which the battle between good and evil is inflected with issues of gender, implying that the biggest threat to the safety of Harker and his companions is not, as one might suppose, the rampaging of a lecherous demon, but rather the rise of female empowerment and the sexual role reversal that may accompany this. The embodiment of this threat is represented throughout the narrative by each of the female vampires, including the transformed figure of Lucy. Possessing both strength and assertiveness, these women are portrayed as acutely terrifying and treacherous.

compare to Buffy

In *The Monstrous-Feminine*, Barbara Creed notes that the demonization of powerful women within literature is not a practice particular to Stoker's era. In fact, according to Creed, fear of female sexuality and power is both timeless and universal: "Fear of the castrating female genitals pervades the myths and legends of many cultures."[12] This is supported by the prevalence of myths concerning the *vagina dentata*. The image of the castrating female reveals itself in various forms, one such manifestation being that of the vampire. Though the idea of vampires as the blood-sucking undead is indeed terrifying, it is their overt and confident sexuality that produces the biggest threat to the decent, upstanding male heroes of Stoker's story. According to Ernst Jones:

> The female vampire's blood sucking is equivalent to oral sex. She sucks innocent male's blood as if she were sucking the semen from his penis. . . . But the vampire also threatens to bite, to draw blood and sever the penis. Vampirism combines a number of abject activities: the mixing of blood and milk; the threat of castration; the feminization of the male victim.[13]

The idea of the female vampire being a "vagina with teeth" is given credit by Harker's description of his nemeses. While initially the women appear to him as attractive, voluptuous ladies, he is eventually unable to see them as anything other than "a mouth filled with sharp white teeth," suggests Carol Senf in her article "Dracula: Stoker's Response to the New Woman."[14] With the threat of castration paired alongside uninhibited sensuality, the vampires in *Dracula* become objects of lust, desire, terror, and disgust all at once. In order to deal with these conflicting sensations, Stoker turns to the fate that must befall all women, Senf (338) adds, "who renounce their traditional feminine roles—they must be destroyed."

While the fear of the castrating female may be timeless, it is a concern that is arguably brought to the fore during particular moments throughout history. In the case of *Dracula*, it is the emergence of feminism at the turn of the twentieth century that appears to ignite his castration anxiety. As Senf (332) argues, *Dracula* can be read as Stoker's "ambivalent reaction to a topical phenomenon—the New Woman." These women are portrayed in Coppola's film as decadent beauties preying on the moral, unsuspecting members of the male sex, including not only Reeves's Harker, but also Anthony Hopkins's Van Helsing and Elwes's Holmwood. Descriptions of this emerging female figure are often given by the characters of Mina Murray, later to become Mina Harker, and her friend Lucy Westenra, each of whom possesses certain qualities linked to the idea of the "New Woman." For example, Mina has "a responsible profession (assistant schoolmistress)," Senf (341) adds, "and a means of economic independence." She is also proficient in various secretarial duties, such as typing and writing in shorthand, skills that aid her in the telling of her tale. The events of *Dracula* are recorded using a bevy of modern devices. Each character tells her or his own separate story via the means of various tools, such as "by typewriter, in shorthand and on phonograph."[15] Also included within the text, Botting (147) notes, are "telegrams, newspaper cuttings, train timetables [and such other] signs of contemporaneity as . . . medical and psychiatric classifications, the legal documents and the letters of commercial transaction." It is through the inclusion of this contemporary equipment that we first see the hint of power being bestowed upon a number of the women within the story. Using the example of Mina, Stoker manages to show the gradual progression of the "woman's place," which moves out of the home and toward the workforce. While by no means a "New Woman," Botting (147) points out, Mina does acknowledge in her abilities as secretary "shifts in the nature of work within and outside the family." However, given Stoker's anxiety concerning the "New Woman," Mina is only allowed employment, and the opportunity to travel, on the condition that she uphold all patriarchal ideals of feminine purity and gentility. This saves our heroine from succumbing to the temptation of an independent life. As a result, Mina is spared the horrible fate of Lucy, who chooses to stray from her allocated path and is duly punished with a stake through her heart.

As might be expected, Mina looks upon the revolutionary behavior of "New Women" with disapproval, as expressed in her journal entries, and her voice-over narration, which is heard throughout Coppola's film. Given that she is the key female character in the story, as evident by her first-person perspective and constant voice-overs, we as the audience are encouraged to respect her opinions, and therefore, when our heroine denounces the "New Woman" as unseemly, we are encouraged to agree. However, an overt disregard for empowered females is not always evident within Mina's writing.

During her visits with Lucy, our heroine often shows signs of yielding to the temptation of becoming a "New Woman." One particular passage of Stoker's novel shows the pair spending an afternoon alone, free from male supervision. At first Mina acknowledges the existence of the "New Woman" with a passing comment about Lucy's and her behavior during luncheon. She writes: "I believe we should have shocked the 'New Woman' with our appetites."[16] However, as the scene progresses, it is possible to argue that their appetites are not wholly gastronomic. This passage abounds with sexual innuendo, never more vivid than the scene in which Mina admires Lucy's beauty in bed. Stoker writes (118): "Lucy is asleep and breathing softly. She has more colour in her cheeks than usual, and looks, oh, so sweet." Here Stoker seems to confuse feminism and the celebration of female power with lesbianism. This is further made apparent when Mina comments on a number of cows grazing in a field, an idyllic scene threatened by the intrusion of bulls. Stoker continues (118): "Some dear cows . . . came nosing towards us. . . . Our hearts full of constant dread of wild bulls." By depicting Mina and Lucy in this way, Stoker reiterates the danger of allowing women too much autonomy, for even a simple walk in the country may lead to "unnatural" sexual desire. The innuendo of the novel is replaced in the film with a scene of Mina and Lucy cavorting together during a rainstorm. This visually stunning scene is intercut with flashes of Dracula's menacing eyes, reiterating that it is his presence that has caused this unseemly behavior in the formerly well-mannered women. Coppola ends this scene with a kiss between his female protagonists, deliberately indicating the novel's association between female independence and lesbianism. The character of Mina, however, does not retain her view of autonomous, free-thinking, and free-spirited women as harmless for long. As Stoker's chosen heroine, she reflects the opinions of the author, and thus she begins to fear that the emergence of these liberated females will lead to an immoral change in female sexual behavior. This opinion is especially evident in the novel, in which Mina's innermost thoughts appear in journal form. Stoker writes (119):

> Some of the "New Women" writers will some day start an idea that men and women should be allowed to see each other asleep before proposing or accepting. But I suppose the New Woman won't condescend in future to accept; she will do the proposing herself.

The appearance of independent women in society represented a very real threat to the "comfortable Victorian sexual and familial life"[17] so revered within Stoker's tale. The representations of gender and depictions of relationships in both novel and film are reminiscent of those celebrated in the popular nineteenth-century poem "The Angel in the House" by Coventry Patmore. In this poem, the domesticated female is likened to a saint. She is charming, meek, devoted, and pure, and lives for nothing more than to serve her husband: "Man must be pleased; but him to please / Is woman's pleasure."[18] This kind of feminine identity is praised by Stoker throughout his writing. For example, Mina is portrayed as admirable because she, despite feeling the temptations of independence, remains faithful to the roles allocated to her by patriarchal rule, such as dutiful wife and mother. As Mina states early on, once she is married, she will give up her position as assistant schoolmistress in order to be "useful to Jonathan."[19] Her faithful devotion to the rules enforced by this phallocentric society results in Mina's ultimate re-

fusal of the freedom and power she is offered by vampirism. While Lucy succumbs to Dracula's thrall and ultimately welcomes the transformation, Mina
rejects it, and when eventually lured in by the Count, she immediately repents
and marks herself as "unclean"[20] and unworthy of her husband's touch. This
"rejection" is particularly evident in the film, both immediately after the seduction scene with her self-condemnation of "unclean," and also in a previous
scene, in which Mina is forced literally to choose between her relationship
with Jonathan and her burgeoning romance with Dracula, whom she believes
to be a foreign prince. When she is informed of Jonathan's predicament in
Transylvania, she must make a decision between her loyalty to her fiancé and
her lust for the Count, the outcome of which ends in a scene in which Mina
tears any mention of "the Prince" from her journal, both making clear her decision to return to her role as the dutiful and devoted wife, and also providing
a convenient explanation to those critics who feel the film strays dramatically
from the path set by the novel, as to why her liaison with Dracula does not
appear in the "journal entries" and "articles" that are supposedly compiled
within the final text. The character of Mina manages to destroy all evidence
of her relationship with Dracula, thus salvaging her image as a well-behaved
woman.

The intense relationship shared between Mina and her "prince" is just
one example of where the plots of film and novel differ. Unlike Stoker's vision, Coppola allows his female leads to behave in a highly sexual manner,
both toward their male counterparts and even, at times, each other. The heroines within the novel, therefore, are markedly less "wicked" than their filmic
equivalents. Significantly, despite the fact that both of Stoker's female leads
become engaged, their associations with their significant others never become
sexualized (at least not while they remain human). As Judith Roth points out,
"only relations with vampires are sexualized in this novel; indeed a deliberate
attempt is made to make sexuality seem unthinkable in 'normal relations' between the sexes."[21] This serves as a stark contrast to the "New Women" who,
rather than conform to the rules so valued by Stoker and his patriarchal society, chose to feel free "to initiate sexual relationships," Senf (333) writes, "to
explore alternatives to marriage and motherhood, and to discuss sexual matters such as contraception and venereal disease."

Such shocking and untoward behavior, however, finds its way into the
story via the character of Lucy Westenra. Even before she becomes a vampire, Lucy is a threat to the patriarchal values Stoker upholds, given that, as
an heiress, she has her own source of income and therefore doesn't *need* a
man to protect and provide for her. But what is more threatening is her reaction to the pursuit of her multiple suitors. In his film, Coppola uses Lucy's

relationships with men to convey her flirtatious and independent nature, and in doing so, further highlights the difference in character shown between Lucy and Mina. As Lucy behaves in an overtly sexual and almost reckless manner toward her three suitors (using phrases like "it's so big" and "can I touch it?" when admiring one man's knife), Mina stands back and watches, both in awe of, and slightly shocked by, Lucy's demeanor. While Mina's reactions illustrate her role as the representative of social conscience, the blatant sexualization of Lucy is used to indicate her adoption of the "free" lifestyle exhibited by the "New Woman." Her attraction to this new way of life is also evident in the novel. For example, when proposed to by three men on the same day, she raises the question: "Why can't they let a girl marry three men, or as many as want her, and save all this trouble?"[22] Stoker is quick to suppress this sinful desire by having Lucy follow her query with a retraction: "But this is heresy, and I must not say it."[23] However, unable to follow her own advice, Lucy succumbs to the thrall of the independent lifestyle offered her by Dracula, a transgression for which she is severely punished. After being transformed into a vampire, she is hunted down, staked, and beheaded by *Dracula*'s male heroes. This serves as a grave warning to all women who entertain thoughts of following Lucy's wayward example. Stoker has used Lucy as a cautionary tale, warning women of what will befall them should they choose to stray from the path.

From the beginning of the story, Lucy shows signs of dissatisfaction with her lot in life, and a tendency to emulate the behavior of the "New Woman." She is active and charming, and she dislikes the notion of being bound to a single man. As her frustrations increase, so too does her state of vampirism, and it is only during sleep, when her unconscious desires take hold, that she is able to vent these frustrations. As Senf puts it, "by day Lucy remains an acquiescent and loving Victorian girl. By night the other side of her character gains control; and Mina describes her as restless and impatient to get out. It is this restlessness which ultimately leads her to Dracula and to emancipation from her society's restraints."[24]

As Lucy begins her transformation into the vampire (or "New Woman"), audiences are encouraged to view her as a danger to the natural order by portraying her as an ugly, wanton wretch, who preys on not only men but on children. During the early stages of her transformation, she attempts to initiate a kiss with Arthur, but such forwardness in a female must be monstrous, and thus she is denied. The next time Lucy attempts to instigate intimacy between Arthur and herself, her behavior clearly imitates that of a "New Woman," and Arthur, behaving like Van Helsing's "obedient pupil,"[25] dutifully hides from temptation. As described in the novel, "when she advanced to him with outstretched arms and a wanton smile, he fell back and hid his face in his hands."[26] This confident, sexually assertive behaviour of their once-beloved leading lady stirs in the men a desire to (among other things) put her to rest, and in doing so, restore the natural balance of their misogynistic society. Senf writes:

> Significantly it is the twenty-eighth of September, the day after he and Lucy were to have been married, that Arthur Holmwood plunges a stake into her breast and ends her vampiric existence forever. It is a vicious attack against a helpless woman, but it succeeds in destroying the New Woman and in reestablishing male supremacy. Only when the traditional order has been restored does Van Helsing permit the kiss which both Arthur and Lucy had desired during her lifetime.[27]

It is telling that Arthur, in the role of the husband, punishes his wife for her untoward behavior. By penetrating her with his stake on what should have been their wedding night, he puts an end to her "unseemly" independent lifestyle. In death, Lucy is restored to her once-passive self, no longer a threat to masculinity. She becomes "Lucy as we had seen her in her life, with her face of unequaled sweetness and purity."[28] After staking and decapitating Lucy in the name of all that is holy, the men set off to Dracula's castle in order to do away with the gender-defying Count and his three threatening females. Stoker's condemnation of desire in women leads David Punter to suggest that the author almost appears to be "traumatized by a specific sexual fear, a fear of the so-called 'New Woman' and the reversal of sexual roles which her emergence implies."[29]

Despite his recognition of the newfound independence sought by women around him, Stoker suggests that an excess of freedom only serves to corrupt innocent women, as represented by Lucy's gradual descent into vampirism. Like Lucy, Mina is intelligent and inquisitive, but she is protected by her willingness to submit to male authority. Throughout both novel and film, Mina is often described by her male companions as intelligent, or as possessing "a man's brain."[30] Indeed, her husband, Jonathan Harker, acknowledges that "it is due to her energy and brains and foresight that the whole story is put together."[31] And yet, while the film ultimately shows Mina defying patriarchal bonds and choosing her own fate, Stoker's novel remains true to its tone, and when the final battle approaches, Mina allows the men to go on without her rather than run the risk of having "her heart fail her in so much and so many horrors."[32] Harker's relief at her submission is expressed in his journal: "I'm so glad that she consented to hold back and let us men do the work."[33] Thus, due to her compliance and obedience to the will of her male companions, Mina is saved from Lucy's doomed fate: the fate of the independent woman.

Therefore, women, and the anxiety they inspire in men, create the true foundation of Stoker's novel: a notion that is examined visually by Coppola in his film version of the tale. Each woman of the story has a profound effect on the male characters. Lucy and Mina are treated as motherly figures of purity, at least up until the time they become contaminated by Dracula, and are viewed by the men as angelic creatures in need of security and chaste love. The female vampires, on the other hand, inspire conflicting emotions, from revulsion to longing. As Fleenor suggests, "the social division of women into either pure and chaste, or as impure and corrupt, defines the basic dichotomy of patriarchal thinking."[34] It also makes up the basic categories seen within Gothic fiction over the ages. Stoker certainly engages with these stereotypes, enforcing them on his characters. We see this in the scene in which Mina is caught drinking Dracula's blood. Though Coppola's film presents her as a willing victim during the encounter itself, the guilt she feels as a result is in no way lessened, due to the fact that her behavior openly defied patriarchal bounds. Knowing this, she becomes hysterical with shame. In her eyes, her purity is irrevocably stained.

Stoker attempts to place his control over each of the women in the novel. Mina and Lucy are subjected to patriarchal rule, which, if flouted, is quick to punish wanton women. After the once-innocent Lucy seeks her independence by means of vampirism, all affection for her is lost, and she is, as Botting writes, "presented as 'a Thing' just before the band of men symbolically subject her to phallic law by driving a stake through her heart and decapitating her. Restoring the boundaries between life and death . . . the ritualised killing of vampires reconstitutes properly patriarchal order and fixes cultural and symbolic meanings."[35] Here, Botting suggests that it is indeed the sexual and emotional independence of women that creates the story's true source of horror.

However, while the idea of female sexuality does indeed form a major plot point of the story, it is never truly examined. Instead, as Botting argues, Dracula "subordinates feminine sexuality to a masculine perspective in which women serve as objects of exchange and competition between men."[36] Any attempts made by the female characters to explore their sexual identities away from their male counterparts are met with dire consequences, thus forcing them to remain under the safe control of patriarchy. In addition, female sexuality is, as Fleenor argues, limited by patriarchal thought, which denies women the power linked to procreation and the female form. "The clitoris, breasts, uterus, vagina; the lunar cycle of menstruation; the gestation and fruition of life which can take place in the female body"[37] are foreign to this system, and therefore considered evil. Any female attempt to regain control of her own sexual and biological power creates a fear in men that results in

D calls Buff
a murderer

women being depicted as murderous monsters. As noted by Stein, "It is precisely this male disgust with woman's sexuality, the male hatred and fear of woman's awful procreative power and her 'otherness,' which lies at the root of the Female Gothic. A male strategy for alleviating this fear is to define woman as 'Other,' to simplify and stereotype."[38]

Stoker's biased depiction of powerful females is best noted when they are seen through the eyes of male characters. This is not an uncommon occurrence in his writing, given that each time a female character becomes too wayward, she is no longer allowed a voice of her own, and is seen only through the eyes of men. This is especially true for the "New Women," the best example of which is Lucy. Once she has achieved empowerment and defined her own individual personality outside the bounds of patriarchal society, Lucy is no longer heard in the first person. This pattern of strong-minded, liberated women becoming subject to male objectification can also be seen early on in the tale, when Jonathan Harker is kept prisoner at Count Dracula's castle. It is here that Harker is "disturbed"[39] by the trio of female vampires who seek to make him their willing victim. These women are denied a first-person voice in the novel, while the film reduces them to sexualized monsters. Furthermore, by presenting Harker as the individual in distress in this situation, Stoker is playing on the Gothic tradition of having the female lead placed in dire peril before having her ultimately rescued. Also, he has reversed yet another common theme of Gothic fiction, that of having "a woman caught between a chaste lover and a demon lover."[40] While the film version of *Dracula* actually reverts back to this theme by including the subplot of the Dracula-Mina romance, Stoker's original text instead sees Jonathan Harker torn between his love for Mina and his yearning for the vampire brides of Dracula. And despite all his goodness and chastity, he does indeed yearn for these sinful sisters, as his journal states:

> There was something about them that made me uneasy, some longing and at the same time some deadly fear. I felt in my heart a wicked, burning desire that they would kiss me with those red lips . . . I lay quiet, looking out under my eyelashes in an agony of delightful anticipation. . . . The fair girl went on her knees, and bent over me, fairly gloating. There was a deliberate voluptuousness which was both thrilling and repulsive, and as she arched her neck she actually licked her lips like an animal. . . .[41]

His immoral desire for a kiss from these decadent beauties causes Harker to consider the three female vampires as more dangerous than any other monster. These wanton women trigger in men a longing to forget themselves. Harker experiences a desire to give in to his primal side, joining them in their uncontrolled pursuit of pleasure. The presentation of the women who stir these desires as horrible, dangerous monsters is an indication of the fear produced by female independence, assertiveness, and sexuality that takes precedence throughout Stoker's story. As Senf writes, "their aggressive behavior and attempt to reverse traditional sexual roles"[42] shows the female vampires to be "New Women," and they are therefore treated with the same dread and contempt suffered by Lucy when she began to show signs of her own empowerment.

For the majority of characters represented in the Gothic fictions of the time, sexual desire is "fraught with complex emotions of guilt and anger," suggests C. Griffin Wolff in her article "The Radcliffean Gothic Model: A Form for Feminine Sexuality."[43] It is due to the conflicting nature of the emotions attached to the act of sex and objects of sexual desire, Wolff (208) adds, that we see many authors of Gothic fiction seeking to manage these difficult and dangerous feelings by "projecting" them onto the "other" creatures, such as Dracula's three brides, that could be consequently destroyed. Characters such as these were "titillating. At the same time, however, they were unimpeachably safe," Wolff (214) explains, "for the fiction is constructed in such a way that the figure who embodies explicit sexual passion is *always* repudiated."

Fear and subversion of female power form the basis of many of *Dracula*'s horrific aspects, as is continually highlighted by the presence of the "New Woman." After introducing audiences with female characters who are both active and unashamed of their sexuality, Stoker proceeds to strip them of any power they may possess by having his heroes drive into their breasts the symbolic stakes of masculine superiority. Both Lucy Westenra and the three female vampires meet their doom at the hands of Jonathan Harker and his gang of male "champions." This is portrayed quite graphically within Coppola's film when, having been subjected to the licentious behavior of the vampire brides, and seen its effect on the formerly chaste and modest Mina, Van Helsing comes upon the brides in their sleep and, one by one, singlehandedly decapitates them and throws their heads from the castle, thus ridding the world of these wicked women. This example of masculine supremacy over female corruption supports the argument that, while Coppola's narrative does tend to verge on becoming more of a love story than its Gothic predecessor, the film continues to highlight many of the significant themes present in Stoker's novel. Feminine power is a continuing issue throughout the story, and the role of women is perhaps even more central to the film than it was in the book. An example of this power can be seen in the film during the final showdown, in which Mina manages to prevent Jonathan and his men from completing their destruction of Dracula by taking up a weapon herself and fending them off, forcing them to back down and allowing her to be alone with the Count during his final moments. This kind of proactive behavior would never have taken place in the book, given that Mina was perceived as being too weak to even watch the battle, let alone take part in it. And yet, as with Stoker's novel, given the amount of time devoted to the demise of Lucy, the death of Dracula seems somewhat anticlimactic. Stoker has his heroes spend a great deal more of their energy suppressing the rise of the "New Woman" than fighting the title villain. However, by the story's end, we see each and every one of these demonic beings destroyed by the heroic hands of Harker and his crew. Thus, as summed up by Botting, "in the face of the voluptuous and violent sexuality loosed by the decadent licentious vampire, a vigorous sense of patriarchal, bourgeois and family values is restored."[44]

NOTES

1. Cynthia Griffin Wolff, "The Radcliffean Gothic Model: A Form for Feminine Sexuality." In *The Female Gothic*, ed. Julian Fleenor (London: Eden Press, 1983), 207.

2. Barbara Creed, *The Monstrous-Feminine: Film, Feminism, Psychoanalysis* (London: Routledge, 1993), 61.

3. Fred Botting, *Gothic* (London: Routledge, 1996), 150–51.

4. Bram Stoker, *Dracula* (London: Chancellor Press, 1982), 54.

5. Stoker, *Dracula*, 55.

6. Stoker, *Dracula*, 55.

7. Botting, *Gothic*, 145.

8. Stoker, *Dracula*, 363.

9. David Punter, *The Literature of Terror*, vol. 1 (London: Pearson Education, 1996), 22.

10. Creed, *The Monstrous-Feminine*, 61.

11. Stoker, *Dracula*, 208.

12. Creed, *The Monstrous-Feminine*, 105.

13. Creed, *The Monstrous-Feminine*, 70.

14. Carol Senf, "Dracula: Stoker's Response to the New Woman," in "General Introduction," *Gothic: Critical Concepts in Literary and Cultural Studies*, vol. 1–4, ed. Fred Botting and Dale Townshend (London: Routledge, 2004), 338.

15. Botting, *Gothic*, 147.

16. Stoker, *Dracula*, 118.

17. Punter, *The Literature of Terror*, 20–21.

18. C. Patmore, "The Angel in the House," *The Victorian Web: Literature, History, & Culture in the Age of Victoria*, www.victorianweb.org/authors/patmore/angel/9.html (accessed September 10, 2006).

19. Stoker, *Dracula*, 74.

20. Stoker, *Dracula*, 366.

21. Senf, "Dracula: Stoker's Response," 336.

22. Stoker, *Dracula*, 81.

23. Stoker, *Dracula*, 81.
24. Senf, "Dracula: Stoker's Response," 338–39.
25. Senf, "Dracula: Stoker's Response," 340.
26. Senf, "Dracula: Stoker's Response," 271–72.
27. Senf, "Dracula: Stoker's Response," 341.
28. Stoker, *Dracula*, 278.
29. Punter, *The Literature of Terror*, 20–21.
30. Stoker, *Dracula*, 302.
31. Stoker, *Dracula*, 319.
32. Stoker, *Dracula*, 302.
33. Stoker, *Dracula*, 319.
34. Julian Fleenor, ed., *The Female Gothic* (London: Eden Press, 1983), 15.
35. Botting, *Gothic*, 151.
36. Botting, *Gothic*, 145–46.
37. Fleenor, *The Female Gothic*, 14.
38. Karen F. Stein, "Monsters and Madwomen: Changing Female Gothic," in *The Female Gothic*, ed. Julian Fleenor (London: Eden Press, 1983), 124.
39. Stoker, *Dracula*, 53.
40. Wolff, "The Radcliffean Gothic Model," 214.
41. Stoker, *Dracula*, 54.
42. Senf, "Dracula: Stoker's Response," 337.
43. Wolff, "The Radcliffean Gothic Model," 208.
44. Botting, *Gothic*, 149.

5

The Borg as Vampire in *Star Trek: The Next Generation* (1987–1994) and *Star Trek: First Contact* (1996): An Uncanny Reflection

Justin Everett

$\mathscr{T}$he optimistic future envisaged in *Star Trek: The Next Generation* (hereafter referred to as *The Next Generation*) is permanently darkened when the ominous and powerful shadow of the Borg is introduced in the episode "Q-Who." In this installment, Jean-Luc Picard's omnipotent nemesis, Q, prematurely introduces the Federation to this cyborg race by flinging the Enterprise-D to the other side of the galaxy (which we later learn is the Delta Quadrant, the opposite corner from the Federation's own Alpha Quadrant). The Borg are an inhuman "other," a humanoid race (later we learn they are an amalgamation of races) that has been so eclipsed by its own technology that it has become absorbed into a computerized "Collective" in which all individuality and freedom of choice is erased. The Borg are explored over a series of episodes that focus on their collective machine intelligence ("The Best of Both Worlds," parts I and II) and on their suppressed humanity ("I, Borg," "Descent," parts I and II). In these incarnations, the Borg are used to explore the relationship between humanity and machine intelligence, and particularly the themes of individuality, perfection, and the desirability or horror of human-machine interfacing.

This would change, however, with the debut of *Star Trek: First Contact* (hereafter referred to as *First Contact*). Though the Borg display some vampiric characteristics in the early episodes, it is in this film that stronger parallels to vampires, and particularly to Bram Stoker's *Dracula* (1897) through the character of the Borg Queen (as a Dracula-type figure), become most evident.

This article was one of a three-part panel titled "Genre Hybridities, Trans/Nationalities and Victimology: Profiling Dracula(ness) and Identity in Science Fiction, Asian, and Mainstream Cinema" presented at the National Conference of the Popular Culture Association and American Culture Association (Boston, MA, April 2007). I wish to thank John Edgar Browning for his insightful and helpful suggestions, which assisted me in laying the initial groundwork for this article.

Alice Krige (as the Borg Queen) and Patrick Stewart (as Captain Jean-Luc Picard). *Courtesy of Paramount/PhotoFest*

Further, like vampires, the Borg generally, and the Borg Queen particularly, can be seen as reflective opposites of the humanoids they pursue, as soulless creatures who reflect what they once were. Moreover, the same Gothic imagery that has become standard in vampire cinema is reworked in the Borg episodes and in *First Contact*; for example, the structuring of the Borg "cube" ship as a sort of Gothic labyrinthine edifice, and the manner in which we see the Borg sleep (i.e., regenerate) in coffin-like "nodes" in a dark, technologized crypt setting.

THE CY/BORG AS POSTHUMAN

For anyone familiar with the history of science fiction, the origin of the Borg in the cyberpunk movement, which was still in full swing when the Collective made its first appearance in "Q Who?" seems fairly clear. Though its beginning is generally traced to the appearance of William Gibson's virtual reality novel *Neuromancer* (1984), the term first appeared a year earlier in a story in *Amazing*.[1] Originally associated with virtual reality, the term was also applied to stories with an anticorporate tone with an emphasis on urban culture, including tales involving nanotechnology and the dangers of human enhancement.

The discussion of the benefits and dangers of altering the human with technology moved from the sphere of science fiction to science fact with the 1999 publication of N. Katherine Hayles's *How We Became Posthuman: Virtual Bodies in Cybernetics, Literature and Informatics*, in which she argues that "the *human* is giving way to a different construction called the posthuman."[2] Essentially, the posthuman view sees the body and mind not as synonymous with what it means to be human, but as malleable entities that can be shaped and redesigned. According to Hayles:

> First, the posthuman view privileges informational pattern over material instantiation, so that embodiment in a biological substrate is seen as an accident of history rather than an inevitability of life. Second, the posthuman view considers consciousness, regarded as the seat of human identity in the Western tradition long before Descartes thought he was a mind thinking, as an epiphenomenon, an evolutionary upstart trying to claim that it is the whole show when in actuality it is only a minor sideshow. Third, the posthuman view thinks of the body as the original prosthesis we all learn to manipulate, so that extending or replacing the body with other prostheses becomes a continuation of a process that began before we were born. Fourth, and most important, by these and other means, the posthuman view configures human being so that it can be seamlessly articulated with intelligent machines. In the posthuman, there are no essential differences or absolute demarcations between bodily existence and computer simulation, cybernetic mechanism and biological organism, robot teleology and human goals.[3]

In posthumanism, the association of humanity with a "natural" (unenhanced) mind and body is reduced to an "accidental" "biological substrate." Elsewhere, Hayles argues that by viewing the human as an existence without essence, "as a pattern rather than a presence," the body can be disposed of, and the mind uploaded to a database; the body, replaced with a cybernetic prosthesis; the mind, enhanced and "improved" using computer software.[4] The line that separates human and machine, mind and computer is dissolved, and can become anything the designer wishes it to be.

Most curious of all, this appears to be something that Hayles, and other posthumanists, find desirable. Hayles dismisses fears that technological advancements will lead to the end of humanity. Instead, she anticipates "social, technological, political, and cultural changes"[5] that will ultimately be beneficial for transformed humanity:

> If my nightmare is a culture inhabited by posthumans who regard their bodies as fashion accessories rather than the ground of being, my dream is

a version of the posthuman that embraces the possibilities opened up by information technologies without being seduced by fantasies of unlimited power and disembodied immortality; that recognizes and celebrates the finitude as a condition of human being; and that understands that human life is embedded in a material world of great complexity on which we depend for our continued survival. If the posthuman can accomplish this, who would mourn the passing of the human?[6]

Moving from the realm of thought experiment to reality, it is possible to say that the march toward making Hayles's dream a reality has already begun. Recent advances in cybernetics—in particular the introduction of artificial limbs that respond to nerve impulses and are approaching the full functionality of their biological counterparts (Woodard)—and a recent operation to keep a disabled child in a permanent childlike state (Saletan)—testify that we have begun to proceed in this direction. Among the strongest proponents is Ray Kurzweil, who looks forward to a merging of humans and computers by the end of this century.[7] One could easily imagine early Borg scientists making similar arguments.

This does not mean that posthumanism does not have its detractors. On the academic side, Daniel O'Hara has argued that the technology that posthumanists embrace shows no sign of heralding a new age for humanity. It is quite to the contrary. Reflecting on the influence of the Internet and other technologies, O'Hara writes that "all these developments have only enhanced the spread of capitalist power into every nook and cranny of existence, proliferating and accelerating the alienated and alienating work rhythms of our lives" and have confused fictional worlds with realistic futures.[8] Others are more fearful. Though O'Hara seems to dismiss some of the posthumanists' predictions as fanciful, Francis Fukuyama suggests that as the first steps in the posthuman program are taken, it would be wise to set up "a regulatory framework"[9] that would serve as a gatekeeper to preserve the essence of what collective human history has defined as *human*, in effect resisting the sort of transformation Hayles embraces.

It should be evident at this point that in both worlds of fiction and reality, the discussion focuses on the dividing line between the "human" and "posthuman," or it put it in the more common parlance of cultural studies, between *human* and *other*. When the *posthuman other* is viewed from the perspective of the human, it comes in the form of a threat, a usurper, as something that would destroy the human and replace it. It is a monster ruled by extremes of perfection and reason, divorced of its animal nature, which is the strange opposite of the vampire, a personification of uncontrolled animal degeneracy.[10] The posthumanist views his own reflection with disgust and views himself as a subject from the position of the *other*, inversing the relationship, and turning the *human*, the flawed pattern in need of remaking, as the *other*. It is this perspective that is taken up by Donna Haraway, in her discussion of kinship and race as cultural and genetic categories that infect American society with division and corruption. Viewing humanity from the outside, she embraces the position of the vampire, which she sees as

> . . . the one who pollutes lineages on the wedding night; the one who effects category transformations by illegitimate passages of substance; the one who drinks and infuses blood in a paradigmatic act of infecting whatever poses as pure . . . the one who is undead, unnatural, and perversely incorruptible.[11]

For Haraway, the vampire becomes a symbol of posthuman transformation. It "infects" the old categories that she sees as divisive, crosses boundaries, destroys, and in the act of destroying, creates something new. This newness is a posthuman who has shed the human, who no longer has a center or point of origin, "the one who speaks too many languages and cannot remember the native tongue."[12] In either vision, whether from the perspective of the human or the posthuman, it seems that human and vampire cannot live with each other. The posthuman dream necessarily, like the vampire, consumes the human, eventually transforming the entire species into itself, so there is no longer a point of reference to remind the vampire of its status as a reflection of the human.

At first, it may seem metaphorical at best to relate the posthuman—the cyborg in its most common literary application—to the vampire. After all, Stoker's Dracula is a fetid reminder of a bestial past that is defeated by combining Van Helsing's arcane knowledge with the science of the Victorian age (represented in part, by Van Helsing's recorder and Mina's typewriter). However, in twenty-first-century culture, the cyborg and the vampire can be seen in relation to a more contemporary threat. Rob Latham argues that these figures can be viewed as "metaphors possessing an uncanny ability to evoke the psychological and social experience—the relationships of desire and power—characteristic of postmodernist culture."[13] A paragraph later, he clarifies this point: "The vampire is literally an insatiable consumer driven by a hunger for perpetual youth, while the cyborg has incorporated the machineries of consumption into its juvenescent flesh."[14] Following a Marxist line of thought, Latham proposes that in consumer-driven culture, the body itself becomes a prosthesis, an extension of the technological society of which it is a part.[15] When the cyborg and vampire are combined into a single idea,

> . . . the power of the cybernetic vampire as metaphor [lies] precisely in its fusion of the contradictory elements of technological progress and primitive

horror: the machines of industrial capitalism preyed upon the worker while at the same time arguing for a utopian transformation.[16]

It is not necessary to take a Marxist line of argument to see the relevance of the figure of the cyborg as vampiric. As a type of postmodern vampire, the cyborg represents the human in the posthuman state following infection. The cyborg has become literally infected by the industrial machinery the human created, and as such, is an uncanny reflection of the posthuman future. The cyborg, however, does not necessarily see it this way. The cyborg can either be disturbed by what it has become (thus still identifying itself as *human*, and connected to the human past) or embrace the transformation as an improvement over the human condition (thus identifying itself with a utopian vision of a posthuman future).

POSTHUMANISM, VAMPIRIC BORG, AND THE *UNHEIMLICH* IN *THE NEXT GENERATION*

In *The Next Generation*, Data (though technically an android modeled after his creator, Noonian Soong) may be seen as a cyborg of the first type. He looks with childlike curiosity upon the human past after which he has been modeled, seeking always to better emulate the human or become "more" human—if he can ever become truly human at all. He is not vampiric in the sense that he does not seek to reproduce himself (though he did create a "child" in one episode), and certainly does not seek reproduction by infecting and destroying others. Data satisfies his own desire to be more human by studying and emulating the behaviors of those around him. The Borg, on the other hand, are cyborgs of the second type. They are posthuman because they have cast off their human identities and believe that they have found within the unity of the Collective (which can be thought of as a type of utopia from the Borg perspective). They are vampiric in the sense that they "spread" their infection in vampire-like fashion (i.e., penetration) by injecting their victims with nanoprobes (microscopic machines—literally microcosms symbolic of the consumerist/capitalist culture in which we live) through fang-like appendages that will begin the transformation from human to posthuman. Broderick observes that "the Borg really *are* just high-tech vampires," though his analysis does not proceed beyond examining the more obvious surface features of this comparison:

> The threat they pose to humanity is the same as the threat posed by the undead cult of Count Dracula: when they appear before you, they over-

whelm you ("resistance is futile"), penetrate your flesh (with elongated metal fingernails),[17] suck out your "essence" and turn you into one of them: a drone which now does the bidding of the darker forces of nature. The Borg "sleep" in regenerative pods, unconscious until they receive a signal which wakes the collective; vampires sleep in coffins, unconscious until the sun sets and thy are awakened by the rising of the moon. They even dress the same: dark colored outfits over pallid skin.[18]

What is most instructive in this superficial definition is the use of the term *essence*. This term presumes that the Borg remove something from their victims, and in the process, introduce an alien substance that transforms them into something decidedly nonhuman. *Essence* can be taken in at least two ways here: 1) as a literal sampling of human flesh (and in doing this, tasting or eating some part, however small, of the victim); and 2) as removing that immaterial quality that makes humans, well, *human*. The first meaning is merely a part of the physical process of making a Borg in the *Star Trek* universe. The relationship of this act as an attack of vampiric fangs (and, through penetration, "rape"[19]) is less interesting than its spiritual analogue. As with a vampire bite, when a Borg injects someone with nanoprobes, that person "dies" in the sense that his human "essence" is lost, though the body continues (though it could hardly be called living), obeying not its own will, but that of the Collective, just as the vampire is a slave to its own bloodlust. Thus, like vampires, the Borg represent a contradiction, an uncanny infusing of the alien with the human. It is exactly this kind of irreconcilable intermixing that, in the words of Sigmund Freud, "arouses dread and horror."[20]

In Freud's famous essay "The Uncanny," he struggles to understand this sense of an elusive fear tinged with a strange familiarity (or resemblance) that is so changed that something that once was recognizable and comfortable becomes a sort of opposite that continues to echo what was familiar in it. Freud uses the German word *unheimlich*[21] to characterize this strangeness; the word, unfortunately, does not translate well into English. Though *heimlich* can be seen as familiar, homely, and comforting, *unheimlich* is not its opposite. It is not the absence of the sense of familiarity or comfort, but a situation in which something formerly comforting remains familiar, but becomes tainted with a repulsive strangeness. It is this play on opposites—between attraction and repulsion—that may be said to characterize an uncanny experience. In somewhat more poetic language, Nicholas Royle, in his book *The Uncanny* (2003), describes the experience in this way:

> The uncanny is ghostly. It is concerned with the strange, weird and mysterious, with a flickering sense (but not conviction) of something supernatural. The uncanny involves feelings of uncertainty, in particular regarding the

> reality of who one is and what is being experienced. . . . But the uncanny
> is not simply an experience of strangeness or alienation. More specifically,
> it is a peculiar commingling of the familiar and unfamiliar.[22]

It is perhaps the word *commingling* that is most compelling in this description. Without *heimlich*, the familiar, *unheimlich* cannot even be apprehended. It remains alien and utterly without reference. It can only be gazed at in wonder and fear, like glaring dumbstruck into the blinding face of God. Many works of science fiction attempt to relate the sheer awe of encountering something completely unknowable. In film, Stanley Kubrick's *2001: A Space Odyssey* (1968) is perhaps the best known example of this. *Star Trek* has also wrestled with the problem of facing the unknowable. *Star Trek: The Motion Picture* (1979) is perhaps the most visually stunning attempt to relate this idea. However, even in this case, the unknowable is most often brought down to the level of the knowable, of the merely ordinary. V'Ger, in spite of its vastness and power, is reduced to a mere twentieth-century space probe that is thwarted with a little hand-tapped Morse code; in *Star Trek V: The Final Frontier* (1989), an alien masquerading as God is taken out with some fancy gunning by Mr. Spock. Even the omnipotent Q is cut down to size when the Continuum robs him of his powers. In the end, these ineffable entities become ordinary.[23]

The Borg cannot be stared at in awe. They are a collection of known races—of Humans, Vulcans, Klingons, Cardassians, and others, who have become *unheimlich* by being absorbed into the Collective. The Collective, by itself, would be a vast, unknowable intelligence, like V'Ger, before its humble beginnings are revealed. But the Collective cannot be separated from the *heimlich* individuals that it comprises. For this reason, the Borg, unique in a universe populated with the unknowable on one extreme and the familiar on the other, are uncanny.

THE BORG QUEEN IN CASTLE DRACULA

In my title, I have implied that the Borg are a reflection of the vampire, and in fact, I mean this in two ways. The Borg in *The Next Generation* follow the motif of the vampire, as developed in the eighteenth- and nineteenth-century literary Gothic tradition and as further refined (to the point of convention) in both print and film over the last century. In arguing that the Borg are an "uncanny reflection," I mean not only that they reflect the motif of vampire fiction, but also that the Borg, like vampires generally, are a reflection of the human. They are uncanny not because they are unknowable, but because they are necessarily apprehended in relation to humanity—the "essence" mentioned earlier in this chapter.

Like vampires, the Borg are people, but people with a difference, an otherness, that makes rational interaction with them impossible. They are dominated by a hunger—the vampire is dominated by an insatiable thirst for blood (and as a side effect, makes other vampires) while the Borg are driven by a mechanical need to assimilate (and as a direct effect, make other drones). I would now like to turn to the ways in which *First Contact* contains particular parallels to Stoker's novel. In particular, I would like to consider the ways in which the Borg Queen may be seen as representative of Dracula, or Dracula-type character, and the ways in which Captain Picard can be compared to Van Helsing.

In *Dracula*, Stoker intensifies the reader's experience of the uncanny by introducing the novel's two most significant vampires, Count Dracula and Lucy Westenra, first as human and later as a vampire. Though Dracula is clearly a vampire when Jonathan Harker first meets him, Harker only gradually apprehends him as such. Dracula is at once monstrous and hospitable, corpse-like and gentlemanly, repulsive and cultured. The illusion of Dracula's humanity continues even after Harker realizes that his host has no reflection in a mirror and reacts to the sight of a trickle of blood from a shaving nick: "When the Count saw my face, his eyes blazed with a sort of demoniac fury, and he suddenly made a grab at my throat."[24] A moment later, after Dracula composes himself, Harker records in his journal, "He must be a very peculiar man!"[25] It is finally, in the next chapter, after witnessing Dracula descending the castle wall *"face down* with his cloak spreading around him like great wings"[26] that Harker realizes that his host is not human: "What manner of man is this, or what manner of creature is it in the semblance of a man? I feel the dread of this horrible place overpowering me; I am in fear—I am encompassed about with terrors that I dare not think of. . . ."[27] It is in this moment that Harker experiences the uncanny, because it is in this moment that he is unable to reconcile the human with the inhuman and can do little else but tremble in terror. The awe Harker feels here is *unheimlich*, uncanny; he has entered an existence that operates by a different set of rules from the one he knows and understands. Until he understands the creature he is dealing with, until he is able to apply Victorian reason and the rule of science to the situation, he is helpless to act.

The confrontation between Dracula and Harker in Dracula's castle, and the sense of revelation Harker undergoes, is the same faced by Captain Picard's crew in the episode "Q Who?" in *The Next Generation*, the first time they encounter the Borg. In what amounts to a celestial temper tantrum, the super-being Q hurls the Enterprise to the other side of the galaxy into Borg space, which he does in order to demonstrate to Picard and his crew the arrogance in their belief that they "belong" in space and, consequently, are prepared to confront whatever they discover. The Enterprise is attacked by a Borg "cube" fifty times the size of a Galaxy Class starship, which seems as much an entity as it does a starship. As the Enterprise attempts to fight the cube, which self-repairs as soon as it is attacked, Picard is overcome with a feeling of helplessness, of facing something he cannot reconcile. He cannot reconcile the Borg because they are uncanny—they are *unheimlich*. They are a race, much as humans are a race, but one that operates not as a society or a collection of individuals, but as a single massified collective. Because the Borg can neither be fought with nor reasoned with, because they are at once similar to the galaxy's other races and utterly unlike them, Picard is faced with a moment of despair similar to Harker's sense of hopelessness.

Like Harker, Picard cannot act until he is able to better understand the Borg, and bring them from the realm of the unknown into the realm of the known. Though the mass consciousness of the Collective keeps them, to a large extent, *unheimlich*, through experience and education they become more "knowable" (or perhaps just a bit less "uncanny") and can then be dealt with through the application of reason and science. In Stoker's novel, Dracula himself is uncanny to Harker and his companions, but is clearly understood, through a combination of occult knowledge and science, to Van Helsing, who must then educate his friends if they are to be successful in defeating the creature. Perhaps the best example of this movement from ignorance and impotence to knowledge and power occurs when Dr. Seward, himself a scientist and perhaps the novel's best example of a Victorian rationalist, is unable to reconcile what he has experienced and his understanding of the natural world. Van Helsing attempts to reconcile this contradiction with these words:

> You are a clever man, friend John; you reason well, and your wit is bold; but you are too prejudiced. You do not let your eyes see nor your ears hear, and that which is outside your daily life is not of account to you. Do you not think that there are things which you cannot understand, and yet which are; that some people see things that others cannot? But there are things old and new which must not be contemplated by men's eyes, because they know—or think they know—some things which other men have told them. Ah, it is the fault of our science that it wants to explain all; and if it explains not, then it says there is nothing to explain.[28]

In *Dracula*, as this passage suggests, the path from a state of helpless ignorance to actionable knowledge is provided by the careful mentorship of Dr. Van Helsing. In *The Next Generation*, however, the obvious mentor we see in Q takes a sadistic pleasure in watching Picard squirm, even if this results in the assimilation of the entire United Federation of Planets. Picard must find his own way. This he and his crew accomplish through a series of episodes that climax with the battle of Wolf 359, in which the Borg seem to have been definitively set back in their plans to assimilate the Alpha Quadrant.

Picard's journey, however, is a more personal one. After having been assimilated by the Borg as the drone Locutus, Picard has a unique understanding of his enemy that others, as he points out to Lily in *First Contact*, may not be able to understand. As the film evolves, comparisons between Picard and Ahab are drawn as his behavior becomes increasingly obsessive and irrational, even to the point that he is willing to commit atrocities, as he does in the Holodeck, when he mows down an assimilated crewman with a Thompson submachine gun. Though there is much that is Ahab-like in Picard's character—indeed, he seems willing to sacrifice both ship and crew to accomplish his purpose—he is equally similar to Van Helsing in his intimate knowledge of the Borg Queen, and in the final scene, of his suppressed memory of his relationship with her when she assimilated him. Picard, addressing the Queen Borg in *First Contact*, recalls, "That's right. It was not enough for you to assimilate me. I had to give myself to you willingly." Though Van Helsing was never a vampire, through his research and his life as a vampire hunter he has obtained a unique knowledge that he must use to defeat Dracula. Similarly, Picard must suppress his own Ahab-like rage in order to draw upon this knowledge and defeat the Borg. By the end of *First Contact*, Picard's journey has taken him through several stages. From a moment when he is unable to act because of his inability to reconcile the uncanny interplay of opposites present in the Borg, through his crew's exploration of the nature of the Borg in a series of episodes, to his final vampire-like transformation into a Borg drone in the person of Locutus. He eventually arrives at a moment when he is able to reconcile this opposition, suppress the rage associated with his rape-like assimilation, and confront his oppressor in the person of the Borg Queen.

Another parallel between Stoker's novel and *First Contact* is represented in the character of Data, whom the Borg Queen kidnaps, takes to her dungeon-like "lair" in the partially assimilated engineering room of the Enterprise, and attempts to seduce him into willingly becoming Borg. It is here, perhaps, that the Borg Queen becomes most identifiable with Dracula, though she is more akin perhaps to Frank Langella's seductive, fang-less[29] Dracula from the late 1970s than to Max Schrek's rat-like fanged Graf Orlok from the early 1920s. In a scene both reminiscent of Bela Lugosi's grand entrance in the Universal *Dracula* (1931), and one that would have been at home in any Karloff-era Gothic horror flick, the Queen makes a grand entrance on a crane as the cadaver-like remains of her head and torso, sporting a mechanical spine that flexes like a serpent's tail, are lowered into the voluptuous mechanical catsuit that makes up her lower body. The lowering is as slow and graceful as Lugosi's descent down the grand staircase to welcome Renfield. One could even imagine Elizabeth Bathory, the Blood Countess, herself making such an entrance after having beautified herself by bathing in the blood of a freshly killed female servant.[30]

The Borg Queen, whose undead flesh is little more than that of an animated corpse, demonstrates Dracula-type qualities. Like the Count, who belongs to the former aristocracy (i.e., a form of authority long discarded), she too is an aristocrat infesting a modern, science-driven world, and as such, represents at once a long-forgotten past and the very real threat of a future in which humans could be hunted into extinction by drones who are at once insect-like and vampiric. She is a Dracula-type character not only in her corpselike pallor, her "royal" status, or her ability to create other Borg through blood infection by introducing nanoprobes with the use of fang-like appendages, nor through her sole endeavor to acquire (i.e., assimilate) property (i.e., worlds) to which she is a foreigner, but through her role as a sensuous devourer.

The very topography of the Queen's body is a commingling of irreconcilable opposites: she is beautiful, yet fetid; womanly, yet mechanical; alluring, yet terrifying. Unlike the Borg Queen's emotionless drones, her facial expressions are passionately human and convey her underlying thirst for assimilation in the same way that the sensuous vampire desires the blood (and sex) of his victim. Yet her pallor is whitely mottled like a corpse, and her head sprouts loops of cable, which reminds the viewer that her mind is synonymous with the Collective. When Data asks if she is the leader of the Borg, she replies, "I am the Borg." The rest of her body, which the viewer knows to be no more than a mechanical extension of her head, is feminine and lithe, engaging the viewer in an irreconcilable play of attraction and repulsion. Unlike the drones, who are horrors of machination, the Borg Queen's physique, and the sensuality of her movements as she brings Data ever closer to desiring assimilation, is a twin topography of horror and desire.

The final matter concerns the reversal of Data's assimilation. As every dedicated viewer of *The Next Generation* knows, Data's nickname is Pinocchio, a reference to his desire to become human.[31] This is not only an ironic reversal of the Borg practice of assimilation (in which flesh becomes dominated by the mechanical), but a reversal of the vampire-victim relationship. In the relationship between the vampire and his victim, the "undead," positioned halfway between death and life, seeks to maintain his presence among the living by literally drawing the life out of the living like a parasite, and eventually, after "killing" his victim, effectively reproducing himself. In Data's case, he has never been alive, so he can't be assimilated. He is a machine. Instead of taking life from her victim, the Borg Queen offers Data what he has always wanted: life—human flesh—which she gives to him in the form of implanted skin on his forearm and face. The Borg Queen cannot "take" from Data as a vampire "takes" from his victim; instead, she must seduce him into becoming her reflection, her opposite, a mechanical thing made human by desire rather than a living being made mechanical by an act of force.

As the end of the film approaches, the Borg Queen appears to have won. Much of Picard's crew has been turned into drones (mechanical vampires); much of the ship has been assimilated (Gothicized); the remaining members of the crew have abandoned ship; the self-destruct sequence has been set; and Data appears to be in the Borg Queen's corner, seduced by the pleasure, for the first time in his life, of feeling truly *alive*. It is at this moment that Data rejects the Borg Queen, rips open a warp plasma conduit, flooding the lower portion of the engineering room with warp plasma, which dissolves all human flesh, including his own. As Picard climbs to safety, the human parts of the Queen's body are destroyed, and the mechanical parts that are left to slither on the floor, helpless without flesh to inhabit. It is, ironically, Data's choice that shows him to be the most human of all, in spite of his losing his chance to be, at least in part, corporeally human. His choice, his freedom as an individual to choose his actions, is clearly accentuated in this scene. This is something the Borg cannot do: to choose. As a part of the collective, they are prisoners of its will, just as vampires are prisoners to their blood (and by extension, sexual) lust. Though Dracula's victims do not choose to become vampires, the openness to seduction (the potential for sin, the weakness of will) that many victims demonstrate leads them into the undead state in which all humanity, all freedom of will, has vanished.

CONCLUSION

To conclude, among the larger aims of this article has also been to show that, while the Borg display some vampiric qualities in the early episodes of *The Next Generation*, parallels to vampires, and particularly to Stoker's novel through the characterization of the Borg Queen with Dracula-type qualities, are more fully developed in *First Contact*. Veronica Hollinger has suggested that "while the intrusion of the vampire into [science fiction] heralds a relatively untraditional treatment of this typically Gothic archetype, [the] conflation of vampire with alien maintains the role of the former as the threat-from-outside, the quintessential Other."[32] Like vampires, soulless and ever-seeking, the Borg and their Queen visibly reflect, through a glass darkly, the humanoids they have sought from afar to assimilate. They are posthuman shells of their former human identities. In scenes and through imagery that revisits Universal and Hammer cinematography, the Borg surround themselves with dark Gothicized technology, sleep in coffin-like "nodes," and in vampire-like fashion, "turn" (i.e., assimilate) their victims by infecting them through double fang-like appendages.

Like her Gothic predecessor Dracula, the Borg Queen is both seductive and aristocratic. Her undead flesh is little more than that of an animated corpse, but like Dracula, she too goes on living: by using blood infection to populate modern, science-driven worlds with others like herself, and by acquiring property—through assimilation, however, rather than acquisition. Through the Borg Queen's black body-tight suit and red lips, the same coloration with which Dracula has been continuously envisaged,[33] she simultaneously modernizes and feminizes Dracula's enduring legacy. Thus, the hybrid presence of the Gothicized Borg in *The Next Generation* and *First Contact* allows new narrative possibilities to be explored and elicits a range of emotional responses, from fear and repulsion to fascination and attraction. What therefore distinguishes *The Next Generation* and *First Contact* from other horror/sci-fi hybrid genres has been their ability to effectively incorporate classic horror themes.

Thus, the Borg come to us as a warning. When they first appeared on television in the 1980s, they were a fanciful vision of a dark, distant, and impossible future. However, at that time the decoding of the human genome was a dream, the first mammal had yet to be cloned, and people did not walk around with their cell phones wired to their ears. It has been less than a generation since these dark predictions, and look at how science has evolved in that time. How many more discoveries in artificial intelligence, nanotechnology, and genetic engineering will be made in the next twenty years? Bill Joy, the founder of Sun Microsystems, is extremely worried. In a 2001 article in *Ethics and Medicine*, Joy ponders the possibilities for a bleak future:

> We are being propelled into this new century with no plan, no control, no brakes. Have we already gone too far down the path to alter course? I don't believe so, but we aren't trying yet, and the last chance to assert control—the fail-safe point—is rapidly approaching. . . . The breakthrough to wild self-replication in robotics, genetic engineering, or nanotechnology could come suddenly, reprising the surprise we felt when we learned of the cloning of a mammal.[34]

What message does the broader Borg narrative within *The Next Generation* give us? In a world where combining the human with the mechanical is becoming increasingly realistic, I think it is a warning. The Borg are an uncanny reflection not of the past, as Stoker's *Dracula* suggests, but of a posthuman future that must be avoided. In the vision of the future posed by *Star*

Trek, a forked path lies before us. One leads to a future in which science and technology free human beings to become better than they are now, to shape a utopian vision. The other directs us to the end of humanity, a destiny in which humans become slaves of their own mechanical creations.

NOTES

1. Michael M. Levy, "Cyberpunk and Beyond, 1984–2004," in *Anatomy of Wonder: A Critical Guide to Science Fiction*, 5th ed., ed. Neil Barron (Westport, CT, and London: Libraries Unlimited, 2004), 73.

2. Katherine N. Hayles, *How We Became Posthuman: Virtual Bodies in Cybernetics, Literature and Informatics* (Chicago and London: University of Chicago Press, 1999), 2.

3. Hayles, *How We Became Posthuman*, 3.

4. Katherine N. Hayles, "The Posthuman Body: Inscription and Incorporation in *Galatia 2.2* and *Snowcrash*," *Configurations* 5.2 (1997): 244.

5. Hayles, *How We Became Posthuman*, 285.

6. Hayles, "The Posthuman Body," 266.

7. Raymond Kurzweil, *The Age of Spiritual Machines* (New York: Viking, 1999), 1–6.

8. Daniel T. O'Hara, "Neither Gods nor Monsters: An Untimely Critique of the 'Post/Human' Imagination," *Boundary 2* 30.3 (2003): 121.

9. Francis Fukuyama, *Our Posthuman Future* (New York: Picador, 2002), 17.

10. David J. Skal, *Screams of Reason* (New York and London: W. W. Norton and Company 1998), 81.

11. Donna J. Haraway, *Modest Witness@Second Millennium. FemaleMan Meets OncoMouse: Feminism and Technoscience* (New York and London: Routledge, 1997), 214.

12. Haraway, *Modest Witness@Second Millennium*, 215.

13. Rob Latham, *Consuming Youth: Vampires, Cyborgs, and the Culture of Consumption* (Chicago and London: University of Chicago Press, 2002), 4.

14. Latham, *Consuming Youth*, 4.

15. Latham, *Consuming Youth*, 15.

16. Latham, *Consuming Youth*, 10.

17. Broderick's description of the Borg is not quite accurate. The "elongated fingernails" he mentions probably refer to the "extraction tubules" mentioned in the *Star Trek: Voyager* episode "Drone." More often, the Borg do not "suck out [the] 'essence'" of their victims. Instead, through what I term *fang-like appendages*, the Borg penetrate their victims and infect them with nanoprobes, viral machines that transform their victims into Borg.

18. James F. Broderick, *The Literary Galaxy of Star Trek: An Analysis of References and Themes in the Television Series and Films* (Jefferson, NC: McFarland, 2006), 111.

19. For further discussion of rape, the vampire, and science fiction, see Veronica Hollinger, "The Vampire and the Alien: Gothic Horror and Science Fiction," in *Bram Stoker's* Dracula: *Sucking through the Centuries*, ed. Carol Margaret Davison

(Toronto: Dundurn Press, 1997), 225–26; and Roger C. Schlobin, "Children of a Darker God: A Taxonomy of Deep Horror Fiction and Film and Their Mass Popularity," in *Journal of the Fantastic in the Arts* 1 (1988): 25–50.

20. Sigmund Freud, "The Uncanny," San Diego State University, www.rohan.sdsu.edu/~amtower/uncanny.html (accessed January 23, 2007).

21. Freud, "The Uncanny," www.rohan.sdsu.edu/~amtower/uncanny.html.

22. Nicholas Royle, *The Uncanny* (New York: Routledge, 2003), 1.

23. There are, of course, hidden races in *Star Trek* that remain unknown. In *Star Trek* (1966–1969), it is these "super-advanced" races that often get the crew of the Enterprise in the most trouble. The Organians, who force a peace between the Federation and the Klingons, are one example of this. More often, however, omnipotent aliens move from the unknown to the known through the application of science and reason. In *Star Trek* (1966–1969) episode "Who Mourns for Adonais?" the "god" Apollo is rendered powerless when the Enterprise uses its phasers to destroy his temple, in reality a machine that supplies his apparent "powers."

24. Bram Stoker, *Dracula*, in *Three Vampire Tales:* Dracula, Carmilla, *and* The Vampyre, ed. Anne Williams (Boston and New York: Houghton Mifflin, 2003), 172.

25. Stoker, *Dracula*, 172.

26. Stoker, *Dracula*, 178.

27. Stoker, *Dracula*, 179.

28. Stoker, *Dracula*, 307.

29. Frank Langella, in the role of Dracula, never appears in the John Badham film (Universal, 1979) with fangs. The same, however, may not be said for Langella's vampiric women in the film. Similarly, while we repeatedly observe the Borg's fang-like appendages, we do not see those of the seductive Borg Queen.

30. For a study of Elizabeth Bathory, I recommend Raymond T. McNally's *Dracula Was a Woman* (McGraw Hill, 1983). Attempts to draw a comparison between Bathory and the Borg Queen, however, would be tenuous at best.

31. Data received this nickname from Commander Riker in the pilot episode of the series, "Encounter at Farpoint" (which, incidentally, also introduced the superbeing Q).

32. Veronica Hollinger, "The Vampire and the Alien: Gothic Horror and Science Fiction," in *Bram Stoker's* Dracula: *Sucking through the Centuries*, ed. Carol Margaret Davison (Toronto: Dundurn Press, 1997), 225.

33. Wayne Stein and John Edgar Browning's chapter in this volume, "The Western Eastern: Decoding Hybridity and Cyber*Zen* Goth(ic) in *Vampire Hunter D* (1985)," points out that this black-red coloration hearkens back to the "recognizable (i.e., marketable) stereotypes that the London and Broadway stage adaptations of *Dracula* helped to engender in the 1920s. These stereotypes were then extended and universalized in film, appropriately by Universal in the 1930s–1940s, then by Hammer in the 1950s–1970s."

34. Bill Joy, "Why the Future Doesn't Need Us," *Ethics and Medicine* 17.1 (2001): 30.

· 6 ·

When Women Kill: Undead Imagery in the Cinematic Portrait of Aileen Wuornos

Caroline Joan (Kay) Picart and Cecil Greek

VIRTUAL REALMS OF FACT AND FICTION

In reflecting upon serial killing, it is apparent that criminological fact and literary fiction have become irretrievably intertwined. The focus on the twilight region of fact, fiction, and myth is important because it gets at the ambivalent workings of the social construction of these contemporary monsters. Rather than assuming that film (and particularly fiction film) is a medium that tells us little about the reality of criminological phenomena, Gothic criminology as envisaged here recognizes the complementarity of academic literary and aesthetic popular accounts of deviant behavior. What prompts this chapter is thus an explosion of books and films that link violence, images of monstrosity, and Gothic modes of narration and visualization in American popular culture, academia, and even public policy. As Edmundson noted:

> Gothic conventions have slipped over into ostensibly nonfictional realms. Gothic is alive not just in Stephen King's novels and Quentin Tarantino's films, but in the media renderings of the O. J. Simpson case, in our political discourse, in modes of therapy, on TV news, on talk shows like *Oprah*, in our discussions of AIDS and of the environment. American culture at large has become suffused with Gothic assumptions, with Gothic characters and plots.[1]

Adapted from "Crime and the Gothic: Sexualizing Serial Killers," Caroline Joan (Kay) Picart, *Journal of Criminal Justice and Popular Culture*, 13: 1 (Spring 2006): 1–18. Edited by Caroline Joan (Kay) Picart and Cecil Greek by permission of the *Journal of Criminal Justice and Popular Culture*, University at Albany, School of Criminal Justice, Draper Hall #221D, 135 Western Avenue, Albany, NY 12222, sunycrj@albany.edu.

The term *Gothic* is crucial; it is generally understood as a literary or aesthetic term that was coined during the eighteenth and nineteenth centuries, and can mean "primitive" (which runs the gamut from being barbaric and uncivilized—the earlier eighteenth-century characterization).

But the Gothic can also connote a nostalgic search for the true or lost foundations of modern European culture, suppressed by neoclassicism and the Enlightenment, with their obsessive search for order and rules.[2] Vampires possess this mythic primitivism that is both a positive and a negative; and as this chapter points out, so do male serial killers. Male serial murderers are typically construed as having vampiric qualities and display the primordial evil that such murderers seek to inspire, assuming the status of a vengeful deity in relation to their victims. If Katz, one of the leading experts on serial killers (and fictionalized as Clarice Starling's mentor, Jack Crawford, in *The Silence of the Lambs* [1991]) was correct, serial killer films should bring to audiences a "sensual awareness of evil in the forms of dread, defilement, transgression, vengeance, sacrilege and sacrifice."[3] Such psychoemotional elements should be discernible in the films that paint converging portraits of serial killers and vampires, which we examine, using a Gothic aesthetic.

This is significant because traditionally, as Pirie pointed out, though there is a natural link between serial killers and vampires, the two are usually set apart because of a conventional desire to separate a realistic account from an account of fantasy.[4] Thus, he argued, "the true life psychopath is very rarely a source for vampire movies. There is a world of difference between the psychological horror of mass murder and the dreamy romantic atmosphere of the undead."[5]

Yet contemporary characterizations of male serial killers converge with those of vampires, making the Gothic aesthetic not an obscure eighteenth-century oddity, but a rhetorical feature of everyday life. However, as the chapter ultimately shows, once a *female* serial killer (and particularly a lesbian one) becomes the object of the narrative, it is less the vampire (which is aligned with the archetype of the male serial killer in popular film) than the Frankensteinian Monster who becomes the main analogue, as we shall show in the main body of the chapter.

The topic of this chapter is focused specifically on depictions of Florida's rogue killer Aileen Wuornos (and in particular actress Charlize Theron's interpretation of Wuornos) as a Frankensteinian Monster. Of course, larger criminological implications that flow from this case study can be pointed to. Female criminals, particularly those who commit violent crimes, are depicted as not women or bastardizations of a woman or as counterfeit women. There is a long history in criminology that aligns the transmogrification of women with criminality, with Lombroso being one of the most infamous.[6] When men kill, these actions are naturalized as males simply doing what is natural to men (violence, domination) but who stepped slightly outside of the rules about what is acceptable behavior, such as a football player who makes a late hit. In other words, men who violate social norms/laws are seen as untamed men or uncontrolled men. Male serial killers may be detested as aberrant, but the audience often ambivalently view the male serial killers' skills of tracking, trapping, and physically overcoming their prey as skills that normal or real men are supposed to have as men (no matter how far these actions are criminalized). Within the popular imaginary, as we point out in a later section, male serial killers who escape detection and capture for long periods are seen as brilliant (as in the case of the mythic Hannibal Lecter). Male serial killers possess traits that are "desirable" even if these skills are used for evil. In contrast, incarcerated violent women are seen as strange, alien creatures; often, beings beyond redemption.

An examination of Wournos's criminal record reveals that she is very different from male serial killers. Henry Lee Lucas may have killed hundreds; Wournos killed only six. Though definitions generally vary, most experts would agree that it takes at least four victims to be considered a serial killer— so she just barely qualifies.[7] Ted Bundy was often described as someone who had charm, cunning, and even brilliance in his killing, while Wournos lumbered along like someone on a very slow killing spree. Wournos was sloppy with her killing and even if her motive wasn't robbery, she appeared in the *Monster* movie to be a cheap hood who killed as part of a robbery.

Wournos, even if she is given the title of being "America's first female serial killer," in comparison with heterosexual male serial killers, is not generally perceived as a "skilled serial killer but rather, as being a woman who didn't know how to be a 'real woman'" (as defined by the patriarchy).[8] The observation is very much in line with the gendered (and raced and classed) dimensions of being a female criminal; Chesney-Lind's work, for example, demonstrated how, even within gang culture, female gang members, relative to their male counterparts, are placed in a lower prestige ranking, and are often seen as sexual auxiliaries to their male counterparts, which is reinforced through the female gangs' adoption of names that mirror the male gangs they pair with, often for economic and physical protection (e.g., the Vice Queens in relation to the Vice Kings). Ironically, as Chesney-Lind also pointed out, there are very few empirical studies that confirm the "stereotype of the hyperviolent, amoral girls found in media accounts of girls in gangs."[9] Indeed, the face of today's demonized woman is a "violent African American or Hispanic teenager."[10] In Aileen Wuornos's case, it is possible that her whiteness was canceled out by both her class and sexuality; yet her whiteness may also have contributed to her being given the double-edged title of being "America's first female serial killer"—a title ambivalently tinged with some prestige, but also with some derogation.

Thus, the criminological ramifications that extend from this analysis stem from not only a critique of gender and sex (feminine behavior as natural to female bodies, and the criminalization of deviations from this norm) but also from the pathologization of lesbian female bodies. Lesbianism, in Theron's case, becomes tautologous with man-hating behavior; her serial killing of men becomes understandable precisely because lesbianism *is* man-hating behavior. As Schmid astutely pointed out:

> In an article written for *Glamour* magazine, Susan Edmiston quotes Robert Ressler as saying, "There may be an intrinsic hatred of males here, as well as an identification with male violence which helped push her across the line into what has been considered a "male" crime . . . In stark contrast to the complex motives attributed to male serial murderers, and the evocation of those male murderers as essentially unsolvable mysteries, Wuornos's motives are presented with absolute clarity: she is a lesbian; *therefore* she hates men and *therefore* she killed them.[11]

CULTURAL COMMENTARIES ON THE CONTEMPORARY FASCINATION WITH SERIAL KILLERS IN REAL/REEL LIFE

Other theorists have focused on the cultural significance of the serial killer craze. Caputi saw both the rise in serial killing and the cultural fascination with the phenomenon in fiction and film as indicative of male sexual dominance. Defining sexual murder as sexually political murder or functional phallic terrorism, Caputi argued that serial killer films include the following typical elements:

1. The films refer to Jack the Ripper and the established tradition of sex crime.
2. The killer corresponds with or Gothic-ally doubles with the police or media.
3. The mother is blamed for her son's criminality, as a result of psychological or physical abuse.
4. The killer claims to love his victims, helping them by killing them.
5. The female victims are ultimately responsible for their own demise (either the killer mentions this or the plot construction naturalizes this).

6. The killer is waging a holy war against women, punishing them for their sexuality, aggression against men, feminism, etc.[12]

Newitz similarly focused on the gender identity anxieties of (hetero)sexual murder as "the serial killer kills off the 'feminine vulnerability' in himself when he kills women, and thus proves himself a man."[13] In contrast, Jenkins criticizes Caputi for ignoring female serial killers (who more often work in health-related professions) and limiting her analysis to feminist perspectives. He views the rise of conservative Protestantism in the 1980s and 1990s as a major factor in the shift from images of serial killers as psychologically damaged human beings to monsters.[14]

While Jenkins also discusses the decline of interest in the psychological background of serial killers, Grixti sees the rise of depictions of real-life monsters as indicative of the uncertainty in which we currently live and its resulting fears. "Feelings of fear . . . derive from the conviction of loss of control and the sense of helplessness . . ."[15] When real-life policies for controlling crime are perceived as weak, and a general atmosphere of social malaise prevails, magical solutions for controlling the monstrous are sought, often imaginatively worked out through narratives in film and popular culture. As each era has its own fears, certain crime-related genres tend to dominate during these periods. Thus, gangster films emerge in the 1930s, *film noir* in the 1940s, science fiction in the 1950s, horror films in the 1970s, and serial killer films in the 1990s; each dealt with their era's most troubling tensions.[16]

Along a parallel track, Seltzer discussed the rise in interest in serial killing as an example of America's wound culture—the "public fascination with torn and open bodies and torn and opened persons, a collective gathering around shock, trauma, and the wound."[17] As those who pass traffic accidents cannot seem to help but look at the carnage, the exploits of serial killers are depicted in documentaries, docudramas, and fictional films, and large audiences avail themselves of these images. Similarly, Tithecott describes the different ways in which we, as a society, construct the serial killer in our own image. We are both "thrilled and horrified by what we see, that we exist in a kind of horror movie which we write and perform for ourselves daily."[18] All these point to the gendered and Gothic dimensions of portraits of serial killers in popular culture as well as criminological theory.

Unnoted in previous literature until Simpson's is a striking similarity between the mythic characterization of a vampire and the description of a serial killer: both kill out of an overpowering compulsion, and in similarly periodic and patterned ways. It is this thought-provoking convergence between criminological theory and popular cultural representations that formed a significant section of this analysis. As Simpson points out, ". . . while serial murder indeed remains a favorite staple of tabloid journalism and cheap fiction, it has also compelled a variety of serious contemporary American writers and film directors to grapple with its philosophical implications."[19] The chapter thus builds upon Simpson's position: that the (white male) serial killer genre results from a combination of earlier genre depictions of multiple murderers, inherited Gothic storytelling conventions, and threatening folkloric figures that have evolved into a contemporary mythology of violence. Contemporized and repackaged for popular consumption, the Gothic villains, the monsters, the vampires, and the werewolves of the past have morphed into the fictional serial killer, who clearly reflects American cultural anxieties at the start of the twenty-first century.

In other words, what enables the Gothicization of crime and in this particular case, serial killers, is a narrative mode that moves across fact (*verité*) and fiction (horror, melodrama). This movement across the narrative visual modes of the authentic documentary and the fictional is particularly evident in purported true stories of serial killers like Henry Lee Lucas and Ed Gein. In each of these accounts, the attempts to sketch the portraits of real men and to explain their supernatural compulsions to kill become reduced to Gothic tropes. These real men, Gothicized into reel archetypes, become either a monstrous cipher (in Gothic literature—a zero or an unreadable or inscrutable code—that is, a monster beyond human understanding or rationale) (*Henry*) or an offspring of *Psycho*'s Norman Bates, the conventional victim-monster (*Ed Gein*).[20]

Before proceeding, it is crucial that we review some of the most relevant points of our prior chapter, on vampires and male serial killers, in order to reestablish what we mean by *Gothic criminology* and then apply that framework coherently to a new test case—that of Aileen Wuornos, in reel and real life. In *The Silence of the Lambs*, *Immortality* (1998), and *Hannibal* (2001), the figures of the vampire and the serial killer blur into each other. For example, the face of the monstrous in *The Silence of the Lambs* is initially visualized through Hannibal Lecter (Anthony Hopkins), a brilliant but institutionalized psychiatrist known as Hannibal the Cannibal. Admittedly, there are technical differentiations between cannibals and vampires, but *The Silence of the Lambs* and *Hannibal* conflate these two, such that Hannibal's vampiric and hypnotic gaze (which is characteristic of vampires, not cannibals) becomes inextricable from his blood-soaked, man-eating teeth (which are ambiguously placed in between cannibalism, an atavistic real-life horror, and vampirism, a supernatural horror). More pertinently, in terms of the history of film (as opposed to literature), there is certainly precedent for the conflation of cannibalism with vampirism in zombie films like George Romero's *Night of the Living Dead*

(1968), which spawned a host of derivatives, like *Horror Express* (1972), *Children Shouldn't Play with Dead Things* (1972), *The Living Dead at Manchester Morgue*, also released as *Don't Open the Window* (1974), *Fear No Evil* (1981), *One Dark Night* (1982), and *Zombie* (1978). According to Gregory Waller, Romero's presentation of the living dead in *Night of the Living Dead* was derived from Richard Matheson's novel *I Am Legend*, which strips vampires of their ability to transform themselves in mists or bats, their legendary wealth, and of their need to be invited into a home in order to invade it.[21] George Romero's *Martin* (Rubenstein & Romero, 1977) focuses on the demystification theme in another way in his documentary-style film of a young boy who believes himself to be a vampire but can only drink human blood by use of surgical means. *The Silence of the Lambs* and *Hannibal* continue this conflation of vampirism and cannibalism, but restore to the serial killer–cannibal the vampire's aristocraticism, combined with a supernatural intelligence and the ever-present threat of his barely contained physical power, which rationally explain Hannibal's ability to terrorize and feed on others' terror.[22] What is new about this chapter is that it emphasizes how the serial-killer-as-vampire analogy is very clearly *gendered* and thus insufficient for understanding how serial killer mythology, in both popular and criminological literature, is generated. The vampire-male connection needs to be expanded by introducing the Frankensteinian Monster model as a female counterpart. *The Silence of the Lambs* is an interesting film to cite in this context because Buffalo Bill, the Other (in more ways than one) male serial killer also fits the Frankensteinian Monster model in one aspect: she/he craves acceptance and wants to remake himself/herself into an image of what she/he wants to be (and wants society to see her/him as). Such a deviation from the vampire–male serial killer mold is both possible and believable, precisely because of the gender deviations written into Buffalo Bill's characterization. Buffalo Bill's pathological and aberrant masculinity, which prefers imagined femininity to normal masculinity, thus ends up as the villainous counterpart to Hannibal's elevated Dark Angel status. Yet what happens when the body of the serial killer is now female, and her gender is lesbian, rather than feminine? To answer that question, we turn to a detailed examination of *Monster*.

GENDER, CLASS, AND SEXUALITY IN RELATION TO SERIAL KILLING: THE CASE OF AILEEN WUORNOS

No discussion of the representations of serial killers in media is complete without a discussion of Patty Jenkins's highly acclaimed docudrama or biopic,

Monster (Alvarado and Jenkins, 2003) alongside Broomfield's second documentary on America's first female rogue serial killer,[23] Aileen Carol Wuornos: *Aileen: Life and Death of a Serial Killer* (Human and Broomfield, 2003). Both films were released during the same year, and a media account reveals that Broomfield shared information and outtakes from his film with Patty Jenkins and Charlize Theron, reasoning that "a good Hollywood movie about Aileen would be preferable to a bad one."[24] Since the focus of this chapter is on fictional films, *Monster* remains the central fulcrum, with the documentary drawn in mainly for comparative purposes and to demonstrate the difficulty in sifting fact from fiction. Ultimately, the focus of the chapter is how the films on Wuornos call attention to the inadequacy of the vampire–serial killer analogy and suggest a corollary one: the (lesbian) Female Serial Killer as Frankensteinian Monster.

Unlike the male serial killer films we have surveyed in our previous chapter in this collection, Aileen's portrait in *Monster* is neither vampiric, like Hannibal Lecter, nor that of a cipher, like Henry Lee Lucas. The Gothic monster who returns our gaze in this film is the Frankensteinian Monster. The principal features of the Frankensteinian Monster that are relevant to this argument are the following: 1) the Frankensteinian Monster is characterized as a lumbering, clumsy, and ugly body (compared with the glamorous, erotic, and often sophisticated body of the [male] vampire); 2) the Frankensteinian Monster, like its body, is a social misfit and a lonely child in need of love, rather than a brilliant and dangerous rebel who flouts society's rules, which fits the typical characterization of vampires. This portraiture of female serial killer as Frankensteinian Monster is evidenced in the following ways: 1) the heavy media emphasis (thus a construction by the media outside of the film's production history) on the transmogrification of Charlize Theron's physical perfections into a grotesquely real simulation of the actual Aileen Wuornos (with a stress on Wuornos's ugliness as a form of physical deformity symptomatic of social alienation and emotional abuse); and 2) the framing of Wuornos's serial killing within the context of an overwhelming loneliness and an obsessive desire for love and companionship. Both these traits are very much attributes of Mary Shelley's Frankensteinian Monster (an internal construction that could be characterized as an intentioned narrative shaped by Patty Jenkins, the director of the film). One could argue that these two realms are not necessarily too disparate by saying that Jenkins shaped or elicited the media response to some extent precisely through the choices she made regarding the portrayal of Wuornos. But intent is not the point of the chapter; the important thing is the interesting convergence between precisely the narrative content of the movie *Monster*, which teems with allusions to the Misunderstood Social Outcast (i.e., Frankensteinian Monster), to the rhetorical tropes critics of the film repeatedly fell back on, particularly in relation to the transmogrification of Charlize Theron's glamorous body as lumbering and ugly (still Frankensteinian). In other words, despite the difference in the sources of the texts (external and internal), they resulted in a coherent narrative.

Perhaps one of the things that compounds the Wuornos case is the attention given in particular to the uglification of Charlize Theron, the ravishingly beautiful blonde star. Media accounts regarding Theron's transformation from ultrafeminine, gorgeous starlet to menacing homeless streetwalker scopophilically hyperanalyze the details of this uglifying makeover. Repeatedly, references are made to the splotchy makeup, protruding false teeth, dark contact lenses, and extra 20 to 30 pounds that produced the illusion of the real Aileen Wuornos so convincingly. Stephen Holden of the *New York Times* remarked: "With crooked yellow teeth that jut out from a mouth that spews profanity in a surly staccato, a freckled weather-beaten face and a prize-fighter's swagger, Charlize Theron pulls off the year's most astounding screen makeover. . . ."[25] Perhaps the wittiest gloss of this Oscar-angling transformation, with a comparison to its cinematic precedents, was coined by Sinagra:

> If you're willing to glug a few hundred cans of Ensure, wear prosthetic teeth, conjure terminal impairment/homosexuality, and dredge up an Oxy-contin-slurred drawl that would scare the banjo off the inbred *Deliverance* boy, importance can be yours. And thus, with . . . [a] performance that swings from muscularly sympathetic to pre-*Extreme Makeover* crass, the bulked-up, butch-struttin', perma-frownin' Theron is poised to ride the tribulations of state-executed Florida prostitute and john-sniffing serial killer Aileen Wuornos straight to Slingbladin' Hilary Swankdom.[26]

David Edelstein used the protruding teeth to make a vampire analogy, but the analogy is in jest, and it is clear, based on tone, that a Filipino vampire is more comical and exotic than fearsome: "Although some of her features are bare, her skin has been lightly speckled (to simulate the ravages of the Florida sun on Wuornos's white Michigan complexion), her eyebrows plucked, her cheeks affixed with jowls, and her mouth with choppers that recall a Filipino vampire movie."[27]

Yet even more consistently noted than the simulation of Wuornos's physical imperfections through makeup magic by Toni G. was Theron's adoption of a lumbering and clumsy gait, a spastic head twitch, a corporeally hulking yet uncontrolled body, and a general nervousness that could explode into violence at the slightest provocation—all these being traits of the Frankensteinian Monster, particularly in its cinematic iterations.[28] Witness, for example, Boris Karloff's poignant interpretation of the lumbering and speech-deficient creature, capable of playing innocently like a child, or suddenly erupting in violence (largely in self-defense) in James Whale's 1931 *Frankenstein*; or Christopher Lee's menacing interpretation of Monster as silent, grotesquely mangled and unthinking killing machine, characterized by a clumsy gait and spastic body twitches in Terence Fisher's 1957 *The Curse of Frankenstein*. Roger Ebert observed:

> Aileen's body language is frightening and fascinating. She doesn't know how to occupy her body. Watch Theron as she goes through a repertory of little arm straightenings and body adjustments and head tosses and hair touchings, as she nervously tries to shake out her nervousness and look at ease. Observe her smoking technique; she handles her cigarettes with the self-conscious bravado of a 13-year-old trying to impress a kid. . . .[29]

Along a parallel track, Meyer perceptively remarked: "The actress slides a palpable fear beneath a weary frown and lumbering gait," as she uncovers the vulnerability and childlikeness that lurks underneath the raucous boisterousness and bravado of Wuornos's shell.[30]

Despite his freakish appearance and lack of self-confidence, the Frankensteinian Monster seeks human contact. In Kenneth Branagh's (1994) cinematic rendition of Mary Shelley's *Frankenstein*, the mirror-imaging qualities of creator and created are magnified by their common search for an eternal love. Victor Frankenstein (Kenneth Branagh), in this version, creates the female monster motivated by the desire to enable a love that overcomes death, as his creature (Robert De Niro) is determined to have a mate with whom he can share all the passions of his heart at all costs. In *Monster*, which appears to be based on letters she shared with Patty Jenkins before her execution, Wuornos is similarly obsessed with hanging on to Selby at all costs, even killing if necessary.[31] Selby Wall is the pseudonym of Aileen Wuornos's real life lover, Tyria Moore. Christina Ricci portrays Moore in the movie *Monster*. Moore looked nothing like Ricci—who is presented as a vulnerable, doe-eyed brunette with a delicate constitution. Tyria Moore had red hair and was a big-boned, overweight girl.

This, rather than simply the desperate need for money, constitutes the rational or sane part of why Wuornos turns from being a prostitute to becoming a serial killer. Yet it is also equally clear that there is a thick miasma of mixed motivations and powerful passions that incite her to kill: self-defense and revenge for having been violently raped, penetrated by a stick, sadistically tortured, and almost murdered in the first instance; then a deep-seated hostility against men rooted in her childhood experiences of sexual abuse, moralized as a form of vigilantism later on. In one sense, this version of Wuornos's life does not fit the compunction model easily because Wuornos is not moved to kill in a patterned, compulsive manner; with one exception, one sees the effort it takes for Wuornos to get herself into the mind-set of being a justified avenger: she verbally prepares herself by casting her potential victims in the roles of child molester or someone who enjoys sadistic rough sex. If they do not protest, and even relish the role playing involved, she pulls the trigger several times without remorse. When one of the men who picks her up turns out to be a shy, socially awkward virgin with a speech impediment, Wuornos cannot go on with her prepared script, and with downturned, set lips, perfunctorily gives him a quick hand job; when he thanks her, she grabs his wallet, extracts her due fee, and says, "You're welcome" sullenly. Finally, guilt, pain, and shame mingle in her cry for forgiveness as she reluctantly pulls the trigger on her last victim: a man who had genuinely wanted to help her, but who presented a danger as he could now identify her to the police; all these details still show the remnants of a sane and rational mind, even if one perpetually racked and tortured. As Holden noted: "What makes these encounters all the sadder is Wuornos' obvious horror, and guilt at the pattern she has been repeating."[32] It is this characterization that brings *Monster*'s portraiture of Wuornos at odds with Broomfield's documentary rendition of her last days in *Aileen: Life and Death of a Serial Killer*. For Amy Taubin, *Monster*'s most hideous misrepresentation was this:

> The movie's unforgivable flaw is that it portrays Wuornos not as the totally insane person that, on the basis of the Broomfield documentaries, she clearly was, but as a woman who merely had a problem with anger management, a woman who was a fool for love. If anything, *Monster* supports the sanctimonious assertion of Florida governor Jeb Bush (then up for re-election) that the three psychiatrists he ordered to examine Wuornos on the eve of her execution (they spent all of 15 minutes with her) found her to have been of sufficiently sound mind to be dispatched by lethal injection.[33]

And indeed, the portrait that emerges from Broomfield's documentary is different in terms of its depiction of Wuornos's sanity. As Winter eloquently described Wuornos's conduct: "Wuornos spills streams of damaged consciousness and contradictory half-inventions, while her puffy, ravaged face freezes into nervous cheer or contorts in molten rage. The condemned woman appeared to have a tenuous hold on reality: she proclaimed that after her death, she was going to heaven and returning to earth with Jesus in a spaceship like the one in 'Independence Day.'"[34]

Since Wuornos was an uneducated homeless prostitute, Hannibal Lecter's mythic erudition, high-class refinement, and vampiric charisma could not be part of her portraiture. Though she occupied a similar economic sphere and suffered from a similar background of abuse as Henry Lee Lucas and Ed Gein, she is not given the Gothic trope of the cipher; in fact, the movie strains to make Wuornos as emotionally transparent as possible in order to create empathy for the character. Nevertheless, references to Wuornos's heartbreakingly tragic history of abuse and alienation are kept to a minimum. Based on the two documentaries by Nick Broomfield, we find out about the mother who deserted Aileen; the grandfather who consistently beat her up and threw her out of the home, thus forcing her to live in woods after she got pregnant and had an abortion as a young teen; her subsequent relationships that ended in betrayal, making her a predictably paranoid person. Her life leading up to meeting Selby—a life marred by rape, incest, violence, and abandonment, and on the brink of suicide—is barely hinted at in Jenkins's script. Instead, the focus remains on the period from 1989–1990, when the hitchhiking prostitute killed six male clients—crimes for which she was executed by the state of Florida in 2002.

During this two-year period, Aileen happened to meet and fall in love with the aptly (re)named Selby Wall (Christina Ricci) [fictitiously renamed for legal reasons].[35] The cinematic depiction of Wuornos's relationship with Selby is important to note in detail because the changes from fact to fiction underlines the melodramatic character of the narrative; *Monster* is conceived as a love story, not principally as a horror story. A telegenic love object must therefore possess certain acceptable feminine traits, and Selby in particular must be a believably appealing character to make the audience understand why Wuornos would kill to keep her.

The real name of Wuornos's former lesbian paramour is Tyria Moore, and she did function as the prosecution's chief witness against Wuornos. Those who stayed on top of the media coverage immediately take issue with the film characterization, as Moore was a tough, masculine-looking redhead.[36] In contrast, Ricci's small stature, large doe-like eyes, smooth features, soft-spokenness, childish rebellion, and physical infirmity (she has one arm in a cast when the two meet) make the character easier to like, and it is thus easy to see her through Wuornos's besotted, overprotective gaze. Selby is trying to tiptoe out of the closet, attempting to escape a domineering family; she clings on to Wuornos as a potential savior, provider, and soul mate. Wuornos, so long accustomed to rejection, eagerly assumes the role of the husband and breadwinner; her desire to keep Selby's devotion at all costs drives her to justify killing and robbing her tricks to support them both. Ricci infuses her interpretation of Selby's weak character with a cloying neediness, materialism, and fickleness that delicately balance Theron's brash bravado and armor of cocksureness. Finally, Selby's feigned ignorance of her lover's nocturnal fundraising activities "establishes an air of complicity that suggests Wuornos is not the only monster in this little domestic unit."[37]

Ricci's acting and scripted role in this movie have been panned by several critics. For example, Carla Meyer decribed "Selby's fuzzy motivation [that] boxes the actress into a performance that's often unreadable. The character didn't have to be much to attract a lost soul like Wuornos, but for viewers convinced by Theron's magnificent show of ardor that this girl means the world to her, she should have been more than this."[38] There seems to be a direct proportion between the degree of transparency and empathy encouraged in the portrayal of Wuornos, and the degree of opacity and distance from the aptly named Selby Wall, who occupies the position of the cipher and traitorous beloved in this story.

Nevertheless, it is clear that Ricci deliberately portrayed Wall's character in this manner because that is the way she interpreted the script. In an interview, the young actress claimed that a significant source of attraction for Ricci was the idea of "playing someone who was such a weak person, someone so motivated by fear that they really couldn't do anything." The young actress added, "That to me was interesting, because I generally don't play very weak people."[39]

Despite the use of composer BT's nerve-jangling music, and Steven Bernstein's sharp, controlled cinematography, both of which serve to intensify the flesh-crawling reality of these horrifying events, *Monster* is shot, not as a horror film, as the prior serial killer films we have written about in this chapter, but principally as a romance and a melodrama. Both the film's formal properties and promotional packaging seem to enact a complex rhetorical dance between the realms of fact and fiction. Though the film's trailers moved across color and frozen black and white images (thus contributing both to its grittiness and seeming authenticity), the final film stays fully in color. Thus, the film's form from the start is ambiguous, straddling the realms of documentary reality (thus, in some sections, its gritty look) and feature fantasy (particularly in its depiction of the love story, or of Wuornos's dreams of becoming a star and of being beautiful).

Hints of Wuornos's childhood begin with a colorful snapshot of a beautiful blonde child playing dress-up in front of a mirror as a voice-over narrates the young girl's dreams of being discovered as a movie star by a prince who would rescue her from the overwhelming poverty that surrounded her. The screen widens, still in color, though no longer shot in soft focus and heightened color, to reveal a teenager who lifts her shirt to reveal her breasts to a small crowd of fascinated boys who, after ogling her body, rush off as if in fear of becoming infected with a dreaded disease. Then during a nocturnal scene, she is shown being picked up by a man in a car, where a transaction occurs before she is thrown out of the car and abandoned, underlining the heavy irony of her dreams in contrast with the realities that weigh her down. Particularly during the violent scenes, the movie generally adopts the cinema verité look characteristic of *Henry: Portrait of a Serial Killer*, and the camera work is almost seamlessly invisible. During the disturbing scene in which Wuornos is raped and penetrated by a stick used by her assailant, the camera focuses mainly on her face as she grimaces and begins to struggle in pain, anger, and protest; in a quick set of shot-reverse shots, we look down upon her as she manages to grab her gun, and assume her point of view as she guns down her attacker before moving into a medium shot as she repeatedly mangles her attacker's corpse, with the barest hint that her panty is still pulled down. As if in deference, the camera then moves into a long shot as Wuornos staggers about, howling like a primeval beast.

The juxtaposition of the rape scene with the lesbian lovemaking scene is important because it highlights the conflicting properties of the Frankensteinian Monster, which is capable of wreaking violent havoc as much as of being vulnerable and childlike. During the much-publicized lesbian lovemaking scene, despite extreme close-ups on lips touching in ardent kisses or hands traveling over bodies that remain clothed for the most part, the camera resists the scopophilic gaze so characteristic of lovemaking scenes, particularly of the lesbian variety shot for heterosexual patriarchal consumption. Persall complained that "when the women are shown making love, Tommy James and the Shondells' *Crimson & Clover* makes it seem more like prom night than a porn film. Writer/director Jenkins never misses a chance to remind us these kids are in love, as if that's justification for what Wuornos does."[40]

Nevertheless, what is also equally clear in this scene is that a role reversal occurs: it is now Selby who initiates the act of seduction and lovemaking. It is her small figure, dressed in jeans and a masculine shirt, that lies atop Aileen's body, which is draped merely by a towel. Later, after they have made love, as they embrace, Selby's head is above Aileen's as if she were the one cradling the larger woman. The majority of the scene is shot in low key lighting, infused with deep blue, as if in romantic nostalgia.

Thus, despite the meticulous detail put into simulating reality, such as shooting in the very locations Wuornos used to frequent (and which were reputed to be haunted by her ghost), the film ultimately cannot make a claim to being a realistic or objective depiction.[41] It is clearly shot from Wuornos's point of view, several years after the events have transpired, and it is the emotions that sear in the memories that animate the portrayal. In fact, the film aroused considerable controversy as the relatives of the men victimized by Wuornos took offense at the generally unflattering portrayal of the men she killed. The film also aroused the ire of John Tanner, the Florida state attorney who prosecuted Wuornos and who claimed he was never consulted by the filmmakers. John Tanner dismissed the film's depiction of what occurred as a total lie. In defense of the film, producer Brad Wyman attempted to pacify its detractors by claiming that "it's not a documentary... It is a dramatic portrayal searching for a greater truth than a factual truth."[42]

Rabin summarizes the formal and thematic contents of the film in this manner: "Patty Jenkins combines the gritty, claustrophobic neo-realism of *Dahmer* with the unlikely gutter romanticism of *Boys Don't Cry*, creating a haunting portrait of how a person can feel so desperate and hopeless that murdering for a few crumpled bills and maybe a beat-up car can begin to seem like a reasonable option."[43] (One could make the argument at this point that it is the dark side of the American Dream—that is, the "cultural emphasis on achievement, which promotes productivity and innovation, also generates pressures to succeed at any cost"[44] that produces monsters like Wuornos, but that is not the focus of this chapter.)

What is crucial to this chapter is that there are Gothic elements to this portrayal of Aileen Wuornos: the polluted urban highways and dark woods in which Wuornos and her customers furtively do their commerce display the mimetic correspondence between the Gothic setting and its characters. In an interesting parallel, Wuornos's depiction as both childlike and animal-like in her stunted moral development resembles Van Helsing's description of Dracula as operating as if motivated by a "child-brain in much ... and it is of the child to do what he have done."[45] This childlikeness is crucial to what makes both vampires and the Frankensteinian Monster Gothic, because childlikeness is actually construed as a form of primitivism, and as freedom from conventional morality. This is not to collapse one into the other, but to show the key affinities they possess in common, which make them repositories of Gothic imagery.

Nevertheless, the principal Undead creature who emerges from this narrative is the Frankensteinian Monster—a lumbering, lonely misfit desperately in search of love; a neglected child in a body too large for it to control; a creature who ends up a fallen Eve despite the purity of her aspirations. In the end, it is hardly surprising that Wuornos meets the fate of female monsters or the feminine-as-monstrous characters who inhabit the classic horror versions of the evolving Frankensteinian cinemyth: it is either they commit suicide (such as Helena Bonham Carter's composite Elizabeth-Justine in *Mary Shelley's Frankenstein* [Barron and Branagh, 1994] or Susan Denberg's Christina Kleve in *Frankenstein Created Woman* [Keys and Fisher, 1967]) or someone else, usually a white, masculine aristocratic figure, or an establishment upholding this hierarchy, kills them off (e.g., Elsa Lanchester's monstrous bride in *Bride of Frankenstein* [Laemmle Jr. and Whale, 1935]).

Broomfield's second documentary on Wuornos reveals an eerie parallelism between the two narratives: before her execution, not realizing the camera was still rolling, Wuornos admitted that she changed her story of self-defense to one of robbery and murder in order to hasten the execution, which, after twelve long years on death row—a period not immune from further abuse and exploitation, she claimed—she welcomed.

CONCLUSION: OF MONSTERS AND *DOPPELGÄNGERN*

This chapter began by gesturing toward the overlap of vampiric themes in male serial murder films; in contrast, it is the implicit portrait of the Frankensteinian Monster that surfaces in the depiction of the lesbian female serial killer Aileen Wuornos. This chapter also broadly outlines a significant change in the depiction of the vampire in more recent literary Gothic popular novels. In Fred Saberhagen's *The Dracula Tape* (1975), Anne Rice's *Interview with the Vampire* (1994), and Jody Scott's *I, Vampire* (1984), vampires acquire the authorial voice. In crafting their own narratives, they become more sympathetic, more superhumanly human and much less radically the "other." "They are more likely to offer a site of identification rather than a metaphor for what must be abjected, and with the movement from the metaphorical to the metonymical, the vampire increasingly serves to facilitate social commentary on the human world."[46] This grows even more pronounced in the most recent characterizations of Aileen Wuornos, known in tabloids as the first female serial killer, as a Frankensteinian Monster—a neglected social misfit in search of love—both in fictionalized and documentary treatments of her story.

Arguably, the move toward establishing the monstrous other as a site of identification becomes particularly disturbing in the case of the serial killer, one of the most compelling monsters that dominate the last part of the twentieth century. While *sympathy* is not precisely the word to describe the response encouraged by serial killer narratives, as we point out in our analysis of fictional serial killer films, there is often nevertheless a certain ambivalence in the representations of modern monsters. In docudramas such as *Henry: Portrait of a Serial Killer* and *Ed Gein*, the serial killer as an abused abuser emerges; in horror films such as *The Silence of the Lambs* and *Immortality*, vampiric aristocraticism and Byronic sex appeal become key features of the mythic serial killer. Often viewed as merely symptomatic of an increasingly violent and alienated society, the serial killer might seem to call for the most emphatic reassertion of social norms and the strongest reaffirmation of conservative values, which happened in the creation of the new FBI Behavioral Science Unit (Punter, 2004, p. 265). This is, however, rarely the case in fictional and popular narratives (Surrette, n.d.).

Rather than being established as the demonic other that must be exorcised from mainstream society, the serial killer is explicitly identified as that society's logical and inevitable product: society, rather than the individual, thus emerges as a primary site of horror. In such narratives, there is rarely any assurance that the threat can be contained; rather than being staked, the serial killer, society's monstrous progeny, is simply left to carry on. Even in the most reassuring serial killer narratives, often those in which a criminal profiler is offered encouraging evidence that the monstrous can be identified and contained, the majority of texts remain at the very least ambivalent about the repudiation of the monstrous. The stability and autonomy of the self and the other, and the clear separability of good and evil, are frequently undercut through a particularly emphatic use of the traditional Gothic *Doppelgänger*. The killer may ultimately be caught and punished, but this is often brought about by the profiler's overidentification with the killer, as in Clarice Starling's pursuit of Buffalo Bill under the mentorship of Hannibal Lecter. Popular narratives such as these are actually more complex and force us to confront the realization that the potential for corruption and violence lies within us all, and the horror comes above all from an appalling sense of recognizing ourselves in our Others.[47] Ultimately, one could argue that the Frankensteinian Monster archetype is perhaps more frightening than the vampire archetype precisely because it elicits sympathy (and in so doing, questions the self-other dichotomy) more than the male vampire model. And perhaps precisely because it is more frightening, it is harnessed within a predominantly feminized film genre: the melodramatic.

NOTES

1. Mark Edmundson, *Nightmare on Main Street: Angels, Sadomasochism and the Culture of Gothic* (Cambridge, MA: Harvard University Press, 1997), xii.

2. Linda Bayer-Berenbaum, *The Gothic Imagination: Expansion in Gothic Literature and Art* (London and Toronto: Associated University Press, 1982), 32.

3. Jack Katz, *Seductions of Crime: Moral and Sensual Attractions in Doing Evil* (New York: Basic Books, 1990), 292.

4. David Pirie, *The Vampire Cinema* (London: Quarto, 1977), 17.

5. Katz, *Seductions of Crime*, 292.

6. Freda Adler and Rita James Simon, *The Criminology of Deviant Women* (Boston: Houghton Mifflin Company, 1979), 2.

7. Charles Bahn et al., *Mind of a Serial Killer* (Cambrix Publishing, 1995), CD-ROM.

8. We are indebted to one of our reviewers for these astute observations.

9. Meda Chesney-Lind and Lisa J. Pasko, *The Female Offender: Girls, Women and Crime*, 2nd ed. (Thousand Oaks, CA: Sage Publications, 2004), 72.

10. Chesney-Lind and Pasko, *The Female Offender*, 53.

11. David Schmid, *Natural Born Celebrities: Serial Killers in American Culture* (Chicago and London: University of Chicago Press, 2005), 238.

12. Jane Caputi, *The Age of Sex Crime* (Bowling Green, OH: Bowling Green State University Popular Press, 1987), 64.

13. Annalee Newitz, "Serial Killers, True Crime, and Economic Performance Anxiety," in *Mythologies of Violence in Postmodern Media*, ed. Christopher Sharrett (Detroit: Wayne State University Press, 1999), 65–84.

14. Phillip Jenkins, *Using Murder: The Social Construction of Serial Homicide* (New York: Aldine de Gruyter, 1994), 81.

15. Joseph Grixti, *Terrors of Uncertainty: The Cultural Context of Horror Fiction* (New York: Routledge, 1989), 153.

16. Martin Rubin, "The Grayness of Darkness: The Honeymoon Killers and Its Impact on Psychokiller Cinema," in *Mythologies of Violence in Postmodern Media*, ed. Christopher Sharrett (Detroit: Wayne State University Press, 1999), 42.

17. Mark Seltzer, *Serial Killers: Death and Life in America's Wound Culture* (New York: Routledge, 1998), 1. One could also point to the popularity of TV programs dealing with forensics and police work, such *CSI*, as well as the constant "pilgrimages" to 9-11's Ground Zero as further evidence of the prevalence of this "wound culture."

18. Richard Tithecott, *Of Men and Monsters: Jeffrey Dahmer and the Construction of the Serial Killer* (Madison: University of Wisconsin Press, 1997), 9.

19. Philip Simpson, *Psycho Paths: Tracking the Serial Killer through Contemporary American Film and Fiction* (Carbondale: Southern Illinois University Press, 2000), ix.

20. Caroline J. S. Picart, *Remaking the Frankenstein Myth on Film: Between Laughter and Horror* (Albany, NY: State University of New York Press, 2003), 43.

21. Gregory A. Waller, *The Living and the Undead: From Stoker's* Dracula *to Romero's* Dawn of the Dead (Urbana and Chicago: University of Illinois Press, 1986), 275.

22. Picart, *Remaking the Frankenstein Myth on Film*, 51.

23. Wuornos represents the first criminologically recognized female rogue serial killer. Traditional female serial killers have fallen into two major categories, which can be labeled here as the "angel of mercy" and the "serial killer mail order wife." The angel of mercy typically works in hospitals or nursing homes and chooses as her victims the terminally ill. She believes she is ending the patients' miseries and is sending them perhaps to a better place. The mail order serial killer uses newspaper and magazine ads to attract "lonely hearts men" (usually long distance), and then murders them shortly after they move in (Peter Vronsky, *Female Serial Killers: How and Why Women Become Monsters*, New York: Berkley Books, 2007). Finally, some criminologists have

noted the institutionally sanctioned serial torture and killing carried out by women at the Nazi death camps, and most recently at Abu Ghraib and Guantánamo (Mc-Tara Kelvey, ed., *One of the Guys: Women as Aggressors and Torturers*, Emeryville, CA: Seal Press, 2007).

24. Internet Movie Database, "Documentary Filmmaker Helping Hollywood Producer," *Movie and TV News* (2004): www.imdb.com/SB?20030909 (accessed February 20, 2004), 1.

25. Stephen Holden, "A Murderous Journey to Self-Destruction," film rev. of *Monster, New York Times* (2003): http://movies2.nytimes.com (accessed February, 20, 2004), 1.

26. Laura Sinagra, "The Butcher Girl," *The Village Voice* (2004): www.villagevoice.com/issues/0352/sinagra.php (accessed February 20, 2004), 1.

27. David Edelstein, "Portraits of a Serial Killer: The Life and Death of Aileen Wuornos, *Slate Magazine* (December 26, 2003): http://slate.msn.com/toolbar.aspx?action=print&id=2093192 (accessed February, 20, 2004), 1.

28. Caroline J. S. Picart, *The Cinematic Rebirths of Frankenstein: Universal, Hammer and Beyond* (Westport, CT: Praeger, 2001).

29. Roger Ebert, "Monster," film rev. of *Monster, Chicago Sun-Times* (January 9, 2004): www.suntimes.com/cgi-bin/print.cgi (accessed February, 20, 2004), 1.

30. Carla Meyer, "Theron gets gritty as prostitute murderer in 'Monster,'" film rev. of *Monster, San Francisco Chronicle* (December 26, 2003): www.sfgate.com/cgi-bin/article.cgi?file=/c/a/2003/12/26/DDGOF3THB71.DTL&ty (accessed February, 29, 2004), 1.

31. Stephanie Snipes, "Behind the Making of a 'Monster,'" film rev. of *Monster, CNN.com* (January 19, 2004): www.cnn.com/2004/SHOWBIZ/Movies/01/19/jenkins.monster/index.html (accessed February 20, 2004).

32. Holden, "A Murderous Journey to Self-Destruction," 2.

33. Amy Taubin, "Monster," film rev. of *Monster, CityPages.com* (2004): www.citypages.com/filmreviews/detail.asp?MID=5337 (accessed February 20, 2004), 1.

34. Jessica Winter, "Verdict on Aileen Sequel: The Execution Left a Lot to Be Desired," *The Village Voice* (January 7–13, 2004): www.villagevoice.com/issues/0401/winter.php (accessed June 20, 2004), 1.

35. Nick Broomfield [producer and director], *Aileen Wuornos: The Selling of a Serial Killer*, 87 min., Hollywood: DEJ Productions, 1992, documentary film.

36. Steve Persall, "'Monster' mishmash," film rev. of *Monster, St. Petersburg Times Online Tampa Bay* (2004): www.sptimes.com/2004/01/22/news_pf/Weekend/_Monster__mishmash.shtml (accessed February 20, 2004), 1.

37. David Germain, "'Monster' reveals Theron's more than just pretty face," *Oakland Tribune* (December 26, 2003).

38. Meyer, "Theron gets gritty as prostitute murderer in 'Monster,'" 1.

39. Brett Buckalew, "Sympathy for the Devil," *FilmStew.com* (December 29, 2003): www.filmstew.com/showArticle.aspx?ContentID=7582 (accessed February 20, 2004), 3.

40. Persall, "'Monster' mishmash," 1–2.

41. Internet Movie Database, "Theron Spooked by Aileen's Ghost," *Movie and TV News* (2004): www.imdb.com/news/wenn/2004-01-06 (accessed February 20, 2004), 1.

42. Internet Movie Database, "Monster Movie Sets Off Debate over Accuracy," *Movie and TV News* (2004): www.imdb.com/SB?20040216 (accessed February 20, 2004): 1.

43. Nathan Rabin, "Monster," film rev. of *Monster, Onion AV Club* (January 5, 2004), www.avclub.com/content/node/17443 (accessed February 20, 2004), 1.

44. Steven F. Messner and Richard Rosenfeld, *Crime and the American Dream*, 3rd ed. (Belmont, CA: Wadsworth, 2001), 13.

45. Bram Stoker, *Dracula (Case Studies in Contemporary Criticism)*, ed. John Paul Riquelme (Boston: Bedford/St. Martin's Press, 2001), 336.

46. David Punter and Glennis Byron, *The Gothic* (Oxford, UK: Blackwell Publishing, 2004), 271.

47. Punter and Byron, *The Gothic*, 266.

Part II

WORKING THROUGH CHANGE AND XENOPHOBIA IN EUROPE

Vlad Dracula stamp (Romania). *Courtesy of John Edgar Browning*

· 7 ·

Return Ticket to Transylvania: Relations between Historical Reality and Vampire Fiction

Santiago Lucendo

The vampire was created and introduced to the public in the first half of the eighteenth century by means of a number of newspaper articles and treatises that preceded its graphic representations in fiction. This was the moment at which the idea of the vampire, as a vehicle for stories and images, was invented, at least as we know it.[1] It was not until 1732, however, that it rose from the grave and became popular, contrary to the "Universal Vampire" concept.[2] Since time immemorial, the vampire's relationship with the world around it has been a reactionary one and contributed to social, economic, and cultural instability, and the image or images the literary vampire has assumed are derived from this tensioning. As shared interest in and fascination with monstrous figures spread in the main capitals in Western Europe, the public began to divorce the vampire from other subjects of popular superstition like werewolves, witches, and demons. It should be acknowledged, however, and shall be the principal argument of this chapter, that the vampire is not a figure imported from the "East," but rather a series of fears and fancies projected over a geographic territory badly or totally unknown. The vampire is a construction developed through national exchange and negotiation, based upon words, images, and places assembled in a fashion that makes it resemble a Frankensteinian creature. From the very beginning, the vampire has occupied a culturally "stitched" body, reflecting the historical, political, and social frameworks surrounding it, and it has served, both racially and geographically, as a space in which the fears and desires of a particular (i.e., dominant, "ruling") culture can be played out.

I am indebted to those who assisted me in translating this chapter from Spanish into English. I am also grateful to John Edgar Browning, among others, whose insightful comments and revisions helped this chapter tremendously.

115

Authors of the nineteenth century, depending on their sources, took what they had on hand to create an image that could satisfy the public's interest. They used folklore, Classic mythology, Gothic novels, or travel literature, often mixing them with each other. All of these sources have in common an interest in provoking sensation and an impulse to recover the past. In most cases, the vampire was used as an excuse with which to treat other matters[3]—for example, human relationships (politics, sexual relationships, conflict in the workplace, or dealings with the dead)—but always with certain patterns that permit us to speak of a vampire stereotype. In terms of this stereotype, Dracula himself has become an open text that has never stopped growing, and his native land of Transylvania has played an active role[4] in the development of the larger stereotype. This land has suffered the same process of fictionalization as endured by its most famous inhabitant.[5] The importance of geography, where vampires are concerned, transcends mere location. It is not only about pointing out the characteristics of the landscape and its location on a map, but highlighting the connections and intentions that link those places with a fictional landscape. Maps, architecture, and journeys affect/effect the image of the monster as much as its actions and its iconographic attributes.

Transylvania, for most of us, is not a region of contemporary Romania, nor just the setting for Stoker's novel, but a place constructed by years of images from literature, cinema, TV, or Halloween. These geographical and architectural settings, some of them real and others imagined, are not themes secondary to the vampire but essential ones, and they are the result of many versions and remakes of the same stereotypes. As the superstition whirlpool of Europe, Transylvania was neither introduced by Stoker, nor was it the first place the vampire inhabited. Rather, it was made familiar in the writings of others before *Dracula* (1897), not just in fiction, as we see with Jules Verne's *The Castle of the Carpathians* (1893),[6] but in many travel accounts that preceded Stoker's novel. Some of these travel writings were used by Stoker himself (which I will discuss in more depth later on) as references out of which he constructed a cardboard model of Transylvania, without ever actually having been there.[7] Sublime landscapes, superstitious peasants, and the omnipresent castle were features that Stoker knew only from the writings of others. He was not alone, nor the first, in taking such materials from various sources and appropriating them into a particular subcategory of Gothic fiction.

Before Stoker chose Transylvania as the quintessential vampire homeland, Sheridan Le Fanu's *Carmilla* made Styria (Austria) the place we would most likely find vampires.[8] Influenced by his Irish comrade, Stoker also chose Styria at an early stage in the writing of *Dracula*, changing it later on to the now-familiar location "beyond the forest."⁹ Both authors, it would seem, constructed their exotic or foreign villains in a very similar manner. By Count Eric Von Stenbock's account in *True Story of a Vampire* (1894), we can see what the *real* Styria looks like:

> Vampire stories are generally located in Styria; mine is also. Styria is by no means the romantic kind of place described by those who have certainly never been there. It is a flat, uninteresting country, only celebrated for its turkeys, its capons, and the stupidity of its inhabitants.¹⁰

Stenbock's humorous description points out the problem that Transylvania posed before Stoker's rendering. He moved the setting of *Dracula* from Austria to Transylvania, where Jonathan Harker's business travels lead him to meet the Count. Extending the vampire's geographical limits, Stoker minimized Dracula's accessibility by removing him further away to "one of the wildest and least known portions of Europe."¹¹ We can see how vampire geography has changed during the nineteenth century, relocating from Greece, to Styria, to Transylvania, where it has rested ever since. Perhaps it was the modernity, intellectualism, and urbanity of the places that produced vampire fictions that made it necessary to move the vampire to more and more exotic terrain. In these places, the novel's fantastical elements could be rendered plausible by their very nature of being unknown.¹² Jonathan's train, itself an emblem of modernity and sophistication, could now transport people (by extension, through "time") from the metropolis to "strange, far places."¹³ In the end, however, it is the traveler who must journey (or imagine the journey) to his final destination; no time machine can bring him there, and no invention can offer security from the "unconscious" projections that accompany him to rather than await him in Transylvania.

The journey operates as a spatial retrogression of sorts, linking normalized and hegemonic worlds with far-reaching, fantastical ones (or "mytho-realistic landscapes"¹⁴). In "Locating *Dracula*: Contextualising the Geography of Transylvania," Gerald Walker and Lorraine Wright conclude:

> Thus, Stoker, while rigorously following a realistic style, carefully crafted his presentation to both transform the landscape he found in his researches into something mythic while preserving much that was actually there, including the disposition of geographic features. The basic regionalisation Stoker uses . . . is a device that helps to enhance the horrifying and fantastic elements of his story. It is not a regionalisation that may be attributed to the on-the-ground realities of Transylvania. Stoker's *Dracula* thus evokes an imaginary world rendered realistically by the way of intricate landscape detail.¹⁵

In order to soften what would otherwise have been strange experiences, the fictional traveler we encounter in Jonathan Harker's character utilizes narrative strategies to overcome these experiences. Prejudiced against unfamiliar people and places, at first Jonathan uses his diary to digest his "queer" surroundings by the use of language; later in the novel, this of course becomes destabilized as Jonathan's trip is fraught with increasingly unfamiliar and uncanny experiences. As Chloe Chard notes in her book *Pleasure and Guilt on the Grand Tour: Travel Writing and Imaginative Geography, 1600–1830*, the traveler has a way of recording what he has experienced,[16] using description as a tool for coping with the reality he sees. Some of Chard's terms provide a useful framework for contextualizing the descriptions of Transylvania Jonathan records in his diary: "opposition"[17] ("there are no maps of this country as yet to compare with our own Ordnance Survey maps"[18]), "profusion and excess,"[19] "enumeration"[20] ("In the population of Transylvania there are four distinct nationalities: Saxon in the south, and mixed with them the Wallachs, who are the descendants of the Dacians; Magyars in the west, Szekelys in the east and north"[21]), or "gastronomic products"[22] to which Jonathan makes constant allusion ("I asked the waiter, and he said it was called 'paprika hendl,' and that, as it was a national dish, I should be able to get it anywhere along the Carpathians"[23]). All these rhetorical strategies contribute to the sensationalism of Jonathan's journey, at the same time making it possible to transform the experience into an object of consumption, which is what has become of Transylvania.[24] However, no book or lecture at the British Museum in London, where Jonathan has "made search among the books and maps in the library regarding Transylvania,"[25] can adequately prepare him for the terror living at Castle Dracula, despite his futile attempts at rationalizing the irrational: "Let me be prosaic so far as facts can be; it will help me to bear up, and imagination must not run riot with me. If [it] does I am lost."[26]

The novel repeatedly signals the wondrous and fascinatingly non-Western aspect of the country to which Jonathan travels, not in the least through his discussion of the strange figures of the "Slovaks, who are more barbarian than the rest" and who "on the stage . . . would be set down at once as some Oriental band of brigands."[27] In particular, the atmosphere becomes more unreal and dream-like as the journey draws nigh, and the landscape itself strays from something picturesque into something more or less sublime. Akin to Marlow's voyage deeper into the Congo in Joseph Conrad's *Heart of Darkness*, Jonathan's journey has been read as a descent into Hell, an adventurous excursion into the unconscious,[28] or into the past. However, Jonathan's progression to Castle Dracula seems less like a journey that moves deeper into an interior, per se, than one that moves further and further away to the outside (i.e., away from civility). He writes, for example, "The impression I had was that we were leaving the West and entering the East."[29] More crucially, these critical readings have one thing in common: they converge on images and themes of *real* fear, both projected and unconscious ones. Eventually, Jonathan, and his band of "God's madmen,"[30] must also inhabit the space that is Transylvania and perform a sort of exorcism there, ridding it of the vampiric presence while replacing it with something civilizing and human even if equally violent.

Stoker constructed (i.e., conceptualized) Transylvania from works such as Emily Gerard's *The Land Beyond the Forest* (1888) and Major Edmund Cecil Johnson's *On the Track of the Crescent* (1885), and from other books like Andrew F. Crosse's *Round the Carpathians* (1878), Charles Boner's *Transylvania: Its Products and Its People* (1865), Willian Wilkinson's *An Account of the Principalities of Wallachia and Moldavia* (1820), and Sabine Baring Gould's *The Book of the Were-wolfes* (1865).[31] Stoker also used the testimony from his brother George,[32] and perhaps his own experience of Irish landscape.[33] Gerard's is one of the main sources from which Stoker draws to develop Jonathan's fears. In the opening of *The Land Beyond the Forest*, a book written during Gerard's two-year stay in Transylvania, she observes:

> Whoever wishes to study the history of Transylvania in its past, present, and future aspects, who wants to understand its geological formation or system of agriculture, who would thoroughly penetrate into the inextricable net-work of conflicting political interest which divide its interior, must seek his information elsewhere.[34]

Early on, Gerard cautions us against finding political accounts or detailed geographical information in her book. Thus, we are not talking about Transylvania (i.e., Romania), but Gerard's "Transyl-fantasia" from which Stoker constructs his own version. Many have commented on the fragments of Gerard's book that Stoker appropriates, and on the article version in which she discusses superstitions in more depth and the possible mistranslations of the word *Nosferatu*. However, nothing has been said about the images and plates included in her book, the material she, and many others, use to (mis)construct the Transylvania with which most of us are familiar. Did Stoker consult the illustrated version or just the article? This is probably an important question. We know for sure he consulted the article, from the Rosenbach Museum's papers, but did he see the illustrations and the colored map in the complete edition?

I am inclined to think that Stoker wrote the novel with these illustrations and the map Gerard includes in her book in mind. If we take a look at the map (in the English rather than the American version, which presents a different black and white map), we see not only the path clearly taken by

Jonathan, in addition to various other locations noted by Stoker that may be found in other maps, but we can see that after the Borgo Pass, the top of the mountain seems like a volcano, to which Stoker also refers in the novel as the power source of Dracula:

> The very place, where [Dracula has] been alive, Un-dead for all these centuries, is full of strangeness of the geologic and chemical world. There are deep caverns and fissures that reach none know whither. There have been volcanoes, some of whose openings still send out waters of strange properties, and gases that kill or make to vivify. Doubtless, there is something magnetic or electric in some of these combinations of occult forces which work for physical life in strange ways; and in himself were from the first some great qualities.[35]

What's more, in and around the frontier of the three states noted by Harker himself ("Transylvania, Moldavia, and Bukovina"[36]), we literally see the "imaginative whirlpool" Jonathan describes: "I read that every known superstition in the world is gathered into the horseshoe of the Carpathians, as if it were the centre of some sort of imaginative whirlpool; if so my stay may be very interesting."[37] In either case, the resemblance between the illustrations in Gerard's book and *Dracula*'s imaginary landscape, developed further in popular fiction of the twentieth century, is significant. In Gerard's book, we find castles, ruined abbeys, mountain passes, old kings, and even a Baron whose resemblance to Dracula is remarkable; it is a complete illustrated catalog of Edmund Burke's Sublime images.[38] The similarities between these worlds, both found in travel writing and in cinematic landscapes, point to a common link between the Gothic novel's vocabulary and the elements of Burke's Sublime.

Another of Stoker's sources, not as frequently cited in the scholarship as the Gerard text, is Major Edmund Cecil Johnson's *On the Track of the Crescent: Erratic Notes from the Piraus to Pesth* (1885). The attitude of Johnson, the book's traveler, is a very significant example of that of the nineteenth-century traveler to Transylvania, and it explains some of the ideas that we have about this place. He is a military officer who travels around Eastern Europe to countries like Greece, Turkey, and Romania. In this book about his journey, he records his observations of different peoples and races, on occasion making anti-Semitic comments and racial slurs against Gypsies. In general, he expresses an attitude of superiority, and he makes repeated comparisons between the things he sees and the conditions in his native land, as Jonathan does with his taxonomization of races and comparative commentaries. It is interesting that Johnson stays at the homes of the nobility; like Jonathan, he travels from count to count and mentions the Székelys,[39] Voivodes,[40] Ospodars,[41] and Wallachs.[42] In addition, Stoker uses Johnson's text to portray the Gypsies, the one ethnic group represented most stereotypically in both Johnson's and Stoker's books. Johnson's comments include: "[Gypsies] are generally wild and nomadic in their habits rarely working themselves, but living in preference off the toil of others,"[43] and "Though attempts to domesticate and tame them have been, in some cases, successful in Hungary and Spain, they are generally wild and nomadic."[44]

One of the most memorable scenes in Johnson's book is his encounter with a group of naked Gypsy children who run after him: "These children of nature are very often dangerous, especially when cold and hungry, as no one, of course, would wish to shoot, or in any way injure them, flight is the only escape from their importunities."[45]

Johnson describes Gypsies like animals and with especial resemblance to wolves. So it is not surprising that Stoker should unite them, Gypsies and wolves, as allies of the vampire. It is also interesting to compare the Major's flight with *Dracula*'s final chase scene, where wolves and Gypsies mix in the defense of the Count: "Neither the levelled weapons or on the flashing knives of the gypsies in front, or the howling of the wolves behind, appeared to even attract their attention."[46] It is important to note here that the "wild and nomadic" inhabitants of Transylvania, using Johnson's descriptors, are an important part of the landscape in the construction of this scenario.

The Transylvania represented here in plates and descriptions is part of a "prescientific" Europe in which Gothic heroes/heroines (though typically male) wandered about, which is in stark contrast to the Victorian metropolis where Stoker lived.[47] A dialogue has emerged—between the countryside and urbanity, between the old castle and the new industrial architecture, and between the East and the West—as part of an Orientalist discourse in which *Dracula* engages and participates.[48] Stoker's book, on the other hand, opposes the past and the present. The different places he describes not only represent various settings but different times and lifestyles. Jonathan is the "occidental tourist" traveling from the supposed modern world to a past clearly constructed by Stoker,[49] and the train on which Jonathan travels doubles as a sort of time machine that makes it possible for him to get there. One of the central points with which I would like to conclude this chapter is that if Transylvania is for many of us an imaginary (i.e., fancifully and culturally constructed) place, could we not say the same about the city's landscape and the world to which *it* is opposed? Is not Victorian London, for example, another imaginary place then? And if so, what is the function of this dialogue between these two imaginary places? What is our position relating to them? Maybe the Victorians invented Transylvania as we invented them to reaffirm ourselves by opposition to other,[50] less modern subjects.

Today we may travel to Transylvania, but because most of us are subject to the same artificial constructions, we would be traveling to *Draculaland*, as the Romanian art group subREAL has so named it (implying a comparison to Disneyland). The difference between these two places is that the first is the result of the transformation of a real place into an imaginary one, a territory dominated by the tyranny of fiction, and the other is the physical realization of an imaginary world. Although each of these places has its own specific problems, which should be addressed individually, they have something in common: that is, both have been created by fantasy. Our fictions say a great deal about us and the way we project our realities into fantasy worlds and into the strange, fanciful creatures that inhabit these imaginary places. In either case, or perhaps more importantly, we must (re)consider what lies behind these creatures themselves—monsters who are as fancifully and culturally constructed as the lands in which they inhabit—because it is less of the monster with which we should be concerned, but ourselves.

NOTES

1. From this date we have two important groups of documents. On one side is the news in the press that referred to the Arnold Paul case, in which the word *vampire* appeared for the first time in English in *London Paper* March 1732, but also the responses to these in *Applebee's Original Weekly-Journal* or *The Craftsman*. On the other hand, we have the scholarly treatises published in Leipzig around the same year that treated Arnold Paul's case and also Peter Plogowitz's, but with an erudite and elaborate approach. Arnold Paul's case and the polemic discussion around it, in both public and scholarly circles, present the main features of the vampire from which, I understand, Europe derives much of its vampire folklore.

2. The "Universal Vampire" concept held by many authors can be found in numerous publications, such as Montague Summer's *The Vampire: His Kith and Kin* (New York: E. P. Dutton and Company, 1929) and *The Vampire in Europe* (New York: E. P. Dutton and Company, 1929), or Ken Gelder's *Reading the Vampire* (London and New York: Routledge, 1994). It implies that we can find vampires anywhere and at any time in the world. In line with Markman Ellis, though not agreeing with all his arguments, I contend that the vampire is a quite modern creation related to the controversy created in the press around it. See Ellis's *The History of Gothic Fiction* (Edinburgh: Edinburgh University Press, 2003), 162.

3. As James B. Twitchell explains in *The Living Dead: A Study of the Vampire in Romantic Literature* (Durham: Duke University Press, 1981), "The Romantics really did not care about vampires; in fact, they rarely if ever wrote about vampires as vampires; instead the vampire was the means to achieve various ends. For an explanation of these various ends[,] we need to examine the works themselves" (38).

4. It is often noted that "Dracula has never been out of print," but equally worth mentioning is Gelder's observation in *Reading the Vampire* that Dracula has never stopped growing in his readings, reproductions, and reinterpretations: "it has become productive *through its consumption*" (65).

5. When interviewed (circa 1973) for a magazine article titled "The Art of Haunting" (facsimile reproduced in Peter Haining, *The Dracula Scrapbook* [New York: Bramhall House, 1976]), American film producer, director, and actor William Castle (remembered most notably for *Rosemary's Baby* [1968], *Mr. Sardonicus* [1961], *13 Ghosts* [1960], *The Tingler* [1959], and *House on Haunted Hill* [1959]) comments on Dan Curtis's telefilm *The Night Stalker* (1972), in which a Dracula-type vampire terrorizes Las Vegas:

> "The Dracula theme was successful in 1927 [for the Horace Liveright–produced Broadway stage adaptation written by Deane-Balderston] and again 45 years later [for the Dan Curtis telefilm]," said Castle. "Take the Dracula theme out of Transylvania and put it in Las Vegas as *The Night Stalker*. Transylvania is Never-Never Land. Las Vegas gives it more credibility." (102)

6. In works on the region of the Carpathians, Jules Verne names two other authors who also described Transylvania, Auguste de Gérando (probably referring to the book *Le Transylvanie et ses habitants*) and Elisée Reclus on his "travel accounts." It would be interesting to compare these two sources to those of Bram Stoker, because very likely they will contain descriptions of a savage landscape, represent the castle as the source of evil and fear, and refer to the Carpathians as a land of superstition.

7. The same could be said of Ann Radcliffe and her *Mysteries of Udolfo* with respect to Italy, and Prosper Mérimée, who had never traveled to Serbia before writing *Guzla* (and who is said to have used Augustin Calmet's comments on vampires).

8. Carmilla LeFanu, in *Three Vampire Tales: Dracula, Carmilla, and the Vampyre*, ed. Anne Williams (New York: Houghton Mifflin, 2003).

9. Clive Leatherdale, *Dracula: The Novel and the Legend* (Southend-on-Sea, Essex: Desert Island Books, 2001), 91.

10. Count Eric Von Stenbock, "A True Story of a Vampire," in *The Vampire Omnibus*, ed. Peter Haining (London: Orion, 1995), 159–60.

11. Bram Stoker, *Dracula: The Norton Critical Edition*, ed. Nina Auerbach and David J. Skal (New York: W. W. Norton and Company, 1997), 10.

12. With the advent of space exploration, the vampire's new origins and fantastical landscape would become outer space; for example, in films like *Queen of Blood* (1966) and *Lifeforce* (1985). And now that traveling to Mars seems closer, we start to wonder where space invaders will come from once we have discovered that Martians are actually some small docile bacteria.

13. "Searchers after horror haunt strange, far places" writes H. P. Lovecraft. "The Picture in the House," in *Wolf's Complete Book of Terror*, ed. Leonard Wolf (New York: Clarkson N. Potter, Inc., 1979), 171.

14. Gerald Walker and Lorraine Wright, "Locating *Dracula*: Contextualising the Geography of Transylvania," in *Bram Stoker's Dracula: Sucking through the Centuries*, ed. Carol Margaret Davison (Toronto: Dundurn Press, 1997), 72.

15. Walker and Wright, "Locating *Dracula*," 72.

16. Chloe Chard, *Pleasure and Guilt on the Grand Tour: Travel Writing and Imaginative Geography, 1600–1830* (Manchester and New York: Manchester University Press, 1999).

17. On the term *opposition*, Chard writes in *Pleasure and Guilt on the Grand Tour*:

For much of the eighteenth century, this device of constructing binary, symmetrical oppositions between the familiar and the foreign constitutes one of the most common strategies for translating foreignness into discourse—both in accounts of the imaginative geography of the Grand Tour and in writings concerned with other domains of alterity. Proclaiming a power of comparison conferred by the experience of travel, the speaking subject adopts his or her own native region as a constant point of reference. (40)

18. Stoker, *Dracula*, 10.

19. These terms are included in the chapter "Opposition and Intensification" in Chard, *Pleasure and Guilt on the Grand Tour*, 56.

20. Of "enumeration," Chard writes in *Pleasure and Guilt on the Grand Tour*, "One of the tropes most commonly employed is a hyperbole of enumeration" (62).

21. Stoker, *Dracula*, 10.

22. In *Pleasure and Guilt on the Grand Tour*, Chard writes, "From early in the nineteenth century onwards, the traveller, in a great many writings, displays an interest in the gastronomic products to be encountered as he or she moves from one region to the next" (240).

23. Stoker, *Dracula*, 9.

24. Commenting on Transylvania's history of invasion and occupation by, among others, the Romans, Hungarians, Turks, and Germans, Nina Auerbach and David J. Skal write, "In essence, fittingly for vampires, the history of Transylvania is a history of whom it belongs to" (9n7).

25. Stoker, *Dracula*, 9.

26. Stoker, *Dracula*, 30.

27. Stoker, *Dracula*, 11.

28. Geoffrey Wall fittingly contends that "Transylvania is Europe's unconscious" (20). Geoffrey Wall, "'Different from Writing': *Dracula* in 1897," *Literature and History* 10 (1984): 15–23.

29. Stoker, *Dracula*, 9.

30. Stoker, *Dracula*, 111.

31. See Paul Murray, *From the Shadow of Dracula. A Life of Bram Stoker* (London: Pimilico, 2005), and Harry Ludlam, *A Biography of Dracula: The Life Story of Bram Stoker* (London: Quality Book Club, 1962).

32. Barbara Belford, *Bram Stoker: A Biography of the Author of Dracula* (New York: Knopf, 1996), 128. Cited in Jimmie E. Cain, "'With the Unspeakables': Dracula and Russophobia," in *Dracula: The Shade and the Shadow* (Southend-on-Sea, Essex: Desert Island Books Limited, 1998), ed. Elizabeth Miller. Cain writes, "George's book . . . provided background for *Dracula*'s opening chapters, which so admirably evoke the

geography, customs, and ethnic complexities of Transylvania, the 'land beyond the forest'" (109).

33. In *Vampires, Mummies and Liberals* (Durham, NC: Duke University Press, 1996), David Glover sees "the Transylvanian topography of *Dracula* as a kind of mirror image of the mountainous Irish terrain of *The Snake's Pass*, and indeed there are brief moments when these twin geographies seem to be indistinguishable" (35). Glover also points out Major Edmund Cecil Johnson's book *On the Track of the Crescent* (London: Hurst and Blackett, 1885) as a referent for Stoker that compares the Szekelys and the Wallachs with the Irish (34).

34. Emily de Laszowska-Gerard, *The Land Beyond the Forest: Facts, Figures, and Fancies from Transylvania* (Edinburgh and London: William Blackwood and Sons, 1888), 7. Of Transylvania's more sublime, fantastical nature, Gerard writes Chapter 1 (Introductory):

> Just as Robinson Crusoe getting attached to his parrots and his palm trees, his gourds and his goats, continued to yearn for them after his return to Europe, so I found myself gradually succumbing to the indolent charm and the drowsy poetry of this secluded land. A very few years more of unbroken residence here would no doubt suffice to efface all memory of the world we had left behind and the century in which we live.
>
> I remember reading in some fairy tale, long ago, of a youthful princess who, stolen by the gnomes and carried off into gnomeland, was restored to her parents after a lapse of years. Their joy was great at recovering their child, but it turned to grief when they discovered that she had grown estranged from them, and had lost all interest in the actual world. The sun was too bright, she said, it hurt her eyes, and the voices of men were too loud, they scorched her ears; and she could never feel at home again amid the restless glitter of her surroundings. (1)

35. Stoker, *Dracula*, 278. It is not surprising to see after reading this paragraph that Murnau converged the vampire with the powers of nature in his film *Nosferatu* (1922).

36. Stoker, *Dracula*, 10.

37. Stoker, *Dracula*, 10.

38. In *A Philosophical Enquiry into the Origin of Our Ideas of the Sublime and Beautiful* (Oxford: Oxford University Press, 1998) originally published in 1757, Edmund Burke provides an enumeration of the different causes for our strongest emotion: the sublime.

39. Major Edmund Cecil Johnson, *On the Track of the Crescent: Erratic Notes from the Piraus to Pesth* (London: Hurst and Blackett, 1885).

40. Johnson, *On the Track of the Crescent*, 107.

41. Johnson, *On the Track of the Crescent*, 108.

42. Johnson, *On the Track of the Crescent*, 281.

43. Johnson, *On the Track of the Crescent*, 150.

44. Johnson, *On the Track of the Crescent*, 151.

45. Johnson, *On the Track of the Crescent*, 150.

46. Stoker, *Dracula*, 324.

47. Cristopher Frayling, *Nightmare: The Birth of Horror* (London: BBC Books, 1996), 100.

48. Edward W. Said, *Orientalism* (New York: Vintage Books, 1979). *Dracula* is not discussed in Said's book, but the novel fits perfectly with his description of Orientalism.

49. "The Occidental Tourist: *Dracula* and the Anxiety of Reverse Colonization" is the title of Stephen D. Arata's article in which he reads *Dracula* in terms of a cultural fear and guilt after imperial colonization, and in the context of late-Victorian fiction. Originally published in *Victorian Studies* (Summer 1990): 627–33.

50. In *Inventing the Victorians* (London: Faber and Faber, 2001), Matthew Sweet addresses this relationship and the problems it poses:

> Suppose that everything we think we know about the Victorians is wrong. That, in the century which has elapsed since 1901, we have misread their culture, their history, their lives—perhaps deliberately, in order to satisfy our sense of ourselves as liberated Moderns. It comforts us to imagine that we have escaped their influence, freed ourselves from their corseted, high-collared world, cast off their puritanism and prejudices. But what if they were substantially different from the people we imagine them to have been? (ix)

Racism and the Vampire: The Anti-Slavic Premise of Bram Stoker's *Dracula* (1897)

Jimmie Cain

*D*uring the 1880s and 1890s, thousands of Eastern European and Russian Jews immigrated to England to flee the pogroms that followed the assassination of Czar Alexander II. Their arrival in England engendered a profusion of anti-Semitic literature. In 1895, for example, Herbert Beerbohm Tree's exceedingly successful stage adaptation of George Du Maurier's novel *Trilby* featured a sinister Jew, Svengali. Jules Zanger suggests that such works as *Trilby* "owed much of their vitality to the way in which they embodied and alluded to a number of popular apprehensions that clustered around the appearance in England of great numbers of Eastern European Jews at the end of the century."[1]

Foremost among these apprehensions was the belief that Jews spread disease and contamination. Essayists such as Robert Sherard and Joseph Banister popularized the image of the new Jewish immigrants as a "brutalized race," one with a "repulsive Asiatic physiognomy [and] flat feet, fat legs and loathsome skin and scalp diseases," a people whose bodies were "black with filth and red with sores" and whose East End dwellings manifested an extraordinary lack of hygiene and a concomitant foul smell.[2] Jews, therefore, posed a threat because of their "propensity to carry and spread disease and thereby infect and weaken other elements of the population."[3] As fellow anti-Semite John Foster Fraser lamented in the *Yorkshire Post*, England had no provisions for preventing the influx of "smallpox, scarlet fever, measles, diphtheria" with the "unwashed verminous alien" from Eastern Europe and Russia.[4]

This chapter is reprinted from *Bram Stoker and Russophobia: Evidence of the British Fear of Russia in Dracula and* Lady of the Shroud © 2006 Jimmie E. Cain Jr. by permission of McFarland & Company, Inc., Box 611, Jefferson, NC 28640, www.mcfarlandpub.com.

In the villain of his 1897 novel *Dracula*, Bram Stoker apparently incorporates such accounts of the immigrant Jews crowding the dilapidated and poorly drained slums of London's East End. The Count's residence at Carfax, in Purfleet, for instance, is well to the east of downtown London, near the Whitechapel district, the epicenter of the London immigrant community. In addition to its dense Jewish population, Whitechapel was also noteworthy as the scene of the murders ascribed to Jack the Ripper, a figure often represented in newspaper stories and sketches as an Eastern Jew.[5] Further marking Carfax and Dracula's other lairs as Jewish residences is their foul smell. Thus the laborer who delivers Dracula's boxes to Carfax tells Jonathan Harker that one "might 'ave smelled ole Jerusalem in it."[6] When the Crew subsequently enter the estate in search of the Count, they encounter a "malodorous air."[7] Even upon stepping into the Count's upscale digs in Piccadilly, Godalming remarks, "The place smells so vilely."[8]

The Count has singularly Jewish features. Describing Dracula's "very marked physiognomy," Harker records that his

> face was a strong—a very strong—aquiline, with high bridge of the thin nose and peculiarly arched nostrils; with lofty domed forehead, and hair growing scantily round the temples, but profusely elsewhere. His eyebrows were very massive, almost meeting over the nose, and with bushy hair that seemed to curl in its own profusion. The mouth . . . was fixed and rather cruel-looking, with peculiarly sharp white teeth; these protruded over the lips . . . .[9]

Harker also cannot help but notice that the Count's "breath was rank."[10] Thus in his conception of Dracula, Stoker undoubtedly includes attributes of the dangerous, pestilential Jewish immigrant. However, I contend that Stoker projects anxieties about a much more real and powerful threat to England and Victorian culture in the figure of the monstrous count: the Slavic menace posed by imperial Russia.

When Stoker began preparations for the novel, England and Russia had been imperial rivals for over one hundred years, a rivalry that eventuated in the tragic Crimean War of 1854–1856. A *Punch* illustration from September 1853, just prior to the outbreak of the Crimean War, entitled "A Consultation about the State of Turkey," communicates the profound distrust of Russia that John Howes Gleason has shown to be widespread amongst Victorians of all stripes. It also exhibits intriguing parallels to the figure of Count Dracula. Above the recumbent patient, a gravely ill Turkey, hovers a spectral image of the Czar, rendered as a winged skeleton adorned with a plumed helmet and brandishing a cat-of-nine in one hand while the other hand menacingly reaches toward the patient's neck. Beside the bed sit representations of John

Bull and his French ally, here pictured as physicians deliberating upon a suitable course of therapy. Notably, the image of the Czar recalls Dracula's associations with bats and death, his ability to emerge from mists and miasmas, and his power to absorb living creatures. Moreover, the physicians are as unaware of the menace to their patient as are Seward and Van Helsing at first.

In his research for *Dracula*, Stoker consulted a number of relatively contemporaneous documents about the geography, peoples, and customs of Eastern Europe, works that gave him the matter for constructing a Slavic, Russian villain. Among the books, Clive Leatherdale notes, "written by British official servants—soldiers, administrators, or their wives"[11] that Stoker consulted, William Wilkinson's *An Account of the Principalities of Wallachia and Moldavia: With Various Political Observations Relating to Them* of 1820 gave Stoker the material for Dracula's racial and ethnic identity, an identity with pronounced Russian and Slavic antecedents. Wilkinson writes that toward the end of the seventh century

> a nation, known under the names of Slaves and Bulgarians, came from the interior of Russia to that part of Maesia, which has since been called Bulgaria. Soon after a great number of Slaves . . . crossed the Danube and settled in Dacia, where they have since been known under the name of Wallachs. . . . The modern Wallachians, however, exclude it altogether from their language, and call themselves "Rummunn" or Romans, giving to their country the name Roman-land, "Tsara-Rumaneska."[12]

Thus Stoker learned that in their inception, the Wallachians, and by association the Moldavians, the predecessors of the modern Rumanians, descended from Slavic peoples immigrating to the region from Russia and sharing close blood relations with the Bulgarians.

Dracula's description of his own heritage shows marked vestiges of Wilkinson's text. But more importantly, Dracula's genealogy reveals clear Russian and Slavic origins. In his "veins flows the blood of many brave races," especially that of the "Ugric tribe," who "bore down from Iceland the fighting spirit that Thor and Wodin gave them, which their Berserkers displayed to such fell intent on the seaboards of Europe . . . Asia and Africa." So fierce were they that their victims believed "that the were-wolves themselves had come." Among his progenitors Dracula also claims Attila the Hun, who descended from "those old witches . . . expelled from Scythia."[13] In his explanatory notes to this passage, Leonard Wolf points out that the Ugric tribe "denotes an ethnological group that included . . . related people of western Siberia" and that in the "early stages of the superstition in Eastern Europe, werewolves and vampires were closely akin." Moreover, he indicates that Scythia refers to "a region in southeast Europe and Asia lying north of the

Black and Caspian seas,"[14] an area that included Russian Armenia and bordered on the Crimean peninsula.

Wolf does not point out, however, the associations to Russia suggested by Dracula's Scandinavian heritage. The word *Russia* is derived from *Rus*, a corrupted form of *Ruotsi*, a Finnish term describing the Varanger, the Vikings, the "Berserkers" who settled in conquered towns and villages along the Volga beginning in the ninth century.[15] Furthermore, the Vikings have been credited with organizing the first Slavic state in Russia, and the first Russian Chronicle glorifies the exploits of the Viking prince of Novogrod, Rurik.[16]

The Huns further connect him with the Slavs in general and Russia in particular. Bernard Pares has shown that in the course of his conquests in the West, Attila subjugated much of the territory that comprises modern-day Russia and the Balkans. Furthermore, Attila incorporated many Slavic people in the Hunnish Empire. When Attila's short-lived empire broke up in 453, the Slavs coalesced into a united group, spreading throughout what is now Eastern Europe, the Ukraine, and Russia.[17]

Significantly, Stoker situates Castle Dracula "in the extreme east . . . just on the borders of three states, Transylvania, Moldavia, and Bukovina"[18] near the conjunction of the Pruth and Seret rivers[19] and, interestingly, at almost the exact terminus of Attila's western conquests, deep in the heart of the Slavic region. This location is further significant because it recalls the memory of Peter the Great. Pares describes Peter as "a barbarian in his habits, direct and practical in his insistence on knowing everything that was to be learned, and with the kind of genius that consists in extraordinary quickness of thought."[20] What Peter most wanted to learn was the military and bureaucratic practices of the West. So in 1697 he began a "journey of education to Europe,"[21] taking in the secrets of the Swedish fortress at Riga and working incognito in the shipyards of Amsterdam and London so as to master modern shipbuilding theory, all the while trying to hire the best experts in the military and practical sciences each country could provide.[22] Equipped with this new knowledge, he proceeded upon his return to Russia to prosecute successful wars of expansion on his neighbors to the north, west, and south. Fortunately for Western Europe, Peter was not always victorious, and one of his most famous defeats came at the hands of the Turks at the Pruth river, in the vicinity of Castle Dracula, in 1710.[23]

Stoker's research for *Dracula* revealed an association between Vlad Dracula and one other famous czar as well. According to Clive Leatherdale, after reading of Vlad Dracula's penchant for impaling his victims, both domestic and foreign, Stoker added staking to the list of measures for killing vampires. Further investigations of the subject would have shown that within a century of Vlad's death, his impaling exploits [were] seized upon by Ivan the Terrible in Russia. Vlad had shown himself to be a hero of the Orthodox faith and a model of the harsh, autocratic ruler. As such he was taken to justify Ivan's supposed divine right to tyranny and sadism.[24]

Felix Oinas, a student of Slavic folklore, weighs in with Leatherdale on this point, for he reports that tales of Vlad Dracula's cruelties "were especially popular in Russia, since the Russians associated him with the person of Ivan the Terrible."[25] Oinas goes one step further in establishing a correspondence between vampires and Russia by arguing that vampires are a predominantly Slavic and Russian phenomenon.

> There are clear indications that the beliefs in vampires have deep roots among the Slavs and obviously go back to the Proto-Slavic period. These beliefs are also well documented among the early Russians. The term "vampire" (*upyr'*) appears as the name of a Novgordian prince (Upir Likhyi) as early as 1407 and resurfaces in 1495 as a peasant name. This term has also been recorded in western Russia as both a personal and place name. The previous existence in Russia of a vampire cult is illustrated by the fight clerics waged in encyclicals against sacrifices made to them.[26]

Furthermore, Oinas shows that the vampire's ability to assume the form of a bat appears first "among the Slavs."[27] It is well within the realm of possibility, then, that Stoker would have uncovered much of this information about the vampire tradition among the Slavs and in Russia during his research and incorporated it into his novel.

Stoker's inherited antipathy to Russia combined with the links he discovered to Vlad Dracula, the Eastern vampire myth, and Russia would therefore account for the prominent allusions to Russia and to Slavic vampire folklore that the author placed in or considered for the opening chapters of *Dracula*. The original first chapter of the novel had Dracula saving Jonathan Harker from a vampire attack in Germany during Walpurgis Nacht. However, Stoker later removed the chapter, which his wife Florence published after his death as a short story entitled "Dracula's Guest." The story has obvious connections with the vampire legends among the Russians, Bulgarians, Rumanians, and Serbians enumerated by Oinas. For example, Oinas records that among the Slavs, vampires

> are believed to lie in their graves as undecayed corpses, leaving at mignight [*sic*] to go to houses and have sexual relations with or suck the blood of those sleeping, or to devour their flesh, sometimes causing the death of the victims. If the grave is opened, the presence of a vampire can be recognized by finding the body in a state of disorder, with red cheeks, tense skin,

charged blood vessels, warm blood and growing hair and nails; in some cases the grave itself is bespattered with blood, doubtless from the latest victim.[28]

Similarly, in "Dracula's Guest" Jonathan Harker learns from a carriage driver that in a deserted village near their route

long ago, hundreds of years, men had died there and been buried in their graves; and sounds were heard under the clay, and when the graves were opened, men and women were found rosy with life, and their mouths red with blood.[29]

Later in *Dracula* after Lucy Westenra has become a vampire—a "*nosferatu*, as they call it in Eastern Europe,"[30] says Van Helsing—she is described in her coffin as "more beautiful than ever. . . . The lips were red, nay redder than before; and on the cheeks was a delicate bloom."[31] When he next encounters the vamped Lucy, Dr. Seward notes that her "lips were crimson with fresh blood, and . . . the stream had trickled over her chin and stained the purity of her lawn death-robe."[32]

Also like the Eastern European vampires described by Oinas, Lucy becomes sexually active after her vamping. Just before she is staked, the "undead" Lucy tries to seduce her fiancé, Arthur Holmwood, later Lord Godalming, in language fraught with sexual allusions: "Come to me, Arthur. Leave these others and come to me. My arms are hungry for you. Come, and we can rest together. Come, my husband, come!"[33] Such behavior violates Victorian sexual mores, characterized by "male-initiated and male-dominant genital intercourse."[34] Lucy, therefore, elicits horror as a vampire victim and as a sexual predator, what Elaine Showalter terms "the nymphomaniac or oversexed wife who [threatens] her husband's life with her insatiable erotic demands."[35]

"Dracula's Guest" features a significant direct reference to Russia as well. Harker becomes intrigued with the driver's story and asks to be shown the village in question. When the driver refuses to accommodate his wishes, Harker sends the driver back to Munich and proceeds alone on foot. Once Harker reaches the deserted town, a sudden snowstorm breaks, forcing him to seek refuge in the only available refuge, "a great massive tomb of marble."[36] As he enters the structure, a sudden flash of lightening reveals "a beautiful woman, with rounded cheeks and red lips, seemingly sleeping on a bier."[37] Before he can investigate further, however, an unseen force hurls him back out into the storm, he loses consciousness, and when he awakes, he discovers a giant wolf gnawing at his throat. Fortunately, he is saved by a group of mounted troopers. What makes this scene important, other than the obvious allusions to

Slavic vampire myths, is that before entering the tomb Harker notices a most unusual inscription on its back, "'The dead travel fast,'" a message "graven in great Russian letters."[38]

The really substantial proof, however, that Stoker had a Slavic, Russian menace in mind when penning *Dracula* is a travelogue coauthored by him and his younger brother George. George, a physician, had served two years as a volunteer first with the Turkish army and later as Chef de L'Ambulance du Croissant Rouge, the Turkish version of the Red Cross, during the Russo-Turkish war of 1876–1878. Upon his return to England in 1878, George published with his brother's assistance his observations of Bulgarians and Russians in *With the Unspeakables; or Two Years' Campaigning in European and Asiatic Turkey*. In one notable section, George recounts the depredations of Bulgarian and Russian troops on the Turkish colonists residing around Andrianople in Turkish occupied Bulgaria. According to George, "twenty-one Turkish villages were burnt and sacked, and the women violated"; in other instances "young Turkish girls were carried off and confined in houses for the Russian officers, who visited them in relays, sometimes for a period lasting over two days."[39] When the Bulgarians and Russians captured the village of Kara Ach, they imprisoned the male population in a house "while the women were violated and the village sacked."[40] After reading many more similar accounts of Russian brutality, one might quite reasonably come to see in the foul-smelling, rapacious, and licentious Russians of this travelogue an analogue for the aromatic count who invades Britain to prey promiscuously on its female population.

NOTES

1. Jules Zanger, "A Sympathetic Vibration: Dracula and the Jews," *English Literature in Translation* 34.1 (1991): 33.

2. Colin Holmes, *Anti-Semitism in British Society, 1876–1939* (New York: Holmes and Meier, 1979), 38, 40.

3. Holmes, *Anti-Semitism in British Society, 1876–1939*, 40.

4. Holmes, *Anti-Semitism in British Society, 1876–1939*, 38.

5. See chapter 4, "The Jewish Murderer: Jack the Ripper, Race, and Gender," in Sander Gilman, *The Jew's Body* (New York: Routledge, 1991).

6. Bram Stoker, *The Essential Dracula: The Definitive Annotated Edition of Bram Stoker's Classic Novel*, ed. Leonard Wolf (New York: Plume, 1993), 276.

7. Stoker, *The Essential Dracula*, 302.

8. Stoker, *The Essential Dracula*, 356.

9. Stoker, *"The Essential Dracula*, 25.

10. Stoker, *The Essential Dracula*, 26.

11. Clive Leatherdale, *Dracula: The Novel and the Legend* (Wellingborough, Northamptonshire: The Aquarian Press, 1985), 97.

12. William Wilkinson, *An Account of the Principalities of Wallachia and Moldavia: With Various Political Observations Relating to Them* (London: Longman, Hurst, Rees, Orme and Brown, 1820), 92.

13. Stoker, *The Essential Dracula*, 40.

14. Stoker, *The Essential Dracula*, 40.

15. Bernard Pares, *A History of Russia* (New York: Vintage Books, 1965), 28.

16. Pares, *A History of Russia*, 19; and *The Columbia History of the World*, 8th ed., ed. John A. Garraty and Peter Gay (New York: Harper and Row, 1987), 470.

17. Pares, *A History of Russia*, 11–12.

18. Stoker, *The Essential Dracula*, 3.

19. Stoker, *The Essential Dracula*, 417.

20. Pares, *A History of Russia*, 198.

21. Pares, *A History of Russia*, 197.

22. Pares, *A History of Russia*, 198.

23. Pares, *A History of Russia*, 206.

24. Leatherdale, *Dracula: The Novel and the Legend*, 216.

25. Felix Oinas, "East European Vampires and Dracula," *Journal of Popular Culture* 16.1 (Summer 1982), 115.

26. Oinas, "East European Vampires and Dracula," 113.

27. Oinas, "East European Vampires and Dracula," 109.

28. Oinas, "East European Vampires and Dracula," 109.

29. Bram Stoker, "Dracula's Guest," *The Essential Dracula: The Definitive Annotated Edition of Bram Stoker's Classic Novel*, ed. Leonard Wolf (New York: Plume, 1993), 448.

30. Stoker, *The Essential Dracula*, 261.

31. Stoker, *The Essential Dracula*, 245.

32. Stoker, *The Essential Dracula*, 257.

33. Stoker, *The Essential Dracula*, 257.

34. Anne Cranny-Francis, "Sexual Politics and Political Repression in Bram Stoker's *Dracula*," in *Nineteenth-Century Suspense*, ed. Bloom Clive, Brian Docherty, Jane Gibb, and Keith Shand (New York: St. Martin's, 1988), 65.

35. Cranny-Francis, "Sexual Politics and Political Repression," 180.

36. Stoker, "Dracula's Guest," 451.

37. Stoker, "Dracula's Guest," 452.

38. Stoker, "Dracula's Guest," 451.

39. George Stoker, *With "The Unspeakables;" or, Two Years' Campaigning in European and Asiatic Turkey* (London: Chapman and Hall, 1878), 116.

40. Stoker, *With "The Unspeakables,"* 124.

·9·

The Grateful Un-Dead: Count Dracula and the Transnational Counterculture in *Dracula A.D. 1972* (1972)

Paul Newland

"The monster has become a portrait of ourselves and of the kind of life we have chosen to lead."[1]
"The dream is over."

—John Lennon/Plastic Ono Band, "God" (1970)

The issue of *Time* magazine published on June 19, 1972, featured a striking blood-red cover on which a darkly clad disciple of the Devil menacingly stared from behind a mask. The headline blazed "The Occult Revival: Satan Returns." For many readers this image would have effectively captured the *zeitgeist*. This was a moment when it felt like a counterculture that had developed internationally during the 1960s had either been inculcated by mass culture or had effectively moved away from peace and love toward something altogether more sinister. By mid-1972, then, many young people across the West had begun to look elsewhere for their "kicks"—it seemed that Satan had become cool. The Beatles had been the avatars of the transnational counterculture during the late 1960s as it had increasingly moved away from Christianity toward Eastern religious practices, mysticism, spirituality, and meditation. But now something more evil was stirring. Testifying to this, the *Time* magazine image looks as if it could have been pilfered from a late-1960s Hammer horror film. It certainly appears to suggest potential points of cultural convergence between the enduring popularity of fictional horror figures such as Count Dracula, low-budget horror movies, and the developing countercultural interest in satanic occult practices. But another text that appeared in 1972 demonstrated the ways in which countercultural practices and occult practices had become imbricated—the British film *Dracula A.D. 1972* (Alan Gibson, 1972).

135

Dracula A.D. 1972 has received very little critical attention. It was once even dismissed as being "beneath discussion"[2] and has long been considered one of the lesser films of the Christopher Lee *Dracula* cycle. Indeed, James Craig Holte has even called it "a complete failure."[3] But I want to suggest here that *Dracula A.D. 1972* is an interesting film that resonates with the ruptures occurring across Western popular culture during the late 1960s and early 1970s. Indeed, I hope that a reappraisal of *Dracula A.D. 1972* might perhaps facilitate a broader understanding of the ways in which a complex array of transnational cultural identities came into conflict during this period, and how and why, at the same time, underground cultural practices were effectively inculcated into mass cultural forms. I want to try to demonstrate how far the film exploits the codes and conventions of a transnational counterculture whose original practitioners had sought to "discover new types of community, new family patterns, new sexual mores, new kinds of livelihood, new esthetic forms, new personal identities on the far side of power politics, the bourgeois home, and the consumer society."[4] By doing this I hope to show how *Dracula A.D. 1972* played an (admittedly small) part in pulling the counterculture toward mass culture; thus condemning the hippie dream to what we might now consider to be a perpetually "un-dead" existence. Finally, I want to consider how and why this process appears to relegate the un-dead figure of Count Dracula to the periphery of the narrative of this particular film.

FOR WHAT IT'S WORTH

Dracula A.D. 1972 was the penultimate film in the *Dracula* cycle produced by Hammer films that starred Christopher Lee as the eponymous Count. This cycle began with the popular and critically acclaimed *Dracula* (Terence Fisher, 1958) and continued with *The Brides of Dracula* (Terence Fisher, 1960), *Dracula—Prince of Darkness* (Terence Fisher, 1965), *Dracula Has Risen from the Grave* (Freddie Francis, 1968), *Taste the Blood of Dracula* (Peter Sasdy, 1969), *Scars of Dracula* (Roy Ward Baker, 1970), *Dracula A.D. 1972* (Alan Gibson, 1972) and *The Satanic Rights of Dracula* (Alan Gibson, 1973). *Dracula A.D. 1972* saw Peter Cushing return as Professor Van Helsing for the first time since *The Brides of Dracula,* released twelve years previously.

The setting of the last two films in contemporary times clearly echoes US films of the period such as *Count Yorga, Vampire* (Bob Kelljan, 1970), *Blacula* (William Crain, 1972), and the TV movie *The Night Stalker* (John Llewellyn Moxey, 1972), but also *Night of the Living Dead* (George Romero, 1968) and *Rosemary's Baby* (Roman Polanski, 1968).[5] David Sanjek has pointed out that in these films "victims in several cases became themselves monsters, thereby muddying the distinction between the monstrous and the normal as well as locating the terror in the everyday world."[6] Sanjek (196) further argues that Romero's film, in particular, "underscored the increasingly inoperative moral allegory of Hammer's output and Hammer's predilection for dramatizing the intrusion of the 'abnormal' monster into a 'normal' human community." A number of British horror films produced from around 1968 certainly appeared to move away from representing good and evil within clearly discernible oppositional terms. As Sanjek (197) puts it, "To remain worthy of attention, the British horror film would have to embrace the monstrous in audience and viewer alike." Films that attempted to problematize the location of the monstrous that were produced in Britain during this period include *Doomwatch* (Peter Sasdy, 1972), *Death Line* (aka *Raw Meat*) (Gary Sherman, 1972), *Asylum* (Roy Ward Baker, 1972), *Don't Look Now* (Nicholas Roeg, 1973), and *The Wicker Man* (Robin Hardy, 1973), as well as, of course, *Dracula A.D. 1972* and *The Satanic Rites of Dracula*.

Writing specifically about the vampire films of the period, Andrew Tudor has commented that "vampires stalk their prey in downtown Los Angeles or London's West End; they have become part of our everyday environment, no longer safely insulated in mythic history."[7] So it seems that when vampirism was located in the quotidian contemporary world of the late 1960s and early 1970s, figures that had traditionally operated as straightforward embodiments of evil in gothic narratives could suddenly be seen to become morally ambiguous. The shift in time that occurs in *Dracula A.D. 1972* from 1872 to 1972 clearly articulates a movement away from a world of moral clarity toward a world of moral ambiguity. As I show, the sense of moral ambiguity captured in the film is dependent upon both its depiction of the conflicting interests of countercultural practices and the continuing inculcation of aspects of these practices into mainstream Western mass culture.

In some ways, of course, *Dracula A.D. 1972* still functions as a vampire tale in the traditional sense. We see Count Dracula dispatch his victims in the time-honored style. And the Count does have a traditional foe in the film in the figure of Van Helsing (Peter Cushing). But both men are from an older generation. They seem better suited to a time when moral codes were more clearly drawn and policed. In *Dracula A.D. 1972* Count Dracula does appear once again as a monstrous figure, but his monstrousness is greatly diminished. This is because the monstrous is primarily located within the countercultural practices of an intercontinental, interracial, and intersexual underground community in the contemporary sequences of the film. These practices are instigated by the Mansonian leader of this "family"—a young man who goes by the name of Johnny Alucard (Christopher Neame).[8] Johnny hangs around the

Chelsea of 1972 looking for "kicks" with a bunch of "kids" that include a young black American woman, Gaynor (Marsha Hunt);[9] a raven-haired white temptress, Laura (Caroline Munro); and a good-natured working-class Londoner, Bob (Philip Murray), who, rather going against Johnny's hedonistic "free-love" philosophy, appears to want to have the central virginal female character, Jessica Van Helsing (Stephanie Beacham), all to himself.

Searching for the ultimate "way-out" experience, Johnny summons Count Dracula at the black mass ceremony that he arranges for his pals in a boarded-up church near the Embankment. This interesting sequence distinctly echoes the "Rising Forth" ceremony conducted by Anton LaVey, the High Priest of the Church of Satan, in a candle-lit chamber of the "Black House" in San Francisco on the night of August 8, 1969. LaVey and his group sought to place a curse on a hippie movement that they regarded as flawed in its Utopian belief in universal free love and its refusal to recognize the bestial, sexual nature of humanity.[10] If the ceremony in *Dracula A.D. 1972* conducted by Johnny Alucard resembles this real event in terms of occult practice, it also clearly, at the same time, celebrates the hippie counterculture. After all, it is presented as a "happening" replete with "far-out" dancing and a space rock soundtrack. The "kids" are not all wearing black—some wear hippie clothes. So the film effectively resurrects stereotypical countercultural behavior at the same time as it celebrates the rise of occult practices. This lends the narrative a certain ambiguity.

When the Count eventually reappears at the climax of the ceremony, rising up from underground in the foggy graveyard, there seems to be some confusion over why he is there. Johnny believes it to be the result of his psychedelic occult powers, but the Count suggests "it was my will." Although this contemporary manifestation of Dracula occurs as the result of a subterranean hippie "happening" and we are thus encouraged to view him through the prism of countercultural practices, the Count, as a figure from the older generation and, of course, as a figure from the past, appears not to understand this counterculture, and furthermore does not recognize any possible connections between its occult practices and his own. The Count's ambiguous role in the events that bring about his resurrection helps to set up the ambiguities surrounding good and evil developed in the narrative. But at the same time, this moral ambiguity effectively relegates him to the purlieus of this narrative.

If the film separates Count Dracula from the lives of the youths upon whom he preys, it is primarily because the London into which he is resurrected has apparently moved beyond dualistic Christian concepts of good and evil.[11] It is no coincidence that Count Dracula discovers that the working churchyard in which he was buried way back in 1872 has been deconsecrated in 1972. He is resurrected into a godless space. The shots of real contemporary London locations featured in the film also set up the city as an ambiguous space. We can see that it is a modern, well-developed city full of life and commerce; but it is also a confused, crowded, polluted city built on conspicuous consumption, tired-looking and depressed, evidently in danger of devouring itself. However, it could be said that this city appears in some ways closer to the space depicted in the carefree "swinging London" films such as *Darling* (John Schlesinger, 1965), *The Knack . . . and How to Get it* (Richard Lester, 1965), and *Alfie* (Lewis Gilbert, 1966) than it is to the decadent *fin-de-siècle* playground in which vampirism once flourished. So while *Dracula A.D. 1972* does suggest that the "swinging" city harbors dark secrets, it is clearly no longer the dark labyrinthine territory staked out in Bram Stoker's novel *Dracula* (1897), the novels of Dickens, or countless other texts published in the late nineteenth century.[12] Indeed, the London of *Dracula A.D. 1972* cannot in any way be said to operate as a bifurcated space in which East End and West End sit in clear moral opposition, or in which over ground and underground spaces are similarly conceptualized within a binary spatial paradigm. Instead, this stylized contemporary London of the film, constructed by a combination of studio setups and location shots, operates as a morally ambiguous, socioculturally confused space. The morally ambiguous nature of the city of 1972 depicted in the film is clearly heightened through its juxtaposition with a vision of the London of 1872 as a city in which the primeval battle between light and darkness can still be clearly played out.

WHEN THE MUSIC'S OVER

The opening sequence of *Dracula A.D. 1972* is set in 1872 in London's Hyde Park. It features Van Helsing (Peter Cushing) battling with Count Dracula (Christopher Lee) on a speeding horse-drawn carriage. The chase ends as the carriage crashes and Dracula becomes impaled on a wooden spoke from one of the smashed wheels. This section of the film, then, fulfills the generic conventions of traditional Dracula/vampire narratives in terms of period setting, characterization, iconography, and even the Gothic font utilized for the titles. The battle between the two characters clearly suggests a Manichaean divide between Van Helsing as a figure of good and Count Dracula as a figure of evil. But when the film suddenly shifts to the London of 1972 by means of a hundred-year jump cut, and we see a jet plane leaving a vapor trail high in the sky over London; traffic jams polluting the city air, and sex shops liberally dotted along the streets, this Manichaean division between good and evil suddenly dissolves.

This moral ambiguity of the London of 1972 (connoted, then, by the appearance of images of steadily decaying modern technology and urban spaces of consumption) is cleverly echoed in the musical score composed by Michael Vickers, perhaps best known for his work with the successful pop group Manfred Mann. While the 1872 battle sequence is accompanied by extradiegetic orchestral music, sudden bursts of Hammond organ suggest an impending updating of this language. Indeed, as the image track shifts to 1972, Vickers's music continues to further transgress the syntactically codified boundaries of classical music and contemporary rock music (which of course has roots in both the Christian spirituality of gospel music and the dark, devilish tones of Robert Johnsonian blues).[13] The extradiegetic music in the film then shifts in register, moving away from orchestral modes of signification toward a hybrid, blues-influenced rock. It should be noted that by the early 1970s in Britain, classical music had become a sign of bourgeois gentility and (for the lower-middle classes especially) aspiration. Rock music, it goes without saying, broadly signified secular or occult-inspired youthful rebellion. But, as Vickers's music suggests, the white male-dominated bourgeois world of the established British order and the world of the countercultural transnational, interracial, and intersexual younger generation depicted in the film are about to come into conflict. They soon appear in danger of merging with each other—a danger made explicit in the next major sequence of the film.

In the front room of a large London house a party is taking place. Extradiegetic film music is replaced here by a diegetic musical performance. A large band is set up, featuring musicians (male and female, black and white) playing a hybrid brand of rock music that clearly bears the influence of the blues. A number of young people, dressed in the countercultural fashions of the late 1960s, are dancing wildly around the room. But also in the room are a number of older white people who stand dumbstruck and motionless in amazement at the spectacle. They are dressed in dinner jackets and expensive dresses—stereotypical signifiers of upper-middle-class gentility. This stark juxtaposition of iconography effectively pits British upper-middle-class concepts of taste and decorum against a transnational concept of a "free," hedonistic counterculture. The hippie youths, obviously "turned on" by the promise of sexual experience and drug-taking at the party, are effectively staging a carnivalesque "happening" under the noses of their bourgeois masters. Here, then, traditional, established notions of Britishness and British culture are threatened by a subculture in which divisions between race and gender seem not to hold sway. There is a real sense of fear in the gray faces of the older generation—a fear perhaps that these young people are about to vampirically suck the blood out of a Britain that they feel they have given birth to and wish, at all costs, to keep alive. However, a number of the younger bourgeois partygoers look as if they might be being turned on by the events. One young woman in particular appears ready to copulate with a hippie on a sofa. It seems, then, that the "free love" ideology of the counterculture might be on the verge of vampirically infecting the bourgeois youth who remain, for now, under the gaze and control of their elders.

Meanwhile, the figure of Johnny Alucard—the youthful womanizer and drug-taker—straddles these initially clearly marked cultures. While dressed as a countercultural dandy, he also sits very still in the center of the room. His stillness thus marks him as bourgeois, but his appearance and sexualized gaze also clearly align him with the countercultural revelers. He thus becomes perhaps the one truly monstrous figure in the film, primarily because he is the only character that actively transgresses bourgeois culture and the counterculture. Count Dracula, though, whom Johnny comes to call upon and consider as his "master," can only remain a peripheral figure because he finds that he cannot transgress cultures in the same way as the young man. He cannot carve out a clear role for himself in this contemporary world of cultural conflict— his power to shape the narrative in 1972 has greatly diminished.

But are Johnny and his friends truly countercultural? There is the clear sense in the party sequence in *Dracula A.D. 1972* that what might once have been thought of as an authentic counterculture is being emptied of life; or, indeed, is "un-dead." As the police arrive at the house to break up the proceedings, a young copper catches a couple "making out" under a table. The young man looks up at the policeman and says "peace, man," a countercultural linguistic sign that had become part of transnational Western mass-cultural discourse (and thus emptied of any potentially authentic force or meaning) by 1972. It is no surprise, then, that we then see a close-up of the policeman grinning at this utterance. He appears to acknowledge its ludicrous, anachronistic nature. This party sequence does not offer the only example of the cynical appropriation of the linguistic codes and conventions of the transnational counterculture that occurs in the film. In a later scene that takes place in the Cavern coffee bar in Chelsea, Johnny asks his companions, "Where are the new experiences, the new happenings?" He wants to know if they are ready for something "way way out." And the comfortably bourgeois Jessica Van Helsing refers to the police as the "fuzz" when she drives around town in her boyfriend Bob's psychedelic Citroen, while also utilizing linguistic anachronisms such as "weird, man, far out" when speaking to her grandfather. Furthermore, before Dracula's resurrection—which is brought about, of course, at the ultimate underground "happening"—Johnny begins his black mass ceremony with tape-recorded space rock, urging his friends to "dig the music, kids." In order to further my argument about the ways in which *Dracula A.D. 1972* exploits the transnational counterculture, I want to suggest that the identity of the band featured in the party sequence is highly significant. Orig-inally from San Francisco, California, Stoneground had been previously fea-tured in *Medicine Ball Caravan*, a documentary film directed by François Re-ichenbach. Hoping to capture the countercultural experience of the late 1960s in the United States, Reichenbach had initially aimed to film the seminal West Coast acid rock band the Grateful Dead driving across the country in Ken Kesey's bus Furthur, the type of trip mythologized in Tom Wolfe's book *The Electric Kool-Aid Acid Test* (1968). But the film did not work out the way that Warner Brothers had hoped. The Grateful Dead, although signed to the recording and publishing arm of the company, declined to take part. So Stoneground and various hangers-on were enlisted. They did not get to use Furthur, but were instead offered a similar (but alas inauthentic) bus painted in psychedelic colors in which to tour the country. However, the footage that Warner Brothers executives were eventually presented with was effectively useless—the work of stoned cameramen. The then little-known filmmaker Martin Scorsese was employed to try to edit the footage into a coherent film, but the finished product was nothing more than "a mundane rock concert film with some barely watchable *cinéma vérité* of hippies daubing face-paint on each other."[14] After the failure of *Medicine Ball Caravan*, Warner Brothers en-couraged Hammer to use Stoneground on *Dracula A.D. 1972*.[15] The employ-ment of this band in the party sequence of the film thus effectively drains it of any countercultural authenticity. What we effectively see here is the crass stereotyping of particular modes of hippie behaviour, and the emergence of the counterculture as an "un-dead" phenomenon doomed to haunt main-stream Western culture.

SYMPATHY FOR THE DEVIL

But what exactly was the counterculture, and how did it manifest itself transnationally? In his book, *The Making of a Counter Culture* (1969), Theodor Roszak argued that the counterculture could be best understood as a reaction against the "technocracy," which he described as "that form in which an industrial society reaches the peak of its organizational integra-tion."[16] For Roszak (19), the technocracy was the product of both advanced capitalism and mature and accelerating industrialism. The counterculture was thus engaged in a sustained resistance against this technocracy, which it saw creating "a civilization," Roszak (47) states, "sunk in an unshakeable commit-ment to genocide, gambling madly with the extermination of our species." Roszak (1–4) clearly advocated that the counterculture was a transnational phenomenon. Indeed, this counterculture reached a truly transnational audience with the first-ever global television broadcast, which featured the Beatles performing "All You Need Is Love" on *Our World* on June 25, 1967. Interestingly, Michael Vickers, the composer of the music for *Dracula A.D. 1972*, had been the conductor of the orchestra on this famous session—fittingly present, then, at the moment when the counterculture went transnational. This was the "summer of love": a period, it seemed, when anything was possible for young people of the Western world who were prepared to embrace the practices of mysticism, spirituality, and meditation.[17]

But a number of individuals and groups (such as Anton LaVey's Church of Satan) soon sought to position themselves at odds with the "peace and love" aspects of the counterculture. Interestingly, Roszak pointed out that

> it strikes me as obvious beyond dispute that the interests of our college-age and adolescent young in the psychology of alienation, oriental mysticism, psychedelic drugs, and communitarian experiments comprise a cultural constellation that radically diverges from values and assumptions that have been in the mainstream of our society at least since the Scientific Revolution of the seventeenth century.[18]

There was a real sense that certain aspects of countercultural practice were grounded in pre-Enlightenment, premodern cultural practice. As such, it could be argued that particular underground groups had much in common with the figure of Count Dracula and his many fictional acolytes. That is, they shared with the Count the desire to exist free from the shackles of rationality in a world in which sexual freedom was celebrated and madness acknowledged as the sociocultural construct that Foucault showed it to be.[19] They, too, desired to embrace a Freudian "return of the repressed." This desire was often marked as evil. So the counterculture was seen to grow a darker side. The Rolling Stones famously titled their 1967 LP *Their Satanic Majesty's Request*, and the Jagger and Richards song "Sympathy for the Devil," released on the following LP *Beggar's Banquet* (1968), brought the voice of the devil to a transnational audience. Interestingly, Johnny Alucard effectively calls on Jagger and Richards during his black mass scene in *Dracula A.D. 1972*, when he cries out "I demand an audience with His Satanic Majesty!"[20, 21] But other characters in the film appear torn between trying to revive the late-1960s spirit of peace and love and exploring this coeval interest in links between blues, rock, and the veneration of the occult.

Interestingly, Roszak also suggested that the counterculture was not a disciplined movement but instead "something in the nature of a medieval crusade."[22] Johnny Alucard's summoning of Count Dracula certainly appears to confirm this. After all, the Count's origins lie in medieval, pre-Enlightenment

Europe. Perhaps Johnny believes that the Count can assist him in breaking free from a staid bourgeois culture that had developed out of the progressive European Enlightenment project and apparently remains entrenched in London in 1972. After all, the figure of Dracula has always embodied elements of the gothic, uncanny unknown; aspects of an increasingly modern experience that cannot be accounted for through rational scientific means. Indeed, in Bram Stoker's novel, *Dracula*, Jonathan Harker recognizes that "unless my senses deceive me, the old centuries had, and have, powers of their own which mere 'modernity' cannot kill."[23] Johnny Alucard seeks to tap into this ancient force in order to try to revolutionize London culture. Interestingly, Roszak argues that "over and again it is the same story throughout Western Europe: the students may rock their societies; but without the support of adult social forces, they cannot overturn the established order."[24] It appears, then, that Johnny wants to rock the bourgeois London society of 1972, Roszak (166–7) explains, by summoning the "adult" force of Count Dracula in a move that clearly resembles Timothy Leary's infamous psychedelic experimentation, and search for "rich and exotic religious traditions, occult powers, salvation [. . .]."

But the problem for Johnny is that Count Dracula soon demonstrates that he has no knowledge of (or interest in) the underground youth culture of the early 1970s, and he refuses to be commanded and put to work by this generation. In Stoker's novel, Jonathan Harker recognizes early on that Count Dracula "was the being I was helping to transfer to London, where, perhaps, for centuries to come he might, amongst its teeming millions, satiate his lust for blood, and create a new and ever-widening circle of semi-demons to batten on the helpless."[25] But what becomes apparent in *Dracula A.D. 1972* is that this difference between the "helpless" and individuals who have already become "semi-demons" had become very hard to distinguish by the 1970s. Indeed, the Count appears to see little point in infecting these young people with bodily desire and lust when they clearly (in the case of Gaynor, Laura, and Johnny, at least) have already been infected. He does choose to infect these characters, but as he does so he appears unusually unsure of himself and his role in their sexual world. Indeed, he is especially reticent to infect the male characters (this happens offscreen). Count Dracula arrives in the London of 1972, then, to find that much of his work has already effectively been done by a transnational counterculture.

A series of very real events saw to it that many of the more obviously positive countercultural ideals died off by the beginning of the 1970s. The documentary film *Gimme Shelter* (David Maysles, Albert Maysles, Charlotte Zwerin, 1970) captures the famously gruesome events surrounding the deaths that occurred at the free Altamont Speedway concert in the United States in

December 1969 that featured the Rolling Stones—often held up as the moment when the counterculture died. Other historical events produced as evidence of the death of the counterculture include the Manson family murders, the militant action of the Weathermen, and the Kent State killings. Interestingly *Dracula A.D. 1972* can be read within this context, as the policeman assigned to the case, Inspector Murray (Michael Coles), clearly relates these fictional London murders to the recent "occult murders" in America. And the youthful group portrayed in the film, "bored with acid, sex and British decadence," can certainly be read as "archetypes of disillusioned youth who, no longer believing in good, want to identify with evil."[26] They function, then, as avatars of an underground counterculture that had all but died in 1972.

HUNGRY FREAKS, DADDY

It is significant that we see the body of Dracula rise up from underground in *Dracula A.D. 1972*. He is, after all, summoned by subterranean cultural practices. But other British horror films of the period can be seen to articulate the sense of anxiety felt by mainstream mass culture concerning the counterculture and the cultural underground. In the British film *Death Line* (aka *Raw Meat*) (Gary Sherman, 1972), the existence of a cannibalistic subculture in the London Underground railway system shows us what might occur if an underground movement is left unregulated and allowed to develop out of the sight of hegemonic sociocultural forces. David Sanjek has argued that in this film "there is the less than fine line between the 'monster' and the 'hero.'"[27] Perhaps, as Sanjek (207) advocates, "the compartmentalization of the monstrous from the normal is no simple matter." In other words, the monstrous is seen to be present not only in one character but instead in a variety of characters. It reaches across the whole of the decaying, multicultural city. Indeed, the contemporary London depicted in this film, like the contemporary London of *Dracula A.D. 1972*, has already been infected by hedonistic sexual practices—witness the opening credits, which essentially offer a tour of Soho's sex shops accompanied by extradiegetic music evoking a striptease.

But it seems that the spatial politics of *Death Line* clearly locate the source of the monstrous "underground," lurking in the tunnels by a disused tube station. If the monstrous remains ambiguous in this early-1970s film, it is certainly manifested in the body of a longhaired figure, known only as "The Man" (Hugh Armstrong), who exists below the surface threshold of mass culture. Perhaps the sobriquet The Man operates ironically here, as this was a common countercultural epithet for a figure that became the personification of the technocracy. *Death Line*, then, seems to suggest that underneath every decent citizen, a hedonistic hippie is waiting to break loose. Indeed, the cannibalistic practices of The Man can be seen to operate as a sign of his potential to attack and distort the sociocultural practices of those who exist on the surface of London life. His behavior does not appear to overly concern the working-class or lower-middle-class policemen investigating the case. Inspector Colquhoun (Donald Pleasance) and Detective Sergeant Rogers (Norman Rossington) treat middle- and upper-class figures (dead and alive) with irreverent scorn. Instead, it is a young proto-bourgeois couple that effectively discovers this underground world—Alex Campbell (David Ladd) and Patricia Wilson (Sharon Gurney).

Alex is a longhaired American male student in London studying international economics (perhaps with one eye on a successful, moneyed future), and Patricia is the young woman he lives with (but, importantly, is not married to—they live "in sin"). Significantly they have a poster of the recently dead transnational countercultural icon Jimi Hendrix on the wall of their flat. Like Johnny Alucard in *Dracula A.D. 1972*, they manage to transgress cultural space. They not only come into contact with a dangerous underground culture but also, all the while, oscillate between respectable bourgeois culture and what was left of a transnational counterculture. It is this cross-cultural movement that effectively produces the horrific consequences of the narrative. The film seems to suggest, then, that by making particular lifestyle choices, this transatlantic couple experience dangerous un-dead underground cultural territory, when perhaps they should just have got proper jobs, got married, settled down, and had kids. The cultural underground is thus marked by the film as horrific, debased, primitive, and uncivilized.

IF YOU WANT BLOOD (YOU'VE GOT IT)

One of the most important points made by Roszak in his book, *The Making of a Counter Culture*, is that "as it approaches maturity, the technocracy does indeed seem capable of anabolizing every form of discontent into its system."[28] Roszak (110) draws on Herbert Marcuse's concept of repressive desublimation in order to argue that from 1968, countercultural ideals began to fall prey to the "technocracy's ingenious assimilation of the 'erotic danger zone.'" If we think of film production companies such as Hammer as being located within the technocracy (especially through their relationship with the Hollywood major production company Warner Brothers), we can perhaps begin to see how a film like *Dracula A.D. 1972* could operate as a tool of repressive desublimation, providing audiences with a narrative that foregrounds a denatured permissiveness that arguably had the effect of masking social control and weakening the full potential of the type of eroticized sexual energy it celebrates.

Indeed, other horror films of the period vampirically preyed on the hippie phenomenon in similar ways. Tigon's *Blood on Satan's Claw* (Piers Haggard, 1971) features Linda Hayden as Angel Blake, an overtly sexualized adolescent girl who holds power over a group of "flower children."[29] This film clearly recalls aspects of the Manson cult and, specifically, the story of Mary Bell, the 11-year-old who was convicted of strangling and killing a smaller child, Martin Brown, in England on May 25, 1968. But *Blood on Satan's Claw*, like *Dracula A.D. 1972*, also exploits the countercultural embrace of free sexuality and hedonism by effectively inculcating it into an increasingly permissive mass culture that sought, through the act of repressive desublimation, to maintain a technocratic social order driven by ideologies of economic rationality and industrial progress.

As a cultural text, then, *Dracula A.D. 1972* amounts to a relabeling and redefinition of apparently deviant underground countercultural behavior by what remained of a dominant bourgeois group.[30] Paul Willis has argued that it was the homology of this alternative value system, hallucinogenic drugs, and acid rock that made hippie culture function as a coherent way of life.[31] But it was the very homology of this countercultural experience that left it open to exploitative acts of repressive desublimation. That is, the mythical coherence of the counterculture was the very thing that made it vulnerable to attack from the established technocratic sociocultural order. In his examination of the underground movement of the 1960s, *Playpower* (1971), Richard Neville points out the efforts made by some European authorities to ward off the horror of the hippies:

> Everything was done to make the hippies disappear. Munich police confiscated sleeping bags, Amsterdam council workmen hosed benches around the Dam. The Eros fountain at Piccadilly was discreetly turned up to splash the surrounding steps—symbolizing society's wishful reaction to their alienated children. Wash them away. To prevent youngsters congregating beneath the statue of King George III, Dorset council used the ultimate deterrent: "the dried blood, which smells like rotten meat, was sprayed twice and the hippies did not come back."[32]

It seems, then, that *Dracula A.D. 1972*, while exploiting the homology of an un-dead counter culture, also attempts to place a stake through the heart of its codes and conventions.

Whereas Stoker's 1897 novel has the forces of modernity emerging victorious over the forces of tradition and the world of the past, *Dracula A.D. 1972* inverts this, reinforcing conservative bourgeois ideology in the face of this threat of cultural change as it charts the movement of the central female member of the young group, Jessica Van Helsing, away from the lure of youthful freedom toward an adulthood of British bourgeois conformity. After all, the two young men with whom she might have had "free" sexual relations, Johnny and Bob, both die before the end of the film. She ends up in the arms of her professorial grandfather (Cushing), telling him "I'm sorry," thus apologizing for her brief dalliance with the alternative lifestyle that the established order in the late 1960s had found so threateningly horrific. So Jessica is saved from one kind of living death—the existence of the vampire—by choosing another—bourgeois normality. Interestingly Judith Clavir has pointed out that "in the 1970s, an era of secular technology, hopelessness, heroin and Quaalude, Living Death is for many a not so unattractive solution."[33]

So as *Dracula A.D. 1972* works through this conflict between (and within) cultures, it clearly exploits the countercultural codes and conventions of the 1960s. It presents stereotypical hippie figures that indulge in the type of countercultural practices being inculcated into the discourse of mass culture by 1972. As such, in *Dracula A.D. 1972* we see what is left of the transnational counterculture become effectively "un-dead." But the film also offers a vision of a historical moment when boundaries between cultures were shifting and breaking down. If the cultural transformations of the vampire that shook Stoker's late-nineteenth-century text were closely linked to discourses of gender, disease, and the decline of the imperial (British) race,[34] *Dracula A.D. 1972* depicts a Britain that is undergoing another such cultural transformation. As Noël Carroll has pointed out, it is often remarked that "horror cycles emerge in times of social stress, and that the genre is a means through which the anxieties of the era can be exposed."[35] The Britain depicted in *Dracula A.D. 1972* is a country in sociocultural crisis, infected by "Other" cultures and hedonistic, underground cultural practices involving illicit sex and drug-taking, but also trying to cling to the resolutely bourgeois vision of healthy family lives working in the service of an economically healthy state. The horrific narrative of the film thus outlines the dangers to the established order inherent in what Jock Young termed (in 1971) the "subterranean world of play"—drug-taking, hedonism, a disdain for work, and other delinquent behavior that might appear not to be of benefit to the workaday practices of mainstream society.[36] But as I have shown, the film clearly problematizes the identity of Count Dracula. Although he is resurrected by subterranean countercultural occult practices, and he clearly gets involved in old-fashioned evil activity, he also in some ways (especially through the significatory properties of his tailoring and Christopher Lee's age, performative gestures, and accent) embodies aspects of traditional white bourgeois culture that the hippies sought to break away from. As such, the central female character who almost falls prey to the Count, Jessica Van Helsing, appears far more horrified by the lifestyle decisions she is being forced to make than she is by the attentions of the Count. This old man means little or nothing to her. Her attention is focused elsewhere, on to a lifestyle choice—should she choose a lifestyle of free love and hedonistic drug-taking or a lifestyle of secular bourgeois respectability in a society still driven by ideologies of economic rationality and productivity? This is not a decision that the old Count can make for her. She has to make it herself. Perhaps the old Count shouldn't have bothered turning up at all.

NOTES

1. Rudolph Arnheim, "A Note on Monsters," in *Toward a Psychology of Art*, ed. Rudolph Arnheim (Berkeley: University of California Press, 1972), 257.

2. Leon Hunt, *British Low Culture: From Safari Suits to Sexploitation* (London: Routledge, 1998), 143.

3. James Craig Holte, *Dracula in the Dark: The Dracula Film Adaptations* (Westport, CT, and London: Greenwood Press, 1997), 63.

4. Theodor Roszak, *The Making of a Counter Culture* (New York: Anchor-Doubleday, 1969), 66.

5. Michelle Perks, "A Descent into the Underworld: *Death Line*," in *British Horror Cinema*, ed. Steve Chibnall and Julian Petley (London and New York: Routledge, 2002), 145.

6. David Sanjek, "Twilight of the Monsters: The English Horror Film 1968–1975," in *Re-Viewing British Cinema 1900–1992: Essays and Interviews*, ed. Wheeler Winston Dixon (Albany: State University of New York Press, 1994), 195.

7. Andrew Tudor, *Monsters and Mad Scientists: A Cultural History of the Horror Movie* (Oxford: Blackwell, 1989), 66.

8. Judith Clavir, "Black Spookery: *Blacula, Dracula A.D. 1972*," in *Film in Society*, ed. Arthur Asa Berger (New Brunswick and London: Transaction Books, 1980), 119.

9. Marsha Hunt was in the cast of the London production of *Hair*. Interestingly, she was also the mother of Mick Jagger's first child, Karis (b. 1970), and apparently the inspiration for the 1970 Rolling Stones hit "Brown Sugar."

10. Gavin Baddeley, *Lucifer Rising: Sin, Devil Worship and Rock 'n' Roll* (London: Plexus, 2006), 67.

11. Peter Hutchings has noticed that the Count also becomes a relatively marginal figure in *Scars of Dracula* (Roy Ward Baker, 1970), a film in which the relationship between the young lovers remains healthy, and they are kept apart from Dracula, who

cuts a peripheral figure until he dies an accidental death. Moreover, *Taste the Blood of Dracula* (Peter Sasdy, 1969) is also characterized by "a degree of confusion and even contradiction in the handling of Dracula" that arises from "the cycle's inbuilt inflexibility in the face of social change." See Hutchings, *Hammer and Beyond: The British Horror Film* (Manchester and New York: Manchester University Press, 1993), 125–7.

12. London is represented as a bifurcated space in novels and collections of short stories including Charles Dickens's *Our Mutual Friend* (1864), Walter Besant's *All Sorts and Conditions of Men* (1882), Arthur Morrison's *Tales of Mean Streets* (1894) and *A Child of the Jago* (1896), and William Black's *Shandon Bells* (1893). For more on this representational history of Victorian London see Paul Newland, *The Cultural Construction of London's East End* (Amsterdam and New York: Rodopi, 2008), Lynda Nead, *Victorian Babylon: People, Streets and Images in Nineteenth-Century London* (New Haven and London: Yale University Press, 2000) and Judith Walkowitz, *City of Dreadful Delight: Narratives of Sexual Danger in Late-Victorian London* (Chicago: University of Chicago Press, 1992).

13. Writing about the famous myth of how the bluesman Robert Johnson sold his soul to the devil, Alan Lomax, in *The Land Where the Blues Began* (London: Minerva, 1997), has argued that "every blues fiddler, banjo picker, harp blower, piano strummer, and guitar frammer was, in the opinion of both himself and his peers, a child of the devil [. . .]." Many white blues rock musicians tried to connect with the occult side of the blues (365).

14. Joe Boyd, *White Bicycles: Making Music in the 1960s* (London: Serpent's Tail, 2005), 245.

15. Denis Meikle, *A History of Horrors: The Rise and Fall of the House of Hammer* (Lanham, MD: The Scarecrow Press, 1996), 262.

16. Roszak, *The Making of a Counter Culture*, 5.

17. In *White Bicycles*, Boyd has described the late-1960s underground in London as "a subculture of drugs, radical politics and music built around the *International Times*, Indica bookshop, *Oz* magazine, UFO, the London Free School, Release, Granny Takes a Trip, the 14-Hour Technicolour Dream and the Arts Lab" (133).

18. Roszak, *The Making of a Counter Culture*, xi–xii.

19. Michel Foucault, *Madness and Civilization: A History of Insanity in the Age of Reason*, trans. Richard Howard (London: Routledge, 1995).

20. Other major British rock bands would go on to gain huge transnational followings by playing a brand of blues rock and heavy metal that had no problem celebrating the devil and the occult. On Led Zeppelin's third album (*Led Zeppelin III*, 1970), the band's updating of Robert Johnston's devilish blues and Jimmy Page's obsession with the teachings of the occult figure Alastair Crowley reached new heights. Page even had the runoff groove of the LP inscribed with Crowley's dictum "Do what thou wilt shall be the whole of the law." And the ZOSO symbol was partly derived from the work of the British occult artist Austin Osman Square (see Baddeley, *Lucifer Rising*, 96). The Birmingham-based band Black Sabbath took the worship of evil further. Interestingly, both bands had relationships with cinema: Led Zeppelin included short fantasy sequences in their concert movie *The Song Remains the Same* (Peter Clifton, Joe Massot, 1976)—during Page's sequence the guitarist experiences the

seven ages of man. Black Sabbath was named after the film *Black Sabbath* (Mario Bava, 1963). For more on the relationship between late-1960s and early-1970s rock music, Satanism, and the occult see Baddeley, *Lucifer Rising*, 89–97.

21. Hunt, *British Low Culture*, 143.

22. Roszak, *The Making of a Counter Culture*, 48.

23. Bram Stoker, *Dracula*, ed. Maurice Hindle (Harmondsworth: Penguin, 1993), 51.

24. Roszak, *The Making of a Counter Culture*, 3.

25. Stoker, *Dracula*, 71.

26. Clavir, "Black Spookery," 119.

27. Sanjek, "Twilight of the Monsters," 206.

28. Roszak, *The Making of a Counter Culture*, 14.

29. Leon Hunt, "Necromancy in the UK: Witchcraft and the Occult in British Horror," in *British Horror Cinema*, ed. Steve Chibnall and Julian Petley (London and New York: Routledge, 2002), 93.

30. Dick Hebdige, *Subculture: The Meaning of Style* (London and New York: Routledge, 1987), 94.

31. Hebdige, *Subculture*, 113.

32. Richard Neville, *Playpower* (London: Paladin, 1971), 217–18.

33. Clavir, "Black Spookery," 119.

34. Alexandra Warwick, "Vampires and the Empire: Fears and Fictions of the 1890s," in *Cultural Politics at the Fin de Siècle*, ed. Sally Ledger and Scott McCracken (Cambridge: Cambridge University Press, 1995), 202.

35. Noël Carroll, *The Philosophy of Horror; or, Paradoxes of the Heart* (New York: Routledge, 1990), 207.

36. Jock Young, "The Subterranean World of Play," in *The Subcultures Reader*, ed. Ken Gelder (London and New York: Routledge, 2002), 149.

Isabelle Adjani (as Lucy) and Klaus Kinski (as Dracula). *Courtesy of Werner Herzog Film-produktion/PhotoFest*

• *10* •

Nosferatu the Vampyre (1979) as a Legacy of Romanticism

Martina G. Lüke

*N*osferatu the Vampyre (*Nosferatu: Das Phantom der Nacht* [German title]) has fascinated audiences since its release in 1979. Werner Herzog's movie version of Bram Stoker's literary classic *Dracula* (1897) was highly celebrated and, amongst other prizes, was warded the German *Filmpreis in Gold* and Film Award for Outstanding Individual Achievement for actor Klaus Kinski (who plays Dracula in the film). The newly released DVD version (2001) topped the US DVD charts for two weeks. Leading questions in this context are: What are the factors that influence people in our modern-day life to still celebrate in a film adaptation of *Dracula*? What is the novelty, since the movie was supposed to be a remake of Friedrich Wilhelm Murnau's *Nosferatu-Eine Symphonie des Grauens* (*Nosferatu: A Symphony of Terror*, 1922),[1] the first Dracula movie and a masterpiece of Expressionism? Why is a *Dracula* film[2] still popular today, especially since the story is familiar to most people? What makes this version so special for a global community? I claim that Romantic ideas and ideals in the movie still have an impact on people today, since they embody repressed desires and offer an escape from modern life.

German filmmaker Werner Herzog is often seen in perspective to New German Cinema,[3] while he himself states that he is "not concerned with aesthetics."[4] However, in this essay I would like to portray *Nosferatu the Vampyre* as a legacy of Romanticism. Brigitte Peucker, for example, states: "It is not too much to say that more than any other current writer, and more than any other filmmaker, Werner Herzog is the profoundest and most authentic heir of the Romantic tradition at work today."[5] Indeed, the legacy of Romanticism[6] can be seen in *Nosferatu the Vampyre* in topics and themes such as the conflicts of the individual and the society, love and death, sanity and insanity, dream and reality, as well as in the setting or the use of music. In my analysis, I want to

153

describe these Romantic aspects in *Nosferatu the Vampyre* with respect to Romantic beliefs that have endured throughout the centuries and continue to intrigue a worldwide audience.

When Herzog began shooting his dual-language (English-German) version of *Nosferatu* in the late 1970s, he ensured it would not be a mere imitation of Murnau's *magnum opus*.[7] In particular, one of the central features of Herzog's adaptation lies in his restylization of the Dracula figure. Herzog's vampire is portrayed as neither a blood-crazed monster (e.g., in such movies as Stephen Norrington's *Blade* [1998] or Quentin Tarantino's *From Dusk Till Dawn* [1996]), nor as an elegant and seductive nobleman (e.g., as played by such actors as Bela Lugosi and Christopher Lee), nor as the mechanical nightmare we find in the Murnau version. Instead, Herzog's remake reveals a deeply disturbed Dracula who longs for redemption. Repelled by the pain and death he brings, Herzog's Dracula is the lonely outsider who yearns for inclusion—to join and grow old with the rest of humanity.[8] Wherever Dracula and his frightening aspect (long fingernails, white skin color, eyes deeply sunken into the skull[9]) appear, others fear and reject him. For example, when Jonathan stops at a roadside inn in the Carpathians, he mentions the name Dracula. Immediately, the whole room goes silent, then everybody tries to warn Jonathan against going there. The Count is at the same time a horrifying monster and a pitiable creature desperate for love and sympathy; for example, in one scene Dracula reaches out for Lucy (Isabelle Adjani) and is rejected and quickly withdraws, emotional pain quite visible in his face and gesture. From this perspective, death pales in comparison to the desolate life without love and approval that Herzog's Dracula has been forced to live for centuries: "Death is not the worst. There are things more horrible than that." Dracula has the fate of an outsider: "Time is an abyss, profound as a thousand nights. Centuries come and go. To be unable to grow old is terrible." The contrast between individuality and society, as well as the tension between contradictory inner feelings and tensions of the individual, are main aspects of *Nosferatu the Vampyre* and show influences of the Romantic legacy.

The feelings of futility, alienation from society, perceptions of contradictions, and even tendencies toward self-destruction are typical themes in the works of Romantic authors or authors with Romantic tendencies; for example, E. T. A. Hoffmann's *Die Serapionsbrüder* (*The Serapion-Brothers* [1819–1821]), Nathaniel Hawthorne's *Ethan Brand* (1850), or Byron's *Manfred* (1817). In this perspective, Dracula's hopeless search for normalcy and love can only end in the most tragic way possible: death. The motif of the exceptional outsider, as in the *Künstlermotiv*, who is both driven by inner tensions and misunderstanding from the outside world and who often suffers a tragic ending, in the tradition of Johann Wolfgang von Goethe's *Die Leiden* *des jungen Werth*er (*The Sorrows of Young Werther* [1774]), can be found in various texts, from one of the earliest of the Romantic period, Wilhelm Heinrich Wackenroder's *Herzensergießungen eines kunstliebenden Klosterbruders* (*The Emotional Outpourings of an Art-Loving Friar* [1797]), to Mary Shelley's *Frankenstein* (1818) or Alexander Pushkin's *Eugene Onegin* (1823–1831).

In the Romantic tradition, the outstanding hero or the heroine is especially plagued by inner feelings in conflict with external reality. In *Nosferatu the Vampyre*, the female protagonist Lucy feels the danger that threatens her beloved, Jonathan (Bruno Ganz), her community, and her existence but is not able to bring it to an end. She desperately tries to find a cure for Jonathan's mysterious illness and to stop the plague. Finally, Lucy has to give her own life to save her husband and the community. Tragically, even this sacrifice does not serve its purpose, since it comes too late after Jonathan has already himself become a vampire. Therefore, her lover has died in one way or another before she made her sacrifice. Here is also a difference from Murnau's work, where the heroine Ellen is able to save the city of Wismar and Hutter. Werner Herzog's version is also in contrast to Bram Stoker's original text, where Lucy Westenra cannot be saved and instead has become a vampire herself. She is killed by her fiancé and Van Helsing, while her friend Mina Harker can be rescued by a similar coalition. In *Nosferatu the Vampyre*, Lucy has to fight all by herself, against her inner self and an outside threat; she is tormented by nightmares, is able to face these demons, and nevertheless becomes the (tragic) Romantic heroine *par excellence*. Herzog does not present the conception of an *omni vicit amor*. In his version of Dracula, love cannot conquer all but is portrayed as a very influential force, since Lucy's inner suffering, her determination, and her tragic death are evidence for the power of love. In the end, Dracula cannot resist this emotional feeling and pays for this strong feeling, which he desired, with his own death.

Again, we see a Romantic tradition in *Nosferatu the Vampyre* since (absolute) love is considered one of the most powerful and noble emotions imaginable. Lucy's unconditional love for Jonathan,[10] her beauty and grace, and her charming personality stylize her as the incarnation of the lovable woman. She bears a resemblance to the *dâmes* of the courts of the Middle Ages that have been so highly celebrated and idealized by Romantic poets and writers, such as in the novels of Sir Walter Scott and poems of Ludwig Uhland. The cultural and religious unity of the Holy Roman Empire of the German Nation (800–1806), as well as the medieval literature and art, fascinated Romantic writers and political conservatives during the Romantic period and Neo-Romantism. *Nosferatu the Vampyre* reveals similar motifs: Lucy appears as a pure and innocent character, often wears white, and resembles an angel or a martyr.[11] She behaves more like a nun, celebrating a life full of virtue and spirituality, than a flesh-and-blood woman, as portrayed in her practical friend Mina. For the Romanticists, religion often stood in the center of philosophical concepts because religion provided the direct way to infinity and eternity. Similar to the Romantic tradition, as in Richard Wagner's *Tannhäuser* (1845), Herzog expresses the essence of erotic and religious duality. Lucy appears as the faithful Christian maiden who willingly sacrifices her life in order to save others. Dressed in white like a heavenly bride, covered with ornaments of flowers, she awaits the vampire, her devilish antagonist. As in Murnau's *Nosferatu*, Lucy (Ellen) gives herself to Dracula. He is a pitiful creature and not the erotic seducer hungry for approval and love that he becomes in Herzog's version. When Dracula enters her chamber, he approaches Lucy at first as a gentle lover, carefully approaching her bed. Nevertheless, his animal-like other comes through (again Herzog presents opposing feelings), and he drinks her blood in a gruesome way. In this context, the topic of the *Belle et la Bête* is easily recognizable, and Johann Heinrich Füssli's famous and disturbing painting "Nightmare" (1781) comes to mind. But the only "love" the vampire can give another person is death, or, in the case of Jonathan, the curse to be undead himself. Instead, Herzog drastically portrays the murderous beast killing Lucy. Again, contrary perceptions and ecstatic feelings, which are so typical for Romantic conceptions (e.g., pure innocence and evil lust, shy desire and blood-lust, or passivity and activity) are exposed.

The Romantics' fascination with the demonic aspects and the destructive sides of love and sexuality can be seen in works such as in E. T. A. Hoffmann's *Die Elixiere des Teufels* (*The Elixirs of the Devil* [1813]) or Heinrich Heine's poem *Die Lorelei* (*Lorely* [1824]). Many Romantic poets have focused on the contrast between vivid beauty and terminal death. E. A. Poe writes, in his *Philosophy of Composition* (1846), that "the death of a beautiful woman is, unquestionably, the most poetic topic in the world." One also has to think of texts such as Novalis's *Hymnen and die Nacht* (*Hymns to the Night* [1800]), where Novalis captures his personal and mystical experiences during his deep grief at the death of his beloved Sophie von Kühn. Film critic David Denby captures this combination and reviews in *New York*: "[. . .] the young German director has made not a conventional horror film (there are no shocks) but an anguished poem of death."[12] The figure of Lucy in *Nosferatu the Vampyre* shows a similarity to the symbiosis of life and death in Romanticism: right from the beginning she appears fragile, almost a vampire herself. Lucy is constantly suffering and passive; she dreams and feels rather than actively participating, so that even her inner strength cannot help to defy fate. From this perspective she appears as a beautiful prey in a desolate world or a sacrifice in the fight of good and evil.

Similar connotations in relation to religious perceptions of the Romantic period can be found throughout the movie *Nosferatu the Vampyre*. The Romantics structured many of their works on a triadic principle that derived from religion (the Divine Trinity) and the three historical stages in the Romantic theory: the lost ideal state, its unharmonious change and destruction, and its harmonic reappearance as a "Golden Age." Many Romantic texts leave the reader in the second state, longing for the lost past and a better future (e.g., Friedrich Hölderlin's *Hyperion* [1797–1799]). In *Nosferatu the Vampyre*, we have similar constructions; for example, in the beginning of the film there is the idyllic harmony of Lucy and Jonathan, a biblical paradise. When Jonathan dares to leave the idyll, he brings (indirectly) death and destruction; his wife dies and the paradise is lost. The viewer is left with his own hope for a better future.

Religion and beliefs appeared as important factors for the Romantics. In contrast to the Age of Enlightenment, linked with names such as Immanuel Kant, Jean-Jacques Rousseau, or Gotthold Ephraim Lessing, for the Romantic, philosophical reasoning alone appeared to be an inadequate tool to explain the world. For Johann Gottlieb Fichte, for example, the objective world was dependent on a powerful self. Thus, imagination functions as a key aspect for the exploration of the world. Gotthilf Heinrich Schubert's *Ansichten von der Nachtseite der Naturwissenschaft* (*Views of the Nightside of Natural Science* [1808]) supported this point of view, since Schubert declared that rational science cannot bring irrational forces and phenomena into a system. A similar fascination with these ambiguities can be seen in *Nosferatu the Vampyre*. After his return, Jonathan is no longer sure about his experiences in Romania. He transmogrifies from a human being to an undead creature who has to leave human society. Lucy's walk along the sea, the piles of dead bodies in Wismar, or the piles of coffins carried through the streets resemble nightmares or fever dreams. Herzog's long shots evoke and intensify these surreal impressions and feelings. The exploration of borders between fantasy/imagination and reality/rationality is an important aspect in Romantic texts, such as E. A. Poe's *Raven* (1845) or *Fall of the House of Usher* (1839) or Achim von Arnim's *Der tolle Invalide auf dem Fort Ratonneau* (*The Mad Invalid at Fort Ratonneau* [1818]).[13] Herzog's *Nosferatu*, as well as Murnau's *Nosferatu*, in contrast to other film versions "manage[s] to signify elusiveness rather than excess."[14]

Thus, Klaus Kinski appeared as the ideal actor to cast in Herzog's version of Dracula: "If Klaus Kinski would not have done it, I would not have shot the movie [my translation]," the director stated in an interview in 1983.[15] In movies such as *Aguirre der Zorn Gottes* (*Aguirre the Wrath of God* [1974]), *Cobra Verde* (1987), *Kinski Paganini* (1989), or even the early Edgar Wallace movies, the legendary Kinski had shown his ability to play obsessed, ambitious men who behave on the verge of madness.[16] Chaffin-Quiray describes a similar fascination with these figures in the works of Werner Herzog, who deals with "documentary impulses, poetic grandeur and epic journeys into the souls of madmen." In *Nosferatu the Vampyre*, Kinski continued this role, portraying a vampire who is at the same time horrible, mad, and sensitive, thus adding psychological depth to Max Schreck's eerie presence as Dracula (Count Orlock) in 1922.[17] In addition, Kinski showed no aggressive behavior[18] during production but willingly endured the four-hour makeup for his Dracula mask every day.[19] The actor declared in a 1979 interview his inner acquaintance with the vampire: "Nosferatu ['the undead']. That is me. I was never an actor who plays a role. That, what I portray, is in me. It is a cry for love, the expression of desperation or of hope. [. . .] Therefore, I am Nosferatu myself [translation mine]."[20, 21]

Feelings, not rationality, are important factors in *Nosferatu the Vampyre*. The movie also reflects the Romantic fascination with fairy tales as escapes from everyday life (e.g., the collection of sagas and folktales, the *Volksmärchen*, by the brothers Jacob and Wilhelm Grimm or Hans Christian Andersen). Jonathan appears in the beginning of the movie as the knight or hero who leaves his country on horseback to explore the world and in the end, leaves again on a horse. Similarly, Klaus Kinski declared in an interview about the contents of *Nosferatu*: "I was interested in the magical, the unexplainable, the fairytale-like quality of this material [my translation]."[22] In the Romantic tradition, simple country folk in particular are perceived as open for unspoiled nature and purity, as well as for the supernatural and mystical. In *Nosferatu the Vampyre*, Herzog highlights this perception of country folk by using their original language. The intrusion of supernatural and powerful forces on everyday reality and their consequences on the human mind are important issues in *Nosferatu the Vampyre*. Jonathan and Lucy's idyll and that of the people of Wismar are destroyed by the undead Dracula, a supernatural power, which they first denied to believe in. Individuals like Renfield (Roland Topor) cannot bear the world and the influence of Nosferatu anymore and turn mad.

Akin to Romantic works such as Heinrich von Kleist's gruesome *Penthesilea* (1808), Herzog adds animal-like behavior to portray irrationality or madness. "Where the nightmare exaggerations of Murnau, preditary [*sic*] wolves, Venus flytraps, the rat-like vampire and his kingdom of vermin are easily recuperated into a scheme of symbols for a repressed but vital Nature, Herzog's expressionism is pure spirit, a sulfuric image of hell," writes critic John Azzopardi.[23, 24] Consequently, in Herzog's movie, the rats, which Murnau also involved in his version, appear in huge masses,[25] and Dracula moans in pain as if a wounded animal. The Count's deadly combination of nature and wildlife seems to dominate and conquer human society.[26]

In this perspective, dreams became important phenomena for the Romantics, since in dreams, ideas and objects that appeared finite in a state of consciousness emerge as "eternal" and without boundaries. In dreams the unconsciousness of the mind is able to break free. These dreams are often linked to the mystery of love, because in Romantic texts lovers often see each other in dreams or have the impression that they know each other from dreams; for example, Tatjana in the already-mentioned *Eugene Onegin* by Alexander Pushkin or Käthchen in Heinrich von Kleist's play *Käthchen von Heilbronn* (*Käthchen of Heilbronn*, 1808). As I will clarify later in this chapter, in *Nosferatu the Vampyre* the aspect of dream is often closely linked to the landscape. Throughout *Nosferatu the Vampyre*, Lucy is led by presentiment and by indistinct feelings that derive from her dreams. After the arrival of the Count and the return of her totally changed husband Jonathan, her uncanny impressions lead to Lucy's determination to sacrifice herself. Close to the Romantic tradition, these psychological aspects are woven into the plot and are also expressed by facial expressions and gesture. In a manner corresponding with Bram Stoker's, Herzog creates a "dream-like unreality."[27] Herzog increases the dream-like effect in *Nosferatu the Vampyre* by using mostly pale or bright colors instead of Murnau's strict Expressionistic black and white contrasts.

The landscape Herzog uses in *Nosferatu the Vampyre* resembles classic paintings of the Romantic period or visions and paintings from the Expressionists Arnold Böcklin or Albin Grau.[28] For example, Lucy's stroll along the sea resembles Caspar David Friedrich's marine paintings of (lonely) people at the seaside, especially the famous *Mönch am Meer* (*Monk by the Sea*, 1809–1810) or *Mondaufgang am Meer* (*Moonrise at the Sea*, 1822). When Jonathan walks along the river toward Dracula's castle, he looks like the wanderer in Friedrich's picture of the *Wanderer im Nebelmeer* (*The Wanderer above a Sea of Fog*, 1818). Bruce Kawin, for example, compares Lucy's walks along the sea with "meditations on her husband" (46).[29] There is the same dream-like approach to a surrounding landscape. While the Enlightenment attempts to analyze and separate, the method of Romanticism is to synthesize and lend to mysterious facets. In an infinite landscape, the free poetic imagination is without boundaries. Herzog similarly uses the 360-degree camera shot for similar visions. In the Romantic tradition, nature reflects the human being. Derived from Friedrich Wilhelm Schelling's *Naturphilosophie* (1795), nature and self became equally important; since the unconscious is at work in nature, the "world-spirit" is in a dialectical process with the consciousness of the human mind. Thus, in *Nosferatu the Vampyre*, Herzog's depiction of the landscape almost reaches a hypnotic intensity. Film critic Theobaldy states: "Herzog's movies crave to make drunk, to capture."[30] The contemplation of nature and its landscape evokes emotions and moods within the spectator. Romantic paintings that deal with this issue easily come to mind; for example, Caspar David Friedrich's *Zwei Männer in Betrachtung des Mondes* (*Two*

Men Contemplating the Moon, 1819). In *Nosferatu the Vampyre*, one senses similar Romantic perceptions of nature and feelings when Herzog's long shots intensify these feelings. As Lawrence O'Toole writes, "Herzog will hold an image until it seeps into the stem of the senses and acquires an undefiled beauty."[31] The director is even declared as "nature poet of the German cinema."[32]

Travel and escape to distant lands and countries function in many texts of the Romantic period as substitutes for inner turmoil or the (unbearable) pressure of the outside world, such as in Byron's *Ritter Harolds Pilgerfahrt* (1812), Chateaubriand's *René* (1802), or Joseph von Eichendorff's *Aus dem Leben eines Taugenichts* (*From the Life of a Good-For Nothing*, 1826).[33] In *Nosferatu the Vampyre*, Jonathan travels to the fascinating landscape of the Carpathians, driven to earn a living for his beloved Lucy, while Dracula travels from his castle in the mountains to Wismar, the town by the sea, driven by a desire for Jonathan's wife, whose picture he saw in Romania. Both men travel for the same purpose, a desired woman, and again we see the romantic topics of love and longing. The movie even ends with a voyage; the final shot shows Jonathan escaping by horse, traveling toward an elusive and infinite horizon. It is "not an ending but more precisely a beginning, a narrative opening or return rather than a closing."[34] Another escape in the Romantic tradition is the use of irony, which allows at the same time freedom and the destruction of excessive (inner) tension. Similarly, there are a couple of ironic comments and situations in *Nosferatu the Vampyre*, such as when Dracula tells his visitor Jonathan, "Can you imagine enduring centuries and each day experiencing the same futilities?" and "Unfortunately, the servants are not at our disposal."

The music supports all the mentioned Romantic aspects of *Nosferatu the Vampyre*. Since Romantics considered music as the universal yet divine language, their enthusiasm is expressed in personal letters as well as literary works. At the same time, Romantic music, linked with names such as Ludwig van Beethoven, Robert Schumann, Franz Schubert, or Carl Maria von Weber, was highly celebrated. In the Romantic perspective, music as an almost sacred unity of word, sound, and feeling directly reaches the listener on both the unconscious and conscious levels, since no words are necessary. The magic power of music enables the listener to let his soul fly and therefore elevates the listener. Herzog uses classical excerpts of Richard Wagner's *Rheingold* (1869) and the choirs by Charles Gounod, both incarnations of Romantic or sentimental music; or, in the case of Wagner, the Romantic opera *per se*. Additionally, as in other movies (e.g., *Aguirre)*, he involves the transcendental music of Popul Vuh. Likewise, the poets of the Romantic period considered tones and rhythm as a spiritual experience that transfers emotion and impressions.

The movie *Nosferatu the Vampyre* enables Herzog to synthesize picture and sound to an intertextual *Gesamtkunstwerk*; it presents Romantic elements in a visual and acoustic narrative. It combines fantastic elements and contrary conceptions of the world in aesthetic beauty. The result is at the same time terrifying and amazing. In this global community, life appears to be faster and more intense than twenty or thirty years ago. I claim that the ambivalent topics in *Nosferatu the Vampyre*, as analyzed in this essay, are essential experiences in everybody's life. Questions concerning love, the meaning of life, and individual contentment might be seen as contrasts to a modern lifestyle and a technical and industrialized society. Combined with a romantic stylization and haunting images, these ambiguities are aesthetic perceptions of the never-ending tensions between reality and fantasy and a quest for transcendental experiences through art, which still fascinate the contemporary audience:

> When Kinski's tortured monster first appears, but even more impressively when he hunts Lucy in her bedroom, he becomes one of the master icons of the cinema. His extended fingertips and open mouth outline his monstrosity turned into familiar desire and materialise our repressed fantasies, neither spoken nor dictated in everyday life. As a result, Nosferatu [Dracula] is part of us and Herzog's film reflects on this condition with impressive vigour.[35]

NOTES

1. For the various adaptations of Friedrich Wilhelm Murnau's *Nosferatu* and the influence of the movie on subsequent revisions of Stoker's *Dracula*, see Saviour Catania, "Absent Presences in Liminal Places: Murnau's *Nosferatu* and the Otherworld of Stoker's *Dracula*," *Literature Film Quarterly* 32, no. 3 (2004): 229–36; and Wayne E. Hensley, "The Contribution of F. W. Murnau's *Nosferatu* to the Evolution of *Dracula*," *Literature Film Quarterly* 30, no. 1 (2002): 59–64.

2. Bram Stoker obviously intended to copyright *Dracula* but he never did. See Barbara Belford, *Bram Stoker: A Biography of the Author of* Dracula (New York: Alfred A. Knopf, Inc., 1996), 272, 326; and Catania, "Absent Presences in Liminal Places," 61, 63–64. So technically, Murnau could have used the same story but instead invented his own names: Count Orlok (Dracula), Knock (Renfield), Hutter (Harker), Ellen (Mina). Obviously, the resemblance was still very noticeable, so Bram Stoker's widow, Florence, sought to prevent this or any other "unauthorized" film version of her husband's book by asking the German courts to destroy all copies of Murnau's version. Thus, all copies of *Nosferatu* should be destroyed. Herzog, who intended *Nosferatu the Vampyre* as *homage* to Murnau's masterpiece, kept the title name *Nosferatu* but changed the names of the protagonists back to Stoker's original.

3. See, among others, Russell A. Berman, "The Recipient as Spectator: West German film and Poetry of the Seventies," *The German Quarterly* 55, no. 4 (November 1982): 499–510; Garrett Chaffin-Quiray, "An Adaption with Fangs. Werner Herzog's *Nosferatu: Phantom der Nacht* (*Nosferatu the Vampyre*, 1979)," *Kinoeye* 2, no. 20 (December 16, 2002): no pagination; Timothy Corrigan, *New German Film: The Displaced Image* (Bloomington and Indianapolis: Indiana University Press, 1994); and William Luhr, "*Nosferatu* and Postwar German Film," *Michigan Academician* 14, no. 4 (Spring 1982): 453–58.

4. Werner Herzog, *Herzog on Herzog*, ed. Paul Cronin (New York: Faber and Faber, 2002), 107.

5. Brigitte Peucker, "Werner Herzog: In the Quest of the Sublime," in *New German Filmmakers: From Oberhausen through the 1970s*, ed. Klaus Phillips (New York: Friedrich Ungar, 1984), 193.

6. The terminus *Romanticism* is expansive, since Romantic philosophy and literature, which spans from early Romanticism at the end of the eighteenth century to the Neo-Romanticists in the twentieth century, deals with dualities and dichotomies. Therefore, this chapter will focus on a variety of topics and themes of Romanticism that can be found in all Romantic movements and in different national contexts. Since Werner Herzog has a German background, texts from German Romanticism in particular will be considered to frame the Romantic aspects in *Nosferatu the Vampyre*.

7. The homage to Murnau's movie can be seen in almost identical camera shots; for example, the travel on the ship, black and white shadows, and the short dialogue texts, which would fit the captions of a silent film.

8. Herzog's fascination with the outsider or the exceptional human being can be seen in other works throughout his career; for example, *Jeder für sich und Gott gegen alle (The Enigma of Kasper Hauser* [1974]), *Woyzeck* (1979), *Fitzcerraldo* (1982), or *Grizzly Man* (2005).

9. Herzog adopts Murnau's perception of a (rat-like) vampire who has adjacent incisors, while other movies, such as Francis Ford Coppola's *Dracula* (1992), portray Dracula with two long separated incisors.

10. She even states that "nothing, not even God, can touch [her love for Jonathan]."

11. Similarly, Jonathan, who wears bright clothes in the beginning of the movie, seems to lose his innocence, since he is dressed in dark clothes as soon as he is bitten by Dracula.

12. David Denby, "Nosferatu," *New York* (October 22, 1979): 89, quoted in Garrett Chaffin-Quiray, "An Adaption with Fangs. Werner Herzog's *Nosferatu: Phantom der Nacht* (*Nosferatu the Vampyre*, 1979)," *Kinoeye* 2, no. 20 (December 16, 2002): no pagination.

13. Indeed, Achim von Arnim's novel inspired Herzog's first feature film, *Signs of Life* (1968). See Herzog, *Herzog on Herzog*, 38.

14. Lloyd Michaels, *The Phantom of the Cinema: Character in Modern Films* (New York: State University of New York Press, 1998), 68.

15. *Gong*, no. 12 (1983): no pagination.

16. In this perspective, one does not wonder why Klaus Kinski appeared in the role of Renfield in Jesus Franco's 1969 version of *Dracula* (starring Christopher Lee).

17. Max Schreck was surrounded by an air of mystery, since he was never seen without his mask at the set. The enduring myth that Schreck was actually a vampire was later captured in the movie *Shadow of the Vampire* (2000) starring William Defoe (Max Schreck) and John Malkovich (Friedrich Wilhelm Murnau).

18. Occasionally actor and director threatened to kill each other. This love-hate relationship is exceptionally portrayed in Herzog's retrospective documentation of his work with Kinski, *Geliebter Feind* (*My Best Fiend*, 1999).

19. Chaffin-Quiray points out in "An Adaption with Fangs" that Klaus Kinski at that time was "also weathering a personal hell," since his third wife was planning to leave him with their son, and therefore, "Werner Herzog managed to help channel his star's private pain into a form of helplessness more conducive to the part [of Dracula]" (no pagination).

20. Indeed, Kinski's 1988 autobiography is titled *Ich brauche Liebe* (*I need love*).

21. *Cinema*, no. 4 (1979): no pagination.

22. *Cinema*, no. 4 (1979): no pagination.

23. The writer's choice of spelling is quoted intact.

24. John Azzopardi, "Herzog: Last Breath of German Expressionism," *Chelsea News* (October 18, 1979): 11, quoted in Garrett Chaffin-Quiray, "An Adaption with Fangs. Werner Herzog's *Nosferatu: Phantom der Nacht* (*Nosferatu the Vampyre*, 1979)," *Kinoeye* 2, no. 20 (16 December 2002): no pagination.

25. Herzog brought more than 11,000 rats to the Dutch city Delft, where the movie scenes in Wismar took place. The white rats from a laboratory in Hungary had to be painted gray in order to look scarier. Parts of the film had to be shot in nearby Schiedam after Delft authorities refused to release the rats. For a description of the shooting see Beverly Walker, "Nosferatu," *Sight and Sound* 47, no. 3 (Autumn 1978): 202–205.

26. Nature and wilderness as hostile opponents of mankind and human desire are, for example, also topics of Herzog's *Grizzly Man*, *Aguirre*, *Where the Green Ants Dream* (1984), or *Fitzcerraldo*.

27. Clive Leatherdale, *Dracula: The Novel and the Legend* (Wellingborough, England: Aquarian Press, 1985), 169.

28. See, for example, Kent Casper and Susan Linville, "Romantic Inversions in Herzog's *Nosferatu*," *The German Quarterly* 64, no. 1 (Winter 1991): 17–24; Thomas Elsaesser, "Six Degrees of *Nosferatu*," *Sight and Sound* 11, no. 2 (February 2001): 12–15; and Catania, "Absent Presences in Liminal Places," 232–34.

29. Bruce Kawin, "Nosferatu," *Film Quarterly* 23, no. 3 (Spring 1980), 46.

30. Jürgen Theobaldy, "Fahrten ins Ungeheure," in *Werner Herzog*, ed. Günther Pflaum, Hans Helmut Prinzler, Jürgen Theobaldy, and Kraft Wenzel (Munich and Vienna: Carl Hanser, 1979), 11.

31. Lawrence O'Toole, "The Great Ecstasy of Filmmaker Herzog," *Film Comment* 15, no. 6 (November–December 1979): 504, quoted in Russell A. Berman,

"The Recipient as Spectator: West German Film and Poetry of the Seventies," *The German Quarterly* 55, no. 4 (November 1982): 499–510.

32. Corrigan, *New German Film*, 132.

33. Contemporaries have been fascinated by travel reports; for example, like those written by James Cook, Alexander von Humboldt, or Adalbert von Chamisso.

34. Corrigan, *New German Film*, 142.

35. Chaffin-Quiray, "Adaptation with Fangs."

Part III

IMPERIALISM, HYBRIDITY, AND CROSS-CULTURAL FERTILIZATION IN ASIA

11

"Death and the Maiden": The *Pontianak* as Excess in Malay Popular Culture

Andrew Hock-Soon Ng

One of the most fearsome creatures of Malay folklore is the *pontianak*. A vampire-like entity, she (the *pontianak* is always female) is characterized by ear-piercing shrieks, overflowing hair, and a penchant for the blood of children. As haunting as she may be, she is also haunted by ambiguities as to what exactly she signifies. For although the term *vampire* is often attributed to her, and although she has certain defining qualities similar to those of the Western vampire, there are also aspects to her that suggest more ghost-like traits. Indeed, what is known of the *pontianak* is as much derived from folklore as it is recalibrated by Malay popular culture. Specifically through film, many Malaysians have become familiar with this entity, but cinematic representations often multiply—sometimes confusingly—the *pontianak*'s signifiers to the point that it is no longer clear where popular culture ends and traditional belief begins. The various *pontianak* films popular in the 1950s and 1960s in Malaysia (and again in 2004) portray her as a hybrid creature that blends Eastern and Western vampiric characteristics. The first part of this essay explores some of these representations. Here, I highlight the ambiguities surrounding the configuration of the *pontianak* (principally the question of whether or not she is a ghost or a vampire), the way in which folklore is reconstituted by popular culture for mass consumption, and the manner in which cross-cultural fertilization (East-West) has come to inform the construction of the *pontianak*.

The second part of this essay analyzes one of the more recent *pontianak* films produced in Malaysia. *Pontianak Harum Sundal Malam* (*Pontianak of the Tuber Rose* [2004])[1] by Shuhaimi Baba signals the return of the *pontianak* to the silver screen after a thirty-year hiatus. It deploys, I argue, to great effect, the *pontianak* as a metaphor for the Malay woman's schizophrenic identity.

The Malay social system is predominantly patriarchal, and women occupy a subordinate position. Silent and often invisible, it is only within certain limited public spaces—such as the stage (*pentas*)—that a woman can articulate her marginalization, cross gender boundaries (she can play heroic roles), and enact empowerment. In Baba's film, the *pontianak* was a dancer before her untimely death. Similarities between the "sites" of the dancer's body and the *pontianak's* will be drawn to show an important correlation that illuminates the *pontianak's* paradoxical signifiers of transgression and reparation. To contextualize my argument, an extensive discussion on traditional dance and its function will be made. That the multiple meanings of dance at work in the film, sometimes contradictorily, complement my reading of the incongruous signifiers of woman and vampire serves to align all three along a single metonymic plane. Finally, my reading is informed by theories concerning the ideological constructions of Malay gender and sexuality as outlined by scholars such as Khoo Gaik Cheng and Aihwa Ong. I demonstrate that the narrative, through the metaphor of the vampire, critiques dimensions of such a male-biased ideology. I conclude this essay by briefly commenting on the inconsistencies of representing the Malay woman in Baba's narrative, and argue that this is perhaps unavoidable due to the deep-seated interpellation by an ideological system that prescribes strict gender and sexual performances to both Malay men and women

THE *PONTIANAK*: BETWEEN VAMPIRE AND GHOST

Ambiguity is perhaps the *pontianak's* most substantial signifier. Although the *pontianak* is a familiar creature in Malay folklore, definitions of her remain elusive. Folklorists and anthropologists have identified some of her more salient features, but there are aspects to her that remain contradictory and vague. One such area of confusion arises precisely from whether or not the *pontianak* is affiliated with the vampire. For while the *pontianak's* bloodsucking proclivity and her fear of sharp, pointed objects suggest characteristics of a vampire (at least, from a Western perspective), that she also has numinous qualities and could possess another person (not in the sense of hypnotizing) imply qualities of a malignant specter as well. Thus, to say that the *pontianak* is a vampire is only focusing on some of her characteristics. This complication is further reinforced through popular depictions, most notably films. In this section, I want to revisit some of the delineations of the *pontianak* to tease out her various nuances that correlate with (Western notions of) vampirism. In the next section, I discuss how this cross-fertilization has been represented in popular culture, and that despite reflections of the Western vampire in this Eastern configuration, there are also levels of resistance that promote a more sympathetic rendition of this monstrous-feminine.

Walter Skeat's magisterial study, *Malay Magic* (1900) affords a substantial description of the *pontianak* (which means "child-bearing ghost"), although he distinguishes this particular vampire from another, the *langsuyar* (or *langsuir*), the main difference being that the latter is the parent of the former. This distinction, however, is not useful and certainly not a feature in Malay popular culture (evidenced in films that unanimously use the term *pontianak*), primarily because both the *pontianak* and the *langsuir* share the same characteristics. Nevertheless, Skeat's description remains one of the most accurate, and has been foundational in arriving at an understanding of this creature. As Skeat describes (and I quote at length):

> If a woman dies in childbirth, either before delivery or after birth of a child, and before the forty days of uncleanness have expired, she is popularly supposed to become a *langsuyar*, a flying demon of the nature of the "white lady" or "banshee." To prevent this a quantity of glass beads are put in the mouth of the corpse, a hen's egg is put under each arm-pit, and needles are placed in the palms of the hands. It is believed that if this is done the dead woman cannot become a *langsuyar*, as she cannot open her mouth to shriek (*ngilai*) or wave her arms as wings, or open and shut her hands to assist her flight [. . .].² She may be known by her robe of green, by her tapering nails of extraordinary length (a mark of beauty), and by her long jet black tresses which she allows to fall down her ankles—only, alas! (for the truth must be told) in order to conceal the hole in the back of her neck through which she sucks the blood of children! These vampire-like proclivities of hers may, however, be successfully combated if the right means are adopted, for if you are able to catch her, cut short her nails and luxuriant tresses, and stuff them into the hole in her neck, she will become tame and indistinguishable from an ordinary woman, remaining so for years.³

Skeat's identification of some of the *pontianak*'s common features finds resonance in other anthropologists' and folklorists' works, such as the fact that she is a woman who has died from childbirth,⁴ that she can fly, take the guise of a beautiful woman, and has sharp claws. But when it comes to deciding what configuration (one that will be familiar to a Western reader) that a *pontianak* should take, Skeat encounters a caveat. What is evident in Skeat's view is that the *pontianak* is closer to a ghost than a vampire. Skeat is careful to attribute her blood-sucking tendencies as "vampire-like," but directly corresponds her to the "white lady" or "banshee." But that the *pontianak* is able to turn into a woman suggests that she is not altogether disembodied (as ghosts usually are), but is actually flesh, although undead. Perhaps the most obvious characteristic that links her to the Western vampire is the method of her sub-jugation. Unlike Skeat's recommendation, the most common way to over-come a *pontianak* is by thrusting a long nail through the back of her neck, re-sulting in either death or transformation into a beautiful woman who can subsequently function as human (in the case of the Western vampire, it is a fatal stake through its heart).

From this brief outline, it is evident that the *pontianak* has conflicting denotations that suggest that she is both vampire *and* ghost. For unlike a Western vampire, whose identity straddles between the living and the dead (hence, the undead), the *pontianak* embodies qualities of both the undead and the numinous. This is perhaps the unique feature of this Eastern vampire. I am inclined to call the *pontianak* a vampire, but mindful of her spectral affil-iations as well. As much as traditional Malay culture does not view the natu-ral and the supernatural as separate realms, it is perhaps not surprising that creatures of Malay folklore resist rigid classifications. The *pontianak*, vacillat-ing between the (un)dead, the embodied, and the numinous, confirms this seamless transgression of sociocultural spaces. She is the Irigaray-ian woman-as-fluid *par excellence*, whose excessive body breaks apart the Symbolic system that struggles to define and confine her.

THE *PONTIANAK* IN MALAY POPULAR CULTURE

Vampires are ambiguous signifiers, whose meanings shift according to histor-ical and cultural changes.[5] In the case of the *pontianak*, her ambiguity is fur-ther reinforced by the constantly evolving Malay popular culture. In some early *pontianak* films such as *Sumpah Pontianak* (*The Curse of the Pontianak*, 1958) and *Anak Pontianak* (*Son of Pontianak*, 1958), the creature is clearly an undead, having the capacity to function like a human being, except that she does not age (but this does not suggest immortality).[6] She can also take on different guises, such as a beautiful maiden or an old woman. In the more re-cent versions, notably *Pontianak Harum Sundal Malam* (*Pontianak of the Tu-ber Rose*, 2004), she is depicted as a more ghostly configuration who can pos-sess another individual's body.[7] Screen *pontianaks* also manifest, albeit scarcely, vampiric influences of the West. Like her Western cousin, the *pon-tianak* thrives on blood, which she sucks, as Skeat notes, through the back of her neck. But local cinematic representations have transformed this charac-teristic, portraying her instead as fanged (as in *Anak Pontianak* and *Pontianak* [1974]), or has done away altogether with this penchant for blood. Again, like the Western vampire, the method of subduing the *pontianak* is by staking her (although in the latter, it is a nail through the back of her neck). But the hammer and stake (through the neck) analogy has been increasingly manifest in *pontianak* films (the opening scene of *Pontianak HSM* is one example), implying another homage to Western representations. Undeniably, aspects of Western representations of the vampire have crept into the local context, and although they remain peripheral, they have contributed to the coloration of the *pontianak's* portrayal, and have reconstituted her into a more hybrid entity that draws on both Eastern and Western vampiric attributes.

Despite these intercultural influences, however, there is a significant resistance to Western technologies of film horror in the way *pontianak* films often substantially downplay her "monstrosity" to foreground her victimized status instead.[8] In *Sumpah Pontianak*, she is a misunderstood person wrongly accused of murder, and must remain in the margins of the *kampong* (village) to look out for her daughter. In *Pontianak Gua Musang* (*Pontianak of Civet Cave*, 1964), she is a victim of jealousy, murdered because her enemy wants to prevent her from having a happy marriage (although in this film, the *pontianak* is often the guilty conscience of the murderer, and only ever appears in the latter's nightmares). In *Anak Pontianak*, although the *pontianak* executes her husband, it is because of his unfaithfulness. She escapes with her child to a remote part of the village and subsequently lives a normal human existence, caring for her son who has, unbeknownst to both, inherited the contaminated blood of his mother. In the end, she has no choice but to destroy him when he can no longer control his transformation into a were-beast, during which he attacks and kills innocent people. Although this may be construed as the narrative's punishment of the *pontianak*, that she is portrayed as a loving mother who must destroy her son in order to protect others suggests an ultimate sacrifice that cannot be simplistically read as retribution. In fact, to further emphasize her "goodness" in *Anak Pontianak*, she is juxtaposed against the *penanggalan* (a creature that can detach its head from the rest of the body), another creature in Malay folklore that is clearly evil.[9] Indeed, the *pontianak* in local films is often sympathetically portrayed to reflect the plight of women in a social system that clearly privileges men. Even though she is an undead, her duties as wife and (more often) mother continue into the afterlife, and it is often in these capacities that her repressed position in society is most attenuated.[10]

Such sensitive depictions of this "monstrous-feminine" (to borrow a phrase from Barbara Creed [2000]) is a refreshing alternative to Western portrayals of female revenants and monsters, which are often negatively typecast. This negativity has been highlighted in several studies by feminist theorists. For example, in Carol Clover's classic study of horror films *Men, Women and*

Chainsaws: Gender in Modern Horror Film (1992), she claims that women in horror can largely be categorized into three distinct "types": the (monstrous) villain, the victim (who usually requires rescuing), and the "final girl" (who survives the ordeal). In the case of the first (Clover is discussing *The Exorcist* [1973] and *Witchboard* [1987], two classic possession films), the woman is garishly transmogrified, her focus mainly as pure and unrelenting evil to juxtapose (and veil) the "male story" of overcoming (usually a psychosexual blockage). Feminist critics have tried to rectify this problematic construction, but often run aground because of horror films' unrelenting and uncompromising portrayal of feminine evil. Barbara Creed's attribution of the monstrous-feminine as nothing but metaphors of abjection to various Western horror reflects scholarship's ambiguity of desiring a reading of empowered femininity that unconsciously reproduces negative essentialism.[11] For Creed, the monstrous-feminine symbolizes the archaic mother that stands outside, but threatens, the Symbolic boundaries, but the problem with such a reading is obvious: because the archaic mother is necessarily dangerous, she is irredeemable and must be annihilated, which only reinforces the binaristic logic of man=good/woman=evil. And the woman who survives (the "final girl") is usually "masculinized" in the process of battling the creature (examples include *The Texas Chainsaw Massacre* [1974] and the *Aliens* trilogy). Furthermore, that the monster, be it "male" or "female," in many Western horror stories, often in the end becomes invariably subjected to the controlling male gaze, which already suggests its feminization. As Timothy Beal notes, the monster usually occupies a point of terrible power as long as it remains unseen or indeterminate; but this is only temporary because it will always be ultimately "captured" by the camera eye (the male gaze), and be subsequently defeated and destroyed.[12] There is a direct correlation here to Mulvey's famous theory of cinematic fetishizing of the female body for the pleasure of the male gaze.

The *pontianak* films, to a significant extent, escape, and even reverse, such binaristic paradigms. The need to subjugate her under the camera/male gaze is rendered problematic for two reasons: first, the fact that she is a *pontianak* is never in doubt; she already belongs to a recognizable category of knowledge (folklore), which counters the need to "penetrate" her through gradual revelation and recognition. Instead, what often becomes clear as the narrative unfolds is the wrongful suspicion of her on the part of the viewer. As noted, in many *pontianak* films, she is sympathetically represented, often more as a creature misunderstood than as evil. Second, the *pontianak* can hardly be said to be fetishized, because she is persistently depicted in all her grotesque glory. Even when she takes on the guise of the beautiful, erotic woman, this merely attenuates the reality of her hideous, hidden self. In fact, as I will argue when analyzing *Pontianak HSM*, if there is any fetishizing at work in the *pontianak* narrative, it is the returned, or reversed, fetishism that becomes activated, directly punishing the male gaze for its will-to-power.

CONTESTING GENDER AND SEXUALITY IN
PONTIANAK HARUM SUNDAL MALAM

The *pontianak*'s beauty/ugliness reveals the contradictory nature of the woman in the Malay imaginary: the Malay woman performs the symbolic role of upholding communal purity and integrity, but because she is viewed as the "weaker vessel" and her sexuality susceptible to easy compromise, any signification of autonomous or independent behavior (read: refusal to submit to patriarchal policing) is regarded with deep suspicion. In the *pontianak* narratives, the *pontianak* inheres this duality, but often as critique of Malay patriarchy. She is the beautiful wife and mother, but the unfaithfulness or absence of a spouse, coupled by her strong independent streak, result in her becoming, in the end, the *pontianak*—a woman whose resourcefulness and autonomy relegate her as dangerously "unfeminine,"[13] and emplaces her invisibly at the margins of society. But even from this (disad)vantage point, she continues to procure subsistence for herself and offer protection to her loved ones. The *pontianak*, in this sense, takes on a further signifier that indicts patriarchal ideology of its subjection of, and its failure to protect and honor, women. Her grotesquery is as much a trademark of her independence as the battle scar of continuously contesting a male-inflected Symbolic order.

To test some of the points raised thus far, I focus my discussion on one of the more recent *pontianak* films. An important landmark in Malaysian film history, *Pontianak Harum Sundal Malam* marks the return of the Malaysian vampire to the silver screen after a thirty-year lapse due to religious sensitivity and censorship.[14] A tale of love and revenge, *Pontianak HSM* takes the viewer back to 1949, to a sleepy Malay village called Paku Laris (perhaps a cruel, phallic irony, the word *paku* means "nail" in Malay). The beautiful court dancer, Mariam, invites the attention of the village men, in particular Marsani and Danial. Marsani, a merchant, woos Mariam with expensive gifts, but his hopes are dashed when one night, after a performance, Mariam is abducted and almost raped, but is rescued by Danial. Mariam soon after marries Danial, but Marsani continues to harbor desire for her. One day, while Mariam—now pregnant—is alone in her home (Danial is away on business), Marsani and his henchmen pay her an unexpected visit, with the pretext of trying to make amends and to invite her to join him in a business venture. His intention soon becomes evident, and in a brief struggle, Mariam is accidentally stabbed. Before retreating, Marsani steals her prized anklets and tiara, the will to Danial's home, and a gong from the *bonang* (or *kerompong*).[15] Mariam's friends, Laila and Sitam, arrive on time to deliver Mariam's baby (through cesarean) before she expires. Fearing for their lives (because Marsani is a powerful man), the two women decide to separate, with Laila taking the child to Indonesia. Sitam (who is slightly retarded) is soon after killed, possibly by Marsani's men. Mariam returns as a *pontianak* and systematically destroys the perpetrators of her death, except for Marsani, whom she spares in order to make his life a living hell (*hidup dalam kematian*).

The film then cuts into the present,[16] and Marsani, now a wealthy businessman, bears the curse of being heirless. His only son has disappeared and, as he later relates, no women in his family ever make it to full pregnancy, their lives terminated by the *pontianak*. He is accompanied by his two adopted sons, Azmadi (who is slightly retarded, perhaps a retributive gesture for Sitam's murder) and Norman (an engineer). Haunted by guilt and vivid nightmares, his fears finally become enfleshed with the arrival of Maria, a traditional dancer working for Marsani's daughter-in-law, Anna, in a cultural market, and who is the spitting image of Mariam. From this point, the film becomes decidedly ambiguous. It is often unclear if Maria is really Mariam, or if she is the latter's daughter as well as an instrument deployed to further punish Marsani. On several occasions, a nail-induced scar is noticeable at the back of Maria's neck, which, according to one version of folklore, is the mark of a *pontianak* transformed into a beautiful woman. But the film also depicts her as being haunted by strange dreams of a traditional dancer, and there are instances in the narrative of her possession during which she attacks Anna and Marsani.

To further complicate matters, there is evidence, on at least two occasions, that the *pontianak*'s return is nothing but Marsani's guilt projected onto Maria. The false suturing in both scenes heightens the *pontianak*'s indistinctness. In the first, we are shown Azmadi bringing a frightened Maria to Marsani's home because the latter wants to meet her. During the meeting (from which Azmadi is absent), it is obviously Mariam who manifests, accusing Marsani of his crime and demanding that he return her stolen inheritance. But immediately after this, we see Azmadi coming to inform his father that Maria has declined despite his persistent invitation. This implies that Marsani has either just met the *pontianak* disguised as Maria, or is merely playing out the scene in his troubled mind. In the final scene of the film, Marsani and his family confront the *pontianak*, who then forces a confession from him, as well as an apology and the promise to return her inheritance. But using a dissolve, the narrative cuts to a scene where Marsani is strangling Maria and speaking incomprehensibly, while his two sons and daughter-in-law struggle to separate them. As if awaking from a trance, Marsani suddenly asks what he had done; the looks on the faces of his relatives reveal that he has indeed made the confession. Once more, this scene suggests that the *pontianak* is merely the hallucination of a man haunted by guilt. Maria, who minutely resembles Mariam, embodies both his shame and his retribution. Although he fears her, he is also drawn to her because she can potentially "save" him once and for all.

The ambiguities in representing the *pontianak* (vampire or ghost, real or imagined) outlined in the previous sections have important links to my argument with regard to the contradictory roles Malay women play in a sociocultural system that is rigidly patriarchal. In *Pontianak HSM*, the vampire metaphor is utilized to comment on the schizophrenic identity of the Malay woman: her tussle between autonomy and dependence, agency and subservience finds an excessive expression through the potent, dangerous body of the vampire. To a point, this view squares with Linda Badley's assessment of bodily representations in contemporary horror:

> Horror became a hysterical text or a theater of cruelty specializing in representations of the human anatomy *in extremis*—in disarray or deconstruction, in metamorphosis, invaded or engulfing, in sexual difference, monstrous otherness, or Dionysian ecstasy: the body fantastic[. . .]. The fantastic is based in somatic consciousness—in sensational existence that is tragically conscious of its material finitude and the presence of Otherness, in the torture, challenge, and horror-comedy of incessant change.[17]

For Badley, the body becomes the site of fissuring and monstrous transformation in order to reveal the fractured identity that is being pulled and manipulated by opposing forces and desires. The *pontianak* is particularly useful to contextualize the Malay woman's social position, because the image of a woman who is independent, worldly, sexual, and enterprising yet quietly feminine, wifely, and domesticated remains a difficult negotiation under current gender ideologies in Malaysia. Through the *pontianak*, the narrative is able to address the dilemma that besets autonomous women, as well as criticize the Malay Symbolic order that continues to demonize such women. To pursue this line of argument, however, it is important to provide a critical perspective from which gender and sexual issues can be addressed and read against the film. Prominently related to these issues is the symbiotic relationship between Malay custom (or *adat*) and Islam, which have informed and constructed notions of masculinity and femininity. A brief analysis of this relationship will be attempted.

One of the new-wave filmmakers in the Malaysian scene, Shuhaimi Baba's provocative works often question the disenfranchised status of women and problematize the Malay male imperative. Gaik Cheng Khoo claims in *Reclaiming Adat: Contemporary Malaysian Film and Literature* that Baba's films attempt to restore the balance of gender positions in the Malay *adat* (or "customs") that resurgent Islamization in Malaysia in the seventies and eighties have upset. According to Khoo, "while the general tendency is to perceive *adat* and Islam as binary yet complementary forces in some situations, it becomes difficult to tell them apart since Islam has become such an integral part of Malay *adat* and vice versa."[18] Yet despite this intricate symbiosis, there are clearly distinguishing features with regard to gender and sexuality. As Jahan Karim Wazir attests, up until the time when resurgent Islam transformed the sociopolitical landscape of Malaysia, "women are not completely subsumed by Islam except in matters of marriage and divorce, and *adat* held a close rein on all, ensuring equitable distribution of inheritance, property, and status between men and women."[19] This view finds further resonance in Aihwa Ong's (1990/1995) explication that "although men traditionally enjoyed prerogatives in religion and property, women were neither confined to the household nor totally dependent on men for economic survival. Malay society is often cited as an example of a Muslim society that permitted relatively egalitarian relations between the sexes."[20] *Adat*, in this sense, is a more balanced worldview where gender is concerned. One of the integral forms that *adat* takes is the dichotomy between *akal* (rationality) and *nafsu* (passion), which, according to Khoo, promotes "bilaterality in gender relations, an openness about sexuality and sensuality, and a non-Western understanding of power," and which "exist[s] in *both* men and women in Malay *adat*" (emphasis mine).[21] However, resurgent Islam, drawing from this dichotomy, transforms the power structure inherent in *adat*. Women are now invested with more *nafsu* (which increasingly became connoted as lust), which "explains" their penchant for gossiping, material accumulation, and straying libido. Lacking in reason (*akal*, which is now the prerogative of Muslim men), "they have to be saved from evil temptation."[22] Because women are more susceptible to sexual temptation, female pleasure—which *adat* recognizes and even celebrates—is now regarded with suspicion. Ong (1990/1995) notes that the

> Islamic emphasis on female chastity imposed more rigorous restrictions on unmarried women (called *anak dara*, or virgins) than on unmarried youths, although promiscuity in either sex was criticized. Young girls were required to be bashful and modest, but the Islamic emphasis on *aurat* ("nakedness" that should be covered) did not, until recently, extend to covering girls' hair

(an erotic feature), which they wore loose or plaited. Everyday dress consisted of loose-fitting long tunics over sarongs (*baju kurong*).[23]

Women's sexuality, more tolerantly regarded in *adapt*,[24] has become, under resurgent Islam's restrictions, a reason for their repression.

In *Pontianak HSM*, this binarism is reversed, and it is the men who are invested with *nafsu* that leads to greed and atrocities. This reversal is perhaps a subtle criticism of Islamic reorientation of *adat* forms. Whether overtly (Marsani's workers) or covertly (Marsani himself), *nafsu* overwhelms the men in this narrative; and rather than upholding reason and protecting the womenfolk (a duty of village men, see Ong [1990/1995]), they are represented as weak and lustful (save Danial, whose role is decidedly limited). The adage that the sins of the father are visited upon the children seems to find resonance in the film as well. Marsani's two sons metonymically "inherit" their adopted father's guilt and weakness: Azmadi is a half-wit whom no women would go near (save one, who will perish because of her association with the Marsani family), and Norman obviously has wandering eyes, becoming tacitly attracted to Maria, which the *pontianak* later exploits to destroy his marriage. The women in *Pontianak HSM*, on the other hand, are represented as strong and independent. Mariam and Anna, both working women, display integrity and are successful in their own right, yet without compromising their elegant femininity. However, for Mariam, instead of respect, she must constantly fend off men who merely view her as fetish.[25] Because of her beauty and profession, she is a target for ill-mannered villagers who accost her with sexual innuendos (in one scene, a rowdy villager walks up to her and invites her to "dance," an invitation that obviously carries illicit overtones). Here, the implication that an autonomous woman is also sexually liberal is pronounced. The harassments she faces, I argue, is an unconscious display of disdain at her autonomy, and to remind her that however successful she may be, she is still "only" a woman, and must submit (sexually), in the end, to men. The ideal modern Malay woman is one who reflects her "Muslimness" and her modernity by her "identification with domesticity, motherhood and the consumption of religious and material paraphernalia which [marks] the Muslim home."[26]

Because Mariam exemplifies the opposite of this ideal, she is exposed to all kinds of harassment. Even after marriage, Marsani continues to harbor hopes that her independent streak (read: "availability") will translate itself into relations with him. His view, in the end, is a refraction of the misogynistic system that codes women and men in certain ways.

Mariam's feminine "excess" cannot comfortably fit into a social system that requires pronounced definitions. Ambiguities are shunned, and as a

result, Mariam as refused-fetish only ultimately reveals the symbolic castration unconsciously experienced by the men. Žižek has asserted that a back-
lash effect that returns the fetish back to the gaze itself is inherent in fetishizing, transforming in the process the gaze into *the fetish*. Fetishizing works on
the premise of an "impossibility to see the object," which then requires an alternative form of gazing at the object, which, in the case of the village men,
takes the form of "eroticizing." But when this occurs, that "impossibility" becomes embodied—"the impossibility to see the object [reverses] into an object that gives body to this impossibility: since the subject cannot directly see
that, the true object of fascination, he accomplishes a kind of reflection-into-
self by means of which the object that fascinates him becomes the gaze itself."[27] Thus, in fetishizing Mariam, the men are really turning themselves
into fetishes, because she unconsciously reveals their own repulsion, which
must then be recast as desire invested onto Mariam's body. But she refuses to
play the object of their fascination, and is therefore punished.

Mariam's transformation into the *pontianak* becomes, I argue, the exaggerated expression of her excess. Her murder is a castigation of her in-
domitable independence by refusing her entry into motherhood and thereby
achieves the ideal Malay-Muslim woman status. Liminally located between
two configurations (independent and domesticated; a working woman and a
mother) and disallowed from harmonizing them, she takes on the identity of
a monstrous-feminine who would aggressively indict the cruelty of the patriarchal system that offers her no belonging. In the second half of the film,
whether or not it is the *pontianak* in a new guise, or the vampire possessing
Maria (in any case, the scent of the tuber rose always accompanies her arrival),
the crossing of the threshold between the natural and the supernatural plots
the monstrous woman/women along the axis of the interstitial, and from
there, she/they can challenge "the multiple violations of moral boundaries"[28]
enacted but exploited by the men for their cruel ends. The vampire becomes
the site where a woman's liminality can be consolidated and patriarchal im-
peratives resisted and exposed for their duplicity. Through Maria, the *pontianak* continues to assert her punishment and claim to her inheritance.

DANCE AS POSSESSION, DANCE AS CURE

Interestingly, Maria's possession is always accompanied by gestures of dance.
In one dream, Maria hears the dancer (Mariam) speaking to her: *Bila bunyi
bersatu, kau milikku* (*when the sound combines, you are mine*). The sound here
denotes the combination of the gong reverberation and the jingling of the an-

klet bells (those stolen by Marsani). Soon after this dream, both items are discovered in a box by Anna while moving into her new home. As her part is preparing for a cultural function during which Maria will be dancing, this discovery is befitting because the items can be used to enhance the performance. But haunting incidents begin to occur in the house, clearly indicating that Anna and Norman are now spiritually disturbed (Anna also dreams of a beautiful dancer imploring her to return her "inheritance"). Maria's instances of possession escalate, all of which are triggered by the sound, and sometimes merely the presence of, the instruments. In one episode, as Anna observes Maria practicing her dance steps, the latter's movements suddenly take on a "battle" mode (for which Mariam is famous), and Maria reaches out for Anna's throat. Maria almost immediately snaps out of her "trance," her face evincing fear and confusion. Another instance occurs during the cultural performance, when the rhythm of the anklet bells and the gong harmonize. The possessed Maria pronounces a curse against Azmadi, which later transpires in the death of his lover. Anna later asks Maria to deposit the gong at her home, and whilst Maria is there, she becomes possessed once again and ends up seducing Norman. During all these moments, Maria has literally become Mariam's "possession"; Maria performs dances that signal death and seduction, guided by the vengeful Mariam.

Dance, through which Mariam once found subsistence and empowerment, once again empowers her through another's body. There are, to some extent, similarities between the dancing body and the body of horror that Badley discusses. While performing, the dancer becomes a body *in extremis*—ecstatic, sensual, and sexual. Mariam/Maria's dancing evidently invites such responses. Her fluid, gyrating movements clearly arouse the men in the audience (especially Marsani). Dancing allows her to cross boundaries: in one *mak yong* performance,[29] she is the warrior woman engaged in battle with a demonic enemy. Such a representation contravenes, as mentioned, the ideal image of the Malay woman who must embody subservience and domestication. On stage, however—which is a liminal space itself, straddling between reality and fantasy—the female body is able to achieve configurations from which she is otherwise barred. More importantly, the ecstatic body attains a form of dynamism that is beyond merely the physical. According to Ghouse Nasuruddin Mohd, dances like *mak yong* contain aspects of the sublime that

> involves the psychological projection of movement energy which extends the movement after the termination of the physical movements. The movements of these dances are slow, graceful and small, and are frequently held for several seconds at the end of each movement phrase. At the point the physical movement ends, the psychological projection takes

over, extending the movement energy into space. This integral energy is
released through the extremities of fingers, feet, torso and head, thus creating a psychological perception whereby the movements are extended beyond physical confines of the dancer.[30]

A gesture that Mariam frequently makes while performing is to single out an
audience member by pointing her finger or her fan at him. If Mohd's point is
appropriated, such a gesture suggests that Mariam's mesmeric power over her
spectators is also located in her ability to extend psychological energies to
them. Her potency as a performer is as much to do with her beauty as it is her
ability to "transfix" her audience in a conjoined moment of ecstasy.[31] Through
the agency of dance, Mariam is able to transcend both physical and symbolic
boundaries that otherwise confine her bodily expressions and significations.
On stage, not only is she able to break away from the ideological limitations
imposed on women, she is able to manipulate space and energy to "control"
men. But as Badley maintains, the fantastic body of dance is ultimately and
"tragically conscious of its material finitude."[32] Beyond the space of the performing stage, she is a woman entrapped, victimized, and finally punished,
perhaps for daring to extend her stage persona to her everyday being.

Mariam's transformation into a *pontianak* (and later, Maria's possession),
following this argument, can thus be construed as the exaggerated culmina-
tion of the body in dance. Mariam's tragic finitude finds expression beyond
natural materiality, and gains further potency through the guise of the vampire. After all, vampirism and dancing share a similar quality in that they are
both interstitial spaces; both are "sites" through which the repressed body can
find potent articulations of power and subjectivity. Traditional Malay dances
such as the *mak yong*, which are usually performed to appease angry spirits,
become instead deployed in the film to provide a gateway through which a
wronged spirit can return and demand reparation. Yet interestingly, this is
fundamentally in keeping with the function of traditional Malay dances as a
method of communicating with spirits and as a cure. It is finally through
dance that healing comes to Marsani and the restless Mariam. In the final
scene of the film, Marsani, dressed in traditional dance gear (and wearing the
stolen tiara), confronts Maria, whom he believes to be the *pontianak*.

I read this curious gesture as Marsani taking matters into his own hands
through an attempt at defeating the *pontianak* through dance. For the Malays,
being haunted is a form of "sickness," which relegates the patient outside his
community. One form of cure is through the ministration of dance. In Barbara Wright's study of Kelantanese dances, she notes that dances such as *main
pateri* are usually performed to invoke healing. The patient is actively cajoled
into partaking in the dance, guided by the *To' Pateri* (the *bomoh*, or spiritual

teacher), so that he is engaged in his own healing and reintegration into society.[33] Marsani's action, in this sense, affirms such a belief, although his real intent was to "destroy" Mariam. During the confrontation, the *pontianak* overcomes Marsani and his family (who has by then arrived on the scene) and threatens to kill Anna. In an effort to save her, Marsani finally apologizes and confesses his crime, with a promise that he will make the necessary amends. A beautiful, surrealistic scene follows in which Marsani and Mariam are seen dancing together, their movements harmoniously paralleled, suggesting that reparation has been made, and that the two ill-fated "lovers" have made peace. Indeed, Marsani's dance may be enacted in order to destroy, but the outcome—in keeping with the traditional function of dance—is healing instead. His "dance" with Mariam implies his redemption, and directly, his reentry into the community of friends from whom he has become estranged because of the evil he has committed. (During the confrontation, Marsani's confession is also witnessed by the spirits of Danial, Laila, and Sitam.) Soon after this, we are informed that Marsani has passed on, and that Maria has disappeared without a trace.

It is telling that Marsani decides to exorcise the vampire himself and not seek the assistance of a Malay shaman, or *bomoh*, who usually specializes in spirit communication.[34] This is perhaps the narrative's way of emphasizing the woman's role and responsibility in seeking retribution and reparation, and that she achieves this on *her own terms*. To posit a *bomoh* as mediator would directly compromise her agency, because it would imply that it is only through the agency of another man (a *bomoh* is invariably male) that she can attain justice. At the same time, the mediation of the *bomoh* would not have compelled Marsani to exhibit abject remorse and to confess not only his crimes, but the lies he has fed to his family. Finally, the presence of the *bomoh* would also indirectly insinuate that the *pontianak*, if not exactly evil, is in the end, still a menacing presence that must be "dealt with" and sent on its way. This would again reify the male=good versus female=evil binarism. The eliding of the *bomoh's* intervention in *Pontianak HSM* is, in my opinion, fundamentally in line with the sympathetic representation of the vampire, and a critique of patriarchal hypocrisy.

CONCLUSION

The *pontianak* is an enigmatic creature who resists the technology of visual pleasure that would reduce her to a fetish. In *Pontianak HSM*, retributive and reparative agency remains Mariam's alone. Yet despite the evidently sensitive

portrayal of the wronged woman, the narrative continues, in the end, to struggle with the representation of the duality that Malay women embody. In
terms of the *akal* and *nafsu* binarism, despite my argument that it is the men
who are clearly invested with the latter, resulting in their cruelty and animalistic lust (*nafsu binatang*, a term Mariam uses for her would-be rapists),
Mariam's eventual transformation into the *pontianak* can be read as an excessive manifestation of passion (extreme hate) as well. Whether it is the act of
killing an innocent person, or seducing an innocent man, the *pontianak* is re-
playing the attributions of *nafsu* that, in woman, is potentially dangerous and
uncontrollable. Also, Maria's portrayal remains a contentious point: her
timidity and reticence (unless possessed by Mariam) reestablish the image of
the ideal Malay woman. Her being haunted and manipulated by a vengeful
creature reifies, unfortunately, the good woman–bad woman logic. Such inconsistencies, however, are difficult to manage because of the entrenched ideological interpellations that construct Malay gender and sexuality. Women
continue to occupy limited spaces and struggle to find articulation, and the
portrayal of "good" but seductive and castrating women will certainly violate
the strict guidelines for Malaysian filmmaking provided by the Film Censorship Board (*Lembaga Penapisan Filem* [*LPF*]).[35] To circumvent this, Baba
casts such a woman as a vampire, but in a sympathetic manner to highlight,
metaphorically, the plight of women subjected to an often hypocritical social
system. As such, Baba's work is commendable, because despite having to work
within rigid regulations, she has managed to produce a text both eerie and
beautiful, subtle but critically resonant.

NOTES

1. The words *harum sundal malam* can literally be translated as "night scent of the
harlot." Indeed, this title suggests potent, illicit sexuality.

2. While preparing this paper, I spoke to an academic versed in Malay folklore, and
he explained to me that the eggs would symbolize, for the dead woman, her lost child;
tricked thus into believing that she has her child with her, she will therefore not manifest as a *pontianak*. According to another version, though, this egg-placing strategy
does not prevent the woman from turning into a vampire, but merely renders her
flightless: "it is thus restricted to walking, thereby losing some of its supernatural powers; its inability to fly renders it less dangerous and makes the task of catching humans
more difficult" (Nicolette Yeo, *Old Wives' Tales: Fascinating Tales, Beliefs and Superstitions of Singapore and Malaysia*, Singapore: Times Editions, 2004, 82).

3. Walter William Skeat, *Malay Magic: Being an Introduction to the Folklore and
Popular Religion of the Malay Peninsula* (1900) (New York: Dover Publication, 1967),
325–326.

4. Aihwa Ong calls such a creature a "birth demon" in "The Production of Possession: Spirits and the Multinational Corporation in Malaysia," *American Ethnologist* 15. 1 (1988): 31.

5. For example, see Nina Aubrech's *Our Vampires, Ourselves* (Chicago: University of Chicago Press, 1994) for a discussion of the shifting meanings of the vampire in American culture.

6. The earliest *pontianak* film, *Pontianak* (1957), which is now lost, actually detracts from the folklore quite substantially. In this narrative, a woman transforms into a *pontianak* as the result of a snake bite.

7. All together there are about eleven *pontianak* films made in Malaysia: *Pontianak* (1957), *Dendam Pontianak* (*The Pontianak's Vengeance*, 1957), *Sumpah Pontianak* (1958), *Anak Pontianak* (1958), *Pontianak Kembali* (*The Pontianak Returns*, 1963), *Pontianak Gua Musang* (*Pontianak of Civet Cave*, 1964), *Pusaka Pontianak* (*The Pontianak's Inheritance*, 1965), *Pontianak* (1974), *Pontianak Harum Sundal Malam* (2004), *Pontianak Menjerit* (*Scream of the Pontianak*, 2005), and *Pontianak Harum Sundal Malam II* (2006).

8. One example of a *pontianak* film that capitalizes on her evil is the 1974 production *Pontianak*.

9. The *penanggalan* (from the word *tanggal*, "to detach") is not a spirit but the result of black magic. Curiously, in *Anak Pontianak*, it is a doctor schooled in Western medicine who transforms himself into a *penanggalan* (using potions), overtly foregrounding the East vs. West/tradition vs. modernity binarisms. This doctor has designs on the woman who is attached to the *pontianak's* son, and uses his diabolical skills to remove anyone who stands in his way.

10. In my discussion of *Pontianak Harum Sundal Malam* below, I will consider some issues of female victimization.

11. Barbara Creed's theory (see *The Monstrous-Feminine: Film Feminism, Psychoanalysis* (London: Routledge, 1993) has received consistent criticism. For example, see Cynthia Freeland's *The Naked and the Undead: Evil and the Appeal of Horror* (Colorado: Westview Press, 2000).

12. Timothy K. Beal, *Religion and Its Monsters* (London and New York: Routledge, 2002), 165.

13. Malay femininity includes aspects such as domesticity, motherhood, passivity, and obedience, among others. For detailed discussion on the construction of the Malay woman, see Aihwa Ong (1990) and Lucy Healey (1994).

14. The "ban" on supernatural Malay films may be the unconscious result of an increasing number of "possession" episodes among factory girls in the 1970s. Ong (1988) argues that Malay women are especially susceptible to spiritual influences during the transitional periods between life phases (for example, from girlhood to womanhood, from a domestic environment to employment), and the high number of possession occurrences may be correlated to an increasing number of kampong girls entering the workforce, as encouraged by the government to boost the country's rapid economic growth. Perhaps to downplay or undermine the growing concern for such a "problem," representations of the supernatural became a target for censorship, citing "anti-Islamic" contents as the reason. For other studies on "possession" episodes

of factory girls, see Susan Ackerman's and Raymond Lee's "Communication and Cognitive Pluralism in a Spirit Possession Event in Malaysia" (1981) and Vincent Crapanzano's introduction in *Case Studies in Spiritual Possession* (1977). *Pontianak HSM* proved to be highly successful, winning awards both nationally and internationally, including Best Director, Best Cinematography, and Best Music Score at the Estepona Fantasy and Terror Film Festival.

15. "The *bonang* is a made up of a set of small knobbed gongs which are placed horizontally on a rack in two rows"—information derived from www.musicmall-asia .com/malaysia/instruments/bonang.html (accessed November 30, 2006).

16. This is a point of contention in the film. When the narrative temporally shifts, it is to the present (*sekarang*), which, if taken literally to correspond with the production of the film, would be 2004. This is not possible in view of the fact that Maria, Mariam's daughter, would be in her fifties, when in the film she is merely a teenager. Alternatively, it is, of course, possible to construe her "youth" as attributable to her *pontianak* status. But this is also problematic, as Maria is oblivious of her past and is clearly haunted by the *pontianak* who uses her body to tempt and destroy Marsani's family.

17. Linda Badley, *Film, Horror, and the Body Fantastic* (Westport and London: Greenwood Press, 1995), 26, 35.

18. Gaik Cheng Khoo, *Reclaiming Adat: Contemporary Malaysian Film and Literature* (Toronto and Vancouver: UBC Press, 2006), 6.

19. Jahan Karim Wazir, "Introduction: Emotions in Perspective," in *Emotions of Culture: A Malay Perspective*, ed. Wazir J. Karim (Oxford and Singapore: Oxford University Press, 1990), 14.

20. Aihwa Ong, "State Versus Islam: Malay Families, Women's Bodies, and the Body Politic in Malaysia" (1990), in *Bewitching Women, Pious Men: Gender and Body Politics in Southeast Asia*, eds. Aihwa Ong and Michael G. Peletz (Berkeley: University of California Press, 1995), 163.

21. Khoo, *Reclaiming Adat*, 137. For an excellent and detailed analysis of *adat* and *nafsu*, see Michael Peletz's essay "Neither Reasonable nor Responsible: Contrasting Representations of Masculinity in a Malay Society" (1994), in *Bewitching Women, Pious Men: Gender and Body Politics in Southeast Asia*, eds. Aihwa Ong and Michael G. Peletz (Berkeley: University of California Press, 1995), 76–123.

22. Khoo, *Reclaiming Adat*, 137.

23. Ong, "State Versus Islam," 166.

24. Khoo, *Reclaiming Adat*, 137.

25. Interestingly, Anna does not suffer the same fetishizing effect, which can be explained by the fact that the more modern Malaysia is more conscientious of typecasting women. But the narrative offsets Anna's "threat" by casting a non-Malay woman (Kavitha Sidhu Kaur—the first Malaysian woman to win an international beauty contest [Miss Charm International, 1990])—to play her role. In fact, it is not even clear from the film if Anna is a Malay or a Muslim.

26. Lucy Healey, "Modernity, Identity and Constructions of Malay Womanhood," in *Modernity and Identity: Asian Illustration*, ed. Alberto Gomes (Victoria, Australia: La Trobe University Press, 1994), 109.

27. Slavoz Žižek, *Enjoy Your Symptoms: Jacques Lacan in Hollywood and Out* (New York and London: Routledge, 1992), 201–202.

28. Ong, "Production of Possession," 38.

29. The *mak yong* is a court dance drama, although not exclusively associated with the court, that originated from Patani, now part of Southern Thailand. This dance is often enacted during occasions such as after a padi harvest (as a thanksgiving gesture), to placate spirits, and to celebrate important days such as the Sultan's birthday. For a detailed analysis and elaboration of this dance form, see Chouse Nasuruddin Mohd, *The Malay Dance* (1995).

30. Ghouse Nasuruddin Mohd, *Malay Dance* (Kuala Lumpur: Dewan Bahasa dan Pustaka, 1995), 15.

31. This ability will later be deployed for dangerous ends, however, by the *pontianak*. Azmadi is cursed precisely through such a gesture—the extension of the dancer's sublime energy to destroy an enemy.

32. Badley, *Film, Horror, and the Body Fantastic*, 35.

33. Barbara S. Wright, "Dance Is the Cure: The Arts as Metaphor for Healing in Kelantanese Malay Spirit Exorcism," *Dance Research Journal* 12.2 (1980): 8.

34. In fact, *bomoh*s very seldom appear in *pontianak* films. For discussion of the role of the *bomoh* in Malay culture, see Taib Osman Mohd's "The Bomoh and the Practice of Malay Medicine" and "Patterns of Supernatural Premise Underlying the Institution of the Bomoh in Malay Culture" in *Bunga Rampai: Aspects of Malay Culture* (1984).

35. Guidelines include the film must not be too frightening, gruesome or violent; it must not be too "bloody"; it must adhere to religious sensitivities (including avoiding scenes that depict bodies rising from the grave); and that there should be a "moral" to the story, preferably in the form of a "noble gesture" or an element of "goodness" prevailing.

12

Becoming-Death: The Lollywood Gothic of Khwaja Sarfraz's *Zinda Laash (Dracula in Pakistan* [US title], 1967)

Sean Moreland and Summer Pervez

$\mathscr{P}$akistani director Khwaja Sarfraz's film *Zinda Laash* (*The Living Corpse*) offers an ingenious deterritorialization of the spatial logic of anxious alterity implicit in both Bram Stoker's novel and early British and American cinematic adaptations thereof. As Peter Hutchings writes, "Stoker's original 1897 novel can be seen as a kind of invasion narrative in which the vampire, a mysterious figure from the East, threatens to invade both British society . . . and the British body."[1] Sarfraz's Dracula figure, Professor Tabani, is instead the product of an invasion that has already long since occurred. Rather than a racially and linguistically coded outsider, Tabani is recognizably a South Asian domestic, but one who bears stigma suggestive of a deleterious Western influence. Rehan, the actor who portrays Tabani, cultivates a Protean acting style that allows him to appear at times as a *Doppelgänger* of both Bela Lugosi from the American Universal *Dracula* (1931) and Christopher Lee from the British Hammer *Dracula* (1958). This method, combined with his Western style of dress and his abandonment of religious and cultural mores in pursuit of knowledge and power, renders him a striking embodiment of anxieties surrounding the long-term effects of British colonial control, Western cultural influence, and unchecked technological change.

Removing the Dracula narrative from the context of Orientalist xenophobia, *Zinda Laash* simultaneously reterritorializes the conventional story in a way that calls attention to the film's own ambiguous status as an uneasy hybridization of Western cinematic influence and Pakistani cultural identity, which is often perceived as threatened not just by the encroachments of Western culture per se, but also by that of India's booming film industry. In light of this double distinction, Sarfraz's directorial and Rehan's theatrical homages to Western *Dracula* adaptations also serve to distinguish the film stylistically

187

from its Bollywood contemporaries.² In the context of the general development of South Asian horror cinema, it is not until two decades later, with Bollywood directors of the 1980s such as the Ramsay brothers, the Bakhris, and the Talwars, that the region saw a wide range of popular horror films (Khan). Director Sarfraz's conception of a new kind of (horror) film for a culturally Muslim and regionally Pakistani audience was informed both by a desire to emulate the popularity of the British *Dracula*, which had played in select Pakistani theaters before *Zinda Laash*'s production, and a desire to produce a film markedly distinct from the influence of Bollywood.³

The reterritorialization of Dracula's distinguishing Western features is rendered explicit from the opening reel of the film, which places it in an ostensibly Islamic ethnoreligious context. Elevating the religious themes that underlie much of Stoker's novel in a semisubmerged state, the film expands their importance by resituating Dracula's mysterious origins in an explicitly religious narrative framework. *Zinda Laash* begins with the Quranic caveat that "life and death are only in the hands of Allah. There is no being in the world, whether of good or bad intention, who can challenge this right of Allah's. This film is the story of just such a professor, who with good intentions conducted experiments in order to gain power over death [translation ours]." Rather than employing disease-contagion or demonic possession as causal tropes, Sarfraz's film explicitly accounts for the origins of Dracula's condition in Tabani's quasi-alchemical endeavor for eternal life, represented as a Faustian event liminally situated between technological innovation and religious transgression. In this respect, Sarfraz's film seizes upon an oft-overlooked connection in Stoker's *Dracula* between the eponymous antagonist's living studies of science and his un-dead state. According to Dr. Seward's diary, Dracula "was in life a most wonderful man. Soldier, statesman, and alchemist—which latter was the highest development of the science-knowledge of his time. He had a mighty brain, a learning beyond compare, and a heart that knew no fear and no remorse."⁴ Reinforcing the link between Stoker's villain and other hubristically twisted examples of amok science (notably Shelley's Dr. Frankenstein, Stevenson's Dr. Jekyll, and Wells's Dr. Moreau), Sarfraz's Dr. Tabani incarnates the paradoxically magnetic attraction and monstrous abjection of these Promethean figures.

The centralization of Dracula's alchemical studies is one of *Zinda Laash*'s primary sources of narrative novelty. Previous versions of *Dracula*, particularly the widely influential Universal and Hammer adaptations, ignored this association altogether, and it was only visually intimated by the inclusion of alchemical symbols throughout Murnau's *Nosferatu*.⁵ Through *Zinda Laash*'s initial caveat and the scene that follows, this cause is unmistakably presented at center stage, both in terms of the film's narrative development and its mise en scène.

Following the opening message, the film's first scene reveals Professor Tabani raptly at work in his laboratory, a surprisingly Spartan set lacking the visual excesses of most contemporaneous "mad scientist" scenarios, consisting of a few bookshelves and basic chemist's apparatus, overlooked by a large stuffed falcon, with flickering candles lending a Gothic atmosphere while indicating the lateness of the hour. Initially, he is accompanied by his female companion/assistant, played by popular actress Nasreen. She is withdrawn from the next scene, as we see Tabani still hard at work in the same laboratory. The candles are gone, the natural light indicating that Tabani has labored incessantly through the night. His intent excitement indicates that he is close to the completion of his lengthy experiments. The almost erotic quality of his attention is particularly emphasized as Tabani's face is shown in a close-up shot, panting heavily and grimacing in grotesque enthusiasm. This feral expression is suggestive both of the highly sexualized *libido sciendi* that drives his experiment, and the linkage between this *haram*, or forbidden, experiment and the bestial condition that will follow his subsequent transformation.

As he prepares to drink the potion, Tabani utters the ecstatic declaration, "Today I have conquered death! I have conquered death! Death itself will die today. [Addressing potion] The sum of my life's work! Now I shall live until the end of time [translations ours]!" The frenzied affect with which Rehan delivers this line echoes Whale's Dr. Frankenstein's cry ("In the name of God! Now I know how it feels to BE God!") and reemphasizes his Promethean presumptions. This statement is immediately ironized by Tabani's cramping up and toppling over, apparently dead. At this moment, the camera's gaze focuses tightly on the stuffed falcon that was previously presented only in passing, revealing it to be mounted on a globe (the resemblance to the American eagle, as an icon of technocratic imperialism, clutching continents in its grip, is powerfully suggestive in this context). This figure, which becomes one of the film's primary visual motifs, suggests the doubly inflected becoming-animal—or more specifically, becoming-predator—that Tabani will undergo; this becoming animal is expressive both of Tabani's loss of humanity and the new appetites and powers that accompany this loss.

When his female assistant returns, it is to find Tabani sprawled on the floor before this grim raptor, a smear of blood below his nostrils signaling to both her and the audience the end of his human life. Encroaching upon the domain of the divine in his desire to banish death, Tabani is presented as having instead undergone a process of *becoming-death*, a narrative event that reflects Pakistani cultural anxiety over Western (and especially American) technological and military power by offering an uncanny visualization of J. Robert Oppenheimer's sublimely presumptuous statement "I am become death, the shatterer of worlds" (itself a quote from the *Bhagavad Gita*), upon witnessing the effects of the atomic bomb.

As the literary-cinematic icon of this anxiety, the film's adaptation of Stoker's *Dracula*, rather than a more typical monster of amok science, (such as Shelley's *Frankenstein*), is in itself strangely apt. In order to appreciate the significance of this choice, it is necessary to note that the term *vampire* is never used within the film; as aside from its popular incarnations in Western cinema, this legendary creature would have been a stranger to the majority of Sarfraz's Pakistani audience. The transformed Tabani is instead referred to as a *"bad-rooh,"* a folkloric term generally meaning simply an "evil spirit" (*Quranic Teachings*). Part of *Zinda Laash*'s infamy and appeal derive from the fact that both Islamic and Hindu folklore lack a figure that directly corresponds to the European vampire.[6] In this context, this creature's dependence upon the blood of the living exerts a singular fascination/repulsion for a primarily Muslim audience in that it literally embodies a transgression of the most sacred teachings of the Qur'an.

In a consideration of horror films through the lens of Kristeva's theory of abjection in *Powers of Horror*, Barbara Creed writes that

> [i]n relation to the horror film, it is relevant to note that several of the most popular horrific figures are "bodies without souls" (the vampire), the "living corpse" (the zombie) and corpse-eater (the ghoul). Here, the horror film constructs and confronts us with the fascinating, seductive aspect of abjection.[7]

It is precisely this intersection of abjection with seduction that Tabani's transformation elicits, and merges with the abjection/seduction of both perceived Western technological power (Tabani's alchemy) and British-American cultural influence (Rehan's adoption of Lugosi/Lee-esque expressions and mannerisms in playing the role).

Extending Kristeva's emphasis on the persistence of religious taboos in our construction of abject subjects, Creed (71) further observes that "[i]n relation to the construction of the abject within religious discourses, it is interesting to note that various sub-genres of the horror film seem to correspond to religious categories of abjection (blood, cannibalism, the corpse, human sacrifice)." This generality is particularly apropos of *Zinda Laash*, since the narrative logic that links Tabani's violation of divine law with his transformation into a blood-sucking "living corpse" draws on the centrality of blood as a sacred/taboo substance throughout the Qur'an.

There are two contexts in which blood is mentioned in the Qur'an. The first are the dietary restrictions to be observed by Muslims (5:3, 6:145, 16:114).

These inform the hyperabject status of a (formerly) human creature who subsists entirely on a diet of human blood. The second are the passages that outline God's creation of humans through various stages of transfigured matter, including especially "clots of blood" (22:5, 23:12, 75:40, and particularly Surah 96).[8] Here, *Zinda Laash* forms an assemblage between the bodily metamorphoses so often explored by horror film, and the Qur'an's uncanny description of embryonic development, which compares one stage of the fetus's growth to the physical appearance of a leech (*al'alaqh)*. This reminds the audience that, "as the developmental stages of the human foetus suggestively figure, we share common characteristics with our animal and reptile forebears."[9]

Through the sanguinary interference of his experiment, Tabani effectively inverts the Qur'anic logic that links God's transformation of a clot of blood (*al'alaqh;* in Arabic, literally "clinging clot") into a sentient being, by regressing from a man imbued with divine afflatus, to a soulless leech (*al'alaqh)* that sucks the forbidden blood of the living in order to perpetuate its *haram* "half-life." As subsequent events in the film hammer home, Tabani's boast that "now I shall live until the end of time" (in Urdu, "ab main waqt kay intiha tak zinda rahun ga!") will be realized as a spectacularly perverse mockery, as he lives (*zinda)* only as a corpse (*laash)* driven by a nightly logic of conspicuous consumption and compulsive domination that hyperbolically extends his (Western) lust for technological control over the conditions of life and death.

But just as the film's narrative framework resoundingly condemns Tabani's transgressive acts and their abject consequences, its visual presentation offers a celebration of Tabani's excesses, as the audience is itself ravished by the mesmeric gaze of this vampiric antihero, even as the film cautions against such seduction. While the narrative structure of *Zinda Laash* relies on a number of obvious binaries (good vs. evil, religion vs. technology, tradition vs. modernity), these are relentlessly interrogated and transformed by the visual logic of the film.

This ambivalence is emphasized by Tabani's next appearances on screen; his female companion has discovered his body and, following his instructions, placed it in the coffin he had prepared below for such an event. The camera focuses on his still form, which suddenly shudders into renewed animation, his hand grasping convulsively at his chest, drawn to the renewed spasms of his heart, which now pumps his altered blood through his body; his face contorts, and his canine teeth are revealed to have elongated grotesquely (an effect that echoes the Hammer *Dracula* films closely). As he sits up and looks around, a smear of blood appears below his nostrils, identical to the one that signaled his death, testifying to the violent trauma of his perverse "rebirth."

This scene is followed immediately by one that offers a visual inversion of the discovery of Tabani's corpse two scenes earlier. We see his female companion lying asleep in bed, clad in the (practically compulsory) low-cut white nightgown. She awakens and languidly yawns; as we hear the slow creak of an opening door, she sits up, startled. The camera follows her fascinated gaze as the reanimated Tabani appears before her, the pointed stigma of his new state on glimmering white display against his leering face.

The cinematography during this brief but important scene emphasizes the intimacy between the audience and the woman, as our perception is briefly welded to hers in order that we can be "seduced" alongside her. This imbrication is emphasized by a quick close-up on her eyes, ever widening in an ambiguous synthesis of terror and attraction that echoes Tabani's gaze prior to the completion of his potion. As he moves in, she leans back in a posture of abandon. The audience's identification with her viewpoint is reinforced as she closes her eyes, and the scene sinks into blackness, which is broken after a brief pause by the sound of her piercing scream, followed immediately by the film's opening credits. Tabani's seduction of/predation on the audience during this scene reinforces the connection *Zinda Laash* makes between the dangerous, transformative power of his experiments, and that of the cinematic medium itself, which is a viral vector for the technocultural contamination that Tabani so aptly signifies.

The vital tension that *Zinda Laash* sustains between its didactic narrative logic and visual celebration can be foregrounded through Gilles Deleuze's cinema theory.[10] Deleuze's cinematic exploration in *Cinema 1: The Time-Image* and *Cinema 2: The Movement-Image* is useful to an understanding of Sarfaz's horror aesthetic, as Sarfraz reterritorializes earlier Western representations of Dracula through the narrative structure in his version of the story, while also paying attention to the "primacy of corporeal effect," or the "affective" dynamic undergone by his intended audience.[11] Through his complex use of framing and deframing, *chiaroscuro*, and stop-action sequences, Sarfraz is able to offer numerous homages to earlier screen adaptations of *Dracula* while at the same time realigning the Dracula figure radically across national and ethnic borders.

An affective, Deleuzian reading of Sarfraz's film rather than a strictly narratological or psychoanalytic one is useful for an understanding of the director's transposition of Gothic imagery onto the Lollywood screen. In *Deleuze and Horror Film*, Anna Powell suggests that, rather than remaining distant from the screen as an "imaginary spectacle," a Deleuzian approach to film allows the spectator to participate in "the sensational continuum of the filmic assemblage," and the Deleuzian perspective celebrates "anomalous states of consciousness in film . . . both for their stylistic innovations and their affect on the audience who participates in the madness by affective contagion."[12]

Zinda Laash's incorporation of motifs from Western cinematic versions of Dracula and their centrality to the film's affectivity are strikingly presented in the next sequence, which echoes Harker's arrival at Castle Dracula in Stoker's novel. The camera follows Dr. Aqeel as he drives a scenic stretch of country road. The scene is accompanied by a lively symphonic score, a Pakistani rendering of Cesare Sterbini's *libretto* for Rossini's *The Barber of Seville*, evocative of lighthearted effect. This ambience is radically altered as Aqeel arrives at Tabani's starkly brooding estate. Upon entering this shadowy and cobwebbed abode, Aqeel's eyes are immediately drawn to the painted images of bats and birds of prey that adorn the walls. The audience's affective link with Aqeel is suggested as the camera swoops close on each of these images in turn, the close-up shot on each accompanied by a startling surge of music, and then back to a close-up shot of Aqeel's face, superciliously expressive of anxious fascination with these images.

Aqeel's fascination, once again highlighting the seductive logic of the gaze that links Tabani's vampirism to the power of cinema itself, anticipates Tabani's arrival on scene. Hearing a voice, Aqeel looks up to see a mysterious man clad in a long black cloak circling the landing above, and descending via a long staircase. This scene closely emulates the signature scene in the Hammer *Dracula*, which in turn offers homage to the Universal *Dracula*, as Lee/Lugosi descends a web-shrouded, stone staircase to greet his guest, "Renfield." Sarfraz's version, however, eliminates much of the hyperbolically Gothic imagery of Browning's film, while retaining the dramatic irony that pervades the initial dialogue between the characters.

The dialogue that develops during this scenic homage is significant. Aqeel explains to Tabani that he has "heard strange things about this place," particularly that "the undead [*bad-rooh*, evil spirits] walk here [translation ours]." Tabani responds, "I am one of the undead," but Aqeel takes this as a joke. Aqeel's refusal to take Tabani's mocking warning seriously, and his subsequent identification with and fatal seduction by the living corpse, here form an assemblage with the film's allusion to the British (Hammer) *Dracula* that had so recently "seduced" Pakistani audiences. This reinforces the critical continuity the film presents between the cultural contagion of Western cinematic influence on Pakistani society, and the affective contagion of Aqeel's/the audience's identification with the handsome antihero.

Deleuze is also useful for understanding the way in which *Zinda Laash* treats the interrelated elements of time and movement (the traversal of space), which assume significant roles in his overall characterization of the cinema. In *Cinema I*, Deleuze presents the image of pre–World War II classical cinema primarily as a movement-image, where time gets represented only indirectly, dependent upon montage and deriving from the movement-images themselves. But a reversal occurs in the movement-time relationship in post–World War II cinema: "instead of an indirect representation of time which derives from movement, it is the direct time-image which commands the false movement."[13] The war itself made possible such a reversal, as Deleuze explains:

> The fact is, that, in Europe, the post-war period has greatly increased the situations which we no longer know how to react to, in spaces we no longer know how to describe . . . what tends to collapse, or at least lose its position, is the sensory-motor schema which constituted the action-image of the old cinema. And thanks to this loosening of the sensory-motor linkage, it is time, "a little time in the pure state," which rises up to the surface of the screen. Time ceases to be derived from the movement, it appears in itself and itself gives rise to false movements.[14]

In other words, our shift in world-perception after the war—from a rational world of modernity to a postmodern world that is becoming increasingly fragmented and disjointed—can be seen reflected in the development of the cinema itself. Rather than continue to create a sense of overall rational continuity, filmmakers after the midcentury are more interested in depicting false continuity in cinema, more reflective of our very process of perception, in which "the images are no longer linked by rational cuts and continuity," Deleuze (ix) adds, "but are relinked by means of false continuity and irrational cuts."

Such "powers of the false" in cinema feature largely in much South Asian horror cinema. Directors such as Sarfraz in the 1960s and Shyam and Tulsi Ramsay in the 1980s and 1990s not only depict typical horror personae engaged in Deleuzean lines of flight, but through the use of time-images also create false movements in their films to reflect a particular state of postmodern angst that is appropriate to the genre of horror. Cinematically, this fragmentation is reflected in horror films, particularly in the deconstruction of essentialized identities of nation, ethnicity, gender, and sexuality in such a manner that their "internal contradictions, conflicts, and differences become visible and significant" in their mutation into horror personae such as zombies, ghouls, and vampires.[15] By depicting such conflicts in his film, Sarfraz makes self-conscious use of both Hollywood and Bollywood conventions, ultimately generating a new transnational mode of cultural production within Pakistani cinema.

Sarfraz's film both reproduces and critically comments upon the ubiquitous powers of the false associated with postwar cinema. One of the most subtly striking instances of this occurs in *Zinda Laash* as Aqeel, already bitten and on the verge of his own becoming-predator, descends into the vault of Tabani's mansion, seeking to destroy his un-dead antagonists as they sleep away the day. Moving through a dimly lit corridor, Aqeel casts a double shadow, which extends both ahead of and behind his in-transition body. Presenting his imminent passage between states (life and death), this visualization not only creates a state of affective anxiety in the spectator, but also suggests the false movement that arises from the un-dead's disruption of linear temporal progression. This link between the living corpse and postwar cinema's powers of the false also informs the use of time-lapse photography in Tabani's death scene at the end of *Zinda Laash*, discussed below.

Through an affective analysis of Sarfraz's film, which attends to images, sounds, and movements as forms of embodied thought, the narrative constraints imposed by the film are imploded. Deleuze's "opsigns" and "sonsigns" are "pure optical and/or sound situations"[16] that break from the narrative drive of the movement/action image to produce a "moment of pure contemplation"[17] for the viewer. Such an approach reveals that, while the film perpetuates a moralizing and moral representation of reality, it also challenges this conception through its visual and auditory emphases on molecular becoming. While such "becomings themselves," Powell explains (78), "are traditionally positioned as the source of horror," for Deleuze, "rather than the horror of an abject, polarized other, both beauty and terror are located in the transformative condition."

This is figured by Tabani's presentation as an object of desire in the film. His libidinal appeal for the film's female characters (and, even more provocatively, given the film's Islamic context, for Aqeel) becomes a vital synthesis of beauty and terror. The film later visually reinforces this ambivalence in the lengthy car-chase sequence that immediately precedes its conclusion, during which Aqeel's brother pursues Tabani back to his lair. This sequence particularly highlights the fact that it is Tabani, and not his human opponents, who is the "romantic hero" of the film. Racing his latest victim (Parvez's wife Shirin) to his house of shadows, Tabani is shown in a series of shots that emphasize his triumphant smile, driving a blazingly white car that contrasts starkly with his pursuer's slower, black vehicle.

Once again, this depiction both invites and critically comments on the audience's identification with the darkly romantic, and technologically advanced, Tabani. His ambivalent monstrousness can be linked to Powell's (77) recognition that, in many horror films, "the intimacy between anomalous life-forms need not constrain the viewer to horrified repulsion, but initiates congruent becomings." Tabani's libidinal appeal reflects the fact that, having become-death, his altered body is fully able to accommodate the range of his transgressive urges. With his concoction and consumption of the possibility of eternal life, Tabani's experiment dissolved the borders of the self in order to reconstitute it (making him, in Deleuze and Guattari's terms, a Body-without-Organs) and his predatory assimilation of other characters merely extends the scope of this experiment. His old identity having emigrated, Tabani's new body is a plane of immanent desiring in which his own implacable blood-drive mingles with the death-drives of his victims, as well as the audience's drive for the pleasures of image-consumption.

Through the chain of infection that links first his assistant, then Aqeel, Shabnam, and finally her mother Shirin to his own becoming-death, Tabani embodies a process of virally aggressive cultural assimilation, visually anticipated through his association with the American eagle-esque falcon in the film's opening scene. Through this ambivalently coded process of expansion/colonization, Tabani continues to make new connections, or "become," by embracing the possibilities of continuing evolution.[18]

In addition, the liminality of the film itself and its seductive/repulsive antihero are vividly realized throughout by a unique synthesis of the sometimes hyperbolically gestural acting style associated with Expressionist film and the Bollywood/Lollywood conventions of music and dance. With its heavily eroticized musical passages (which, combined with its supernatural displays of violence, were sufficient to earn the film the equivalent of an *X* rating in Pakistan),[19] *Zinda Laash* visually synthesizes the *libido sciendi* of Tabani with the refigured sexuality of Stoker's tale, a reframing of desire that informs Sarfraz's incisive meditation on cinema itself, as the medium of both a perverse contagion and a liberating transformation.

Like Tabani's seduction of/predation on his female assistant, several of the song and dance sequences in the film reflect this paradoxical effect. In the first of these, which replaces Harker's encounter with the three vampiresses in Dracula's castle in Stoker's novel, Dr. Aqeel is seduced by Tabani's now-vampiric assistant. The seduction is conveyed by actress Nasreen's performance of a spastically sexualized dance, the movements of which are deliberately made unnatural; Nasreen bumps, grinds, hops, and twitches like a broken automaton. Unlike the easy fluidity of movement in a later dance sequence depicting Aqeel's fiancé, Shabnam, and her friends frolicking flirtatiously on a beach, Nasreen's dance is redolent of an evil eroticism emphasized not only by her bizarre bodily comportment, but also by the frequent zip-pans to bird and bat imagery in the room (again, images of becoming-predator) and the specific moment in which the dance is framed by columns or pillars as the camera moves across the room to follow the dancer.

The effect of this framing and deframing, in contrast to the intimate audience-character subject identification deployed in Tabani's seduction of Nasreen, is a deliberate distancing of the viewer from the dance as a reminder to him or her not to be seduced. Even Aqeel stands framed by a curtain, a corner of which falls in front of him, partly shielding him from the vampire's lurid invitation. In a suggestive warning to the eager-for-seduction cinema audience, this visual inoculation is overcome as Aqeel's passive scopophilia leads to his being helplessly enfolded in the woman's embrace. It is only Tabani's sudden reappearance that prevents him from becoming her prey. The scene following this dance sequence closely resembles Hammer's *Horror of Dracula*, where the vampiric seductress played by Valerie Gaunt is prevented by a possessive Christopher Lee from feasting on his dinner guest (Hyde). Without resorting to an allegorical reading of the scene, it is worth noting the parallel this triangular encounter suggests between Aqeel (the audience), Nasreen (a perverse impersonation of Bollywood conventions), and Western cinematic influence (Rehan's Christopher Lee-esque performance). In Sarfraz's film, Aqeel is then bitten by Tabani, but manages to ward him off with the aid of the rising sun, to return to the all-too-temporary safety of his room.

The film continues to develop the logic of visual contagion slightly later, during a scene that takes place in the lounge of a hotel, as a crowd of people watch the performance of a band and a dancer, hired by the hotel management per cultural tradition across Middle Eastern nations, including Pakistan, in the 1960s. This scene provides a comment on the film's cultural hybridity by presenting a band playing Western instruments—such as bass, guitar, and saxophone—while the music that accompanies their performance notably features South Asian instruments, not visually represented, but played by the same symphonic orchestra responsible for the entire score of the film.[20] Aqeel's fiancé, whose centrality to the narrative was anticipated by Tabani's admiration of Aqeel's photograph of her earlier, is present in the audience, and quickly becomes the camera's focus. Previously the *object* of Tabani's desiring gaze, Shabnam is presented in this scene as the *subject* of a comparable gaze. As the band plays, another and more culturally customary dance scene occurs. In stark contrast to the unsettlingly spasmodic quality of Nasreen's earlier performance, this dance fluidly combines traditional belly-dancing with elements of the twist, all to the backdrop of modern Egyptian music. The camera focuses first on the dancer herself, and then on Shabnam's apprehension of the dancer. Her look of intent fascination echoes the erotic intensity of Tabani's gaze, first at his potion and then at his assistant, who subsequently reproduces this predatory gaze while attempting to seduce Aqeel.

Shabnam's eventual becoming-predator is intimated during this musical sequence by her fascination with the performance's cultural hybridity. Her inevitable seduction by the compulsively consumptive and quasi-Westernized Tabani is prefigured by her visual seduction here. This scene, like Nasreen's earlier dance, provides the audience with a visual prophylactic in the form of a series of framing and deframing shots, as we observe the dancer, and observe Shabnam observing the dancer, through a vertical frame suggestive of a doorway. This distancing device is subsequently explained by the arrival of Aqeel's brother with Shabnam's father, Parvez, whose viewpoint the audience has shared during this scene. These two then question the hotel proprietor about the sinister Tabani, an interrogation that will eventually lead them to search Tabani's mansion for the missing Aqeel.

The technique of framing and deframing becomes increasingly central in the film's final scenes, as Tabani chases Dr. Aqeel's brother (played by actor Habib) through his great house and eventually down into the vault. This vault is riddled with windows that contain no glass, but are heavily cobwebbed. These dark apertures suggest a space beyond the screen, gestured toward by the camera's attentive gaze and the corollary gaze of the protagonists, a dangerous space that is "out-of-field."[21] The implicit threat of this space is kept at bay by the fragile barrier of the cobwebs that partially block the eye, reflective of the prophylactic distancing devices employed by the film. During earlier visits to the crypt, both Dr. Aqeel and his brother pause to study these windows at length, but do not go through them, confining themselves instead to walking around and through the doorways.

In this final chase scene of the film, however, Tabani deliberately leads Aqeel's brother to and through those windows, suggesting the vampire's invasive fluidity and force in the face of his victims' helplessness; his perpetual motion, which "cuts through the barriers of space-time. The range of his movements is limitless and his impetus unstoppable."[22] This transgression of visually sequestered space again invites the audience to penetrate into the abject/seductive dimensions of the film, belying its narrative forbiddance, which like the pervasive cobwebs serves only tenuously to obscure these dark passages.

The film's contrastive play with shadow and light is intensified in its final scenes, providing a safe closure of the narrative within the moral framework of Islam. Tabani's *becoming-death*, or his desire for eternal life, already critically circumscribed by the film's opening *caveat*, is here foreclosed by the reassertion of traditional, narrative morality. Echoing the initial warning in Arabic and Urdu, the film reminds the audience once again of the ultimate power of Allah. As Tabani is on the verge of making Aqeel's brother his next victim, the latter calls out to Allah in desperation: "Yah Allah! Through the grace of the Prophet please grant me freedom from this evil spirit! [translation ours; in Urdu, 'Ya Allah! Apne rasool ke sadkay se ab is khabees se nijaat dila!')." Immediately following this pious invocation, a blaze of white light

Promotional poster for *Zinda Laash* (*Dracula in Pakistan* [US title], 1967). *ZINDA LAASH*
© 1967. Directed by Khwaja Sarfraz. Produced by Abdul Baqi, Hafiz Chaudhry, and
Qaim Hussain. Image reprinted by permission of BOUM PRODUCTIONS LTD. P.O. Box
6465, Bridport, Dorset, UK DT6 6DU, www.boumproductions.com

(which forces the audience to blink, as though attempting to awaken them from the cinema's vampiric seductions) shines down from the heavens; it is in these rays of divine light that Tabani finally disintegrates.

The film makes excellent use of time-lapse photography in showing the living corpse's gradual dissolution, as his features begin to flake away, until his entire body is reduced to dust, a stark reminder to the audience that Allah "created you out of dust" (Qur'an 22:5). With its compression of years of decay into a few screen seconds, the film's conclusion also embodies postwar cinema's "powers of the false," contrasting this representative technology with, and containing it within, the traditional values of an Islamic ethnoreligious narrative. Thus, Tabani's transgressive Body-without-Organs is undone by the organ-izing power of the film's radiant *deus ex machine.*

This destruction of darkness by divine light and dissolution of the cinematic powers of the false by traditional narrative, suggestive of Tabani's "purposeful trajectory of monstrosity" and initially offering a deterritorialization of the Western Dracula legend, is finally firmly reterritorialized within the cultural context of Islam. At this point in the film, its (and Stoker's) "conventional Gothic morality asserts itself." The "mad scientist," Powell (109) explains, "must be punished for dabbling in forbidden knowledge and unleashing monstrous forces disguised as 'nature.'" And yet, in spite of this narrative containment, the affective contagion figured by the film's un-dead antihero, like the visual and auditory celebration of his transgressions, lingers on. This residual affect informs the suspicion with which the film was greeted by Pakistani authorities and also testifies to its unique position in the history of both Lollywood cinema and that of Dracula's legions of screen offspring.

NOTES

1. Peter Hutchings, *The Horror Film* (London: Pearson Longman, 2004), 45.
2. While Rehan claimed not to have watched earlier British and American versions of the film, his performance of the role is at times incredibly suggestive of both adaptations.
3. On Lollywood, Chris Hyde writes: "Though it is little but a weak sister to India's powerhouse film industry, through the years Pakistan's movie operations have carved out a bit of their own territory in making films mainly in Urdu and Punjabi for audiences across that Asian nation. Primarily based in the city of Lahore, these operations are engaged in making a full range of entertainment for film fans in southeast Asia—though the production values as a whole tend to be at a somewhat lower level than their juggernaut rival next door. Still, Lollywood has proven in the past that it can produce quality pictures that are capable of standing on their own merits, though few of these are ever seen by Western eyes." See Chris Hyde, "*Zinda Laash,*" review of

Zinda Laash, November 11, 2003 (www.boxofficeprophets.com/hyde/livingcorpse.asp [accessed March 12, 2007]).

4. Bram Stoker, *Dracula* (London: Penguin, 1988), 360.

5. David J. Skal, *Hollywood Gothic* (New York: W. W. Norton and Company, 1990), 55.

6. Although neither Indian nor Pakistani culture makes reference to European vampires, several creatures are developed in both local mythologies and in horror films that possess features of the traditional vampire. These include the concepts of the *churail* or *rakshasha* (a female hag often in the guise of an attractive woman, with the unique ability to rotate her feet, who has died in an untimely fashion and for revenge preys on mostly young men via sexual seduction), the *bhoot* (shadowy and ghost-like apparitions that feed on the recently dead), the *gayal* (incorrectly buried and unsatisfied spirits that attack their own families), and the *brahmaparush* (ghouls that devour their victims by first draining and consuming their blood and brains through the skull).

7. Barbara Creed, "An Imaginary Abjection," in *Horror: The Film Reader*, ed. Mark Jancovich (New York: Routledge, 2002), 70.

8. I. A. Ibrahim writes that "literally, the Arabic word *alaqah* [*sic*] has three meanings: 1) leech, 2) suspended thing, and 3) blood clot" (*A Brief Illustrated Guide to Understanding Islam* [Houston: Darussalam, 1997], 6).

9. Anna Powell, *Deleuze and Horror Film* (Edinburgh: Edinburgh University Press, 2005), 68.

10. In *Cinema I: The Movement Image* (Minneapolis, MN: Minnesota University Press, 1986) and *Cinema II: The Time Image* (Minneapolis, MN: Minnesota University Press, 1989), Deleuze contends that the cinema, like horizontal philosophy, is an art form that is capable of deterritorializing the "rigid 'image of thought'" that dominates Western philosophy (Flaxman, Gregory, ed. *The Brain Is the Screen: Deleuze and the Philosophy of Cinema* [Minneapolis and London: University of Minnesota Press, 2000], 3). In these books, as in his other philosophical work, Deleuze engages in a process of concept creation—for philosophy is, after all, not a reflection of something else but the process of inventing concepts, or images of thought. On the whole, in his work on cinema Deleuze invents and classifies cinematic concepts consisting of types of images (perception-, affection-, and action-images in the classic cinema, and the time-image in the modern cinema) and the signs that correspond to each type. His ideas derive from Bergson's concepts of the movement-image and the time-image found in *Matter and Memory* (1896) and *Creative Evolution* (1907), as well as the types of signs advanced by the philosopher Charles Sanders Peirce. Overall, in these two books Deleuze makes the Bergsonian claim that the cinema works with these two complementary givens: "instantaneous sections which are called images; and a movement or a time which is impersonal, uniform, abstract, invisible, or imperceptible, which is 'in' the apparatus, and 'with' which the images are made to pass consecutively" (Deleuze, *Cinema 1*, 1).

11. Deleuze, *Cinema 1*, 2.

12. Deleuze, *Cinema 1*, 23.

13. Deleuze, *Cinema II*, ix.

14. Deleuze, *Cinema II*, ix.

15. Paul Dave, *Visions of England: Class and Culture in Contemporary Cinema* (Oxford and New York: Berg, 2006), 13.

16. Dave, *Visions of England*, 6.

17. Powell, *Deleuze and the Horror Film*, 77.

18. Appropriately, this evolutionary process unrolls in a "body without organs," defined by Deleuze and Guattari in *A Thousand Plateaus* as the *"field of immanence* of desire, the *plane of consistency* specific to desire (with desire defined as a process of production without reference to any exterior agency) [emphasis theirs]" (Deleuze and Guattari, *A Thousand Plateaus: Capitalism and Schizophrenia*, trans. Brian Massumi [Minneapolis, MN: Minnesota University Press, 1987], 154). As Deleuze explains with both Guattari and Parnet, such a body is "made up of different lines which cross, articulate, or impede each other and which constitute a particular assemblage on a plane of immanence" on which "particles are emitted and fluxes combine" (Deleuze and Parnet, *Dialogues* [Paris, Flammarion, 1997], 89). The opponent of the body without organs is the organism itself, or the "organization of the organs called the organism" (Deleuze and Guattari, *Thousand Plateaus*, 158).

19. In his review, Omar Khan writes: "The movie opened on July 7th, 1967 to big crowds as curiosity levels had reached fever pitch as the film made history as the only local release to be awarded an 'Adults Only' certificate. The clever advertising in the papers had filmgoers lining up to see why the film was deemed to be a threat to the fragile moral fibre of society! 35 years on, *Zinda Laash* remains the only local film ever to have been certified 'For Adults Only.'" See Omar Khan, "*Zinda Laash* [*Living Corpse*] (1967)," review of *Zinda Laash* (www.thehotspotonline.com/moviespot/bolly/reviews/xyz/zindalaash.htm [accessed March 12, 2007]).

20. *Zinda Laash* has a musical score that was, and remains, typical of Bollywood/Lollywood films. This soundtrack is traditionally played by a full symphonic orchestra conducted by a musician hired to create the film's soundtrack. Any singing that is done is the work of professional singers and merely lip-synched by the actors and actresses.

21. Deleuze, *Cinema I*, 14, 18.

22. Powell, *Deleuze and Horror Film*, 109.

13

Modernity as Crisis: *Goeng Si* and Vampires in Hong Kong Cinema

Dale Hudson

$\mathcal{R}$icky Lau Koon-wai's 1985 hit *Goeng si sin sang* (aka *Mr. Vampire* [Hong Kong: English title]) initiated a successful cycle of *goeng si* (stiff corpse) films that combined conventions from martial arts, comedy, and horror from Hong Kong, Hollywood, Japanese, British, and other commercial film industries. Drawing from Chinese literary and operatic traditions, as well as from international cinematic conventions, the *goeng si* is a transcultural figure that is generally known in the Anglophone world as a "Chinese hopping vampire."[1] *Goeng si* films provided a new attraction for Hong Kong cinema, one that translated into an exportable commodity for regional, if not global, consumption. With the cycle's exhaustion in the late 1980s, however, emerged a number of films that placed the *goeng si* in dialogue, and sometimes in debate, with the Dracula-like vampire from European/Hollywood cinema.

The aim of this chapter is to situate a few of such films within Hong Kong's crisis of modernity, preceding the transition of Hong Kong after 150 years as a Crown Colony to a future of 50 years as a Special Administrative Region (SAR) of the People's Republic of China (PRC), as well as within post–Cold War globalization. Specifically, Esther M. K. Cheung and Chu Yiu-wai define two patterns of cinematic expression of crisis visions in Hong Kong cinema that I would like to explore in relation to *Yi mei dao ren/Vampire vs. Vampire* [*One Eyebrow Priest*] (Hong Kong 1989; dir. Lam Ching-ying), *Jat aau O.K./A Bite of Love* [*One Bite, O.K.*] (Hong Kong 1990; dir. Stephen Shin), and *Goeng si ji sang/Doctor Vampire* (Hong Kong 1991; dir. Jamie Luk): "crisis emotions" of nostalgia, fear, and despair as discussion about the

I would like to thank Catherine Portuges, Anne Ciecko, Sarah Lawall, Sunaina Maira, and Sheetal Majithia for the comments and insights in the development of this chapter.

handover commenced, and "crisis bodies" bound to Hong Kong as a mutable cultural space that has been subjected to rapid transformations.[2] While the box-office returns for these films paled in comparison with those for *Mr. Vampire* and its official and unofficial sequels, I would like to suggest that these films pose questions about Hong Kong's crisis in a more urgent way than the *Mr. Vampire* films, moving from the spectrality of ghosts to the corporeality of vampires as the handover became imminent.[3]

As Rey Chow has noted, cinematic texts cannot be reduced to symptomatic expressions of their moment and place of production.[4] Nonetheless, I do want to make connections between *goeng si* films and the historical and cultural context in which they were produced, distributed, exhibited, and consumed in order to suggest that the film's potential political content might contribute questions that scholars ask of Hong Kong cinema in general, which have been framed by analysis of art films, such as the work of Wong Kar-wai and Stanley Kwan, or commercial films with higher production values, such as the work of John Woo and Tsui Hark. The emergence of *goeng si* films coincides with accelerated awareness of uncertainties and certainties regarding Hong Kong's future. A colony since the UK acquired a 99-year lease on the Xianggang New Territories in 1898 from the Manchus (Qing dynasty), Hong Kong's past, present, and future have always been entangled with events elsewhere in "Greater China," including the overthrow of the Qing dynasty and establishment of the Republic of China (ROC) in 1912, the exile of the Kuomintang (KMT) government to Taiwan and the proclamation of the PRC in 1949, the Great Proletariat Cultural Revolution from 1966 until the death of Mao Zedong in 1976, and the massacre of students rallying for democratic reform in Tian'anmen Square in 1989.

During the late 1970s and early 1980s, Hong Kong's identity fell into crisis when PRC premier Deng Xiaoping announced the "one country, two systems" idea in relation to Hong Kong, Macau, and, some argue, to Taiwan as well. UK prime minister Margaret Thatcher's 1982 visit to the PRC announced the first tangible steps toward Hong Kong's "reunification with China," which was made official with the signing of the Sino-British Joint Declaration of the Future of Hong Kong in 1984. Hong Kong would be allowed to keep its capitalist system for another half century (1997–2046), thereby maintaining one form of modernity that was often held in opposition to the monopoly power structures in the communist model of modernity advocated by the PRC. Nonetheless, Hong Kong would not realize postcolonial sovereignty in ways comparable to decolonization elsewhere; in fact, its status as an SAR points to fractures and fissures within Chinese modernity like the Special Economic Zones (SEZs), areas where neoliberal economic laws facilitated foreign investment, since the early 1980s. The departure of the British colonists would not bring the realization of the modern, sovereign, territorial nation-state of Hong Kong, along the lines of the nation-states that emerged from the Westphalian state system in 1648—only a few years, incidentally, after the Manchu conquest of China.

Abstract fears and anxieties following 1984 gained physicality after 1989 with the massacre of students in Tian'anmen Square. Images of their mutilated bodies were broadcast live via satellite around the world, visualizing Hong Kong's "crisis emotions" upon the surrogate "crisis bodies" of mainlanders. Fears of disappearance or submergence within the PRC, as well as anxieties over contamination and reemergence as never-a-postcolony, then, are part of the social context in which *goeng si* films emerged. Adding to the complexity of this "crisis," Ackbar Abbas has characterized the mass demonstrations of hundreds of thousands of the middle class in Hong Kong following the massacre as "a rare moment when economic self-interest could so easily misrecognize itself as political idealism."[5]

Since Hong Kong cinema addresses itself to audiences in Hong Kong, east and southeast Asia, parts of Africa, south Asia, Europe, and the Americas, the meanings read into its productions are multiple; thus, they cannot be reduced to a monolithic, collective response to Hong Kong's relation to the UK and PRC. Divergent audiences embrace *goeng si* films for still more divergent reasons. In Europe and North America, for example, the films have appealed to Chinese and other east and southeast Asian diasporic audiences, as well as to local fans of both martial arts and horror films. Stefan Hammond and Mike Wilkin, for example, write, "Our bloodsucking brothers from the East do not traipse about in capes flaunting Old World charm and seductively biting necks—although they do reside in coffins and have healthy incisors."[6,7] Cheung and Chu write, "The attraction of the cinema to fanboys and the like lies in its three-fold allure of the erotic, the exotic, and the kinetic," producing a vast body of "entertainment guides, along with numerous fan clubs, websites, and cinephile magazines" that "propel and sustain the consumption and global circulation of orientalist and stereotypical images of Hong Kong through genre film."[8]

Hammond and Wilkin, then, are invested in reifying cultural differences between "vampires" in Hong Kong and the "Old World," conscious that such constructions are cinematic fantasies. Moreover, their generalization, here in a description of *Mr. Vampire*, obscures variations within *goeng si* films. Characters in *Vampire vs. Vampire*, *A Bite of Love*, and *Doctor Vampire* do "traipse about in capes" like Count Dracula. The vampire's cape, of course, serves as an important, culturally specific prop in European/Hollywood vampire films, as well as films produced in México, Japan, Pakistan, and other places where culturally specific conventions of European/Hollywood films have been adapted transculturally. Like fangs, the cape physically marks the vampire as foreign, a phantom and potentially menacing presence from another time and place, possibly backward or retrograde, perhaps "premodern" or feudal, an immigrant, exile, or refugee that threatens to engulf its host culture.

In an era of global capital, filmmaking often must negotiate between the culturally nomadic and the culturally specific, "getting the mix right," to borrow an expression used in another context by Bollywood *masala* producers, in order to attract culturally sophisticated and culturally naïve audiences alike. Commercial films such as Hong Kong *goeng si* films have been overlooked in the greater academic attention to films associated with the new waves in Hong Kong and Taiwan, as well as the work of the Fifth and Sixth Generation filmmakers in the PRC. As Robert Stam argues, hybridity expresses itself, not merely through cultural objects, but also through its very process of enunciation, its mode of constituting itself as a text.[9] I want to suggest that the presence of the European/Hollywood vampire in Hong Kong cinema reconfigures fears of the handover to PRC into ambivalent anticolonial, antiforeigner, and anti-Christian narratives—ambivalent because they seem nostalgic for an era when different configurations of transnational (or perhaps even prenational) consciousness were still possible.

Vampirism and vampires are tropes and figures that have been adopted by novelists, playwrights, filmmakers, and other artists over the past few centuries to investigate and narrate modern subjectivities. Vampirism and vampires are, additionally, tropes and figures that have been adopted by theorists in critiques of political economy. In volume one of *Capital*, for example, Karl Marx writes that "capital is dead labour which, vampire-like, lives by sucking living labour, and lives more, the more labour it sucks."[10] In everyday journalistic rhetoric, the vampire extends Marx's associations in discussions of transnational media corporations. "It was inevitable: in the rapidly shrinking world of global entertainment, Hollywood was destined to discover Hong Kong," proclaims a US weekly news magazine; "Can a vampire resist fresh blood?"[11] While Marx uses the vampire as a metaphor to describe the most exploitative and undemocratic properties of capitalism, Michael Hardt and Antonio Negri use the vampire as a metaphor for means to oppose "Empire," their controversial conception of the post–Cold War world order of global capitalism.[12] "The vampire is the one figure that expresses the monstrous, excessive, and unruly character of the flesh of the multitude," they write.[13, 14] For them, "Multitude" opens possibilities within Empire's deterritorized and fragmented power structures of global war. It is within these contradictions internal to the meaning of vampire and vampirism—exploitation and resistance, capital and flesh—that I want to situate my analysis of *goeng si* and vampires in Hong Kong films. Vampirism may be understood as a trope for powerful modes of production within the global economies, particularly during an era of accelerated globalization when identities are often traded like commodities.

A TRANSCULTURAL APPROACH TO
TRANSCULTURAL PRODUCTION

Abbas develops the notion of *déjà disparu* to suggest "the feeling that what is new and unique about a situation is always already gone," so what remains is "a handful of clichés, or a cluster of memories of what has never been."[15] Abbas's concept of the *déjà disparu* would seem to resonate with Stephen Teo's reading of the centrality of Taoist priests in the narratives of ghost and *goeng si* films as indicative of "something of the values and ideologies which modern, even postmodern Hong Kong cinema seeks to negotiate, betraying the stubborn survival of pre-modern ways of thinking beyond the historical moment when they ought to have died, just like the cadavers."[16] Although academic attention to Hong Kong comedy-horror films has focused on ghost stories, partially due to their complicated relationship with Chinese literary and operatic traditions, as well as the production of ghost films by new-wave directors such as Ann Hui and Stanley Kwan, I want to suggest that *goeng si* films represent a neglected subject of inquiry—moreover, one that requires a different analytical lens. Although examining the films through a nonlocal lens, invariably, risks misrecognition, ignoring a group of films that were popular, not only with audiences in Hong Kong but with audiences throughout southeast Asia, suggests something potentially worse.[17] What I hope to bring to my analysis of these films, then, is not the sort of false consciousness imbedded in a sense of European/North American authority over Hong Kong films—the sort of criticism that Teo has termed after T. E. Lawrence's exploits in Arabia, "Lawrence-critics," but to work within the space for transcultural comparative analysis.[18, 19] In approaching the subject of the foreign character of the Dracula-like vampire—and, in the case of Hong Kong cinemas, the *doubly foreign* character, since Dracula is defined as foreign to the familiar English, Dutch, and US characters in Stoker's novel—I want to emphasize *appropriation* and *mimicry* rather than *imitation*.

Although critics have taken up *goeng si* films seriously, they have also dismissed the later films for precisely the reasons that I believe the films warrant consideration. In an otherwise analytical examination of *Mr. Vampire*, for example, critics might add evaluative comments; for example, "Gravitating from traditional Chinese beliefs about corpses, ghosts, and that Tao, subsequent films increasingly relied upon stock-Hollywood horror motifs and abandoned the creative mixing, matching, and mystifying of Eastern and Western cultures."[20] Cultures are already mixed and mismatched, both in Hong Kong and in Hollywood, which by 1989 had already begun to recruit talent from Hong Kong. Moreover, the mixing and mismatching have a long history that has served both Hong Kong and European/Hollywood cinemas. "The urge of the Hong Kong film industry to expand into the international market, to find a market beyond the traditional Chinese-speaking market, leads to the possibility of a construction of a global identity," explains Teo; "As the example of *The Legend of the Seven Golden Vampires* [UK–Hong Kong 1974] shows, there are instances when this attempt to find a niche in the global market may yield awkward results, albeit interesting to watch, because of the obvious attempts to incorporate popular elements from both eastern and western cultures."[21] Transculturality, then, is central to Hong Kong filmmaking.

In an introduction of the catalog for the 1989 Hong Kong International Film Festival, which focused on "phantoms," Li Cheuk-to argues that "it was not until 1974, following [on] the heels of the worldwide success of Hollywood's *The Exorcist* [USA 1973; dir. William Friedkin], that a sustainable, recognisable Horror genre emerged in the Hongkong cinema."[22] Ng Ho argues that *Mr. Vampire* "was a breakthrough, showing that Hongkong cinema had at last digested all it could from Western vampire movies and that it was moving on to inject genuinely local Chinese sources of vampire folklore," yet he notes that "Hongkong's 'vampire culture' is at best a bastardized one."[23] Unlike Western vampires, who "symbolise humanity's long-held desire for immortality, for eternity," he finds that Hong Kong vampires are "only 'hallow shells' of moving, rotting flesh." Like all transcultural figures, the *goeng si* destabilizes constructions of cultural purity (Chinese, British, English, Han) by foregrounding the resilience of what is often termed *contamination*.

A basic question in the study of *goeng si* films is whether "vampire stories" exist in China in any way that can be related to European ones. "With the exception of the legend of the 'Xiangxi Corpse Drivers' (Xiangxi is an old administrative region in Hunan province), it is almost sure that no one would have heard of a vampire story," writes Ng Ho; "I had once doubted that vampires existed in China."[24, 25] The "Xiangxi corpse drivers," a legend that remains unauthenticated, is significant:

> This strange practice of transporting cadavers seem[s] to stem from the desire of the Han people (the majority race in China) who have migrated to the desolate and mountainous regions in Upper Yuan River in Hunan. There, the Hans were in a minority. Upon death, the traditional concept of burial in one's native soil was adhered to among the Han migrants.

Because of the inaccessible mountainous terrain, the only way in which corpses could be transported home was through the method so described of "corpse driving," whose practitioners were—and still are—the Daoist *fat si*.[26]

It is unlikely that the significance of "native soil" in this legend, Stoker's novel *Dracula,* and its cinematic adaptations, in which "native soil" serves as a metaphor for Dracula's isomorphic tie to "nation" (Transylvania), is more than coincidental. Still, the legend provides insights into the ways that the *goeng si* and the vampire have come to mix in *goeng si* films. The figure of the *goeng si* is ideally suited for an analysis of Hong Kong identity, often conceived in crisis between despair and hope, disappearance and reinvention, threat and resolution, death and renewal, as well as of practices of accommodating the local and global markets.[27]

Although the term *Chinese hopping vampire* calls attention to the Eurocentrism, Orientalism, colonialism, and other racist legitimizations for the construction of an essentialized Chineseness in the Anglophone imaginary, the term also points to the transcultural as a productive site for resistance, negotiation, and invention. Allegedly, the term *hopping vampires* was a marketing strategy developed by Hong Kong publicists, pointing to strategic essentialism often necessary to gain access to regional and global markets.[28] Often accused of "regional imperialism," Hong Kong is a hegemonic cinema, which, like Bollywood and Hollywood, often downplays markers of national identity in order to accommodate to the expectations of divergent international audiences. At the same time, Hong Kong "national" identity is a misnomer in the sense that national identities are customarily conceived as bound to the modern nation-state. If Hong Kong digested all that it could from European/Hollywood vampire films, as Ng Ho suggests, then it may follow that Hong Kong *goeng si* films produced after 1989 regurgitated or excreted (to extend gastrointestinal metaphors, though other metaphors might be more appropriate) what was digested from these non–Hong Kong vampire films and put it on stage (on screen) with the European/Hollywood vampire itself; that is, Hong Kong horror-comedies were able to compete side-by-side with horror-comedies from Britain and Hollywood. If modernity functions as crisis, then crisis can be recuperated in productive ways.

MODERNITY AS CRISIS—HONG KONG CINEMA

Modernity in China is often understood to begin with the transformation of the Qing dynasty into a modern nation-state; that is, China's proclamation of sovereignty required submission to a world order dictated by Europe.[29] Hong Kong, however, presents a number of special considerations with regard to modernity. Chris Berry and Mary Farquhar characterize "the postcolonial postmodernity of Hong Kong—once a colony, now an SAR, but never a nation-state—as a temporal condition incommensurable with and particularly resistant to modernity's progress."[30] Dia Jinhua has written extensively about the changes effected upon Chinese cinemas in response to post–Cold War globalization, finding that the Fifth Generation filmmakers in PRC were caught between the preindustrial and the postmodern in a "typically modernist attempt to express the inexpressible."[31] About Hong Kong, she notes a particular anxiety in relation to the fading of British colonial democracy and rapidly changing yet constant centralized government of PRC that plays out in such a way that the "cold war 'national' boundary between Hong Kong and the Mainland marks (in reverse) the global division between the North and South, i.e., between global wealth and poverty."[32] Although Hong Kong (and Taiwanese) martial arts films express anxiety in relation to 1997, she finds that they became central to PRC's ability to "locate itself in the process of rapid globalization."[33, 34] More than the changes to the PRC with the creation of SEZs open to foreign investment in 1979, contemporary Shanghai and other cities exhibit slums and sweatshops in the shadows of postmodern office towers and luxury residences, much like Hong Kong, as well as the "global cities" of Tokyo, London, and New York before the collapse of Soviet communism.[35]

Despite its global significance and presence, Hong Kong cinema remains a subcultural ("weird, wacky, zany" or "popular"), regional ("Asian"), or transnational ("Chinese") cinema—one that is generally institutionalized as a "national cinema" or as part of "world cinema," rather than a hegemonic global cinema like Hollywood.[36, 37] However, as Anne Ciecko points out, "it is clearly time to redraw the map of world cinema and put Asia in the center."[38, 39] Meaghan Morris has argued that "dubbed into multiple languages, Hong Kong films circulate not only as 'Hong Kong cinema' or 'Chinese cinema', but as a vital part of the local film culture in particular places."[40] Although Hong Kong produces fewer films than either the Tamil- or the Hindi-language industries in India, its strategies for producing commercially viable and technically innovative films for local and regional audiences suggest a historical precedent for the "Korean miracle" of the early 2000s, though one without South Korea's state-sanctioned policy of globalization (*Segyehwa*). Unlike most constructions of "national cinemas" that define themselves according to modern nation-state-based nationalism in opposition to Hollywood, Hong Kong cinema is predominantly mainstream, with Hollywood serving "more like a model and a partner than an 'other' to be resisted, deconstructed, and repelled."[41] In the mid to late 1980s, Hong Kong cinema was considered "a 'marginal empire' with close relations to Hollywood"; that is, it was more complicit than oppositional to Hollywood.[42] In addition to Hollywood, Hong Kong filmmaking draws upon Japanese traditions of *chanbara* (swordplay) films, of *anime* and *manga*.[43] When difference is stressed, it is "difference from *the other Chinese cinemas*," as Cheung and Chu make clear. Hong Kong films represent Hong Kong, physically as Han ethnicity, and performatively as cosmopolitan, consumerist, and capitalist in opposition to the revolutionary realism and romanticism of the Third Generation "revolutionary film workers" in the PRC.

About Hong Kong cinema's representation of China, Kwai-cheung Lo argues that "Hong Kong filmic production is never asserted as a nationalistic entity against the universalist drive of modernization" because the "local," as a primary source of national identity, "emerges between the national discourse and the global structuralization and remains fluctuating and unsettled."[44] Teo observes that Hong Kong cinema since the 1970s projects an "abstract nationalism" based upon *tian xia*, the moral and cultural traditions of a motherland, rather than specific political allegiance to Hong Kong.[45, 46] Sui Leung Li argues that kung fu films expose Hong Kong's relation to its own Chineseness as ambivalent.[47] Bruce Lee's enemies, for example, were often nonspecific in terms of historical or cultural moment, particularly in export prints for Japan; nonetheless, Lee defeated his enemies. Films produced during the 1970s through 1984 exhibit an optimism that Abbas describes in terms of "colonialism seemed almost an irrelevance, no more than a formal administrative presence that did not interfere with the real life of the colony."[48] Indeed, Hong Kong offered little by way of natural or human resources to exploit until 1949; rather, Hong Kong served as a "space for facilitation" that was simultaneously autonomous and dependent, a place where "'premodern' and 'postmodern' join hands," Abbas (72–75) explains, "without having to acknowledge each other." Since Hong Kong is historically a temporary stopover for exiles and refugees from the Qing court, the Japanese, the KMT, and the Chinese Communist Party (CCP), Abbas (25) has argued that Hong Kong cinema looked toward PRC and ROC (Taiwan) for "legitimate history" until 1984. By the 1990s, most critics agree that it was no longer possible for Hong Kong filmmaking to rely on "pan-Chinese fantasies of authentic 'Chineseness'" or to ignore globalization, so that filmmaking adopted a "new localism" and indirect politics.[49]

Abbas argues that Hong Kong cinema is commercial by necessity (no state funding from the colonizer), but, since Margaret Thatcher's 1982 visit to the PRC to begin discussions of the handover, it is commercial while addressing "a public in the process of changing—a public suddenly anxious about its cultural identity because so many social and political liberties hinge on that question."[50] Hong Kong becomes the subject of Hong Kong cinema, he argues, since a cultural identity would be understood as a prerequisite for claiming political autonomy. More recently, Berry and Farquhar have addressed "cinematic significations of the national" in Chinese cinema, noting that "what is most crucially at stake" is "the production of the collective identity and, on its basis, agency," which is not "unified and coherent" but "multiply constructed and contested."[51] The commercial modes of Hong Kong distinguished its cinema from the "'prescribed' realist modes with melodramatic happy endings for different national purposes" of the PRC (class justice) and ROC (small-scale capitalism), Berry and Farquhar (12, 77) explain, so that realism serves as an aesthetic choice to serve China's construction of itself as a modern nation-state in both the PRC and ROC.

CRISIS EMOTIONS: CONTAGION AND COPRODUCTION

The specific historical settings of *goeng si* films establish the convention that the *goeng si* appears during times of political, social, and spiritual imbalance. Indeed, the emergence of the *goeng si* cycle concurs with a moment of imbalance in Hong Kong following the 1982 discussions of the colony's future. Industrially, the Shaw Brothers faced the new competition of kung fu films after achieving a virtual monopoly in Hong Kong's Mandarin-language commercial film market when the Cathay Organization ceased film production in 1970. Bare-handed boxing (*kung fu*) carries associations of Chineseness that the *wuxia* (swordplay or martial arts) film do not due to their appropriations of conventions from Japanese *chanbara* films and Hollywood films. In the popular imagination, kung fu is linked to Chinese opera, Taoism, antiforeigner patriotism of the Boxer uprisings, and populist Cantonese-language entertainment films.[52] Bruce Lee's decision to sign with Golden Harvest, rather than Shaw Brothers, announced the end of an era. Dai Jinhua has argued that the "emergence" of a special type of films during the 1980s and 1990s—the "classical-costumed tales of anecdotal history" (*guzhuang baishi pain*)—is really a "recurring cinematic phenomenon in the history of Chinese film, popular in times of social upheaval, times of anxiety and uncertainty."[53] The difference, Jinhua (85–86) points out, between Hong Kong martial arts films set during the late Ming dynasty or late Qing dynasty, as each struggled against collapse, suggests different conceptions of the modern Chinese nation-state: in the former, Han China under attack by non-Han forces; in the latter, the minority Manchu ruling the majority Han.

Comparably, critics have argued that vampires emerge in Hollywood cinema at moments of crisis.[54] Faced with the oligopolic control of Hollywood's "Big Five" studios, Carl Laemmle Jr. redefined Universal Studios (USA) in terms of low-cost features with classical horror monsters—Dracula, Frankenstein, the Mummy, the Invisible Man, Fu Manchu—as a means to forestall loss of studio control.[55] Hammer Studios' (UK) horror cycle similarly redefined the studio.[56] Its first vampire film, *Dracula/Horror of Dracula* (UK 1958; dir. Terence Fisher), was actually financed in part by Universal. The exhaustion of the Hammer horror cycle in the mid 1970s coincided with the "kung fu craze," particularly in the lucrative North American market. Teaming with Shaw Brothers, whose dominant position in the martial arts films had also begun to wane during the 1970s, Hammer coproduced *The Legend of the Seven Golden Vampires* (UK-Hong Kong 1974; dir. Roy Ward Baker), which it marketed as "the first kung fu horror spectacular." International coproductions between UK and foreign film companies were rare due to the protective stance of British labor unions.

Shot entirely in Hong Kong, *The Legend of the Seven Golden Vampires* stars Peter Cushing as Professor Van Helsing, who travels to lecture at a university in the provincial municipality of Chungking (Chongqing), the first Chinese inland port open to foreigners in 1891, thirteen years before the film's story is set.[57] Van Helsing learns of the "seven golden vampires" in a Szechwuan (Sichuan) village that has been cursed. A century earlier, Count Dracula had transferred himself into the body of Kah (Chan Shen), the high priest of the seven golden vampires, who had traveled to Transylvania in order to gain Dracula's support. While the faculty of Chungking University laughs at Van Helsing's superstitious beliefs, Hsi Sing (David Chiang) confides in Van Helsing that his grandfather had destroyed one of the seven golden vampires. Assisted and protected by Hsi Sing, his brothers, and Shih Szu (Mai Kwei), Van Helsing and his son Leyland (Robin Stewart) defeat the remaining six golden vampires and Dracula. Swordplay and martial arts are added to Hammer's battalion of traditional weaponry against vampires. Like Dracula, the Chinese golden vampires transform into bats, a Western convention that is generally considered unthinkable to Chinese, as matters of the afterlife require that the physical, human shape remain intact for reincarnation.[58, 59] Typical of the racial economies of British filmmaking of the time, only the white men and a Chinese woman survive.[60]

Teo interprets the coproduction as an attempt for both studios to reposition themselves in the international film market. "Shaw Brothers wanted to exploit the kung fu boom that came about due to Bruce Lee, while Hammer Pictures saw an opportunity to expand its influence and its market share in Asia," he explains. Examining the film as a text, he writes: "In the opening scenes, we see Dracula absorbing the image of a Chinese high priest. 'I will take on your image, your mantle,' Dracula says. The debate about globalization has centered on the question of the hegemony of the global North, US cultural imperialism, and this scene could be seen as an indicator of how globalization proceeds from the idea of dominance and repression." Globalization implies interdependencies, often uneven and unequal. Hammer's coproduction with Shaw Brothers, based in the British colony of Hong Kong, suggests a movement toward the transcultural along imperial lines. Comparably, Hong Kong production companies, such as Golden Harvest, sensed the exhaustion of Bo Ho Film's *goeng si* cycle and turned toward the transcultural, though along postcolonial lines. Bo Ho produced new films with European/Hollywood vampires.

CRISIS BODIES: *GOENG SI* AND VAMPIRES

One well-known example of a Chinese ghost story is the *Liaozhai Zhiyi/Strange Stories from a Chinese Studio* by Pu Song-ling (1640–1715), a writer and chronicler of supernatural tales known as Master Liaozhai. Written in a melodramatic style known as *chuanqi*, Pu's stories emphasize the division of mind and body—the *yin* is the world of ghosts and the *yang* is the world of humans—with the human body as a site for battles. Teo interprets Pu's writing style as resistant to the foreign Manchu occupation.[61] Ghosts and demons search for bodies to possess for reincarnation; and the dead take the form of abstract spirits, usually manifested in Pu's stories as *huli* or fox creatures, or human figures that imbibe life "essences" through sexual encounters. Ghosts were invariably beautiful women, who had died victims of injustice, often love gone wrong. For these spirits, peace comes through rebirth and reincarnation. The ghost story extends back to the golden age of Shanghai cinema, but Stanley Kwan's *Yin ji kau/Rouge* (Hong Kong 1987) became a popular and critical success that reinvigorated the genre by adding the high production values and stars of heritage cinema. In some films, the ghost is exposed as a hoax. History is not represented accurately but imaginatively as "a sense of loss."[62] The films suggest complex processes of recovery, preservation, and intergenerational transmission of this imagined history. Local identity, Berry and Farquhar write, is configured through the past in heritage and postheritage cinemas in response to globalized modernity.[63]

    Examining the ghost as a figure of "haunted time" where past, present, and future collapse upon each other, Berry and Farquhar (39) find that the copresence of past and future "destabilizes the very idea of a clearly defined present, which is the cornerstone of modern linear time." Not surprisingly, the KMT banned ghost stories and martial arts epics in its 1935 "campaign against superstition and moral decadence."[64] Clearly, the linear progression of modernity to realizing China as a modern nation-state was seen as disrupted by these harbingers of the past. They (48) point out that "opera film is a form of cultural nationalism that may be transformed by state directive into political nationalism," yet, until there was a version that valorized social revolutionary ideals, the PRC perceived the operatic mode as problematic due to "its feudal content and regional diversity, the flip side of the grand narrative of an imagined modern nation." While the KMT banned ghosts and martial arts, Berry and Farquhar (59) point out, the CCP appropriated and transformed them into the basis for a class-based nation-state.

Vampires, like ghosts and cadavers, are premodern, remnants of feudal and dynastic order. For Franco Moretti, Bram Stoker's character of Count Dracula functions like monopoly, so that "the nineteenth-century bourgeois is able to imagine monopoly only in the guise of Count Dracula, the aristocrat, the figure of the past, the relic of distant lands and dark ages."[65] Monopoly represents a feudal order, incompatible with ideals of free competition, and, for Moretti, nationalism, combined with money and religion, "coordinates individual energies and enables them to resist the threat." Monopoly capitalism, then, must be tempered by the modern nation-state. "Modernity conquers its foe," writes Steve Pile about the novel *Dracula*, "by its superior use of information available to its agents and by its superior craft—its use of technology."[66] Hong Kong films can equate excessive accumulation of wealth with a loss of humanity that manifests in the appearance of a *goeng si*. Ghosts are liminal figures, caught between time and space.

Gwai chui gwai/Spooky Encounters (Hong Kong 1980; dir. Sammo Hung Kam-bo) is widely considered the first ghost film to depict the *goeng si*, as well as one of Hong Kong's first horror-comedies.[67] Like *Mr. Vampire*, the film features well-known martial arts performers trained in the Chinese Drama Academy (as did Jackie Chan and Sammo Hung) in the role of the *goeng si*. The film establishes a convention of two dueling *sifus* (masters), Chin Hoi (Lung Chan) and his brother Tsui (Fat Chung), and introduces the cadaverous *goeng si* (Yuen Biao). The film's "unrelated sequel," *Gwai aau gwai/ Encounters of the Spooky Kind II* (Hong Kong 1980), was directed by Ricky Lau and starred Lam Ching-ying in the role of the "vampire-busting" *sifu*.[68] The two men would become nearly synonymous with *goeng si* films in these capacities.

The new-style *wuxia pain* draws upon the Japanese *chanbara* to reinvent itself as a film mode, imitating what is necessary yet maintaining certain Chinese traditions.[69] In *Mr. Vampire*, Kou relates that the *goeng si* is motivated because it was once human and may exhibit human characteristics such as vanity, vulnerability, and other foibles. Kou explains that a *goeng si* is the cadaver of a person who died an inauspicious death. The *goeng si* differs from a *sishi* (corpse) in that it retains an "extra breath," awaiting an opportune time to reanimate itself. Unlike the European/Hollywood vampire, which draws its victim's blood, the *goeng si* draws its victim's breath—a trait that is emphasized less in the subsequent *Mr. Vampire* films.[70] *Goeng si* are typically dressed in Mandarin clothing, have long blue fingernails and elongated fangs, and move by hopping with their arms extended. They are generally depicted as blind, locating their victims by sensing their breath. They choke their victims, often piercing the throat with their long fingernails. A *sifu* employs special powers, incantations, and invocations, called *fashu*, to deal with ghosts and spirits.[71] A *sifu* may "tame" a *goeng si* by applying a talisman, a strip of yellow paper onto which Taoist scripture is written, to the *goeng si*'s forehead and directing its movement by ringing a bell, or a *sifu* may destroy a *goeng si* with incantations, wooden swords, or dogs' blood.[72] The films make use of the operatic *liangxiang*, "a frozen sculptural pose that visually conveys 'archetypal images and emotions,'" such as defiance, dedication, or distilled hate—a pose that combines emotion (*qing*) and energy (*qi*).[73] The films accentuate martial arts sequences with fast editing techniques and special effects, most notably wires, erased during postproduction, that allow characters to perform spectacular feats in a technique often called "wire-fu" by fans. Musical cues and small pyrotechnics indicate the magic of *fashu*. Invariably, the *sifu* destroys the *goeng si* and cures its victims. The most spectacular fight scene comes at the close of the films, often followed by a brief comic moment. The films, as Ng Ho argues, are primarily concerned with the relationship between *sifu* and student, master and disciple, so that the *goeng si* serves as a situation in which this comedic conflict finds expression.[74, 75]

Produced by companies like Bo Ho Film and Golden Harvest, the films adopt visual strategies of costume drama. The *goeng si* is often dressed in a Mandarin robe, situating the "cadaver" as either a relic from the past or a marker of tradition, an ancestor whose soul must be put to rest to ensure the family's prosperity and well-being. The *sifu* typically wears a yellow Taoist robe, at least in the fight sequences, so that the narrative battles of "good versus evil" are visually represented through costumes. The films typically situate the crisis bodies of ghosts and *goeng si* within the comedy of human relations, often a playful rivalry between two male characters over the attention or affection of another character, such as a *sifu* or beautiful woman. Humor is both verbal and physical, with physical humor emphasizing the human body as spectacle in ways that invert the body-as-spectacle in martial arts films. Arms and legs may demonstrate physical strength, agility, and balance in martial arts sequences of *goeng si* films, but groins and buttocks attest to bodily weak-nesses for injury or excitement. The body comedy is typically framed for male spectator pleasure.[76] Like the martial arts hero in general, the physical strength and movement of the *sifu*'s body is endowed with the "ability to pro-tect positive social values," which "transforms his victory against evil into a reaffirmation of the system's legitimacy."[77] If the *sifu* tames ghosts and *goeng si* that appear in moments of crisis, the question turns to how crises are de-fined in these films.

Set in Republican China, the plot of *Mr. Vampire* begins with Mr. Yam hiring Kou to supervise the relocation of his father's corpse due to the bad *feng shui* of his present grave.[78] Yam invites them to discuss the transaction over English tea. Afraid he will make a mistake at this foreign custom, Kou brings one of his students to do things first. Yam's daughter Ting-ting (Moon Lee Choi-fung) orders coffee as an opportunity to perform her cosmopoli-tanism. When she learns that they are unaware of the intricacies of coffee drinking, she plays a joke on them. She sips the coffee, sips cream directly from the creamer, and eats a spoonful of sugar. The two follow her lead, much to her amusement. This scene introduces the film's slapstick humor, as well as Hong Kong's colonial ruler, the UK, through one of its most national prac-tices insofar as high tea was often a means for British colonists to maintain a sense of national identity. Yam is a businessman, whose transactions require contact with foreigners (Europeans), perhaps pointing to British control of several important ports following the Opium War, which effectively colo-nized a significant part of China's access to international trade. Michael Hoover and Lisa Odham Stokes have suggested that Yam might be read as "part of the Chinese elite that emerged in the nineteenth-century colonial Hong Kong, establishing themselves as successful merchants or as *compradors* for Western firms (*hongs*) operating in the territory."[79] The bad *feng shui*, then, may be read as a symptom of association with, seduction by, or enslavement to foreigners. Gina Marchetti observes that Hong Kong films set in Repub-lican China, as well as those set during the Japanese occupation and the pre 1949 civil wars, often allegorize the 1989–1997 period.[80] Just as in European/Hollywood costume dramas, slippages in the artifice of "historical accuracy" introduce contemporary issues in a dialectic of past, present, and future. Some films are set in the Qing dynasty (1644–1912); others, in Republican China (1912–1949), the period following the last major occupation of China by the Manchus, the foreign "nation" that established the Qing dynasty. Many films featuring martial arts as a means of combating *goeng si*, ironically, are set in the Republican era, when martial arts and ghost stories were outlawed as a threat to security, a threat to modernization. The imagination of "China" and efforts to construct historical verisimilitude differ from film to film. No longer divided, China is often represented as a single nation, often occupied by another nation, yet it is also represented as a nation that is politically, and to some extent culturally, divided. *Goeng si* films evoke a history, factual or fictitious, that contradicts any imagination of a monolithic Chinese cultural heritage and national identity—Maoist and Nationalist alike. Questions such as those concerning ethnic minorities and foreign intruders in China, as well as ethnically Chinese refugees from Vietnam into Hong Kong, become the context in which a *sifu* fights a *goeng si*. The post-1989 films that I examine imagine Hong Kong as a site of negotiation between traditions coded as Chinese and British.[81, 82]

COLONISTS DEPART, VAMPIRES ARRIVE

If Stoker's novel *Dracula* poses questions about "English" identity during an earlier moment of globalization, then *Vampire vs. Vampire*, *A Bite of Love*, and *Doctor Vampire* pose questions about Hong Kong's identity during a more recent moment of globalization. In these films, European/Hollywood-style vampirism moves from London to the much more economically productive Hong Kong, reversing the directional movement of investment capital, which by 1990 had begun to flow in greater quantities from Hong Kong to the UK. These films imagine Hong Kong identity as a site of intercultural encounters between traditions coded as Chinese and British through the films' representations of the *goeng si*, the European/Hollywood vampire, and, in one case, a "mixed vampire."

British vampirism enters China via Christian missionaries in *Vampire vs. Vampire*, and a little *goeng si* assists the *sifu* in his battle with the European/Hollywood-style vampire. Christian missionaries have a long history in China that can be traced to the Tang dynasty and that is deeply entangled with the bilateral treaties between China and European states following the Opium Wars (1839–1842 and 1856–1860) that, among other unequal benefits, removed foreign subjects from the jurisdiction of Chinese courts of laws; subsequent agreements required the Chinese government to protect Christian missionaries following attacks on Christians by Chinese nationalists, under the name *Yihequan* ("Righteous and Harmonious Fists," called "Boxers" by the British), during the uprisings against foreign imperialism.[83] Among a large body of anti-Christian publications, one pamphlet asserted that Western men drink the menstrual blood of Western women, accounting for their "unbearable stench."[84] In general, European powers used the attacks on missionaries to secure additional economic and political privileges.

Set in Republican China, *Vampire vs. Vampire* foregrounds the tensions between influences coded as "traditional" and "foreign" in China. Summoned to a village to diagnose its recurrent "problems," despite its "good *feng shui*," which promises "wealth and progenies," one-eyebrow priest (Lam) discovers a nest of bats hanging from the branches of a tree submerged in the river. The bats signal the foreign presence in the village, representing China as vulnerable to foreign contamination, particularly since the submerged tree is located near an abandoned Christian mission. Portraying the head sister is the well-known singer Maria Cordero, who moved to Hong Kong at age ten in the mid 1960s and began a career as a singer in the mid 1980s. Cordero was born in Macau, which like Hong Kong in 1997, officially returned to PRC in 1999 as an SAR. Cordero is not Macanese, a term that identifies people of partly Portuguese ancestry, but ethnically Filipino and Chinese, visually signifying the interconnections of globalization. Macau was "founded" (colonized) by the Portuguese in 1557 and granted the title of *Cidade do Nome de Deus, de Macau, Não há outra mais Leal* ("City of the Name of God, Macau, There is None More Loyal") in 1640. Although Macau was a major port of trade between China and Europe, its significance was eclipsed by Hong Kong by the 1840s. Elsewhere in the film, emigration from the colony is presented as a means of self-preservation. One-eyebrow priest divides the profit from some work with his assistants, Hoh (Siu-hou Chin) and Fong (Fong Liu), telling them that they can use it for their "future emigration to Guangzhou," the largely Cantonese-speaking capital of the Guangdong province in southern China, adjacent to Hong Kong, that was called Canton by the British who used the port to import opium into China. This extratextual introduction of Macau and Guangzhou is significant to the film's thematic displacements and substitutions for Hong Kong identity. Further presence of a European/Hollywood vampirism is discovered in a locked "meditation room" in the mission. European/Hollywood cinematic conventions—garlic, bats, crucifixes—are parodied. The head sister interprets garlic hanging from the ceiling beams of the meditation room as a means to exorcise ghosts.

The film's vampire, one of two dead mission priests, is later discovered in a grave by police authorities. Consistent with Hong Kong cinematic conventions that wealth is permissible but greed is foolish, a buffoonish general has his men excavate in search of "antiques." As his men attempt to retrieve a ruby, attached to a buried sword, the sky fills with clouds. When they unearth the sword, they also unearth the priest's corpse. The villagers want to burn the corpse and dump its ashes into the sea to bring "luck" to the village, but the general and his girlfriend take the corpse to their place. While freeing the gemstone from its mounting, the general cuts himself on the sword. His blood drips onto the corpse, which absorbs the blood, begins to breathe, and bites the general's girlfriend on the neck, its body fattening on her blood. The reanimated vampire is covered in mud, wears a black cape, and has red eyes and long dark hair, suggesting stronger visual reference to European/Hollywood vampires than to *goeng si*. In his attempt to "bust" the vampire, one-eyebrow priest discovers that *fashu* is ineffective: the vampire tears a talisman in two. One-eyebrow priest is saved by a little *goeng si*, initiating the "vampire versus vampire" plot of the English-language title. Unlike many European/Hollywood vampire films, particularly the Hammer films, in which the vampire is destroyed by sunlight, the vampire in this film is unaffected by daylight. Ultimately, one-eyebrow priest tricks the vampire into falling into quicksand.

Vampire vs. Vampire adapts and parodies generic conventions from both local and foreign films in conflict, so that it represents a transcultural text, much to the confusion of Western fans, some of whom question the "authenticity" of the European/Hollywood-style vampire.[85] The film does not speculate on the origin of vampirism, suggesting that an explanation resides, nondiegetically and extratextually, outside the film. If the *goeng si* in the *Mr. Vampire* films represents a perilous connection with a Chinese past—one that must be buried properly in order to ensure good *feng shui*, then the little *goeng si* represents a corrective connection with a Chinese past. This Chinese past, however, is not only cultural, but self-referential with the *goeng si* cycle, specifically the very recent past of the emergence of the baby *goeng si* as a figure in *Goung si ga chuk /Mr. Vampire 2* (Hong Kong 1986; dir. Ricky Lau Koon-wai) to assert a specific local (Hong Kong) identity and expel the "vampirism" of British colonization and Christian proselytism, as well as the potential "vampirism" of the handover.[86] Rather than propose a definitive position, however, the film, like *A Bite of Love* and *Doctor Vampire*, is critical of both British and Chinese authority, negotiating productively what can be gleaned from this crisis of an unsettled modernity.

In *A Bite of Love*, Hong Kong identity is a site of conflict between two cinematic antiheroes: the vampire and the triad (organized crime family) boss. The vampire Duke Lee (George Lam Chi-cheung), whose name suggests homage to Christopher Lee who portrayed Count Dracula in most of the Hammer vampire films, is a specter of the past, a romantic nineteenth-century antihero. The wheelchair-confined triad boss Fung (Norman Tsui Sui-keung) is a selfish twentieth-century antihero, who will sacrifice the life of his sister, Anna (Rosamund Kwan Chi-lam), to save his own.[87] The film's opening-credit sequence establishes the anachronisms of Lee's existence. Whereas Fung and Anna travel the streets of modern London in limousines and sports cars, Lee travels in a horse-drawn carriage toward a "gothic" castle, typical of those in the Hammer films. Costume design is self-conscious of cinematic conventions: Lee wears a wig of long gray hair; a white, ruffled shirt; black trousers; a black vest; and a black, high-collared cape with a red lining. Unable to adjust to the world as it has changed over the centuries, he is world-weary and lonely. Although he requires human blood to survive, he does not want to kill for it, so he drinks human blood acquired from a blood bank. As his servant reminds him, however, blood is expensive and his financial situation is precarious. Lee vows that he will not bite humans because it will transform them into vampires, undercutting the conventional associations of vampires with public health crises.

Despite its comedic artifice, *A Bite of Love* addresses issues about citizenship and contagion. The film introduces the legal status of "foreign" workers in London by calling attention to Lee's identification card. Not all Hong Kongers were eligible for British citizenship.[88] Before the handover, conservative UK politicians feared that two and a half million British Dependent Territories Citizens (BDTCs) in Hong Kong would immigrate to the UK.[89] Lee's masquerade, then, would seem a credible, if highly stylized, response to anxieties over the handover. Fung's condition is no less perilous. He suffers from an ailment or blood disorder that requires transfusions of O-negative blood, as does an orphan. At a local hospital, Lee cures the orphan by giving him a direct transfusion of his own blood, which is potent against human disease. Lee's altruistic act irreversibly weakens his vampiric powers, so that Fung is able to entrap Lee. Fung sends Lee and the orphan to Hong Kong in crates as airfreight, ostensibly part of Fung's drug trafficking. To escape, Lee bites Fung, transforming him into a vampire. Suspecting Fung carries the HIV-AIDS virus, Lee asks Anna whether she and her brother have ever "mixed" with foreigners.

The duplicitous Fung tells his sister that he has changed his ways and become "good." Anna was born on June 6, 1966, at 6:00 pm (in the English subtitles), a date and time of birth that makes her blood special. If Fung consumes her blood, he will become "King of the Devils." Aware of her brother's intentions, Anna consults *Fright Night Part II* (USA 1989; dir. Tommy Lee Wallace) to learn about vampire-slaying techniques.[90] She also consults a book on vampires in which she reads that her brother is a "mixed vampire" and that tears of sincerity are lethal to such vampires. In the final battle sequence, Anna offers her neck to Lee, so that he can overpower Fung. After an extended fight sequence in a subterranean chamber, the two vampires burst through the cement ceiling into the sunlight, where the bodies explode. Due to Lee's selfless act of self-destruction, Anna and the orphan will not transform into vampires. They are free to live as humans, as uninfected Hong Kongers. The film closes with Lee's vampire outfit beginning to glow with white light. Anna finds an infant, which, she is told, is Lee come back to life.

Her tears of sincerity over his act have freed him from the eternal life of vampirism and reentered him into the cycle of reincarnation as (an ethnically Chinese) human. Like Fung, Lee was a "mixed vampire," an ambivalent metaphor for Hong Kongers either infected or abandoned by their colonial rulers, suggesting the ongoing negotiations and contestations within Hong Kong's "crisis bodies."

Blood contamination is associated with cultural or national identity in *Doctor Vampire*. In the UK on business, Chiang Ta-tsung (Bowie Lam), a Hong Kong doctor, stops into a bar where female vampires suck the blood of their male victims, later allowing their white vampire master, the Earl (Peter Kjær), to suck this blood from their necks. Blood, here, illustrates Marx's concept of commodity fetish insofar as the Earl refuses to perform the labor of entrapping or seducing victims to procure a supply of blood. The Earl's enslavement of women suggests capitalism's "vampiric" exploitation of human labor. At the bar, Chiang sees an ethnically Chinese woman, who he believes is being assaulted by a white man. "You bully the Chinese," Chiang shouts at the white man, turning to tell the woman, "[the British] always mistreat the Chinese." The woman, Alice (Ellen Chan), is really a vampire; and the man, her victim. Alice takes Chiang to a private room, where she drinks his blood and transmits the vampiric infection. When the Earl drinks his slaves' blood, he is repulsed until he tastes Chiang's blood, which now runs through Alice's veins. "The blood is like your Chinese ginseng," he says before kicking her in the head, tossing into a fire a Taoist charm that Chiang has given her, and ordering her to go to Hong Kong for more ginseng-infused blood. According to the film's ostensibly anticolonial narrative structure, blood functions as a vehicle of infection for Chinese and a vehicle of nourishment for Britons.

The film's comedy pivots on intercultural and intertextual jokes about vampirism and colonialism. Chiang's nurse fiancée, May Chen (Sheila Chan), celebrates his return with a meal of ginseng soup and garlic prawns. He finds the taste of garlic repulsive, as it would presumably be to European/Hollywood vampires. Ironically, May's staple cuisine, the ginseng soup, is what makes Chiang's blood so alluring to the Earl. Chiang's transformation into a vampire is ambiguous and self-conscious, like that of Nicolas Cage's character in *Vampire's Kiss* (USA 1989; dir. Robert Bierman).[91] Chiang begins to believe that sunlight bothers his eyes. While shopping with May, he buys a pair of sunglasses, as well as a tuxedo and long cape. Outside the hospital, he waves his new cape to signal his movement in parody of similar gestures in Hollywood vampire films dating to *Dracula* (USA 1931; dir. Tod Browning). He drinks V8-brand vegetable (mostly tomato) juice through two straws, holding them in his mouth so that they look like elongated vampire fangs. Unlike Cage's character, Chiang acquires the supernatural power to influence telepathically others' movement. As Chiang begins to question whether he might be a *goeng si* ("vampire" in the subtitles), he hops with his arms extended to determine whether it feels natural to "walk" like a *goeng si*. His colleagues later give him a Mandarin outfit like the ones that *goeng si* wear in films. Chiang's identity crisis is visually represented through costumes and props, most notably the vampire film's black cape and the *goeng si* film's Mandarin robe. His identity crisis emerges in a comedic conflation of cinematic conventions for European/Hollywood vampires and Hong Kong *goeng si*. Fears of infection, whether the "English flu" (an inversion of the "Asian flu") or HIV-AIDS, are other sources of the film's jokes that imbed social critique within cinematic and cultural stereotypes.[92] Although blood contagions are potentially fatal, cinematic conventions can cocontaminate with rejuvenating effects.

The film, however, concludes with a confrontation between the Earl and the Hong Kongers. Alice, who has come to Hong Kong to save Chiang, sides with the Chinese characters against her foreign master. "Come back to me," the Earl demands in English. She replies, also in English, "We are not the same." Alice's statement emphasizes cultural difference: a diasporic or overseas Chinese is not "the same" as a Briton, not "the same" as his other (white) slaves. I want to extend this analysis further. On a less literal level, if the current and historical colonial power (UK) is a displacement of a potential new colonial power (PRC), Alice's statement also expresses her difference from other Chinese. Hong Kong Chinese are "not the same" as PRC Chinese. Order and identity are restored in a way that prioritizes Chinese culture that predates the "national consciousness in humiliation" of the Opium Wars when Hong Kong was taken from China by Britain, specifically the power of Buddha as represented in a traditional Chinese opera performance (or ghost ceremony) that functions diegetically as a hospital fundraiser, as well as predates the establishment of the PRC—or the ROC—as the modern Chinese nation-state. As a martial arts fight escalates with increasingly bold aerial displays by characters in traditional operatic costumes, a beam of light radiates from the third eye of a statue of Buddha.[93] Chiang and his doctor friends then use *fashu* to throw light onto the Earl and Alice. The Buddha shines a light on the Earl, who explodes, and the infected Chinese characters are healed. More than with the baby *goeng si* in *Vampire vs. Vampire*, Hong Kong identity is protected from foreign contamination, represented exaggeratedly as vampirism/Christianity, via traditional Chinese culture; however, foreign contamination may also contain fears over the handover.

The film makes only playful criticism of Hong Kong's capitalist system. The hospital manager is depicted as more concerned with profits than with his patients' health. Chiang and his two colleagues repeatedly justify their positions by noting that three doctors are more efficient. Moreover, they perform a series of bogus operations, including a circumcision, on a triad leader to generate profits for the hospital. Committed to overthrowing the Qing and restoring the Ming during the nineteenth century, triads were more associated with organized crimes (smuggling, piracy, racketeering) during times of peace, such as during the early Republican era.[94] Moreover, traditional Chinese culture is commodified—the opera functions as a hospital fund-raiser, the *sifu* offers his knowledge to anyone who will pay, perhaps suggestive of a capitalist "compromise" in relation to Chineseness. The film represents, then, a defiance of cultural essentialisms: Hong Kongers are not Chinese as imagined through the lens of British colonialism, nor are they Chinese as imagined through Chinese nationalism. Unlike the spectral crisis of ghosts, these three films represent crisis as corporeal, pointing to the overdetermined material effects of the extant and imminent transformations of Hong Kong since the 1980s.

CONCLUSION—CONFLATION AND REIFICATION

From the national "transparency" of Hollywood's invisible style to the radical decentering of its logic by Third Cinema, cinema is an adroit medium for representing, producing, and disseminating the elastic contours of national culture and a means for generating national consciousness. Film itself is a remarkably hybrid medium and form of cultural expression with a complicated and uneven history of colonizing audiences, as well as resisting or opposing such colonizing processes. Cameras lend themselves to Western one-point compositional perspective, yet lens and distances between subject and lens can adapt the camera's perspective to approximate other aesthetic traditions.[95] While such distinctions, according to traditional aesthetics, invariably risk essentializing and ontologizing culture and ignoring the vagaries of audience reception, they do offer insights into different cultural uses of cinematic conventions, as well as cultural conceptions of film. Since the first filmmakers in China were foreign, mostly European, Chinese filmmakers learned to mobilize Western cinematic techniques to emphasize the stylized action, aestheticizing body movements, in Hong Kong cinema.[96] Precinematic traditions provide the basis for what might be called a "distinctive mode of Chinese cinema," particularly the opera, so that the opera film has been placed at the center of a "Chinese 'cinema of attractions.'"[97] Transcultural meaning, then, is often complex and contradictory.

As the *goeng si* cycle neared exhaustion, *Mr. Vampire* director Ricky Lau produced *The Romance of the Vampires* (1994). The film draws from various local and global cinematic conventions, including those of local Category III (violence and erotica) films, which represented almost half of Hong Kong productions in the early 1990s, and Hollywood's *Pretty Woman* (USA 1990; dir. Garry Marshall). The film features Chinese actors portraying European/Hollywood-style vampires. Transculturality—both in terms of Chinese and US/British, vampire and *goeng si*—is no longer marked or represented as distinct, as distinguishable. Transculturality is, simply put, a reflection of lived realities. Sticky rice, an important prop in the *Mr. Vampire* films, is as much a part of the mise en scène as KFC ("Kentucky Fast Food Restaurant," according to the subtitles), in ways that recall the ambivalence in French-Swiss filmmaker Jean-Luc Godard's famous juxtaposition of Marx and Coca-Cola. Contradictions abound. Global culture is contradiction. Although it did better than *Doctor Vampire*, *The Romance of the Vampires* found limited audiences, both in Hong Kong and in North America, perhaps due to its relative absence of essentialized national identities within its transcultural formula. In a recent *goeng si* film, *The Era of Vampire/Tsui Hark's Vampire Hunters* (Hong Kong-Japan-Netherlands 2002; dir. Wellson Chin), comedy is almost entirely absent, prompting IMDb users to write that the film does to the *goeng si* film what *Crouching Tiger, Hidden Dragon* did to the *wuxia* film: Hollywoodizes it. Set during the high Qing dynasty, rather than the late Ming or Qing dynasties or the late Republican period, the film suggests that crisis has been postponed, if not averted, once again; and the "classical" *goeng si*, comedy extracted, is reified.

NOTES

1. Linguist Katharina M. Wilson observes that "although the superstition of vampirism seems to have developed in eastern Europe, the word *vampire* (for which the Slavic cognate is *upir*), which is now universally used to describe the phenomenon, seemed to have gained popularity in the West." Universal, however, seems to refer to the West, which designates eighteenth- and nineteenth-century England, France, and Germany in her study. Katharina M. Wilson, "The History of the Word Vampire" (1985), reprinted in *The Vampire: A Casebook*, edited by Alan Dundes (Madison: University of Wisconsin Press, 1998), 9. Unlike European languages, the term *vampire* has not been widely adopted in Mandarin and Cantonese. The term *goeng si* (*jiang shi* in pinyin) translates literally as "stiff corpse" or "inactive carcass." The term *kap hyut gwai* (*xi xie gui* in pinyin) is often translated as "bloodsucking ghost," though it is less frequently used in relation to the films that I discuss in this chapter.

2. Esther M. K. Cheung and Chu Yiu-wai, "Introduction: Between Home and World," in *Between Home and World: A Reader in Hong Kong Cinema*, ed. Esther M. K. Cheung and Chu Yiu-wai (Hong Kong, China: Oxford University Press, 2004), xxviii.

3. According to Ryan Law, Hong Kong Movie Database (HKMDb), www.hkmdb .com, (no date; accessed December 14, 2002, and January 14, 2007), *Mr. Vampire* earned HK$20.1M, whereas *Vampire vs. Vampire* earned only HK$11.2M, *A Bite of Love*, HK$10.8M, and *Doctor Vampire*, only HK$2.9M. By contrast, *Mr. Vampire 2* earned HK$13.1M and *New Mr. Vampire*, HK$17.1M.

4. Rey Chow, *Primitive Passions: Visuality, Sexuality, Ethnography, and Contemporary Chinese Cinema* (New York: Columbia University Press, 1994).

5. Ackbar Abbas, *Hong Kong: Culture and the Politics of Disappearance* (Minneapolis and London: University of Minnesota Press, 1997), 5.

6. Stefan Hammond and Mike Wilkin, *Sex and Zen: A Bullet in the Head* (New York: Fireside Books/Simon and Schuster, 1996), 25.

7. Later, Hammond and Wilkin write (89–90):

Inspiration is drawn from centuries of Chinese legend, in which legions of hopping vampires are a common part of daily life, and whose existence is put up with as one might tolerate bad weather. Instead of appearing as scheming Eastern European guys in formal wear, charming the ladies and biting their pale, innocent necks, these vampires are corpses in Ming Dynasty garb. Rigid in death, Kyonsi ("hopping ghosts") are scary, but they have a cute, playful side to them as well. And child-vampires are always cute. But vampires are often foot soldiers for more powerful demons and witches. These monsters aren't cute at all.

8. Cheung and Yiu-wai, "Introduction: Between Home and World," xiii.

9. Robert Stam, "Beyond Third Cinema: The Aesthetics of Hybridity," in *Rethinking Third Cinema*, ed. Anthony R. Gunerante and Wimal Dissanayake (New York and Oxford: Routledge, 2003), 40.

10. Karl Marx, *Capital: A Critique of Political Economy* (1867) trans. Ben Fowkes, 364.

11. David Ansen, "Movies: Chinese Takeout." *Newsweek* (February 19, 1996), 66.

12. Michael Hardt and Antonio Negri, *Empire* (Cambridge and London: Harvard University Press, 2000). For critiques of this work, see *Debating Empire*, edited by Gopal Balakrishnan (New York and London: Verso, 2003).

13. Michael Hardt and Antonio Negri, *Multitude: War and Democracy in the Age of Empire* (New York: Penguin Press, 2004), 193.

14. I thank Sheetal Majithia for bringing this reference to my attention. For a critique of *Multitude*, see Lisa Rofel, "Discrepant Modernities and Their Discontents," *Positions: East Asian Cultural Critique* 9.3 (winter 2001): 637–49.

15. Abbas, *Hong Kong*, 25.

16. Stephen Teo, "Ghost, Cadavers, Demons, and Other Hybrids." In *Hong Kong Cinema: The Extra Dimension* (London: British Film Institute, 1997), 224.

17. For a discussion of the complexities of transcultural analysis, see Rosie Thomas, "Indian Cinema: Pleasure and Popularity: An Introduction," *Screen* 26.3–4 (May–August 1985): 116–31.

18. Stephen Leo, "The Legacy of T. E. Lawrence: The Forward Policy of Western Film Critics in the Far East," in *Film and Nationalism*, ed. Alan Williams (New Brunswick and London: Rutgers University Press, 2002), 183–84.

19. This transcultural space has been explored in the essays in *Hong Kong Connections: Transnational Imagination in Action Cinema*, edited by Meaghan Morris, Siu Leung Li, and Stephen Chan Ching-kui (Durham and London: Duke University Press, 2005; Hong Kong: Hong Kong University Press, 2005).

20. Michael Hoover and Lisa Odham Stokes, "At the Hong Kong Hop: *Mr. Vampire* Spawns Bloodsucking Genre," *Para-doxa: Studies in World Literary Genres* 17 (2002): 75.

21. Stephen Teo, "Local and Global Identity: Whither Hong Kong Cinema?" *Sense of Cinema* online (2000), www.senseofcinema.com/contents/00/7/hongkong .html (accessed March 22, 2003).

22. Li Cheuk-to Li, "Introduction," in *Phantoms of the Hong Kong Cinema*, ed. Li Cheuk-to (Hong Kong: HKIFF/Urban Council, 1989), 9.

23. Ng Ho, "Abracadaver: Cross-Cultural Influences in Hong Kong Vampire Movies," in *Phantoms of the Hong Kong Cinema*, ed. Li Cheuk-to (Hong Kong: HKIFF/Urban Council, 1989), 31.

24. Ho, "Abracadaver: Cross-Cultural Influences," 29.

25. Ho (29) continues: "As yet, no one has been able to ascertain the authenticity of the Xiangxi corpse drivers. The late movie producer Zhang Shankun once produced a movie entitled *The Corpse Drivers of Xiangxi* [Hong Kong 1957]. It dealt with groups of smugglers who used corpses as hiding repositories to smuggle illicit drugs."

26. Ho, "Abracadaver: Cross-Cultural Influences," 30.

27. The artwork for the titles of films in publicity posters and video boxes for *gyonshi* films, for example, often includes two small fangs with dripping blood. While these fangs may be read in terms of ghosts or demons, as they appear in many films, the fangs also suggest Western vampires.

28. Stephen Teo makes this point about the Hong Kong publicists in "Ghost, Cadavers, Demons," 219.

29. Chris Berry and Mary Farquhar, *China on Screen: Cinema and Nation* (New York: Columbia University Press, 2006), 23.

30. Berry and Farquhar, *China on Screen*, 38.

31. Dai Jinhua, "Postcolonialism and Chinese Cinema in the Nineties," trans. Harry H. Kuoshu, in *Cinema and Desire: Feminist Marxism and Cultural Politics in the Work of Dai Jinhua*, ed. Jing Wang and Tani E. Barlow (London and New York: Verso, 2002), 49.

32. Dai Jinhua, "Order/Anti-order: Representation of Identity in Hong Kong Action Movies," trans. Zhang Jingyuan, in *Hong Kong Connections: Transnational Imagination in Action Cinema*, ed. Meaghan Morris, Siu Leung Li, and Stephen Chan Ching-kui (Durham and London: Duke University Press, 2005), 82.

33. Jinhua, "Order/Anti-order," 92.
34. In "Order/Anti-order," Jinhua (93) explains:

Whereas at the beginning of the 1990s, the Hong Kong movies popular in the Mainland cinema worked as an imaginary space and cultural release for the real and spiritual post-June-Fourth-1989 pressure, they soon became a reference for the self-identity and self-expression of Mainland young people growing up in the fragmented and ineffective ideological space between the imagination of globalization and local reality.

35. For a discussion of third-world conditions in first-world cities, see Saskia Sassen, *The Global City: New York, London, Tokyo* (Princeton and Oxford: Princeton University Press, 1991).
36. Morris, "Introduction," 3.
37. For examples of studies of Hong Kong cinema as regional, national, or transnational, see *Transnational Chinese Cinemas: Identity, Nationhood, Gender*, edited by Sheldon Hsiao-peng Lu (Honolulu: University of Hawai'i, 1997); *The Cinema of Hong Kong: History, Art, Identity*, edited by Poshek Fu and David Desser (Cambridge and New York: Cambridge University Press, 2000); Lisa Odham Stokes and Michael Hoover, *City on Fire: Hong Kong Cinema* (London and New York: Verso, 2000); David Bordwell, *Planet Hong Kong: Popular Cinema and the Art of Entertainment* (Cambridge and London: Harvard University Press, 2000); *At Full Speed: Hong Kong Cinema in a Borderless World*, edited by Ester C. M. Yau (Minneapolis and London: University of Minnesota Press, 2001); Yingjin Zhang, *Screening China: Critical Interventions, Cinematic Reconfigurations, and the Transnational Imaginary in Contemporary Chinese China* (Ann Arbor: Center for Chinese Studies/University of Michigan Press, 2002); as well as other studies cited in this chapter.
38. Anne T. Ciecko, "Introduction to Popular Asian Cinema," in *Contemporary Asian Cinema*, ed. Anne Tereska Ciecko (Oxford and New York: Berg, 2005), 6.
39. Ciecko cites filmmaker Shekhar Kapur, who argues that the current millennium will shift toward an Asia-centric global media culture.
40. Morris, "Introduction," 4.
41. Cheung and Yiu-wai, "Introduction: Between Home and World," xxiv.
42. Chu Yiu-wai, "Introduction: Globalization and the Hong Kong Film Industry," in *Between Home and World: A Reader in Hong Kong Cinema*, ed. Esther M. K. Cheung and Chu Yiu-wai (Hong Kong: Oxford University Press, 2004), 5.
43. Kinnia Yau Shuk-ting, "Interactions between Japanese and Hong Kong Action Cinemas," in *Hong Kong Connections: Transnational Imagination in Action Cinema*, ed. Meaghan Morris, Siu Leung Li, and Stephen Chan Ching-kui (Durham and London: Duke University Press, 2005), 35–48.
44. Kwai-cheung Lo, "Transnationalism of the Local in Hong Kong Cinema," in *At Full Speed: Hong Kong Cinema in a Borderless World*, ed. Ester C. M. Yau (Minneapolis and London: University of Minnesota Press, 2001), 263.
45. Cited in Bordwell, *Planet Hong Kong*, 40.
46. *Tian xia* is defined as a China-centered view of the world among "barbarians."

47. Sui Leung Li, "Kung-fu: Negotiating Nationalism and Modernity," *Cultural Studies* 15.3–4 (2001): 515–42.

48. Abbas, 30.

49. Marchetti, "Introduction: Plural and Transnational." *Jump-Cut* 42 (1998): 68.

50. Abbas, *Hong Kong,* 23.

51. Berry and Farquhar, *China on Screen,* 9.

52. Jeff Yang, *Once Upon a Time in China: A Guide to Hong Kong, Taiwanese, and Mainland Chinese Cinema* (New York: Atria Books, 2003), 52.

53. Jinhua, "Order/Anti-order," 82.

54. "Dracula evidently appeals to nations in crisis," Kim Newman argues in a review of the film. He provides a laundry list of sites of major economic and social upheavals that coincide with major film versions of the novel *Dracula*—"Germany 1922. America 1930. Britain 1958. America 1979. America 1992."—equating 1992 with "the current recession and the displacement of Bush." Kim Newman, "Bloodlines" *Sight and Sound* 3.1 (January 1993): 12.

55. Douglas Gomery, *The Hollywood Studio System: A History* (London: British Film Institute, 2005), 158.

56. Peter Hutchings, *Terence Fisher* (Manchester and New York: Manchester University Press, 2001).

57. The costume qualities of this film extend to the film's use of local locations to signify central Europe, most visibly in the composite shot of the Castle Dracula on the hills of Hong Kong. Chungking University was not founded until 1929, a full quarter of a century after Professor Van Helsing's visit.

58. Teo, "Ghost, Cadavers, Demons," 219.

59. Teo argues (223) that Hong Kong "horror" films are indebted to Hollywood and Hammer conventions, as well as to local literary and cinematic traditions. The reincarnation theme of the ghost story, Teo writes, allows for "an allegorical tale of betrayal and fate, transforming characters on a journey through a psychic realm where the past determines the present." Decapitation is the ultimate form of capital punishment insofar as the decapitated body is not eligible for reincarnation and condemned to eternal punishment as a lost soul wandering in hell.

60. *The Satanic Rites of Dracula/ Count Dracula and His Vampire Bride* (UK 1973; dir. Alan Gibson) also points to global capitalism, particularly the ways that capital is "sucked" along colonial and postcolonial lines. Dracula's principal disciple in the film is a Chinese woman, Chin Yang (Barbara Yu Ling), suggesting a racialized casting decision as a comment on the UK's anxiety over the more healthy economy of its Chinese colony in Hong Kong.

61. Stephen Teo, "In the Realm of Pu Songling," chapter in *Phantoms of the Hong Kong Cinema,* edited by Li Cheuk-to (Hong Kong: HKIFF/Urban Council, 1989). Teo writes: "The end-of-dynasty fatalism; the nostalgia of the period Ming; the antipathy towards the existing order (as reflected in the tough lot of the scholars), are the under currents of *Liaozhai.* Pu chronicled the stories of the common people which reflected all these undercurrents adopting a seemingly objective stance as part of his 'correct' approach."

62. Natalie Chan Shi Hung, "Rewriting History: Hong Kong Nostalgia Cinema and Its Social Practice," in *The Cinema of Hong Kong: History, Art, Identity*, ed. Poshek Fu and David Desser (Cambridge and New York: Cambridge University Press, 2000), 255.

63. Berry and Farquhar, *China on Screen*, 77.

64. Abbas, *Hong Kong*, 40.

65. Franco Moretti, *Signs Taken for Wonders: Essays in the Sociology of Literary Form*, trans. S. Fischer, David Forgacs, and David Miller (London: Verso, 1988), 91.

66. Steve Pile, "Perpetual Returns: Vampires and the Ever-Colonized City," in *Postcolonial Urbanism: Southeast Asian Cities and Global Processes*, ed. Ryan Bishop, John Phillips, and Wei Wei Yeo (New York and London: Routledge, 2003), 276.

67. In *Hong Kong Action Cinema* (Woodstock: The Overlook Press, 1996), Bey Logan argues (103) that *Maau saan goeng shut kuen/The Spiritual Boxer 2* (Hong Kong 1979; dir. Liu Chia Liang) is perhaps the first recent Hong Kong film to include a *goeng si* in its narrative.

68. The term *unrelated sequel* comes from Frederick Dannen and Barry Long, *Hong Kong Babylon: An Insider's Guide to the Hollywood of the East* (New York: Hyperion/Miramax, 1997): 224. Most Western fans of the film describe it in similar terms.

69. Yung Sai-shing, "Moving Body: The Interactions between Chinese Opera and Action Film," in *Hong Kong Connections: Transnational Imagination in Action Cinema*, ed. Meaghan Morris, Siu Leung Li, and Stephen Chan Ching-kui (Durham and London: Duke University Press, 2005), 46.

70. In "Abracadaver: Cross-Cultural Influences in Hong Kong Vampire Movies," Ng Ho argues: "Regarding the myth of those whose blood being sucked by a vampire, turns into one of that vampiric body. There are no literary sources to back this up in Chinese annals. It is safe to say that this is mainly a Western concept, one utilised and adapted into Chinese form by *Mr. Vampire*" (33). Ricky Lau's *Mr. Vampire* films include *Goeng si sin sang/Mr. Vampire* (Hong Kong 1985), *Genug shut ga chuk /Mr. Vampire 2* (Hong Kong 1986), *Ling waan sin sang/Mr. Vampire 3* (Hong Kong 1987), *Goeng shut suk suk/Mr. Vampire Saga 4* (Hong Kong 1988), and *San goeng shut sin sang/Mr. Vampire 1992* (Hong Kong 1992).

71. In Taoism, *xian* (immortals) gain eternal life and godlike powers, such as the immunity to fire and the ability to fly, through certain rituals and alchemy. Three categories of *xian* are generally recognized: *tianshen* (heavenly immortals), who can fly; *dishen* (earthly immortals), who live in the mountains and forests; and *shijieshen* (corpseless immortals), who give up their bodies after death.

72. Caroline Vié, "Jiang shi," in *The BFI Companion to Horror*, ed. Kim Newman (London: British Film Institute, 1996), 175.

73. This definition and these examples come from Chris Berry and Mary Farquhar, *China on Screen: Cinema and Nation* (New York: Columbia University Press, 2006): 65–66. They reference Geremie R. Barmé, Persistance de la tradition au royaume des ombres: Quelques notes visant à contribuer à une approche nouvelle du cinéma chinois, chapter in *Le Cinéma chinois*, edited by Marie-Claire Quiquemelle (Paris: Centre Georges Pompidou, 1985): 119–20 and Luo Yijun, "A Preliminary Dis-

cussion of National Style in Film" [in Chinese], chapter in *Anthology of Chinese Film Theory*, volume 1, edited by Li Pusheng, Xu Hong, and Luo Yijun (1989): 268–69.

74. Ho, "Abracadaver: Cross-Cultural," 29.

75. In "Abracadaver: Cross-Cultural," Ho describes (31) four "cultural traits" (or cinematic conventions) in these films: (1) a corpse's retention of an "extra breath," which leads to its transformation into a vampire; (2) a human's ability to hold his or her breath to stop a vampire; (3) the victim's transformation into a vampire after having had its blood sucked by a vampire; and (4) the use of wooden swords, string dipped in ink, yellow scrolls, and sticky rice to subdue a vampire.

76. In a typical gag, a snake will crawl up the trouser leg of a male character. The male character will squirm and scream until the snake can make its exit through the man's unzipped fly. Often female characters cover their eyes from this spectacle, but male characters yank on the snake.

77. Lenuta Giukin, "Boy-Girls: Gender, Body, and Popular Culture in Hong Kong Action Movies," in *Ladies and Gentlemen, Boy and Girls: Gender in Film at the End of the Twentieth Century*, ed. Murray Pomerance (Albany: State University of New York Press, 2001), 58.

78. *Feng shui* means "wind, water" and traditionally symbolizes the space between heaven and earth—that is, the environment where we live; underlying philosophy is that we and our environment are sustained by an invisible, yet tangible, energy called *chi*, which moves like wind, but can eddy and become trapped like water and stagnate; the skill of a *feng shui* consultant lies in recognizing where chi is flowing freely, where it may be trapped and stagnant, or where it may be excessive; the work is to create space for chi to flow and activate the opportunities that may be frustrated by obstacles—a harmonious rebalancing of yin and yang, the dark and light of all situations; the principles may be applied geophysically, as well as superficially to placement, design, and decoration.

79. Hoover and Stokes, "At the Hong Kong Hop," 73.

80. Gina Marchetti, *From Tian'anmen to Time Square: Transnational China and the Chinese Diaspora on Global Screens, 1989–1997* (Philadelphia: Temple University Press, 2006), 11.

81. J. A. G. Roberts, *Modern China: An Illustrated History* (Stroud, UK: Sutton, 1998), xiv.

82. The opening sequence to *Fei zhou han shang/Crazy Safari* (Hong Kong 1990; dir. Billy Chan Ping-yiu), for example, includes an educational documentary—perhaps more appropriately described according to it diegetic function as the auction house's marketing video—on the differences between the Western vampire and Chinese *goeng si*, suggesting that cultural differences are distinct and recognizable. Like other "artifacts" stolen under colonialism, the *goeng si* is considered a museum-quality piece worthy of commodification through auction—a "Chinese mummy," as the auctioneers proclaims, recalling J. G. von Herder's term "embalmed mummy" for China during the eighteenth century.

83. Roberts, *Modern China*, 34, 98.

84. Roberts, *Modern China*, 101.

85. Well Worth Tracking Down!" (user comment on *Yi men dao ren/Vampire vs. Vampire*), *Hong Kong Movie Database* (February 20, 2001; accessed December 14, 2002).

86. *Mr. Vampire 2* introduces a *goeng si* nuclear family. A young girl, Chia-chia, befriends a child *goeng si*, offering her hand to the creature as the child Elliott did to the little space alien, abandoned by the other botanist aliens, in *E.T.: The Extra-Terrestrial* (USA 1982 dir. Steven Spielberg). More importantly, the film acknowledges the arrival of ethnically Chinese "boat people" from Vietnam.

87. The lead stars, Kwan and Lam, are both identified, retrospectively, by fans with their work in the "national epic" *Wong fei-hung/Once Upon a Time in China* (Hong Kong 1991; dir. Tsui Hark). Rosamund Kwan portrays Aunt Yee in the film, and George Lam performs the title track.

88. With decolonization after the Second World War, the UK implemented various polities to allow the Commonwealth to remain British while distinguishing these newly independent states from the UK. The British Nationality Act of 1948 created three categories of Britishness, including Citizens of the United Kingdom and Colonies (CUKC), which was divided later into three new categories, including BDTC, in the British Nationality Act of 1981. The Commonwealth Immigration Act of 1962 prohibited Hong Kongers to enter the UK freely. Two acts in 1985 and 1986 created another new category, British Nationals (Overseas) [BN(O)], which included consular protection but did not include the right of abode in the UK. In 1987, the category of Hong Kong Permanent Resident was created. Following the 1989 massacre in Beijing, the UK did grant a limited number of Hong Kongers that status of British Citizen (BC) with right of abode in the UK, as well as BC to non-Chinese ethnic minorities living in Hong Kong. Michiko Ai, "The Transition of Hong Kong People's Nationality after World War II," *E-Journal on Hong Kong Cultural and Social Studies* 2 (August 2002; accessed January 16, 2007), www.hku.hk/hkcsp/ccex/ehkcss01/issue2_ar_ma_01.htm.

89. Michael Dummett, *On Immigration and Refugees* (London and New York: Routledge, 2001), 120.

90. In *Fright Night*, the high school student Charlie is successful in identifying his neighbor, Jerry, as a vampire due to his regular viewing of old vampire films on television. He enlists the assistance of the television show's host, who stars as a vampire hunter in many of the films aired, in destroying the vampire Jerry.

91. In *Sex and Zen: A Bullet in the Head*, Stefan Hammond and Mike Wilkin note this intertextual reference: "Back in HK, the doc finds he's lost his taste for garlic shrimp and starts going around with sunglasses and an Edwardian cloak, like Nicolas Cage in *Vampire's Kiss*" (90).

92. Upon his return to Hong Kong, Chiang boasts to his colleagues that he "did it" in England and is now "a real man." His colleagues joke that he must have slept with a (British) prostitute, but Chiang tells them that he slept with "a beautiful Chinese woman." They later link Alice's bite marks on Chiang's genitals as the source of his infection. When they meet Alice, one of Chiang's colleagues protects himself with a crucifix, but she tells him that crucifixes are "out of fashion" and have no effect. She also tells him that she wouldn't want to drink his blood because he "sleeps around," so

his blood might be infected with AIDS. When the hypochondriac patient, Mrs. Hsieh, complains about not feeling well after a night of heavy drinking, the doctors decide that she should have her blood tested for the "English flu." They draw samples of her blood, which they give to Chiang and Alice as nourishment.

93. The Han brought Buddhism from India to China.

94. Roberts, *Modern China*, 48.

95. Framing and editing strategies suggest alternative aesthetics, so that south Asian popular films draw from Sanskrit aesthetics, emphasizing successive modes of affect, in addition to colonial traces of Aristotelian aesthetics, emphasizing unities and narrative. African cinemas often discard the colonial remnants of Western cinema's linear chronology, which is too simplistic and myopic to express collective chronotopes. Some southeast Asian cinemas elide scenes of dramatic action upon which Western cinemas based their entire meaning. Western audiences often complained that Hong Kong action films emphasize fight choreography over narrative coherence and causality, though, somewhat paradoxically, such audiences often watch the films specifically for the fight sequences.

96. Sai-shing, "Moving Body," 29.

97. Berry and Farquhar, *China on Screen*, 47.

The Legend of the Seven Golden Vampires (*The Seven Brothers Meet Dracula* [US title], 1974). *Courtesy of Dynamite Entertainment/PhotoFest*

· 14 ·

Enter the Dracula: The Silent Screams and Cultural Crossroads of Japanese and Hong Kong Cinema

Wayne Stein

*W*ithin the genres of horror, fantasy, and science fiction, wherein the epic struggle between good and evil has remained a time-honored tradition, no character has endured longer than the vampire. In general, narratives about vampires have approached this power mêlée from a fairly orthodox, and particularly Westernized, vantage point. However, while this approach has certainly seen success in Anglocentric markets, problems have occurred when Eastern markets attempt to appropriate these narratives, which calls into question the effectiveness of translating very politicized themes, like Dracula and vampires, for example, into cultures that have very diverse, non-Western belief systems. More crucially, it raises several questions about the texts themselves that cannot be answered using a purely Western politics that defines normative behavior in terms of its own moral and religious conventions.

Where there is blood, often there are vampires; and where there are vampires, one is likely to find Dracula, or a character resembling Dracula, leading them. His is an old story, and the twentieth century has seen him traverse nearly every part of the world, making Dracula the vampire a transnational phenomenon or "pandemic." The consummate international male, he is virile in both the West and in the East, but Dracula and his kind are also diasporic. The vampire's global presence may indeed make it a multicultural phenomenon, but it seems to me, and this will be the chief argument of this chapter, that not all vampires are successful in communicating the same cultural sense of fear, shock, and alternative morality. Specifically, horror as a genre presents a strong case in point where cultural transparencies can fail.

A shorter version of this paper, titled "The Blood of Hybridity in Postmodern Cinematic Asian Vampires," was presented at the Popular Culture Conference in Boston, Massachusetts, on April 4, 2007.

The cultural subtext provides ample problems for Asian audiences trying to decode Western horror. Some of the initial attempts to merge the Western narratives of Dracula into an Eastern horror genre (e.g., Michio Yamamoto's *Noroi no yakata: Chi o su me* [*Lake of Dracula*, 1971] and Roy Ward Baker's *The Legend of the Seven Golden Vampires* [1974]), in Japan and Hong Kong respectively, met critical and financial failure. Indeed, something more complex, more imaginative, or more aesthetically frightening for Asian audiences is missing in those initial cinematic concoctions. In the following essay, I will present, for reasons of brevity, only a short survey of Eastern films and animes that I take to be the best examples supporting my claims about this cultural (mis)translation, which is made visible when Westernized Dracula and vampire narratives attempt to relocate in Eastern soils.

First I shall discuss what I term the lack of moral authenticity presented in such Western/Eastern narratives; I contend that, for example, the Judeo-Christian religious underpinnings of Westernized materials have not translated well with Asian audiences raised within a non-Western context: the metaphysics of Buddhism and Confucianism and their local traditions of Taoism (Hong Kong) and Shintoism (Japan). This section will focus on a quick overview that contextualizes how conflicting and competing metaphysical features tend to create an internal opposition in Asian audiences to the basic ideas of terror, shock, and evil revealed in the *Dracula* narrative.

Second, what I propose then is to follow the evolution of *Dracula*'s influence, its initial contact and subsequent retraction, and then the reemergence and cultivation of the cinematic horror genre within the important Asian film industries in Japan and Hong Kong. This major section of the chapter will show how both of these Asian industries ultimately developed their own brand of vampire films by mixing elements of martial action with horror. Japanese cinema fuses samurai lore with its vampire tales and further develops this into other creative and original genres for its animated features: specifically, in director Toyoo Ashida's *Banpaia hanta D* (*Vampire Hunter D*, 1985); Toshihiro Hirano's *Kyuketsuki Miyu* (*Vampire Princess*, 1988); and Hiroyuki Kitakubo's *Buraddo Za Rasuto Vanpaia* (*Blood: The Last Vampire*, 2000).

And thirdly, the next section will center on how the Hong Kong cinema has produced a successful new hybrid of *wuxia pian* (sword films) and kung fu films with its vampires: specifically, in Lau Kar-Leong's *Mao shan jiang shi quan* (*Spiritual Boxer II*, 1979); Sammo Hung's *Gui da gui* (*Close Encounter of a Spooky Kind*, 1980); Ricky Lau's *Jiang shi xian sheng* (*Mr. Vampire*, 1985); and Dante Lam's *Chin gei bin* (*The Twins Effect*, 2003). Finally, I shall illustrate how Dracula's influence can precipitate unique cinematic antagonisms that result from regional differences: the by-products of metaphysical, psychological, or even political stimuli.

I. IN SEARCH OF ASIANICITY: A MORAL AUTHENTICITY
FOR ASIAN AUDIENCES

Hollywood has recently embraced and adopted Asian horror films with limited success, like Hideo Nakata's *Ringu* (1998) adaptation into *The Ring* (2000); Takashi Shimizu's *Ju-on* (2003) into *The Grudge* (2004); and the Pang Brothers' *Gin Gwai* (2002) into *The Eye* (2008). The original Asian versions of these films were not released for mass consumption to Western audiences but did manage to find a limited "cult" following via straight-to-DVD release. To a large extent, according to Patrick Galloway, the Asian sense of evil or shock does not translate well into Western standards of evil or shock: "Traditional Christianity simply won't tolerate certain types of exploration in thought, deed, or art, the resultant baffles and filters are so inculcated in our popular culture that it isn't until you watch a film from a country without such conventions that you begin to see what, perhaps, you didn't even know you were missing!"[1] To reiterate, when Asian audiences experience a Western film of horror, the standards for evil, terror, fear, and shock are different. Thus, the message for many Asians watching films like *The Legend of the Seven Golden Vampires* is decoded differently from the original message intended for the Western audiences. The Shaw Brothers had to release a more violent version for its audiences. Strangely, Asian films of horror are often more violent than their Western counterparts. This difference occurs because, to use a Vygotskyan theory of language, the inner speech decodes the outer speech differently: "A word without meaning is an empty sound . . ."[2] Since everything is text, certain aspects from Western films do not translate at all for Asian audiences trying to read the visual cues. Vygotsky provides an explanation that can work to explain this reaction: "In our speech, there is always the hidden thought, the subtext."[3] What was lacking in these first Dracula narratives that entered the consciousness of the Asian psyche was a moral authenticity, signals of cultural subtexts and cathartic nuances from the genre of horror that they expected to experience.

Interestingly, scholar I. Q. Hunter argues against the negative effect of the "inauthentic" in *The Legend of the Seven Golden Vampires*, since films like *The Exorcist* (1973) had a huge impact on Chinese cinema horror films.[4] However, this section of the paper builds on the claim that when a horror film that incorporates significant aspects of Japanese and Chinese ghost lore into its film but then fails to implement some of the essential provisions of that tradition, such factors are crucial and not minor grounds for such films to fail.[5]

The directors of those initial films should have taken into account the way Buddhists viewed death and mortality. They "tend to regard death as a morally insignificant break in the lifetime of an individual."[6] Indeed, funerals are known as "a white happy-event."[7] Furthermore, the premise of being tragically damned forever as one of the undead, as we see in *Dracula*, becomes less fearful or shocking to Asian audiences who, for the most part, grow up believing in or at least being exposed to the idea of rebirth. According to Buddhist traditions, death and even being damned are mere transitory phases of existence, since everyone is reborn. The Festival of the Hungry Ghost in China and the O-Bon Festival in Japan are celebrations concerning the transitory nature of existence, which also commemorates ancestor worship.[8] Both Japanese and Chinese ghost stories are filled with undead ghosts who do not realize they are dead.[9] This aspect is of enormous value to this argument, for examination of some of the basic, distinctive qualities of these stories may provide hints into how Asian audiences construe *Dracula* narratives. They look within their own traditions of undead narratives, within their own inner Eastern speech/text traditions, to decode the message of *Dracula*, and its outer Western speech/text traditions. The following section will look at Japanese and Chinese tales of the undead so as to better understand problems of narrative transparency that occur in defining an Asian moral authenticity.

Let us first look at the Festival of the Hungry Ghost celebrated in Chinese culture, and its variant in Japanese culture, as examples for understanding the dead. The Japanese tradition of the O-Bon Festival, deriving historically from the Chinese festival, is celebrated yearly every July or August, according to the lunar calendar. In Buddhism, everything is transitory or impermanent; death itself is a step in a process leading to rebirth. All beings are reborn only to die and be born again, which is the law of *samsara* (the wheel of death and rebirth). This holiday celebrates remembrance of the spiritual realm. Some spirits do not know they are dead and are termed lost spirits or hungry ghosts or *gaki*, "demons tormented by a terrible hunger and thirst that can never be satiated."[10] Offerings (*segaki*) such as food and other objects are presented to appease the *gaki*, those associated with one's family but also those without a family.[11] On the last day, floating paper lanterns are placed into the water to guide the spirits toward their next transformation. Though this festival is celebrated every year, respect for the dead must be paid every day.[12] In Japan, "when a person has met an unnatural death or died in difficult childbirth, the ceremony of opening the dead person's mouth is the most important service [conducted by a shamaness] for the salvation of his soul."[13] Why worry about tragic deaths? Because when the body dies, the spirit should reunite with its ancestors. This represents the Confucian value of showing respect for one's family.[14] If a woman dies tragically (e.g., if she is murdered or commits suicide), the *spirit* becomes a *yurie*, a vengeful ghost. Such vengeful ghosts may seem real in appearance, but instead of thinking of them as undead, imagine them as the (un)born: those beings of liminality, trapped temporarily between death and rebirth. The female ghosts in *Ringu* (1998) and *Ju-on* (2000) are *yurei*, wandering spirits. The vampires in the Toho trilogy, which used the Dracula narrative for Japanese audiences, possess characteristics of wandering spirits, as they seem to be doomed tragic figures rather than the lustful figures of Western cinema.

As already noted, Chinese folklore has a tradition of vengeful and hungry ghosts.[15] For the most part, Japan adopted this tradition. However, Chinese vengeful ghosts take a form that Japan never adopted: the *jiangshi* (also *chiang-shih, goeng si,* or *kiang shi*),[16] the Chinese vampire. These vampires have perhaps more parallels with the putrid walking corpses we find in the Eastern European tradition of the "revenant" (a zombie-like vampire who typically haunts villages more than their resident peasants), than with the lustful undead found in the vampire genre of the West. Authority on vampire folklore Paul Barber makes this point:

> The archetypal (fictional) vampire, Count Dracula, does not fit the model well at all. . . . In folklore the problems are rather different, the situation less uniform. The vampire or revenant might be of virtually any nationality—such creatures occur (or have occurred) in the folklore of most (if not all) cultures in Europe. . . . He, too, like the fictional vampire, is bound by the constraints of the world of spirits, but they are different constraints and different spirits.[17]

The *jiangshi* appears like a zombie with white skin and long fingernails, moving or hopping around with hands outstretched in a stiff manner because of *rigor mortis*.[18] Chinese folklorist G. Willoughby-Meade is one of the first Westerners to correctly point out how Chinese defined a vampire, explaining that the human body originally possesses two souls and not one: the *p'o* (an animal-like nature) along with the *hun* (god-like nature). Upon death the *p'o* (or *p'ai*[19]) leave the *hun*. Thus, vampires are beings with reconstituted souls.[20] In a Taoist manner, the two parts of the soul live in harmony when alive. However, as Steven Harrell explains, they clash with each other when ill, and finally when the *hun* and *p'o* separate, the person dies.[21] Harrell maintains (521) that the *p'o* (the animal or *yin* nature) decays and becomes *kuei* (ghost) while the *hun* (the god or *yang* nature) becomes *shen* (spirit). Hence, the vampire is a living *kuei*, an undead being or ghost, who thirsts for his or her opposite: the *hun*.[22] The Taoist master is able to keep these opposites artificially united through magic incantations even after death.

Most ghost stories have their origins in *Strange Stories from a Chinese Studio* (1679), written by Pu Songling (1640–1715). G. Willoughby-Meade, for example, recalls a vampire tale about a resuscitated corpse. In many similar stories, women are usually portrayed as the undead attacking defenseless men, since women are *yin* while men are *yang*. In the tale, four travelers, who stopped over at an inn, find themselves fighting for their lives as a dead woman attacks them. Ghosts, since they are animal (*yin*) nature, are attracted to men because of their strong masculine (*yang*) nature. A woman who is also *kuei* symbolizes *yin* twice over, a signification of double trouble. When the one man in the story held his breath, the *kuei,* or vampire, could not sense the *yang* figure before her. This becomes an important feature in all Chinese vampire films. Hold your breath and the vampire cannot "smell" your presence.

Many ghosts in those stories are essentially hungry ghosts, trapped between being dead and becoming reborn.[23] For the Chinese, reincarnation is the "backbone in all ghost stories."[24] To further the understanding of hungry ghosts, it becomes vital to know how the concept of death and rebirth works in Buddhism and Taoism. Funerals are often important aspects of Chinese vampire stories. After someone dies, it takes forty-nine days, Robert John Smith explains, for the soul to completely leave the body to find another body. Family members and Buddhist monks are usually expected to pray or chant for the soul of the dead person, hoping that it successfully experiences a good rebirth.[25] Smith explains (92) that the idea for the forty-nine days of prayer comes from Hindu tradition in India. This tradition then joins the Chinese traditions, likes those we find in the *Sutra of the Ten Kings* (tenth century AD), according to Stephen Teiser, who describes how forty-nine days of chanting for the dead serves as a means of providing verbal offerings to the seven kings of Chinese hell who will help guide and lead the dead safely along their way.[26]

The transition from death to rebirth is not always smooth. Asian audiences often feel empathetic toward the tragic element of the hungry ghost because it might be something that has happened to them in the past or will occur to them in the future. This tragic element becomes a key component in understanding why many tales of Eastern horror differ from Western tales. Those who have difficulties transmigrating become hungry ghosts. A Chinese thinker in 535 BC said, "When an ordinary man or woman dies a violent death, the *hun* or *p'o* are still able to keep hanging about men and do evil and malicious things."[27] They are confused or can become vengeful ghosts, wandering and haunting the living. In *The Legend of the Seven Golden Vampires* (which this essay will examine later), Dracula has somehow transmigrated into the body of a Chinese warlord and sorcerer, whose followers include *jiangshi,* the walking undead or un(re)born. Their appearance as ugly zombie-like beings is accurate, but beyond that, much remains that is inauthentic. How Van Helsing deals with such Chinese vampires is not accurate enough or satisfying enough for Asian audiences. Later this essay will examine this in more detail by reexamining the film's impact on Chinese cinematic horror. Now let's examine the effect that Dracula would have on Japanese horror.

THE DRACULA EFFECT IN JAPAN:
THE TOHO VAMPIRE TRILOGY

On the subjects of vampirism and culture, Daniel Farson writes, "Why would anyone believe in such a weird superstition as vampirism? . . . Yet they did. And have done so from the beginning of time all over the world."[28] However, Japan seems to be the exception in Asia, for it does not possess its own history of vampire tales until such tales invaded from the West in the twentieth century.[29] In the 1970s, foreign films in Japan started to become very popular and began to compete with domestic films. Toho studios decided to produce some vampire films that were quite Western in design: a trilogy of vampire films directed by Michio Yamamoto. The films tried to stay faithful to the Hammer formula. Since Japanese supernatural/horror films like *Kwaidan* (1964) and *Onibaba* (1964) were winning fame and awards overseas in European and American markets, Toho felt that Japanese vampire films might do well too (Galbraith IV 194). *Vampire Doll* (1970) was created and has been called the first Japanese vampire film. In the end, one isn't sure if any vampires in the film are real. *Lake of Dracula* (1971) and *Chui o suu bara* or *The Evil of Dracula* (1974) followed. *Lake of Dracula* is definitely more Hammer-like than its successor. In this film, the protagonist, Akiko, has a recurring nightmare of a tragic event of her childhood and thinks it is not based on reality. In the nightmare, Akiko recalls visiting an old European-style house by a lake, being attacked by lurid vampires, and being saved by an old man. Strange, horrific activities happen to her thereafter as she ages. Indeed, we discover that even her own sister has become a vampire as the nightmares and visions of the past merge into the horror of her current life. In a quest to find out why such tribulations occur, she hunts for the old house and the old man. Locating them, she comes upon and reads his diary, learning that he is descended from vampires (Dracula himself). Being Asian-looking necessitates his "mixed heritage," contrary to Dracula's trademark standards of racial purity imposed in Western markets (in which racial miscegenation is generally avoided altogether). Thus, while *Lake of Dracula* is certainly reminiscent of Hammer's style, it is far from a typical Dracula or vampire product, as some critics have stated. One critic calls it "an acceptable, if unexceptional film."[30] Unfortunately for Toho, these films did not meet with success in the West or East, and neither did the third in the series.

The third film, *Evil of Dracula*, is not as well conceived and is even weaker than its predecessors. As critic Stuart Galbraith states, "the picture is derivative of other films, notably Hammer's 1970 production, *Lust for a Vampire.*"[31] Viewers may actually experience *déjà vu*, for the plot at times actually feels much like *Lake of Dracula*. At the beginning of the film, Professor Shiraki arrives at an old-looking European building, which parallels the opening of *Lake of Dracula* where Akiko enters an old house. At one point, Shiraki is attacked by a vampire, hits his head, and blacks out. Akiko in *Lake of Dracula* also was attacked by a vampire, falls, and hits her head, blacking out. Shiraki reads the diary of the teacher whom he replaced to learn about the past horrors just as Akiko reads a diary, though of the old man, to learn about past horrors. In the endings of both films, the evil male vampire is pierced in the heart, dies a horrible death, and crumbles into dust. Perhaps the director himself felt the movie was too contrived and too formulaic, for the film seems ill conceived, less imaginative, and lacking in logical development. Galbraith adds that "fantastic films already ask their audience to accept characters and events they're not likely to swallow in the real world, and can work only when they follow their own peculiar logic. There doesn't seem to be any logic governing *Evil of Dracula*" (227). By 1976, imported films, mostly from America, started for the first time to outgross Japanese-produced films.[32] Thus, this trilogy of vampire horror films did not take advantage of the reasons such films as *Kwaidan* and *Onibaba* met with some success in the West, because they did not examine how Asians, particularly Japanese, see and treat the undead.

The next generation of Japanese vampire films would be more philosophical, more imaginative, and more successful not only for Japanese audiences but also for Western ones. In the anime *Vampire Hunter D* (1985), *Vampire Princess Miyu* (1988), and *Blood: The Last Vampire* (2000), the Zen spirit of the samurai would intermingle perfectly with the spirit of animism from Shintoism, and the code of honor from Confucianism. The three philosophies combine in all three anime, focusing on hunters looking for demons as a way to restore balance in nature.

II. *BANPAIA HANTA D* (*VAMPIRE HUNTER D*, 1985): THE APOCALYPTIC VAMPIRE HUNTER

The first Japanese film to combine successfully Eastern and Western ideas about vampires is *Vampire Hunter D* (1985), directed by Yoshiaki Kawajiri

(1950–), an anime based on the novel of the same name by Hideyuki Kikuchi (1949–), who has written some seventeen novels on the subject. This film is not only important because it is a multigenre bonanza of horror–samurai and spaghetti Western–science fiction, but it is one of the first anime released in America, helping to ignite the anime craze. Needless to say, American teenagers became cult followers of this strange animation.[33]

An adamant fan of the Hammer films, Kikuchi leads the way, with the help of the American Western, in resurrecting Dracula and vampirism in Japanese cinema: "D is also a Dracula-type character, sporting a long flowing cape and a black cowboy-esque hat, as he wields a sword (instead of a gun). When we first meet him, he is 'riding into town' on a cybernetic horse."[34] D's (in)humanity is emblematic of the struggle his being a vampire represents: to be half vampire and half human, but neither fully one or the other. Additionally, being a *ronin*—a masterless samurai—D, in his quest for a new lord, is hired by Doris Lang, who was bitten by a 10,000-year-old vampire named Count Magnus Lee, a local aristocrat. Doris cannot afford D's fee except with payments of carnal pleasures. However, at a key moment in the story, he refuses her payment of sex, at the same time that he has a deeper hunger for her blood. At that moment of weakness, his samurai spirit (*giri*) conquers his vampire spirit. This sense of *giri* is connected to Confucian values of service, honor, and respect that the samurai must demonstrate.

Because Count Magnus Lee desires to marry Doris, a human, Lee's daughter Ramika tries to kill her. Ramika does not want the impurity Doris's blood would bring to taint the noble purity of the ancient house. The influence of Hammer-style vampirism is emulated through Count Lee, a reference or homage to the actor Christopher Lee (1922–), to whom the novel is dedicated. Moreover, the character of Count Lee gestures, if only symbolically, to an impotent Emperor Hirohito (1901–1989) who was once thought to be of divine origin.[35] At one point, D confronts Ramika and tells her that she is going against the ways of the Ancient One. We are not told directly whom that refers to. After Count Lee is defeated by D, Lee recognizes the source of D's power as Dracula's. D represents true nobility because he is descended from Dracula, the purist, the "first," and the most (un)holy of vampires. The theme of maintaining a purity of the bloodline in the tale parallels the tragic fall of Japan's royal line. D is connected to the Ancient One, just as Emperor Hirohito was thought to have been a living god, an *arahitogami*; indeed, before World War II, ". . . commoners involuntarily would kneel down and bow heads to the ground. . ." to the emperor, since he was connected to the ancient one: the sun goddess, *Amaterasu*.[36] Throughout Japan's long history, the emperor had for every Japanese generation remained an unconquerable deity, since no foreign power had ever defeated Japan until the twentieth century.

The real story here is not that D, a representative of good, is fighting Count Lee, an evil vampire. Instead, it is the fact that an incompetent landlord or ruler, represented by Count Lee, is eliminated. By killing incompetency, D restores harmony, a very Shinto act. In the closing credits, D, the descendant of Dracula, rides into the barren sunset on his cybernetic horse and passes under a green tree, a visual detail emblematic of his achievement. Perhaps D represents all of us. As Rob Latham contends, each of us has become a cybernetic vampire, "an insatiable consumer driven by a hunger for perpetual youth, while the cyborg has incorporated the machineries of consumption into its juvenescent flesh."[37] D transcends such human and demonic consumptions. The green gestures towards the balance that has been temporarily restored.

Vampire Hunter D stands as a cross-cultural pollination that, at the time of its inception, helped to reinterpret and to revamp the worn-out cinematic genres, just as the samurai films helped to reinvent the Western by creating a new type of amoral hero in spaghetti Westerns. Such reinvigorated genres often tell us much about the times in which they emerge. The world that Vampire Hunter D traverses remains a chaotic, unhealthy one. While this film is perhaps a perfect mixture of East and West, its attempt to excavate the richness of a Japanese mythos is overshadowed by another anime: *Vampire Princess Miyu*.

KYUUKETSUKI MIYU (*VAMPIRE PRINCESS MIYU*, 1988): OF DEMONS AND GODS

The episodic *Vampire Princess Miyu*, an Original Video Animation (OVA), demonstrates how Asian metaphysics can be maintained and updated while not sacrificing its essence to Western vampire tropes.[38] This film deviates from Dracula tropes a bit more than did *Vampire Hunter D*. Like D, Miyu is the hero, a hunter while being a vampire, though of half human origins. However, not being your typical Western vampire, sunlight does not harm her. She does not hunt vampires. Instead, she hunts something more deadly: *Shinma*, demon gods, who plan to take over the world. Interestingly, one of her best allies is Larva, who wears a mask and who is himself a *Shinma*, a god demon. She also befriends Himiko, who happens to be a vampire hunter; Himiko herself befriends Miyu because she realizes that *Shinma* are more dangerous. Toward the end of the quest, we learn that Himiko is also a vampire. The short miniseries examines horror in relationship to the animism of Shintoism.

The rocks, the wind, the trees, everything in nature lives and is spiritual because life forces, good or bad, can be located in any object. Virtuous spirits are often used to brawl against ghastly spirits. Larva, a caring spirit, is used to fight against the evil *Shinma*. Returning nature to a sense of balance and harmony is crucial to the narrative.

The OVA series borrows the visual effect of the gothic style from Dracula and vampire films. As Susan Napier notes, *Vampire Princess* is very gothic with its "old dark houses, hooded figures and ancient curses."[39] We also have the ancient city of Kyoto, a very holy place, as one of the backdrops. In this OVA series, the eternal damnation of souls lost to vampirism is not so vital. Because the eternal in Buddhism remains impermanent, even the state of good is, in reality, called good and evil. Indeed, "*Vampire Princess Miyu* is less about the battle between good and evil than about the contest between delusion and reality."[40] Thus, we begin to see why it ultimately does not matter that Miyu and Himiko are vampires, or that Larva is herself a *Shinma*. What really matters is returning reality to a state of harmony. Such unlikely unions demonstrate how opposites can negotiate to restore harmony in the face of chaos. Other anime, like *Blood: The Last Vampire*, examine the need for restoration in a more political manner.

BURADDO ZA RASUTO VANPAIA (BLOOD: THE LAST VAMPIRE, 2000): SAYA, THE BATGIRL

Saya Otonashi, another "young" female vampire hunter, fights various monsters with a sort of demonic vigor and determination. Though this anime is but forty-eight minutes long, its combination of computer-generated techniques and 2-D animation make it one of the most popular and most influential anime in recent years.[41] Set neither in the near future nor the distant past, *Blood* is set during the Vietnam War with American and Japanese characters, speaking English and Japanese. Saya is one of the "originals," a chiropteran (which refers to bats) or a vampire, but like Miyu, she has no fear of sunlight. Sony and Production I.G funded this fully digital animation project. *Blood: The Last Vampire*, however, was not based on any novel or manga, but manga and novel spin-offs were created from the anime. Scott Frasier, who worked on the project, revealed that a team of anime creators working for Mamoru Oshii (1951–) came up with the idea as something different.[42] Oshii had directed the cyberpunk anime classic *Kôkaku kidôtai* (1995) or *Ghost in the Shell*, which gained a cult following, particularly in America, that helped to create interest in this work. Later, Hiroyuki Kitakubo (1963–) was chosen to direct the film.

Saya wears a schoolgirl uniform and looks and behaves like a typical Japanese girl: very feminine and very obedient, as is expected of her. As Neo-Confucianism became part of Japan, the idea of *sanju* or female obedience was maintained in Japanese culture, a series of ideas requiring that women must know their place and show submission to their husbands, to their families (mothers-in-law), and to their sons.[43] However, as ghosts, women return to take revenge when treated unfairly. Thus, Saya is very much in the tradition of the vengeful female ghost, a *yurei*, who seems possessed and intent on getting her revenge. She seems to be a mere "girl," but we learn later that she is "much" older than she looks, which begins to explain why she possesses inhuman demonic powers. Saya pulls out a samurai sword to slash down the vampires, for a sharp wooden staff thrust in the heart is of no use. If enough blood spills out, then these vampires will die. Since something from her past connects to these vampires, this mystery methodically forces the pace of the violence forward. Like D (another vampire hunter), Saya carries the weight of the samurai spirit well.

Like *Ghost in the Shell*, this film contains very graphic scenes of violence, not usually experienced in Western animation. American animators impose a sort of self-censorship in order to sell more to children and teens, while some Japanese animators do not feel obliged to create Disney- or Marvel-like subject matter and treatment. Kenji Kamiyama, one of the screenwriters, explains during an interview that "Japanese animation is created ignoring taboos."[44] This may be a key reason for the great appeal of Japanese animation in America, where the excess is welcomed. The combination of violence and the Vietnam connection help to create a rather political film. Though many of the creators maintain that no political messages were meant, a clear political point seems implied by having the story located in Yokota Air Force Base during the Vietnam War. Kamiyama exclaims (1 of 2): "We weren't really trying to make any kind of ideological statement." Ultimately, the meaning of horror on a military base makes one question the horrors of war that the base represents.

The tragic ending becomes a very Japanese signature way to end a film.[45] Happy endings are not as popular in Japanese films, because the Japanese feel that life is not like that. Films usually end in *mono no aware*, which means the "sadness of things." Japanese audiences desire this: "the savoring of the exquisite pain and grief of mortality."[46] Kamiyama adds that he and other Japanese filmmakers "want audiences to think about what happens after the movie ends. We want them to think more about the film."[47] Some of the vampires are killed, then the film ends, but we hear planes taking off, probably for Vietnam. Saya feeds a dying vampire some of her blood to ease its pain and her own pain as a reluctant hunter, which adds "a realistic quality to a character that might otherwise have been perceived as a cardboard version of the 'tough girl' stereotype."[48] As it were, we begin to think about how many soldiers had died in Vietnam, even perceiving that this reluctant violence is really about the war of reluctance there. Mitshisa Ishikawa, one of the executives of Production I.G, stated during an interview that "vampires kill out of necessity to live. Humans are far more violent because they're violent for political reasons; they're violent when they don't need to be violent, to make a point."[49] But Brian Ruh, a critic, states that the film is about "political vampirism . . . [where] the base itself serves as a form of vampire, taking the Japanese land and sapping its vitality."[50, 51]

With the help of innovative violence and a Gothic, *ronin*-type female as vampire hunter, such geopolitical concerns elevated the film to broader success. While Japan continued to produce mighty postmodern vampire warriors in film, the next section examines how Hong Kong has produced kung fu vampires who traversed a much different evolutionary path.

III. DRACULA REBORN IN HONG KONG CINEMA: *THE LEGEND OF THE SEVEN GOLDEN VAMPIRES*

In 1973, important factors ensured an "unholy" collaboration between Eastern and Western horror cinema traditions. In England, the end of a successful run of Hammer films with Dracula and the undead caused producers to look toward Hong Kong because of its internationally successful kung fu films. Adding to the upheaval was the death of Bruce Lee (1940–1973), the first international Asian action superstar, that same year, thus opening a gap in international cinema as the search for the next Bruce Lee unfolded. Asian film scholar Stephen Tao proclaims that "no other figure in Hong Kong cinema has done as much to bring East and West together in a common sharing of culture as Bruce Lee in his short lifetime."[52] His last film, *Enter the Dragon* (1973), was a joint East-West production between Golden Harvest Pictures and Warner Brothers.[53] For Warner Brothers, *Enter the Dragon* (*Long zheng hu dou*) would become the biggest box office kung fu hit of all time, and for Western audiences, it would define Bruce Lee.[54] However, for Asian audiences, particularly in Hong Kong, it was not as warmly received because "it shows a sullen and sulking Lee forced to submit to the West's perception of him," Stephen Tao (117) is apt to point out, "as a mere action hero. . . . he performs a clichéd characterization of the reserved, inscrutable and humourless

Oriental hero so often seen in Hollywood movies." This perhaps demonstrates perfectly the problem of East-West muddling up of stereotypes and tropes, since Bruce Lee personifies the segregated Oriental Exotic, fighting separately his foes. With the death of Lee, Hammer's gravitation toward genre hybridization (horror–kung fu) became crucial as the studio urgently started to negotiate with the Shaw Brothers to make what they hoped would be cinematic history with Roy Ward Baker (1916–) as the director. Unfortunately, the Hammer-Shaw collaboration would repeat some of the same mistakes as the Warner–Golden Harvest collaboration.

Perhaps something magical or alchemical should have happened in *The Legend of the Seven Golden Vampires* (1974). By the end of 1973, director Roy Ward Baker began shooting in Hong Kong on the Shaw Brothers lot with Chinese superstar David Chiang (1947–) and British horror legend Peter Cushing (1913–1994) playing Professor Van Helsing. Interestingly, the characters include Dracula himself (played by John Forbes-Robertson, 1928–2008), who travels all the way to China in the body of a Chinese Fu Manchu–like sorcerer/warlord named Kah, whom he has possessed. After reaching the small village of Ping Kuei, Dracula takes up residence in Kah's old stronghold and begins raping and sucking the local women dry, but only after he has revivified the legendary seven Golden (mask-wearing) Vampires. In some sort of strange homage to *Shichinin no Samurai* (*Seven Samurai*, 1954), we then meet seven brothers (and one sister) who are charged with fighting off the seven golden vampires (and their army of zombie followers). Naturally, these heroic siblings seek the help of Professor Van Helsing (Hammer's Peter Cushing), who happens to be lecturing in China. Concerning the film's multinationalism and multiculturalism, one author writes, "The film's central conflict is between two white Europeans—the Count and his old nemesis Van Helsing . . . —who, between them, enact a form of mythological colonization."[55] In a sense, the location in China becomes merely an incidental space of exotic otherness, much like the way Hong Kong is treated by the British in many films, as in *Enter the Dragon*.

Unlike *Seven Samurai*, wherein the director, Akira Kurosawa (1910–1998), affords each samurai his own individualized personality (i.e., weaknesses and strengths), *The Legend of the Seven Golden Vampires* does not go into the psychological depth of each brother. Thus, flattened, they emerge as mere bodyguards or workers, protecting Van Helsing, who seems too feeble to fight. Unfortunately, the film concludes with Van Helsing, whose kung fu is terrible, saving the day by fighting hand to hand with the vile Dracula, who unluckily or luckily transforms from the agile Chinese Fu

Manchu/kung fu warlord Kah into a sort of club-footed old European Count. Dracula is powerful but cannot even walk straight and merely trips onto the spear clumsily held by Van Helsing; then he dies, anticlimactically, without much of a fight. The film ends in a sad, pathetic, and boring way, ending with no rising crescendo of violence. Bruce Lee must have turned in his grave. Instead of a masterfully executed climax, the film ends with a whimper.

Action sequences, representing the battle between good and evil, can be entertaining. Often equally important for Asian audiences, however, is how the cinematic heroes combat their own inner demons, just as Siddhartha had battled his own to become enlightened. Buddhism teaches that everyone can become like the Buddha, and everyone must be responsible for his or her own karma or actions.[56] Since people have the opportunity to liberate themselves, this is the ultimate battle that must be fought. Rather than "emphasizing the duality between good and evil, Buddhism distinguishes between wholesome and unwholesome (kusala/akusalamula) tendencies."[57] By fighting such demons, one becomes whole or more rounded. Even for Western action films, an interesting three-dimensional villain makes for a better film.

Unfortunately, the union between East and West in *The Legend of the Seven Golden Vampires* fails to meet either culture's expectations, quickly becoming a quirky cult film hard to categorize. Ray Ward Baker, its director, later said that more could have been done in the film: "One could have done tremendous things with it, but (they) just didn't occur to me until after I'd shot the bloody thing!"[58] Though the undead try to rise up and conquer China in the film, the same cannot be said for the film's attempt to conquer the Asian cinematic world. East-West productions continue to be characterized by cultural miscues and misguided clichés. One critic writes: "While it may not be accurate to describe [it] . . . as a good film[, it's] certainly a memorable one."[59] Dracula and his Western baggage simply fail to impress Asian audiences, and *The Legend of the Seven Golden Vampires*, being neither a good vampire film nor a good kung fu flick, leaves Eastern as well as Western audiences unmoved by the collaboration. It performed in a mediocre manner at best in England but not so well in Asia. Interestingly, Warner Brothers, who initially owned the distribution rights to Hammer films, chose not to release it in America, though the film was later released as *The Seven Brothers Meet Dracula* (1979) with limited success in an edited, shorter version. Though this execution of horror–kung fu genre hybridity is flawed, the idea is not, for the juxtaposition of martial arts and vampires would eventually see light again and bring with it a respect for an authentic representation of Asian metaphysics.

MAO SHAN JIANG SHI QUAN (*SPIRITUAL BOXER II*, 1979): ENTER THE CHINESE VAMPIRES

The Legend of the Seven Golden Vampires, sparking a renewed interest in vampires, particularly for some of its Asian crew members, prompted filmmakers to consider other directions in which the film might have been taken. It had some authentic martial arts stars like Lau Kar Wing (1942–), older brother of legendary fight choreographer Lau Kar Leong (1936–). Leong himself was the fight choreographer of the film. He was also the key fight choreographer of such Cheng Cheh (1923–2002) martial arts masterpieces as *Jin yan zi* (*Golden Swallow* [1968]) and *Ci Ma* (*Blood Brothers* [1973]), which also starred David Chiang. In fact, Cheng Cheh himself helped with the Asian sequences of the film. *The Legend of the Seven Golden Vampires*, indeed, had the potential for success, which is why in 1979, Lau Kar Leong resurrected the hungry ghosts theme by remixing vampires with kung fu once again in a film he would direct himself. With *Spiritual Boxer II*, Leong adds an important ingredient that Jackie Chan's success had helped to inaugurate: humor.[60] This time, he throws out the typical traits held by Western vampires, particularly seen in the tradition of Dracula. Leong adopts the Chinese variation on the vampire with the *jiangshi*, which he resurrects from old folktales, and Lau Kar Wing, who starred in *The Legend of the Seven Golden Vampires*, is also given a role.

Spiritual Boxer II examines the return of the un(re)born (rather than the undead) to their places of burial, their ancestral hometown. The dead should be buried with family ancestors. When someone dies and cannot afford proper transportation, a Taoist priest (*fat-si*) is tasked with "herding" the *jiangshi* back to their hometown to receive a funeral. Rather than carrying bodies home in caskets, Taoist monks use incantations, oral and written, to make the dead walk home. Since rigor mortis has set in and thus the dead are unable to walk, they hop instead. Written incantations (yellow paper with red Chinese characters) are placed on the foreheads of the *jiangshi*, commanding them to stand and move. Humorously, individual incantations must be used for crossing bridges, for stopping, for resting, and so on. (Incidentally, the *fat-si* must carry a large variety of such instructional incantations.)

In *Spiritual Boxer II*, Gordan Lui plays a criminal who escapes in order to seek revenge, all the while managing to elude authorities by pretending to be a *jiangshi*.[61] Also, the apprentice to the Taoist master, played by Yu Wong, fights using a curious and comedic style and shows more vigor by fighting like a vampire with stiff joints. Indeed, he is only successful when he becomes enchanted like a *jiangshi* and fights using his vampire "stiff-joint" style. More importantly, it is here that Leong's genius for invention lies, which unfortunately received little or no attention from the critics. Nonetheless, Leong's absurdly funny but completely fresh action sequences would later become a fundamental tradition of this future genre of horror. In addition, the film concludes in typical Leong fashion with a huge fight sequence between Gordan Lui and his enemies, who, of course, outnumber him. Though the film saw little success at the box office, its contribution to the genre has endured by helping to initiate many of the tropes that future Chinese comedy vampire films eventually adopt. Thus, a new tradition was born, and improvements come when Sammo Hung pushes this new cinematic expression of horror even further.

GUI DA GUI (*CLOSE ENCOUNTER OF A SPOOKY KIND*, 1980): OF HUNGRY GHOSTS

When Bruce Lee died, Sammo Hung (1952–), like other Hong Kong stars, had not yet figured out how to survive in the post–Bruce Lee era. Hung had starred in *Enter the Dragon*, fighting against Lee himself in the opening fight sequence. But he saw something unique in the vision of combining humor and horror that we see in *Spiritual Boxer II*. Stephen Tao acknowledges not only the impact *The Spiritual Boxer II* (1979) had on Hung's *Close Encounter of a Spooky Kind* but also the latter's impact on what was then becoming a successful new hybrid genre.[62] Hung directs, cowrites, and stars in *Close Encounter of a Spooky Kind*, mastering the humorous aspects of the film in much the same way *Spiritual Boxer II* had done. He proves to be a comic genius like his friend Jackie Chan.

The opening of *Close Encounter of a Spooky Kind* is set during a Hungry Ghost Festival, which is a combination of differing religious traditions, but which are not oppositional. In another culture, different religions would be in competition, but in Chinese culture, they are not. The Hungry Ghost Festival combines three different religions: the Confucian idea of respecting ancestors mixed with both Buddhist ideas of rebirth and Taoist ideas about the separation of the soul (*hun* and *p'o*). For Taoists, the soul is reunited when the person is resurrected.[63] For Asian directors, an important part of the success of this new breed of vampire films is the amalgamation of these Asian cultural tropes, themes, and philosophies wherein Taoism mixes with Buddhism. With the addition of Confucianism, a new holy Asian "trinity effect" is birthed.

In Asia, where family reigns supreme, according to Confucianism, ghosts suffering from amnesia is tolerable, but humans must not. Once a year, it is important to remember the dead, especially the hungry ghosts. The festival is based on a story about Mokuren, a follower of Shakyamuni, the Buddha, who saw his mother as a hungry ghost and worried about her. The Buddha tells him to have a ceremony for the dead. In the end, it works, and his mother is at last reborn. Hungry ghosts are spirits who are not being remembered by family members, or who may have died tragically, or who may have suffered injustices during death. Monks and nuns work overtime during the festivals and rites of remembrances.[64] If the ceremonial festival is successful, the ghosts can return to be reborn. Hung artfully places his story within this backdrop.

In *Close Encounter of a Spooky Kind*, Hung plays a character named Courageous (or Bold) Cheung, a pedicab driver, whose wife is having an affair and conspires to use vampires to get rid of him. The Ghost Festival is transformed into a scary setting rather than a festive one in order to frighten Courageous Cheung with phony hungry ghosts; however, it backfires when real ones appear. Yuen Biao plays a real vampire. Instead of sucking blood, Chinese vampires suck out the life force: *chi*. This action becomes one of the major differences between Eastern and Western vampires.[65] Indeed, Courageous Cheung is not sure what is authentic and what is counterfeit. This tension of deception regulates the rhythm of the humor. The film was met with better success than *Spiritual Boxer II*,[66] and the genre would continue to evolve and expand with other Sammo Hung productions.[67]

JIANG SHI XIAN SHENG AND SEQUELS
(*MR. VAMPIRE* AND SEQUELS, [1985–1992])

After *Close Encounter of a Spooky Kind* became an enormous success, Hung continued to modify this new viable formula by producing a series of comedies in Hong Kong during the 1980s with the *Mr. Vampire* films. In them, Ching-Ying Lam, who plays the inspector in *Close Encounter of a Spooky Kind*, plays a Taoist priest. This successful Asian vampire series combines a variety of genres: comedy, horror, and kung fu. Children throughout Asia found themselves with a new likeness to imitate by copying the hopping movements of these zany vampires. Later, this successful series recruited N!xau (1944–2003), the star of *The Gods Must Be Crazy* (1980), resulting in even greater success with *The Crazy Safari* (1991) (aka *The Gods Must Be Crazy III* [*Fei zhou he shang*]), which features future superstar Stephen Chow (1962–)

as the Cantonese narrator. Ricky Lau Koon-Wai (1949–) directed many of the *Mr. Vampire* films (*Mr. Vampire I, II, III, IV,* and *Young Master Vampire*), but he also directed *Close Encounters of the Spooky Kind 2* (*Gui yao gui*, [1990]), which was produced by Sammo Hung.

In the original *Mr. Vampire*, a Taoist *fat-si* (exorcist) is hired to relocate a dead body, or *jiangshi*, because its grave is cursed with bad *feng shui*. A *fat-si* must keep the *jiangshi* in control, because they are attracted to humans and want to suck the *yang* or breath out of them in order to extend their reanimation. The vigor of Yuen Wah as a vampire during the kung fu action sequences heightens the success of the film as well.[68] Lam Ching Ying as the *fat-si* also becomes famous as a result of the film and becomes known as the "Hong Kong Peter Cushing."[69]

The Hong Kong vampire movies had come a long way since Dracula's failed debut in *The Legend of the Seven Golden Vampires*. But after only a few years, the Chinese vampire films begin to lose their appeal for audiences after studios released too many cinematic copycats. However, few could have imagined that what was needed to reinvigorate this genre hybridity once more was actually a return to the East-West collaborative formula initiated during the mid 1970s with *The Legend of the Seven Golden Vampires*. Indeed, "Hong Kong cinema's hybridity, freely mixing elements from East and West," Tao writes, "is perhaps seen to best effect in the horror genre, combing aspects of Western vampire movies, Chinese ghost stories and Hong Kong's own kung fu comedy genres."[70]

CHIN BEI GIN (THE TWINS EFFECT [2003]): COMING FULL CIRCLE, ALMOST

A film that successfully blends Dracula-type tropes with Chinese culture, *The Twins Effect* in many ways transcends previous films in the hybrid genre strain that began with *The Legend of the Seven Golden Vampires*. The film stars the pop singing duo called the Twins, Gillian Chung (1981–) and Charlene Choi (1982–), though they are not twins, and even Jackie Chan makes a cameo appearance.[71] Directed by Dante Lam and codirected by Donnie Yen (1963–), who also choreographs the fight sequences, *The Twins Effect* combines not only horror and comedy but romance as well. The hopping vampires, or revenants, of the previous films give way to a new, yet familiar, breed of vampires who are strikingly Western. Interestingly, the film borrows, among other things, a familiar *Highlander* (1986) plot device. Duke Dekotes (Mickey Hardt), a master vampire/vampire hunter, has killed all the top vampires around the world in order to absorb their energies (*chi*). When he has eliminated them all, he will be transformed into a supervampire with special powers that will allow him to walk in the sunlight (i.e., John Carpenter's *Vampires* [1998]). Prince Kazaf (Edison Chen, 1980–) is the last vampire in the Duke's way. Two vampire hunters, Reeve (Erin Cheng, 1967–) and his young assistant, Gypsy (Gillian Chung), are trying to find the Prince first. However, Prince Kazaf loves Reeve's baby sister Helen (Charlene Choi). In the typical Western vampire fashion, Prince Kazaf avoids sunlight and sleeps in a coffin. However, he is atypically good, for he drinks bottled blood and does not want to kill humans. He also desires to be "hip," sporting a coffin that looks more like a tanning booth with stereo music.

With *The Twins Effect*, we have finally come full circle with a film that offers a viable combination of Western and Eastern metaphysics. The film juxtaposes humor, horror, romance, and beautifully choreographed fight scenes, with two pop singers in the backdrop. *The Twins Effect* is a complete success and achieved a status with Hong Kong audiences that never materialized for *The Legend of the Seven Golden Vampires*. However, *The Twins Effect* is not the crossover hit that *Crouching Tiger, Hidden Dragon* (2000) later becomes. Unfortunately, creating a Dracula-type vampire film with Eastern and Western actors that can achieve the global success we see with *Crouching Tiger, Hidden Dragon* has yet to see reality. So perhaps we have not come completely full circle, but we are close, for undoubtedly the code for success has been decoded. Consequently, what has helped Dracula and his vampire cousins achieve popularity with Asian audiences is perhaps a deeper exploration of the psychology behind Dracula's and the vampire's lust for blood, which is a more Buddhist-centric approach. Asian audiences feel a sense of authenticity in this sort of being, wherein Dracula and vampire narratives finally become meaningful.

CONCLUSIONS: THE BURNING HOUSE OF HORROR

The Twins Effect, *Vampire Hunter D*, and their animated successors are examples of hybridity that work for Asian audiences and, to some degree, for selected American audiences. According to the Lotus Sutra (around the second century BCE), a Buddhist scripture which became popular in the Chinese or Mahayana tradition, a family resides within a house on fire.[72] Within this burning edifice, the children do not seem to notice the ensuing danger, even when the father warns them to leave. Ironically, fiends, devils, and monsters are more enlightened than their human counterparts, for they are responsive to the pain of their skin being roasted: "All of the goblins and ghosts and beasts howled in fear, not knowing how to escape the burning house."[73]

Herein lies the meaning of the parable: humans should know better and should respect the silent screams of demons. The house symbolizes more, for it represents their bodies or realities. Perhaps the initial Dracula and vampire narratives simply forget to decode the empty sounds or the silent howls of horror that Asian audiences expected. The real battle of life is about being awakened to the inner fight, best embodied by the demons we bear within us. We are all trapped in the hypnagogic state of delusion: the Draculas who enter our nightmares parallel the real monsters who surround us everyday, sucking our economies, our minds, our friends. Horror is never a fiction nor a genre; instead, it is a metaphor for the chaotic, mixed vestiges of life, being neither about good and evil, nor about death and rebirth. Hence, horror returns us to our reality and the delusions that inundate us: "In our memories, the reality we believe we've experienced is inevitably mixed with illusion."[74] What can we say is real and what can we say is illusion? Therefore, we stay submerged, immersed, and trapped within, like hungry ghosts imprisoned within the burning house of horror, waiting for *nirvana*.[75]

All is burning. . .
The ear is burning, sounds are burning. . .
The nose is burning, odors are burning. . .
The tongue is burning, flavors are burning. . .
The body is burning, tangibles are burning. . .
The mind is burning, ideas are burning . . .

—"The Fire Sermon"[76]
The Adittapariyaya Sutra

NOTES

1. Patrick Galloway, *Asia Shock: Horror and Dark Cinema from Japan, Korea, Hong Kong and Thailand* (Berkeley: Stone Bridge Press, 2006), 11.

2. Lev Vygotsky, *Thought and Language*, trans. Alex Kozulin (Cambridge: MIT Press, 1986), 212.

3. Vygotsky, *Thought and Language*, 251.

4. I. Q. Hunter, "The Legend of the 7 Golden Vampires," *Postcolonial Studies* 3.1 (2000): 83.

5. In *Hong Kong Cinema: The Extra Dimensions* (London: BFI Publishing, 1997) Stephen Teo, who provides one of the most comprehensive overviews of Chinese vampire films, or what he terms as the "*jiangshi dianying* or cadaver movies" (219),

fails to mention *The Seven Golden Vampires* in the chapter entitled "Ghosts, Cadavers, Demons and Other Hybrids" (219–29), though he does mention Hammer films as being somewhat influential. The chapter focuses on successful Hong Kong films that wove a sense of authentic Chinese folklore into the energy of Hong Kong horror cinema.

6. Monima Chadha and Nick Trakakis, "Karma and the Problem of Evil: A Response to Kaufman," *Philosophy East & West* 57.4 (October 2007): 542.

7. Li Shuang, "The Funeral and Chinese Culture," *Journal of Popular Culture* 27.2 (Fall 1993): 113.

8. See Stephen F. Teiser, *The Ghost Festival in Medieval China* (Princeton: Princeton University Press, 1996), for further discussion of the Chinese version of the festival, and see Robert John Smith, *Ancestor Worship in Contemporary Japan* (Stanford University Press, 1975), for further discussion of the Japanese version of the festival. See also Fernando G. Gutiérrez, "Emakimono Depicting the Pains of the Damned," *Monumenta Nipponica*, vol. 22, no. 3/4 (1967): 278–89.

9. Hungry ghosts are recorded in Pu Songling, *Strange Stories from a Chinese Studio* (1679), a collection of Chinese folktales of the supernatural, and in Lafcadio Hearn, *Kwaidan* (1904), a collection of Japanese folktales of the supernatural. See also Anthony C. Yu, who examines such ghost stories in the Chinese tradition in "Rest, Rest, Perturbed Spirit! Ghosts in Traditional Chinese Prose Fiction," *Harvard Journal of Asiatic Studies*, vol. 47, no. 2 (Dec. 1987): 397-434.

10. Gutierrez, "Emakimono Depicting the Pains of the Damned," 282.

11. Gutierrez, "Emakimono Depicting the Pains of the Damned," 282.

12. In *Ghosts and the Japanese* (Logan: Utah State University Press, 1994), Michiko Iwasaka and Barre Teolken conclude that

> death is not only a common subject in Japanese folklore but seems indeed to be the *principal* topic in Japanese tradition: nearly every festival, every ritual, every custom is bound up in some way with relationships between the living and the dead. . . . death is the *prototypical* Japanese topic—because death brings into focus a number of other very important elements in the Japanese worldview: obligation, duty, debt, honor, and personal responsibility [italics added]. (6)

13. Ichiro Hori, "Japanese Shamanism," from *Religion in the Japanese Experience: Sources and Interpretations*. Ed. H. Bryan Earhart. (Encino: Dickenson Publishing Co., 1974), 98.

14. Confucianism, which originated in China, mixed with Shinto practices found in this festival. See Smith, *Ancestor Worship in Contemporary Japan*, 24.

15. Such vengeful ghosts, Rania Huntington writes, were often in the form of shape-shifting fox spirits (*huli jing*), which were popular for the public who read or knew of Pu Songling's *Strange Stories from a Chinese Studio*, where some thirty-four out of eighty-six stories were about *huli jing* (83). See Rania Huntington, "Foxes and Sex in Late Imperial Chinese Narrative." *Men, Women and Gender in Early and Imperial China*, 2.1 (Jan 2000): 78–128.

16. J. Gordon Melton, *The Vampire Book: The Encyclopedia of the Undead* (Detroit: Visible Ink Press, 1999), 114–16.

17. Paul Barber, *Vampires, Burial and Death: Folklore and Reality* (New Haven, Yale University Press, 1988), 67.

18. Graham R. Lewis points out (38) that a "blurring of definitions" remains between vampire and zombie films in Hong Kong cinema, like *Zombies vs. Ninja* (directed by Godfrey Ho, 1987) and *Spirit vs. Zombie* (directed by Yao Fenpan, 1889). See Graham R. Lewis, "Asian Zombie Apocalypse," *Asian Cult Cinema* 23: (1999): 37–39, 49.

19. See Melton, *The Vampire Book*, 114–16.

20. G. Willoughby-Meade, *Ghost and Vampire Tales of China* (London: East and West, 1925), 21.

21. Steven Harrell, "The Concept of Soul in Chinese Folk Religion," *The Journal of Asian Studies* 38.3 (May 1979): 521.

22. A further complexity exists that G. Willoughby-Meade did not examine. The *hun* is composed of three components, as T. A. Chew shows: "the first component is the 'Sheng-hun' (the Spirit of Growth), the second is the 'Jue-hun' (the Spirit of Awareness), and the third is the 'You-hun' (the Spirit of Thought and Inspiration). 'You-hun' is what most people refer to when they speak of soul" (in *White Sun: Tao of Heaven*, Malaysia: White Sun Enterprise, 2004, www.white-sun.com [accessed March 4, 2007]). The *p'o* has six components: the five sense organs (eyes, ears, nose, tongue, and body) and the mind. When the *hun* and *p'o* are in perfect harmony, the *chi*, the life force, runs smoothly. Though Taoists debate on the number and types of souls, Steven Harrell contends (521) that most folk beliefs keep the number to "two, ten, twelve, three and one."

Walter Liebenthal claims that the ancient origins of the Chinese soul come from the *Book of Rites*. In addition, Liebenthal emphasizes (333) that Taoists or Alchemists were not concerned with the soul but with the immortality of the body. See Walter Liebenthal, "The Immortality of the Soul in Chinese Thought," *Monumenta Nipponica* 8.1/2 (1952): 327–97. Thus, one can begin to understand the origins of the Chinese vampire through such philosophical and religious underpinnings.

23. In ghost stories, the *kuei*, an animal soul, when it is portrayed as a woman, is often revealed literally as an animal. Thus, the *kuei*, disguised as a beautiful woman, reveals herself at the end to be a fox as in King Xu's *Hua Pi Zhi YinYang Fawang* (1993) or *Painted Skin* based on a Pu Songling tale. Of course, Ching-Ying Lam (1952–1997), who played the Taoist master in the *Mr. Vampire* series, plays a Taoist monk in this film. In 2008, a bigger-budgeted version by Gordan Chan (1960–) was released with *Wa pei (Painted Skin)*.

24. Stephen Tao, *Hong Kong Cinema: The Extra Dimensions* (London: BFI Publishing, 1997), 221.

25. Smith, *Ancestor Worship*, 92.

26. Stephen F. Teiser, "'Having Once Died and Returned to Life': Representation of Hell in Medieval China," *Harvard Journal of Asiatic Studies* 48.2 (Dec. 1988): 451.

27. Wing-Tsit Chan, *Source Book in Chinese Philosophy* (Princeton: Princeton University Press, 1963), 12.

28. Daniel Farson, *Dracula: A Biography of Bram Stoker* (New York: St. Martin's Press, 1975), 107.

29. Laurence C. Bush, *Asian Horror Encyclopedia* (San Jose: Writer's Club Press, 2001), 193.

30. Stuart Galbraith IV, *Japanese Science Fiction, Fantasy and Horror Films: A Critical Analysis of 103 Features Released in the United States, 1950–1992* (London: McFarland and Company, 1993), 207.

31. Stuart Galbraith IV, *Japanese Science Fiction, Fantasy and Horror Films*, 227.

32. Stuart Galbraith IV, *Japanese Science Fiction, Fantasy and Horror Films*, xvii.

33. A sequel was released with *Vampire Hunter D: Bloodlust* (2000). Though boasting a higher budget, it seems to lack the gothic rawness and edge of the original. This paper will not examine its failures and prefers to focus on the first film's successes.

34. Wayne Stein and John Browning, "The Western Eastern: Decoding Hybridity and Cyber*Zen* Gothic in *Vampire Hunter D* (1985)," ed. Andrew Hock-Soon Ng, *Asian Gothic: Essays on Literature, Film and Anime* (Jefferson: McFarland, 2008), 213. (See also in this volume, 282.)

35. Emperor Hirohito's "mystical ancestry" was recorded in such ancient texts as *Kojiki* and *Nihonshoki*. For further discussion, see Takie Sugiyama Lebra, "Self and Other in Esteemed Status: The Changing Culture of the Japanese Royalty from Showa to Heisei," *Journal of Japanese Studies* 23.1 (Summer 1997): 265.

36. Takie Sugiyama Lebra, "Self and Other in Esteemed Status," *Journal of Japanese Studies*, 267.

37. Rob Latham, *Consuming Youth: Vampires, Cyborgs, and the Culture of Consumption* (Chicago: University of Chicago Press, 2002), 1.

38. In 1997, *Vampire Princess Miyu* became a twenty-six-episode series. Though there were some interesting changes in the series from the original OVA series, this paper focuses on the original, which I feel is richer and more pertinent.

39. Susan Napier, "Vampires, Psychic Girls, Flying Women and Sailor Scouts: Four Faces of the Young Female in Japanese Popular Culture," in *The Worlds of Japanese Culture: Gender, Shifting Boundaries and Global Cultures*, ed. D. P. Martinez (Cambridge: Cambridge University Press, 2003), 95.

40. Christopher Bolton, "Anime Horror and Its Audience: *3X3 Eyes* and *Vampire Princess Miyu*," in *Japanese Horror Cinema*, ed. Jay McRoy (Honolulu: University of Hawaii Press, 2005), 66–76.

41. A PlayStation 2 version of *Blood* followed. Mamoru Oshii would write a trilogy in novel format about the story. Furthermore, a *manga* version by *hentai* (sexy) artist Benkyo Tamoki would be released (2000) with some nudity and lesbian sex scenes. Later, a TV series *Blood+* (2005) was created, and Chris Nahon (1968–) began directing a live action version, which was then released in 2009.

42. Brian Ruh, *Stray Dog of Anime: The Films of Mamoru Oshii* (New York: Palgrave MacMillan, 2004), 154–55.

43. Richard Storry, *The Way of the Samurai* (New York: Galley Press, 1987), 89.

44. Sara Ellis, "Kenji Kamiyama on Anime," *AkadotRETAIL*, www.akadot.com/story.php?id=222 (accessed March 4, 2007): 2 of 2.

45. James Cameron's *Titanic* (1997) was a huge blockbuster in Japan, the film's sad ending undoubtedly helping.

46. Patrick Galloway, *Stray Dog & Lone Wolves: The Samurai Film Handbook* (Berkeley: Stone Brook Press, 2005), 25.

47. Ellis, "Kenji Kamiyama on Anime," 2 of 2.

48. Dani Cavallaro, *The Cinema of Mamoru Oshii* (London: McFarland and Company, 2006), 168.

49. Luis Reyes, "Chatting with Ishikawa," *Akadot.com*, www.akadot.com/article/article-ishikawa1.html, quoted in Ruh, *Stray Dog of Anime*, 163.

50. Luis Reyes, "Chatting with Ishikawa," *Akadot.com*, 163.

51. Interestingly, *Blood+*, the TV series, is set in Okinawa. Once again, we see Americans as foreign occupiers in Japan demonstrating "political vampirism," but this is also compounded by the perception of the Japanese as original occupiers by the native Okinawans, who feel it was their island first. Thus, we see layers of historical and political bloodsucking. Indeed, *karate* is said to have developed as a special art to fight against the Japanese samurai spirit and occupation. The *nunchakus* was a weapon developed by the Okinawans because swords were illegal. Bruce Lee uses nunchaus in his Hong Kong film *Jing wu men* (1972) (or *Fist of Fury*, which was called *Chinese Connection* in America) to beat up the Japanese. Lee understood the significance of his choice.

52. Tao, *Hong Kong Cinema*, 110.

53. The film was released after Lee's mysterious death, and, Tao (117) adds, ". . . is really an uneasy amalgamation of antithetical East-West sentiments."

54. *Wo hu cang long (Crouching Tiger, Hidden Dragon* [2000]) would pass *Enter the Dragon* as the biggest martial arts moneymaking film of all time and even become the biggest moneymaking foreign film of all time.

55. Leon Hunt, *Kung Fu Cult Masters* (London: Wallflower Press, 2003), 164.

56. Ichiro Hori explains, "Buddhism proclaimed human equality and the equal possibility for all to become Buddhas (Saints of enlightenment)." See Ichiro Hori, "Japanese Folk-Beliefs," *American Anthropologists, New Series* 61.3 (June 1959): 405–24. This becomes one of the key reasons Buddhism is integrated into the philosophy of martial artists in Asia, especially as demonstrated by the Shaolin monks of China (represented in kung fu films) and the samurai of Japan (represented in *chambara* [samurai] films). The martial artist becomes responsible for his or her own success in a battle. Therefore, praying to some higher power is not necessary. This self-reliance remains attractive to warriors who train for years to perfect their craft. Thus, viewers vicariously can see how the hero within can win the day.

57. David Loy, "The Three Poisons Institutionalized," *Tikkun* 22.3 (May/June 2007), rpt. in *The Buddhist Channel*, www.buddhistchannel.tv/index.php?id=8,4046,0,0,1,0 (accessed 11 July 2008): 2 of 4.

58. Bey Logan, *Hong Kong Action Cinema* (London: Titan Books, 1995), 103.

59. Daniel O'Brien, *Spooky Encounters: A Gwailo's Guide to Hong Kong Horror* (Manchester: Critical Vision Book, 2003), 11.

60. *Spiritual Boxer I (Siu Chien* 1975) was not about vampires but about the fake mystical boxers of the Boxer Rebellion, and it perhaps used humor more successfully.

61. Gordan Liu would later play the Shaolin monk in such classics as the *Shao Lin san shi liu fang (36th Chamber of Shaolin* [1978]) and in Quentin Tarantino's *Kill Bill* (2003/2004) films.

62. Tao, *Hong Kong Cinema*, 224.

63. Essentially, the Hungry Ghost Festival becomes an extension of basic Chinese funeral rites remembering the dead. As Li Shuang explains: "Generally speaking, Chinese funerals reveal the core of Chinese religions—Confucian, Taoism and Buddhism." See Li Shuang, "The Funeral and Chinese Culture," *Journal of Popular Culture* 27.2 (Fall 1993): 119.

64. According to scholar Kenneth Ch'en, the Chinese originally rejected earlier variations of Buddhism that tried to enter the country because these variations lacked stories about filial piety. After all, the story of Buddha concerns someone who left his father, wife, and son. When new stories and traditions, like the Hungry Ghost Festival, that respected filial piety were introduced, the Chinese reconsidered and welcomed Buddhism. Ch'en's work offers great insight into how Buddhism in China became more about family. See Kenneth Ch'en, "Filial Piety in Chinese Buddhism," *Harvard Journal of Asiatic Studies* 28 (1968): 81–97.

65. Both Sammo Hung and Yuen Biao grew up together with Jackie Chan in the Chinese Opera.

66. O'Brien, *Spooky Encounters*, 27.

67. Indeed, as Daniel O'Brien explains, *Close Encounter of a Spooky Kind* was an unanticipated hit that led to many copycat productions, causing Hung himself to further develop the newest of subgenres, mixing humor, horror, kung fu, and Chinese vampires. See Daniel O'Brien, *Spooky Encounters*, 27.

68. Yuen Wah also grew up with Sammo Hung in the Chinese Opera, and Wah also did the acrobatic stunts and doubled for Bruce Lee in *Enter the Dragon*.

69. O'Brien, *Spooky Encounters*, 56.

70. O'Brien, *Spooky Encounters*, 219.

71. The film is renamed *Vampire Effect* in America. A sequel starring Jackie Chan's son was also produced, but it is not as original nor as innovative as the first, which shows at the box office.

72. The Mahayana branch of Buddhism (China, Korea, and Japan) differs from the original school of Buddhism, or Theravedan or Hinayana tradition (Sri Lanka and Thailand). As Bernard Faure points out, the Lotus Sutra became popular in both China and Japan. For further discussion on differences between the various traditions, see Bernard Faure, *Buddhism* (New York: Konecky and Konechy, 1998), 105.

73. Burton Watson, *Lotus Sutra* (New York: Columbia University Press, 1993), 64.

74. Mamoru Oshii, *Blood: The Last Vampire, Night of the Beasts*, trans. Camellia Nieh (Milwaukee: DH Press, 2005), 7.

75. To reiterate, *nirvana* literally means "extinguishing the flame."

76. This version of the sutra is from Theravedan Buddhism, the oldest branch, translated by Ñanamoli Thera from the Pali. *The Adittapariyaya Sutra: Three Cardinal Discourses from the Buddha*. Buddhist Publication Society. 1981, www.accesstoinsight.org/tipitaka/sn/sn35/sn35.028.nymo.html.

· 15 ·

Identity Crisis:
Imperialist Vampires in Japan?

Nicholas Schlegel

*A*n often-overlooked aspect of cinema resides in its multicultural origins. Although Thomas Edison and the Lumière Brothers were essentially using the same technology, they were in fact producing aesthetically distinct products. By the time the Soviets were analyzing the cinematic works of D. W. Griffith, it was apparent that emerging techniques were of great interest to other cultures. To this end it is reasonable to assert that film is a collaborative, hybridized, global medium; its power to influence and inspire is undeniable and compelling. Social, revolutionary, and artistic movements are often reflected in the film, literature, music, and art (graphic arts, sculpture, illustration, painting, fashion, civil engineering, and architecture) of a given time and place. In the particular case of film, the power to influence is fierce and reaches millions cross-culturally who only need the ability to see and hear.

To foreground this notion, let us briefly consider the case study of the horror films that defined Universal Studios in the 1930s and 1940s. Examination reveals a wealth of European talent (notably German and English) in front of and, more importantly, behind the camera. This cross-cultural influence produced a body of films that are aesthetically Expressionistic (I refer to the German cinematic context of this movement), but moreover, these texts were created by individuals whose background and training were part of this contemporaneous scene. Every motion picture producing culture has been influenced by outside traditions and aesthetics. This influence is not only unavoidable but provides a wealthy repository that creates and sustains a *pleasure* in viewing and consuming "foreign" or other cinema.[1]

On the subject of the latter, a certain "other" Eastern European Count has been invading soil, blood, nightmares, movie theaters, and living rooms for well over a century. The popularity and resiliency of *Dracula* (and vampires

Legacy of Dracula (Yûreiyashiki no kyôfu: Chi o suu ningyô [Japanese title], 1970). Courtesy of Toho Company/PhotoFest

in general) in literature, film, and popular culture is a testament to the timeless themes of Bram Stoker's novel and the richness of his characterizations. At Universal Studios, director Tod Browning, cinematographer Karl Freund, art director Charles D. Hall, and actor Bela Lugosi set the aesthetic standard by which all other *Dracula* adaptations (or generically, vampire cinema) are measured. Indeed, Browning's *Dracula* (1931) was the first horror picture of the sound era; it constructed the benchmark for other cinema-producing cultures and inadvertently created a model of how vampire films were supposed to look and sound.[2]

This chapter explores the curious existence of a trio of Japanese financed, produced, directed and distributed vampire films from the early 1970s: *Legacy of Dracula (Yûreiyashiki no kyôfu: Chi o suu ningyô* [Japanese title], 1970), *Lake of Dracula (Noroi no yakata: Chi o sû me* [Japanese title], 1971) and *Evil of Dracula (Chi o suu bara* [Japanese title], 1974), and hereafter, the Toho Dracula Trilogy. Under the aegis of legendary genre film studio *Toho*, these three films, all directed by Michio Yamamoto and written by Ei Ogawa, Hiroshi Nagano, and Masaru Takesue, are marked with an odd aesthetic that has motivated the author to structure a formal inquiry into the *raison d'être* behind their inception and creation. In this chapter, I will examine how these three texts draw upon a Western gothic aesthetic (which many critics viewed pejoratively) as an aesthetic device. This device, along with specific thematic developments, allow for manifestations of Japanese national identity to be revealed in the subtext of these films. One of the key ways in which this identity is located is by defining what Japanese identity *is* and what it is *not*.

The Toho Dracula Trilogy, while confusing to some Western audiences, simultaneously through its atmospheric mise-en-scène, provides us access to what is ideologically latent in these texts. The current of fear that runs through the series is that of foreign encroachment; indeed, the very same fear of encroachment or cosmopolitanism that is found throughout Stoker's *Dracula*.[3] The first portion of this study characterizes and explores the cross-cultural properties of these films. The second portion attempts to explain the more formal issues of identity in the modern Japanese horror film. The goal of the chapter is not to affix a thesis as to why these films exist, but rather, what cultural, political, and/or social factors aid in *explaining* their existence.

The genres of horror, fantasy, and science fiction have been the perfect vessels through which ideological tensions and cultural anxieties are transmitted. Both in literature and film, they suppress obvious and direct relations to societal issues and supplant them into stories that are removed from the contemporary social *milieu*. Toho was a home for this type of genre programming. The studio successfully divested its attention and efforts across multiple genre streams: the disaster film, the science fiction film, the Godzilla franchise, the Kaiju series,[4] and the horror film. Toho remains today a major force in contemporary Japanese cinema.

The Toho Dracula Trilogy, however, presents a complicated case study, as the films have been received and indeed, criticized for, bearing a distinctly Western aesthetic in both form and content. The general criticisms leveled against these films appear to eschew the pleasures to be experienced through the promise of repetition and difference, which define and refine the text, reader, and genre triad. I argue that situating and contextualizing these films, bringing that which is "hidden" to the surface, shall more than adequately explain the Toho Dracula Trilogy's admittedly odd aesthetic.

What is at stake in this chapter, then, is the incommensurability of aesthetic signification. Or put another way, how does one measure, or indeed, compare the value of aesthetics? When horror aficionados and critics attack a film (among other things, a social document and cultural product) on the basis of such criteria, what valuable insights are lost in such narrow-minded comparisons? Beyond these concerns, I will provide basic industrial and economic analysis to further contextualize capitalist business practices in the global motion picture industry.

The temptation to incorporate an authorial view into this analysis is attractive; Michio Yamamoto directed all three, and it is probable that this is of some significance. However, it is not the intent of this chapter to evaluate these films through the determinist lens of auteur theory; such an endeavor would likely reduce other very salient factors. Nor do I intend to pass judgment on auteur theory in general; such debates are better left for the theorists to ponder.[5]

Indeed, films are simultaneously works of art, economic products, technological benchmarks, historical documents, cultural artifacts, and so on. To reduce a film (or body of films) to the work of a sole artist will not benefit the broader concerns of this chapter or frame the period in which they were created, exhibited, and received.

As a historical inquiry, this study aims to provide judicious aesthetic, economic, and social contextualization. Beginning with the aesthetic, Robert Allen and Douglass Gomery suggest in *Film History: Theory and Practice* that "the classical Hollywood film style constitutes an aesthetic system that can be used (or reacted against) by filmmakers. For audiences, it represents an important part of their horizon of expectations, establishing what a fictional film is 'supposed' to look and sound like."[6] Of course, when viewing, for example, third world cinema, an American audience is presented with a whole set of content and form variances that don't neatly "fit" into the mainstream diet most audiences consume. This is presumably why the Toho Dracula Trilogy confounds Western audiences. Audiences *expect* to experience uniquely Japanese vampires bound to tropes and conventions associated with Japanese mythology and folklore, yet this is not even remotely the case.[7]

As already stated, all three films would seem to portray in form, content, and aesthetic a distinctly Western identity and seemingly, ideology and sensibility (as I will argue, a false presumption). This Eastern troika of vampire films travels all the way to the Transylvanian Alps for their folkloric and mythological substance, permeating the films with an odd, almost surrealistic quality that is at once both alluring and completely disjointed. The juxtaposition is awkward and confusing for the simple reason that this representation is not part of Japan's past, present, or (I speculate with fair confidence) future, which presumes that Krakauer claimed correctly that cinematic works exist relative to the context of the world around them and to the fidelity of their representation.[8] It is my contention, however, that these three films do in fact exist relative to the culture that produced them, but not manifestly so.

The new aesthetic experience is built upon previous movements in the arts. Tim Burton, Quentin Tarantino, or indeed nearly any Director's Guild member would find himself or herself unemployed if there were a ban on aesthetic influence or reproduction.[9] I would argue that the ownership of an aesthetic impedes its appreciation and progress and undermines salient factors mentioned above. The reasons behind the Western aesthetic that inhabit the Toho Dracula Trilogy are varied and complex, but I shall offer some suggestions as to exactly what they may be.

Why then do we have this Toho Dracula Trilogy and what exactly is it imitative of? There are several reasonable explanations to these questions. The first and most plausible consideration is cross-cultural; Great Britain provides a case in point. In the United Kingdom, the "Hammer House of Horror" reigned supreme from roughly 1957 to 1975. Britain's Hammer Pictures Ltd. was the single most successful independent studio ever to operate outside the Hollywood oligopoly of the studio system era (the vertically integrated Big Five: Paramount, Warner Brothers, MGM, RKO, and Fox). It is crucial here to note that Hammer's influence on the horror film genre is immeasurable. Beginning with the watershed *Curse of Frankenstein* (1957), Hammer ushered in an era of blood, breasts, gore, and ghoulish stories fueled by suppressed Victorian energies and bathed it all in Technicolor washes for audiences to luxuriate in. In Heide Kaye's essay on Gothic film, she notes on Hammer Studios:

> The Hammer films offer a highly coloured, highly sexualized image of the traditional Gothic texts, tending towards the flamboyance of Grand Guignol instead of suspense. These reflect post-war society and its emphasis on youth culture in conflict with an older generation. The buxom starlets, gory scenes and decadent settings glamorize the conflict against sexual repression and the class system. . . . The vampire is clearly a sexualizing force for both men and women.[10]

This statement foregrounds several issues that need addressing and situating in relation to the Toho Dracula Trilogy. The vampire as bloodthirsty foreign invader is a very old and very important thematic characteristic in vampire literature, originating with Stoker's *Dracula* (1897). The ritual of bloodletting, blood ingestion, and blood intermingling associated as a major trope of vampire literature and film can be read as foreign contamination not only of the soil but, more importantly, the host. The "kiss of the vampire" is penetrative and does not concern itself with sperm, but rather blood. This infiltration of "otherness" in a bloodline brings into question issues concerning identity, which I will examine in depth in the second portion of this chapter.

From a managerial perspective, the economic foresight with which Hammer sought to resurrect the dormant literary and cinematic properties of *Frankenstein, Dracula, The Wolfman, The Mummy, The Phantom of the Opera,* and so on, was uncanny. The films, many of which were singularly Gothic in theme and content, did extraordinary box office in the United Kingdom and foreign markets. The result, as is often the case, is that many producers from around the globe were eager to replicate not only the aesthetic attributes of the films but, they hoped, their box office receipts as well.[11]

In summary, Toho studios and the films' creative personnel clearly used Hammer as a template for business possibilities and a model for aesthetic mimicry. Similarly, the Toho advertising campaigns reproduced with detailed accuracy the Hammer layout and the studio's attention to lurid yet salient exploitation factors.

The post–World War II years in Japan were forged upon the greatest geographic destruction a single nation had ever endured. A decade later, motion picture production nearly soared proportionately to the level of devastation Japan witnessed; cinema became an important social glue for the trauma-weary Japanese. In the 1950s, independent producers such as Mitsugu Okura (Japan's most notorious exploiteer) made a lucrative career in producing and exhibiting what would become Japan's own unique brand of exploitation cinema. Patrick Macias notes in *Tokyo Scope: The Japanese Cult Film Companion*:

> [Mitsugu] began operating movie theaters in red light districts and other disreputable areas of town. By the 1950s, the former carnival barker had his very own theater chain. . . . managing some 2000 screens meant that he was constantly in need of more and more product. . . . In 1957 Okura had produced the pioneering erotic-grotesque film *Kenpei to barabara shi bijin* [*The Military Policeman and the Dismembered Beauty*], and it proved to be the model for the sex and spook films that followed. . . . Okura brought such treasures as Roger Corman's Edgar Allan Poe adaptions and Jess Franco's *Awful Dr. Orloff* to Japan for the very first time. But he also had a penchant for drastically cutting his acquisitions, retitling them to play up an often non-existent "sexy" angle, repacking them into anthology formats and sometimes even misleadingly promoting a single feature as a double feature![12]

This statement illustrates an interest in transgressive cinema in postwar Japan. The United States helped to establish the model for exploitation films and the characteristics that define the production, distribution, and marketing strategies for this genre. Mitsugu not only imported exploitation programming from the United States and Europe and built a business model based on American practices, but eventually he bought out Shin Toho studios and began producing a cycle of exploitation films that continues to flourish in Japan today. The substance of Mitsugu's productions was in form and content Japanese. However, the salient exploitation factors were primal and non-culture specific: sex, violence, rebellion, youth culture, and taboos were the necessary ingredients to bolster box office returns. By the 1970s, Japan's exploitation output was competitively prodigious.

Though we may appear to be away from the immediate subject of this chapter, in fact, we are brought back to the question of appropriation and business models. Both *Lake of Dracula* and *Evil of Dracula* are derivative of Hammer's *Horror of Dracula* (1958), *Brides of Dracula* (1960), and *Dracula Has Risen from the Grave* (1968). *Lake of Dracula* combines elements from these three films (the vampire's death, homoerotic undertones, and unintentional impalement) while *Evil of Dracula* cashes in on the British trilogy of lesbian vampire films, better known as the Karnstein Trilogy. *The Vampire Lovers* (1970), *Lust for a Vampire* (1970), and *The Twins of Evil* (1972).[13] In fact, *Evil of Dracula* is very reminiscent of the US production of *Count Yorga, Vampire* (1970), which owes a debt to the very same Hammer films that Toho was imitating.[14] Upon first glance, all of these films would appear to be caught in an endless cycle of *homage* and/or appropriation, but what ultimately begins to separate the Japanese entries is a slow but steady progression from so-called aesthetic replication to a poetic fluidity with the camera and an atmospheric mise-en-scène that transcends imitation. All three films progressively begin to display moments of lyrical horror, and, in some instances, deliver more accomplished effects than the Hammer films.

Yet, in what is a typical review, contemporary movie critics disagree. Hereafter, I refer to reviewers and critics to provide substantive examples regarding the social reception of the trilogy. British film author and editor Jasper Sharp provides the following from a review on the film:

> [*Lake of Dracula*'s attempt] at retaining the iconography of the European gothic just [doesn't] ring true—derelict mansions and candelabras in 70s Japan??? [*sic*] Aside from our cute, mini-skirted, Barbie doll-like heroines, there is nothing endemically Oriental in this film, and the conviction of the inherent psycho-sexual component which underpins this type of horror lies smothered by the superficialities of a script that is 50% amateur Freudianism and 50% genre contrivance.[15]

Callous value judgments aside, Sharp, a Japanese cinema author and critic, sets up his problem with the films, but offers no explanation of the phenomenon he judges. That *Lake of Dracula* should offer a palimpsest of architectural mise-en-scène should not really surprise audiences, particularly when Japanese cities and villages were undergoing massive modernization and especially when the vampire has been shown to be originally from Europe. The film's horror genre clichés or its depictions of repression of adolescent trauma may not be subtly deployed, but film is a culturally hybridized medium, and Hammer unquestionably provided a template for the trilogy. Moreover, Sharp cannot resist the temptation to compare Yamamoto's trilogy to Western equivalents. Creating a binary, he continues: "Just compare this [treatment] with Stephanie Rothman's attempt at relocating the fundamental mythos to California in 1971's *The Velvet Vampire*, for example, or Kathryn Bigelow's sublime reconception of vampirism in 1987's *Near Dark*."[16]

Rather than simply assert that the Dracula trilogy is derivative, the more appropriate question might be, what technological, economic, social, aesthetic, historic, or philosophical conditions led to the creation of these films to begin with? To answer some of these questions, we must look at Japan's era of modernity, the defining characteristics of this era, questions of imperialism, and ultimately—identity.

Arguably, it is the question of identity that plagues these three entries from the Japanese horror canon. At the very least, it troubles Western critics because identity is thematically both manifest and latent in virtually every type of Japanese thriller; it is a central trope that is at the core of nostalgia for the past and a technological naissance that thrust Japan into its place as a major economic power in the late twentieth century.

If citizenship and national identity form a permanent bond, then it may help this discussion to investigate the Japanese era of modernity. Japanese modernity is generally acknowledged as emerging shortly after American Commodore Perry's steamships arrived off the coast of Japan in 1854 seeking commerce treaties with the relatively inexperienced (in Western negotiations, that is) Japanese diplomats. It is a debatable point whether these events entered Japan into imperialistic frontier politics perhaps a bit prematurely, but regardless, international modernization had begun, and a bond formed between the United States and Japan that went beyond mere trade routes. In her analysis of Japanese imperialism, Hilary Conroy notes: "The first stage of Japanese imperialism was remarkable for its restraint, the last for its excess. Yet, the two are observably interconnected. Ideas and attitudes which emerged in, but did not dominate the Meiji era ran rampant in the 1930s to bring Japan to horror and ruin."[17]

The post–World War II period in Japan constituted a comprehensive restructuring at the hands of the victors. Historian Michael Auslin suggests the administration of a "noble" imperialism during the Allied occupation:

> . . . from the beginning of the Occupation in September 1945, relations were surprisingly peaceful. The initial Occupation reforms under Supreme Commander Douglas MacArthur were as far-reaching as anything attempted by the Meiji leaders—land holdings were redistributed, women

given the vote, a Constitution written, and school curricula revamped. This was a crash course in American culture and society, as well as a second period of domestic modernization.[18]

Indeed, one of the more civil aspects of the new political restructuring in Japan was to essentially broaden existing amendments of the Meiji Constitution; economic, educational, and political reform was eagerly implemented during the Occupation. This "crash course" Auslin mentions led to a speeding locomotive of technological and industrial confidence that was bewildering to even the Japanese. And crash the train did, not exclusively with emerging ideologies born out of new constitutional ratifications, but with a sense of *self and of other from the past.* This concept brings us back to the question of identity, or more appropriately, a lack of identity. In his case study on Japanese horror, Ramie Tateishi notes

> . . . a repressing of the past in the name of progress and the so-called "modern" . . . entails a form of active destruction, insofar as it involves a wiping away of the previous foundation in order to construct a new one. The notion of horror implied in this buried/forgotten past is that the remnants of yesterday may turn vengeful as a consequence of being denied, ignored, or otherwise erased.[19]

This notion of a monstrous past is seen in many Japanese films of the 1960s; *Kwaidan* (1964) and *Onibaba* (1964) offer prime examples here. However, was there any fear or anxiety over Western imperialism or contamination on display in other Japanese films or genre programming of this era? At its most basic, *Godzilla* (1954) is an example of experiential trauma at the hands of an invader. The legendary image of Godzilla breathing radioactive fire over a blazing Tokyo skyline while people, buildings, cars, and tanks are demolished is a powerful vehicle for social commentary and a clear metaphor for the destruction of Hiroshima and Nagasaki and the fire bombings of Tokyo and dozens of other cities. It is not coincidental, of course, that the hibernating prehistoric dinosaur was awoken by the hydrogen bomb test "Bravo Shot" conducted in the Marshall Islands in March of 1954. Radioactive material was carried by ocean winds into the harbors of Japan, where radiation contaminated Japanese fisherman and their goods with deadly effects.[20]

True to a genre's conventions and laws, the cycle of ghostly pasts endemic to Japan's culture has enjoyed a current rebirth; ghosts are becoming vengeful spirits from the grave and exerting their powers through videotapes and other technological gadgets in films such as *Ringu* (1998), *Ju-on* (2000), and *Dark Water* (2002). However, the Toho Dracula Trilogy circumvents the implied conventions of Japan's most popular and powerful genre—the ghost story—in favor of the Western gothic tableaux. My contention and belief is that many Western critics and fans failed to see that this tableaux is merely (highly significant) "window dressing" that primitively conceals layered ideologies concerning national identity.

The first entry in the Toho Dracula Trilogy, *Legacy of Dracula* (1970), is embedded with an interesting tri-aesthetic. Here I rely on *Video Watchdog* publisher and editor Tim Lucas for a useful and accurate description:

> [*Legacy of Dracula*] unreels like a delicate mutant fusion of classical Japanese ghost stories and the Mexican folklore involving *la Llorona* [*The Crying Woman*]. . . . *Legacy of Dracula* is a run-of-the-mill haunted house offering with all the familiar locations and scenes—the secluded old house, the midnight investigations of a noise, the fake scares as people rifle through closets—and only a few, all-too-brief flares of poetical horror to make its fairly stingy running time worthwhile. With her night black hair, milky moonlight-blue skin and transfixing stare, Kobayashi's weeping vampire is visually arresting, but too subtly employed; she is a light *frisson* rather than a serious chill.[21]

As such, *Legacy of Dracula* provides an interesting merger of Universal's "haunted house" tropes, Mexican folkloric treatments, and traditional Japanese ghost conventions. Its overall effect is visually stunning; its thematic treatment is clever and unexpected in spite of being slightly tethered to its original sources. Most importantly, it proved successful enough to have laid the foundation upon which the sequels were constructed. Let me briefly indicate here that it is in the two subsequent films in this trilogy that the direct link to Stoker's Dracula is found, but also, where issues of national identity become more salient.

The second entry, *Lake of Dracula* (1971), is more comfortable with the material, more confident in its direction, more derivative of the Hammer model, and indeed, more fun. We are introduced to our five-year-old future heroine, Akiko, in a precredit sequence that provides many international iconographic cues. We fade into an almost "red sky in the morning, sailor take warning" seaside scene. The first visual of the film thus locates us physically and allegorically at the scene of Commodore Perry's negotiations to open up trade with Japan. The trusty and time-honored "chase the disobedient pet" contrivance leads young Akiko to a heavily green- and blue-gelled hut (from the outside)/castle (on the inside), which appears to be a cross between a Caspar David Freidrich painting and a nomadic dwelling. The interior is lavishly adorned with Western gothic flourishes: chandeliers, suits of armor, and cobwebbed arches; in short, a near replica of Hammer's often recycled castle set from *Horror of Dracula*. The home is mere seconds from the coast, suggesting settlement or encroachment of a foreign invader. Shortly after entering the dwelling, Akiko cautiously approaches a vampire bride, long white gown, raven haired, who is seated and playing a piano. When Akiko asks the vampire bride if she has seen her dog, the vampire bride pivots slowly, like a marionette, and we see her pale white visage. As Akiko turns in terror to flee, we cut to an eyeline match of the Count standing atop the massive staircase—glaring at Akiko; in a sudden cut to an extreme close-up, we are shown his bloodstained "eye," which will forever imprint itself on Akiko's psyche. This image is then transposed to a "negative" state where the titles are superimposed.

The film fades to the present, when Akiko, now an adult art teacher, has found therapeutic value through her art; the classic Freudian repression of this trauma has stamped her psyche with blurry horrific visions that she then pours onto the canvas. Shortly thereafter, in what is a distinct nod to nearly *every* Dracula film, we are witness to the arrival of the foreign antagonist; this time, however, in Akiko's town, locating his evil in the here and now as opposed to merely a memory. A truck delivers a crate containing a coffin, and the rest is self-explanatory.

Jasper Sharp's review is certainly justified in its highlighting of psychoanalytic theory; Freud informs much of *Lake of Dracula* and *Evil of Dracula*. However, again, his assertion begs the question what exactly is "amateur" Freudianism? It is a useful plot device to have Akiko continually question her sanity, as her family and friends are well aware of her past traumas and her inability to slay her inner demons.

The bulk of the film situates the diegesis in the *fantastic*.[22] Akiko's fiancé, Saeki, is a doctor who would rather explain away strange occurrences through science and reason rather than superstition and the supernatural. Freud punctuates the beginning of the film powerfully and then reemerges at the end; Akiko and her fiancé return to the primal scene of her childhood trauma and force a showdown with the Count, who has inducted Akiko's sister Natsuko into his cult of vampirism.

A run-of-the-mill battle ensues, and the vampire is destroyed by accidental impalement. Natsuko collapses and, cleansed of her impurities, returns to her normal state. It is of note that there is a basic social unit lacking in all three films. Fiancé Saeki and sister Natsuko represent her family structure. Lacking are any patriarchal figures; especially absent is the role of the father.[23] The "normative" structure of their family has been restored, and the film ends on the ashen image of the disintegrating vampire.

Lake of Dracula sets the story in the present (something Hammer would follow suit with the following year[24]), and the dialectic of Western psychological thought in an Asian setting is continued in the third and final film to be discussed.

In keeping with the semi-loose thread of continuity in the series, the same actor reprises the role of the ubiquitous Count in *Evil of Dracula*. The narrative is loosely based on Hammer's *Brides of Dracula* and *Lust for a Vampire* (1971), especially in its employment of an all-girls' school as its setting.[25] Professor Shiraki begins his tenure as a professor of psychology at his new university; in an interesting scene that highlights Western cognitive thought, he lectures on Freud, psychoanalysis, and Rorschach. Shiraki projects a series of Rorschach inkblots to the students and asks for their initial responses. Sexual innuendo follows, but this is contrasted by a student's hallucination of the inkblot turning bright red and is then animated into a "devil-like" vision. She passes out, and quite hilariously, the other students comment that she "studied too hard for the exam!" This scene, in particular, provides a very provocative analogy to or metacommentary on the Toho Dracula Trilogy. Specifically, the controversy surrounding Rorschach's tool for psychological evaluation, the "meaning making process," is precisely the same issue that is at stake for Western audiences; their confusion at a "Japanese Gothic" aesthetic.

Much of the plot of *Evil of Dracula* centers on the disappearance of Keiko, a student at the university; as such, it is indebted to films such as *The Night Stalker* (1972) or *Blacula* (1972) for the incorporation of the journalist investigation/police procedural mode of narrative discovery in a supernatural or fantastic tableaux. In fact, in another interesting scene, and a distinct nod to Bram Stoker's character of lunatic human familiar Renfield, Professor Shiraki learns that the professor who previously held his post has gone insane and is incarcerated at a mental institution not far from campus. Further, his predecessor kept a "diary" (much like Stoker's character of Jonathan Harker) that provides Shiraki many clues for his investigation.

If we examine the thematic treatment of *Evil of Dracula*, we can plainly see a reasonable if not justifiable sense of xenophobia. Global cinema author Pete Tombs offers this synopsis:

> A flashback tells of a shipwrecked sailor (with red hair, like most "foreign devils" in Japanese films) being tortured for his Christian beliefs. He renounces God and is set loose to wander in the desert. Close to death, he drinks his own blood to survive and is soon draining the life fluid of young Japanese girls.[26]

This brief synopsis is bloated with numerous connotations discussed in this essay. The link to Perry's steamships is certainly more visible and the clash of East-West theologies more manifest. But it is the loss of self and self-mutilation, which then lead to the parasitic preying upon of "young Japanese girls," that ultimately signify what is at the core of these films. It is appropriate that Tombs refers to a "draining of *life* fluid." If we retrace our steps, we remember that at the center of vampire fiction/film is this threat of contamination of blood and land. The Toho Dracula Trilogy thus presents a subtle though perceptible *fear*. Yes, quite naturally it presents fear, but not fear of fangs, cobwebs, noises in the dark, skeletal trees, ominous suits of armor, and decrepit castles. It presents a fear of Western encroachment and imperialism in a Japan that found its cinemas and airwaves heavily censored by SCAP (Supreme Commander of the Allied Powers); in a Japan that itself was an imperialist invader of Manchuria and Korea; in a Japan that attacked swiftly and without declaration the United States of America; in a Japan that entered an era of modernity perhaps prematurely; and in a Japan that ultimately became an unstoppable juggernaut in the world economy. In no uncertain terms then, the approximation of a "Western" aesthetic to present these fears, fascinations, tensions, and anxieties seems perfectly reasonable if not completely logical.

In researching the responses to these films, I encountered many negative reviews of the Toho Dracula Trilogy; it was and continues to be poorly received by primarily American and British critics and film reviewers. The films are generally seen as derivative hodgepodges of vampiric conventions/contrivances with the added "attraction" of a perplexing Western aesthetic. The role of the film critic/reviewer is, of course, to pass judgment on whether a film is "worth" your time and money. That does not, however, adequately explain how so many critics failed to (1) properly situate the films within the period in which they were produced, when nearly every mainstream vampire film was in some way a derivative hodgepodge, and (2) stop and ask *why* the films bear a distinctly Western "look" or "feel." This general complacency has troubled more than one author; for example, Robin Wood addresses this concern when he refers to a " . . . general ambience that encourages opinion mongering, gossip, Guilty Pleasures, and similar smart-assery—and, as an inevitable corollary, actively discourages criticism and scholarship."[27] Wood (113) warns that this bourgeois elitism common to film critics endangers " . . . not merely the evaluation of one movie but quite fundamental critical (hence cultural, social, political) principles—issues that involve the relationship between critic and reader as well as that between film and spectator."[28]

One of the few critics to give Yamamoto's trilogy an evenhanded and nonbiased review was the aforementioned *Video Watchdog* publisher and editor Tim Lucas. His overall impression is that these films (specifically *Legacy of Dracula*) may not be quite as good as their rarity would suggest, and yet

Lucas finds plenty to admire. Here, for example, is a contrapuntal (to Sharp's) summary of *Lake of Dracula*:

> *Lake of Dracula* isn't entirely imitative; its great distinction is the glossily macabre cinematography of Rokuro Nishigaki, rich in lagoonish greens, milky whites and moonlit blues; production design which nicely approximates the stateliness of Hammer; and the screenplay's serious attempt to grapple with the relationships between art and mental disturbance, horror and beauty.[29]

There is a substantial critical gulf between Lucas's " . . . serious attempts to grapple with the relationships between art and mental disturbance, horror and beauty" and Sharp's "50% amateur Freudianism and 50% genre contrivance." Lucas, quite correctly, praises the film's visual attributes, while Sharp seemingly finds nothing of value anywhere in the text.

That the polemic I suggest and moderate through these reviews is contingent upon national context as opposed to aesthetic and thematic "value" perpetuates a precarious, almost Orientalist attitude regarding the reception of Yamamoto's trilogy. Further problematizing the matter is Sharp's claim that Barbie doll–like heroines are endemically Oriental. Much has been written about globalization and commodity fetishism in Asia, especially concerning Barbie dolls and cultural imperialism. In their essay, "Japan, the U.S. and the Globalization of Children's Consumer Culture," Gregory Smits and Gary Cross explain:

> Certainly Japan imported much foreign culture, but always on its own terms. As Mary Yoko Brannen points out in the context of analyzing Tokyo Disneyland, "The process of assimilation of the West, the recontextualization of Western simulacra, demonstrates not that the Japanese are being dominated by Western ideologies but that they differentiate their identity from the West in a way that reinforces their sense of their own cultural uniqueness and superiority, or what we might call Japanese hegemony."[30]

Therefore, while it may be true that the Japanese were cathartically grappling with residual occupation anxieties through cultural documents like film, it is clear that they were also navigating a new national identity. Like a phoenix rising from the ashes, Japan's post–World War II identity has experienced cultural, economic, political, and spiritual rebirth. I return now to Jasper Sharp, who concludes his review thusly:

> Perhaps this will be enough to elevate the film above the status of a cheesy 70s cross-cultural oddity whose sundry Eastern trimmings might just be

enough to satisfy the truly curious. Needless to say, if vampires are your
thing, there's not much else like this out there.[31]

Sharp, for once, comes very readily to the point, " . . . there's not much else
like this out there." This is precisely why the films deserve scrutiny and analysis. His proclamation that *Lake of Dracula* is a "cross-cultural oddity" should
be evidence enough that it might just then require further attention. In short,
the Western "sensibility" of these texts interrogates the political desiring and
fetishization of impulses that were not necessarily socially sanctioned. This
dual consciousness was no doubt a product of post-traumatic stress, occupation, and political reform.

Lastly, should we be inclined to use as a criterion the very aesthetic these
films embrace and re-create (the strategy of most reviews I read), then I feel
justified in asserting that from a technical as well as "aesthetic" standpoint,
they are arguably more graceful, proficient, and skillful than a good deal of
late-1960s and early-1970s Western vampire cinema. Thematically, they are
clearly not as sophisticated as the modernist vampire literature that was
emerging at that particular time and shortly thereafter (*Salem's Lot* [1975], *Interview with the Vampire* [1976], *They Thirst* [1981]), nor are they conversely
as simplistic as some reviews would have us believe.

In spite of its aesthetic curiosities—or precisely because of them—this
trio of films merits attention as a retelling of Stoker's novel. By way of both
similarity and contrast, they allow for remarkable variances that enhance the
text, reader, and genre triad previously discussed. These films are much more
than mere imitation of a successful British economic and aesthetic model.
They are representative of a fear and anxiety of foreign rule and interference
consonant in the period under which they were produced. The world has become a much smaller place in the past decade. The latest research in the field
of global horror cinema addresses this phenomenon. Steven Schneider notes,
"The situation over the last ten years or so has changed drastically due to the
effects of the new global economy, the decline of rigid national boundaries
and the transcultural phenomenon affecting virtually all sectors of cinema
from Hollywood to Hong Kong and beyond."[32]

Yet despite this permeability of national boundaries and the increasing
sophistication of film studies as a field, film critics still cannot resist the comparison of foreign cinema to the dominant structures and practices of classical or contemporary Hollywood or, in this particular case, England. A culture's history, folklore, and mythology are inextricably tied to its fears; by
understanding them, we cut the Gordian knot—unraveling the threads of
culture. In the case of this vampire trilogy from Japan, is it a major surprise
that a country destroyed by war, occupied by foreigners, and confounded by

their own successes in the wake of ruin would make a series of films that are (according to Western critics) confusing?

The thematic and aesthetic qualities of these films could be construed as *homage* or conversely appropriation, but as I have argued, I believe them to be something else entirely. They reveal simultaneously a blossoming fascination with the West and a xenophobic anxiety. The three films are cultural artifacts of a specific time and place that may be odd and confusing on the surface, but underneath, where all horrors dwell, they *do* in fact deliver real horror.

NOTES

1. For a detailed account of the history of Universal's horror canon see Michael Brunas, John Brunas, and Tom Weaver, *Universal Horrors: The Studio's Classic Films, 1931–1946* (Jefferson, NC: McFarland, 1990).

2. I draw attention here to the fact that Bela Lugosi is synonymous with the role of Dracula; his Hungarian accent, widow's peak, and attire are the cues (both auditory and visual) most often associated with this character.

3. By the late nineteenth century, London's East End had become a cosmopolitan hub of immigrants, laborers, criminals, prostitutes, and other lower-class-income residents. Only a few years prior to Stoker's publication, the section known as Whitechapel became particularly notorious for a series of murders committed by another famous Late Victorian villain, Jack the Ripper. Other major cities in Great Britain experienced mass influxes of foreign residents, escalating nationalistic and class biases.

4. *Kaiju*, literally translated, means "strange beast." This cycle of films refers to giant (but non-Godzilla) monsters such as *Rodan* or *Mothra*.

5. In *Film History: Theory and Practice* (New York: McGraw-Hill, 1985), Robert Allen and Douglass Gomery address this concern:

> The auteur approach to film criticism sparked a controversy, still debated in some circles, over who should receive credit for the artistic achievements in Hollywood films. Truffaut and later Sarris argued that in true cinema art the director's vision showed through. This claim prompted other critics to assert, equally vociferously, that a case for authorship could be made for the script writer, producer, star, and even the cameraman. . . . Who has made cinema art? Might be recast as why and how have films looked and sounded the way they have? . . . A close reading of the films of Hawks, Ford, and Hitchcock shows them to bear a distinguishing signature, but their films also reveal the "marks" of studio, Hollywood style, and genre.

6. Allen and Gomery, *Film History*, 87–88.

7. Rarely has Japan made films concerning Western vampires. There is, however, one other example of a curious vampire film prior to the Toho Dracula Trilogy. Directed by legendary genre maestro Nabuo Nakagawa, 1959's *Onna Kyuketsuki* (*The*

Vampire Man) is nearly as "confusing" as the Dracula trilogy. Typifying an East-West binary, the vampire in this story fears sundown as opposed to sunrise.

8. See Siegfried Krakauer, *From Caligari to Hitler* (Princeton: Princeton University Press, 1947).

9. The highlighting of Tarantino and Burton is appropriate, as Burton has "borrowed" very liberally from the visual style of Hammer (see *Sleepy Hollow*, 1999), and Tarantino has also "borrowed" very liberally from several distinctly Japanese aesthetics in his *Kill Bill* series.

10. Heidi Kaye, *A Companion to the Gothic*, ed. David Punter (Oxford: Blackwell, 2000), 186.

11. For a detailed account of the rise and fall of Hammer Studios, see David Pirie, *A Heritage of Horror: The English Gothic Cinema, 1946–1972* (New York: Equinox Books Avon, 1974).

12. Patrick Macias, *TokyoScope: The Japanese Cult Film Companion* (New York: Viz, 2003), 86.

13. The Karnstein Trilogy refers to a trio of films that take J. Sheridan Le Fanu's *Carmilla* (1872) as their central antagonist. The films depict strong lesbian themes, nudity, and violence. They proved very successful for Hammer at a time when the vampire's popularity was beginning to wane. The vampire's tether on Western society in the 1970s relied on new treatments, such as gay vampires, lesbian vampires, black vampires, vampire orgies, and so on.

14. I am indebted here to Tim Lucas's outstanding publication *Video Watchdog* for providing this "appropriation" paradigm. See Tim Lucas, "Toho's Dracula Trilogy," *Video Watchdog* 101 (November 2003): 64–67. A complete list of intertextual references is neither attempted nor encouraged.

15. Jasper Sharp, *Midnight Eye: The Latest and Best in Japanese Cinema*, www.midnigh teye.com/reviews/lakedrac.html (accessed July 24, 2007).

16. Jasper Sharp, *Midnight Eye: The Latest and Best in Japanese Cinema*, www.midnigh teye.com/reviews/lakedrac.html (accessed July 24, 2007).

17. Hilary Conroy, "Lessons from Japanese Imperialism," *Monumenta Nipponica* 21, no. 3–4 (1966): 337.

18. Michael R. Auslin, *US/Japan 150 years. The Next 150 Years: Japanese and American Voices*, www.cgj.org/150th/html/contributionE.htm (accessed July 24, 2007).

19. Ramie Tateishi, "The Japanese Horror Film Series Ring and Eko Eko Azarak," in *Fear without Frontiers*, ed. S. Schneider (Godalming: Fab Press, 2003), 296.

20. Yuki Tanaka explores the creation of *Godzilla* set against the backdrop of nuclear terror in "Godzilla and the Bravo Shot: Who Created and Killed the Monster?" See *Japan Focus: An Asia-Pacific e-journal*, www.japanfocus.org.

21. Lucas, "Toho's Dracula Trilogy," 65–66.

22. For more on the literary applications of this theory, see Tzetvan Todorov, *The Fantastic: A Structural Approach to a Literary Genre* (Cornell: Cornell University Press, 1970).

23. This would later become a central theme in Japanese horror, the "absent father" film, dominating much of the genre in the 1970s. Notable among these films is

Dabide no Hoshi: Bishoujo-gari (*Star of David* [1979]) for its brutal depiction of derelict fatherhood.

24. Hammer brought *Dracula* to the twentieth century the following year in its stylish and "hip" *Dracula A.D. 1972* (1972).

25. The all-girls' school proved to be a "hot spot" for sexual exploration in *Brides of Dracula* (1960)—homoerotic undertones were found in the narrative thread of every major character in this film; the exception being Peter Cushing's Van Helsing, who is victimized by Baron Meinster. Cushing's potency in the role helps reestablish the heteronormative and patriarchal themes of the film's ending.

26. Peter Tombs, *Mondo Macabo: Weird and Wonderful Cinema Around the World* (New York: St. Martin's Griffin, 1998), 179.

27. Robin Wood, "Neglected Nightmares," in *The Horror Film Reader*, ed. A. Silver and J. Ursini (Pompton Plains, Limelight Editions, 2001), 113.

28. Wood is actually attacking Roger Ebert here, claiming Ebert's "critic as superstar" complacency caused him to get many facts and assertions dead wrong regarding Wes Craven's *The Last House on the Left* (1972).

29. Lucas, "Toho's Dracula Trilogy," 66.

30. Gary Cross and Gregory Smits, "Japan, the U.S. and the Globalization of Children's Consumer Culture," *Journal of Social History* vol. 38, no. 4 (Summer 2005): 873–90.

31. Sharp, www.midnighteye.com/reviews/lakedrac.html.

32. Steven Schneider, *Horror International* (Detroit: Wayne State University Press, 2005), 3.

The Western Eastern: Decoding Hybridity and Cyber*Zen* Goth(ic) in *Vampire Hunter D* (1985)

Wayne Stein and John Edgar Browning

"If you do not fear death, there is nothing you cannot do."

Yamamoto Tsunetomo
from *The Hagakure*

". . . by being Japanese I cannot help but feel a strong sense of crisis."

Kenzaburo Oe
Conference at Duke University (1986)

$\mathcal{A}$ccording to Fred Botting, with the dissemination of Gothic(ness) over national boundaries and genres comes the increasing difficulty in attempting to encapsulate the homogeneous parts and subparts of the Gothic.[1] Shadowing the progression of these macabre narratives and their migration have been many (un)familiar monsters, one of which is the vampire, an enduring member of the Gothic. Buried and nearly forgotten under the surge of science, technology, and medical advancement that arose out of the Enlightenment, the vampire was suddenly (re)exhumed by Romantic and Victorian writers and then later rediscovered and reinvented by American writers of the frontier trying to cope with the contradicting realities prevalent in the West. In the case of the latter:

> In forging a native style nineteenth century American writers were responding to European literary influences, but many of them also grappled

From *Asian Gothic: Essays on Literature, Film and Anime* © 2008 Edited by Andrew Hock-Soon Ng by permission of McFarland & Company, Inc., Box 611, Jefferson, NC 28640, www.mcfarlandpub .com. We wish to thank Andrew Hock-Soon Ng, for his insightful and incredibly helpful suggestions on earlier versions of this chapter.

with the most fundamental conflict shaping American experience, the battle between civilization and nature, between mental landscape of European
consciousness and the physical landscape of the New World.[2]

The rich symbolism and cultural malleability shared by (un)invited Gothic
figures have helped to erect particular socially constructed teratologies (studies of the "monstrous"). In the case of the vampire, different cultures have
transplanted this trans/national figure across a network of venues simultaneously to represent social unrest during periods of transition and "crises."

In contemporary Japan, the vampire has found not only a new ethnic
identity, but an innovative medium to manifest as well: the anime. Conceived
in the tradition of the American frontier Gothic,[3] the 1985 Japanese anime
Vampire Hunter D (Bampaia hantâ D), originally a novel (1983) by Hideyuki
Kikuchi, has today become a global cult text amalgamating various genres
(action/horror/fantasy/sci-fi/Western/animation). This hybrid anime is set
some ten thousand years into the postapocalyptic future, where vampires have
come to rule over humans like feudal land barons. Overseeing these barons
(and iconic of the outdated, patriarchal, and other-worldly authority figures
who typify traditional Gothic narratives) is Count Magnus Lee, referred to in
the film as the "noble one," which we are left to infer as meaning the "ancient
one" or "one who is of ancient nobility." Within this animated and highly contested world, a strange hybridity on many levels is engendered, producing a
sense of postmodern frontier Gothic(ness) that oscillates between civilization
and nature, while juxtaposing the syncretic tensions of the Old and New
Worlds onto a Third World mind-/land-/culturescape. Just as D, the protagonist in the film, is a hunter, we too, as viewers, are involved in a sort of hunt
(or journey) as we attempt to define the sense of the Japanese embedded in
Vampire Hunter D. More importantly, this hybrid text uncovers or extends our
understanding of a *Gothic* that is at once American frontier–defined and also
uniquely Japanese.

There is a greater sense within the East Asian Gothic of a complex multiplicity or East Asianicity of merging and interrelated cultural, political, and
social resonances that helps create the construct called the "individual." This
has to do with an intermixing of Taoism (animism and nature), Confucianism (politics, the ethical and the social), and Buddhism (spiritual and psychological). What this essay proposes is to appropriate this generalized system in order to make lucid the (inter-)complexities of what we call
Japanicity—with its rooted practices in Shintoism (which has grown out of
Taoism and Zen), Confucianism, and Buddhism—in an attempt to arrive at
a definition of a Japanese Gothic as typified in *Vampire Hunter D.* As such,
this essay traces the trajectory of the hunt for a Japanese Gothic: first, by ex-

amining the sublime setting in *Vampire Hunter D*, where the frontier Gothic merges with a cyberpunk aesthetic, and reveals in the process a Japanese dystopia; second, by peering into Japan's own hunt for a revised sense of human nature in the (anti-)hero (or "supahiro") who fights against the moral malaise—symbolized by a hunger for blood and identity—of a lost humanity (patriarchal/Confucian values); and finally, by decoding *Vampire Hunter D's* Japanicity in order to cultivate a new form of spirituality that helps define what we call "CyberZen Gothic," a product that merges Eastern and Western Gothic constructs and transcends convention and identity, as well as the forces of hybridity that surface from such a union.

HUNTING FOR THE GOTHIC IDENTITY: GROUND ZERO AT CYBERPUNK AESTHETICS

Vampire Hunter D becomes a backdrop where competing forms of the Gothic come together. As the film starts, we catch the first shadowy glimpse of Count Lee's unsettling castle in the midst of what appears to be the aftermath of some great cataclysm. The castle's superstructure and ramparts ambiguously hint at European design while simultaneously eliciting a sense of Asianicity with the inclusion of temple-like spires protruding from all sides, supported by rocks and steel: a fusion of old and new that almost gestures toward a sort of "Tokyo Noir." Next, the film introduces Doris, the ambiguously gendered lead female character. Doris's skimpy attire and hypersexualized physical features contrast with her bayoneted laser rifle and electrified bull whip, arsenal she uses to defend her farm and younger brother from trespassing creatures. Following a brief skirmish between Doris and one such creature, a werewolf (whose history and very namesake is of European origin[4]) suddenly appears and strips Doris of the cross (another Western symbol, and repellent of vampires) that hangs from her neck. Here, we are introduced to the obscured silhouette that is Count Lee, a Dracula-type character whose cape shrouds him in a way that ambiguously hints at the same bat/cape "form" first introduced by stage renditions of Dracula in the 1920s (and which is later carried over into motion pictures).[5] Count Lee (or simply "the Count," as he is often referred to in the film) and his attire mirror the visual trappings popularized by Universal and Hammer with actors like Bela Lugosi and Christopher Lee (in fact, that D's vampire is called Lee may also echo the latter). The film establishes a European Gothic dynamics very early on in the film: that Count Lee (an aristocrat) targets Doris (farmer), who is merely trying to defend her meager livelihood, echoes the traditional capitalist struggle that

Franco Moretti has so amiably argued in his Marxist reading of *Dracula* in "Dialectics of Fear" (1983).⁶ Also, in the vein of European Gothic, *Vampire Hunter D* foregrounds an outmoded entity—a throwback—which nevertheless radically haunts and vexes the contemporary.

Indeed, *Vampire Hunter D*'s unique mixture of animated narrative style, vampire codes of honor, sword-play, eroticism, and a gamut of European and American Gothic staples distinguishes it from previous Dracula stage and filmic products. Also of interest is the film's setting, which is framed against a postapocalyptic landscape. This essay therefore approaches the question of how situating the film in a decadent future reflects Japanese consciousness, and how this actually serves to culturally enrich, not problematize, the *Dracula* narrative.

The Gothic world of *Vampire Hunter D* parallels two Japanese "mise-en-scène": one filmic, the other historical. In the first instance, the film echoes traces of the Yakuza films that flourished in Japan in the sixties and seventies. These films represent the amoral or "postmoral" (*jingi naki*) society and became "increasingly linked to a dystopic mise-en-scène, providing the diegetic opposition against which the protagonists struggle, both legitimating and masking a spectacularization of the extremities of violence that is central to the genre and spectator pleasure."⁷ Such a morally empty, violent universe is indeed evident in the corruption and moral quagmire ruled by Count Lee. In the second instance, Count Lee's world, if viewed as a metaphor of wartime Japan, could also suggest the nation's capitalistic feudalism and its postapocalyptic aftermath. Like the Emperor Hirohito (whom many Japanese people believed to be deity), Count Lee too is an outdated figure of an overstretched economy who rules over a landscape that echoes Hiroshima and Nagasaki after their destruction. His legitimacy is now in question, and it is only through cruelty that he can maintain his resented authority. But there is another historical dimension to the Gothic landscape of *Vampire Hunter D* as well, one that reflects contemporary Japan, and which we will investigate shortly.

D is also a Dracula-type character, sporting a long flowing cape and a black cowboy-esque hat, as he wields a sword (instead of a gun). When we first meet him, he is "riding into town" on his cybernetic horse. It is clear from this representation that D, more than the Count, is a vampiric construct that merges East and West. He literally embodies both Japanese and foreign significations. Coupled with this pairing is also his human-vampire dichotomy, and together they represent D's difficult struggle with two conflicting identities, both with which he is uncomfortable.⁸ D, who suffers from a similar agony experienced by the *dampiel* (or *dhampir*), is the result of the union between a male vampire and a human female.⁹ The novel clearly expresses this:

With both the cruelly aristocratic blood of the Nobility and the brutally vulgar blood of the humans, *dhampirs* were tormented by the dual destinies of darkness and light; one side called them traitors while the other labeled them devils. Truly, the *dhampirs*—like the Flying Dutchman cursed to wander the seven seas for all eternity—led an abominable existence.[10]

Hideyuki Kikuchi further notes that D's "personality constantly shifts between man and vampire" (in Martin). Met with contempt by both humans and vampires, D, the cowboy half-vampire, finds solace in neither race in his endless search for meaning to his life. This quest for meaning—a *bildungsroman* motif—that D exemplifies finds resonance in American Westerns as well. Here, the protagonist is often depicted as searching out adventures in an attempt to locate personal significance. Discussing a Western film, *The Searchers* (1954), critic James K. Folsom comments that in the film:

> [T]he question of where one is "at home," and the metaphorical exploration of this problem, often falls into the predictable, if disturbing discovery that one does not have a single home at all, but rather two homes, mutually incompatible in their values. Exploration of this duality at the heart of human nature is central to gothic writing.[11]

Appropriating this view to analyze *Vampire Hunter D* can yield interesting insights. In a sense, D's metaphorical search is a quest to heal the split to his personality. Desiring to be "at home" with himself, he nevertheless faces the rejection of both races, which in turn results in an inverted rejection of himself. He cannot, in the end, feel "at home" because his identity is always already rend and undercut by denial and loathing. For D, being at home in his corporeality is tantamount to experiencing the Freudian *unheimlich*, or unhomeliness.

On a macrocosmic scale, the experience of being discomfited by one's identity/home represented by D finds vital resonance in Japan of the 1980s. To further this argument, we want to draw a curious parallel between this anime and the genre known as cyberpunk to show not only the two categories' affinity, but the kind of socio-ideological assertions they make. Like the vampire hunter, the cyberpunk's console raider's quest to evade control by multinational corporations drives her to hack into systems to disrupt, and sometimes destroy, the flow of valuable information of the cyber frontier. Cyberpunk, a dystopic way to examine familiar social categories, questions how power and people are controlled and terrorized by a fear of reality and technology. As such, it lends itself to interesting deployments by genres that problematize such notions, for example, the frontier Gothic. As David Mogen writes, "contemporary American science fiction in particular adapts traditional frontier gothic conventions to modern circumstances. Because futuristic settings allow both for discovering New Frontiers and for recovering old ones."[12] In this curious space of the cyberpunk Western, hackers become the new postcolonial cowboys, trying to control the frontier of cyberspace, while attacking the technologies of oppression. Cyberpunk examines the future when cyberspace has relinquished its virtuality to become a more seductive reality where body and mind can be controlled. Humans acquire a new post-(in)humanity that implies a cyborg-like identity that is nevertheless interpellated by a highly intricate network of systems and machines (especially super-intelligent computers) that now manipulate them. In fact, the more "cyber-technologized" a human is, the more (in)human she becomes, prompting theorist David Mogen to deliberate that "computer-encoded personalities seem to see themselves as high-tech versions of the Undead, trapped in mechanical repetition of old patterns."[13] As such, cyberpunk foregrounds a realm where a new master narrative has metamorphosed out of the ashes of posthuman history, a narrative that, interestingly, has also insidiously Gothic significances. Here, it is not so much that vampire-like automata thrive, but the dread of turning into such an automaton itself that plots the human into perpetual victim-coordinates within his or her own body. What theorists Mogen, Sanders, and Karpinski iterate with regard to frontier Gothic may equally serve to explain this cyberpunk space: terror and horror, feelings of helpless victimization by forces from without that may after all be projected from within, a dread of annihilation more overwhelming than that induced by any merely physical threat.[14]

This brief excursion to cyberpunk now paves the way for a reading of *Vampire Hunter D* as a mirror of Japan in the 1980s, which forms another of the anime's ideological backdrops. Just as cyberpunk is less about some distant future and more about the political presence that helped to define the Reagan Era in the 1980s,[15] *Vampire Hunter D*, it seems, is less a warning about Japan's bleak future or a commentary about the problems of the past, than it is about a spiritual void that Japan has come to experience in the eighties. Charles Inouye argues that contemporary Japan "suffers from . . . affluences and the insatiable contentment of consumer culture"[16] that have resulted in the sense of national *unheimlich*. In its race to become a highly modern and technologized country, what has been left behind, even forgotten, is a sense of originary Japanese-ness steeped in culture, tradition, and religion. Rapid westernization has resulted in an identity crisis in modern Japan, compelling a constant "staging," according to Marilyn Ivy, of old customs, folklores, and beliefs to paradoxically reinforce its own sense of identity and its loss thereof.[17] Read against this contemporary backdrop, *Vampire Hunter D* expresses some of the nation's unconscious fears of the Self becoming dissolved by an unchecked metamorphosis into Western otherness. As much as the anime is set in a postapocalyptic temporality, there is also a sense of personal apocalypse—the denuding of the Japanese Self—that underlies the film's message. Perhaps unsurprisingly, then, it is set in a frontier-like landscape of the West, for as David Mogen notes of frontier mythology, it "is still the vehicle which expresses an ambivalent sense of destiny, projected into dreadful apprehensions of personal or cosmic apocalypse, into visions depicting new forms of consciousness emerging from horror."[18] In the frontier Gothic of *Vampire Hunter D*, the hunter's ambivalent destiny is not merely between his human and vampire halves, but between his Eastern (the samurai) and Western (the cowboy) ones as well.

Vampire Hunter D reverberates with symbolic spirituality of a lost era when demons, humans, and deities intermingle on a similar existential plane. Very much like Ivy's notion of staging, both the novel and the anime are attempting to realize in the *present* something that is vanishing, if not already lost, and may perhaps return again in a distant future. Either way, it is a sense of longing that propels the narrative. In this possible world, the "human" is perpetually vexed by exterior forces that, upon closer scrutiny, may have arisen from somewhere interior in the first place. As Neocleous notes in a different Gothic context but reflective of *Vampire Hunter D*, "human appearance . . . helps to disguise the fact that the enemy is in fact—again contradictory— both superhuman and subhuman: it possesses superhuman powers enabling it to drive the world to perdition and yet is also a subhuman cause of degeneration, disease and disintegration."[19] By prefixing "human" with "super" and "sub," it already suggests that the evil that humans encounter comes ultimately from within him- or herself. Too much power and wealth, or too little, positions the human as either super or sub, reminiscent once again of the hypercapitalist system that modern Japan has come to embody. This is further complicated by Japan's own wartime history: its "superhuman" and living God—Emperor Hirohito—became, overnight, a subhuman to the Allies that defeated him, and directly signaled the triumph of Western science over Eastern spirituality. This "defeat" has never been carefully negotiated, hitherto resulting in a schizophrenia that constitutes the Japanese identity crisis today.

HUNTING FOR A HERO: UNLEASHING THE "SUPAHIRO"

During the 1980s in the "land of the rising sun," a land of seemingly endless bounty and economic prosperities also diffuses into contradicting values of corruption, consumerism, and depletion of cultural meaning, morals, and myths. Whereas Japanese businessmen find inspiration for their own capitalistic beliefs from *A Book of Five Rings* by Miyamoto Musashi, often called the greatest samurai in Japanese history, so too does *Vampire Hunter D* find its inspiration from samurai lore and philosophy, and from Gothic literary traditions. It seems that contemporary Japan's populace—both real and animated—communicates its need for heroes by recourse to warrior figures of old who are also "essentially" Japanese.

Interestingly, both the samurai and the cowboy practice the virtue of loyalty. But while loyalty is an important part of the cowboy's and samurai's separate, but overlapping, codes of ethics, the latter takes it to the extreme in the form of deadly vengeances and suicides. The samurai code of loyalty is also later influenced by Confucianism, thus supplementing a dimension of filial piety as well to its already entrenched creed of retribution. According to Confucius, "one cannot live under the same sky as the man who killed one's father or brother,"[20] a principle that is profoundly advocated in one of the most popular samurai narratives, which has also spawned endless cinematic remakes: the tale of *The Forty-Seven Ronin* by Monzaemon Chikamatsu. Based on a true story, the lord of these forty-seven ronin commits an unforgivable deed and is sentenced by the Shogun to commit suicide. After his death, his samurai become ronin, or masterless samurai. Ideally, they should have committed suicide directly after his death, and inevitably, they do; but before doing so, they avenge the memory of their master by killing his enemy. Their sacrifice becomes the ultimate act of courage and sets itself apart as what it means to be Japanese.

In D, we see such qualities as well: D's unrivaled courage in the film, the memory of his father (Dracula) whom he secretly honors, and his "classical" sense of nobility (a sort of Japanese *noblesse oblige*) are all contrasted to Count Lee's feudal, capitalist, and selfish mentality and disdain for "commoners."[21] That these qualities are infused within a half-vampire (a "monster") may be problematic for traditional European and American Gothic aesthetics that often rely on strict binaries (although this is also complicated by villains who are desirably depicted), but they seem to rest very well with a postwar Japanese consciousness, perhaps because the Japanese have acknowledged its own hauntedness by an other that resides within the Self, as well as the fact that in Eastern religious systems, good and evil are not opposites but dialectically related. As Henry Hughes posits, "the Eastern Gothic more often depicts not a mission against some perceived singular evil but the discovery of an undivided world of good and evil."[22] *Vampire Hunter D* seems to do both: that there is a singular evil—Count Lee—that must be defeated signals the text's affinity with Western Gothic; but that the hero in the narrative is also an amalgamation between good and evil also point to Hughes's notion of Eastern Gothic concerns. Possibly due to his hybrid nature, D, despite the many dangerous situations in which he finds himself throughout his quest, remains *invincible*—a marked characteristic of a *supahiro*. And like most *supahiros*, D also has a sidekick, Left Hand, which is literally his left hand, except that it can talk and act on its own volition. Interestingly D's *supahiro* qualities are the combination of his unique liminal identity. While his vampiric half allows him superhuman strengths and abilities, his human half renders him "very down to earth." Also, although he embodies characteristics of a Western superhero (demure, good-hearted, with a profound sense of justice and rightness and superhuman strength), that he is also in possession of "many of the characteristics of his samurai ancestors"[23] evinces his unique, if unstable, Japanese identity as well.

The conclusion of the film fuses the various identities of D (*supahiro*, cowboy, samurai, Eastern, Western, human, vampire) into a celebration of an ambiguous, contradictory, and heterogeneous whole. The viewer will learn of his past and the motivation for his actions: he is none other than the son of Count Dracula, which not only explains his noble ways, but exposes D's aristocratic background as well. The viewer will also discover, in a pivotal scene, that Doris has fallen in love with D, but that he must now choose between *giri* (duty) and *ninjo* (human emotions). D's human-half lusts after Doris, but his vampire-half gazes down at her neckline and desires her blood; in the end, however, his cowboy/samurai nature prompts his sense of *giri* to rise above both his lusts, thus preventing the "moment of the monster"[24] from becoming realized. Yet, despite D's ability to withstand his vampiric desires, it is not a certainty that he has conquered his vampiric blood. After all, the monster in him "cannot be definitively killed [because] the monster . . . is within the self."[25] And despite his defeat of the Count, D's real enemy is ultimately himself. He is both hero and monster—a duality embodied by many Gothic figures since Walpole's first Gothic novel in 1764.

TOWARD A ZEN GOTHIC

The hero, in samurai terms, does not distinguish himself through great deeds, nor is he measured by the number of his enemies. The samurai is a selfless servant, and thus, the condition of being devoid of self is more important for one who has become masterless. This important trait, we argue, provides a unique perspective on the Gothic impulse in Japanese narratives, one which has been ably argued by Hughes in a pioneering essay on Japanese Gothic. As he explains:

> Desire may cause self-division [. . .] but the Japanese solution is rarely found in the reaffirmation of the self. It is, instead, the emptying of the self that constitutes cosmic achievement. In addition, to the quest for an empty self, the Eastern Gothic more often depicts not a mission against some perceived singular evil but the discovery of an undivided world of good and evil. In translation, life is not a battle ground for God and the Devil—the two grow naturally together in the field of life.[26]

Thus, for a hero, desires of the self must be eschewed in order to render duty faithfully and impeccably; and in the absence of duty (because the samurai is masterless), then the relinquishment of desire must be performed through self-conscious acts of religious adherences, and more extremely, suicide. And because desire is often related to some future reward or gain, or some longing for what has past or has never been, one of the ways in which the samurai can cultivate a distancing from desire is to concentrate on the *immediate present*.

Such a view finds further resonance in Zen beliefs. Zen is about the power of immediacy and being *fully* aware of the here and now. As one Zen philosopher states, "If one fully understands the present moment, there will be nothing else to do, and nothing else to pursue. Live being true to the single purpose of the moment. . . . [Be] true to the thought of the moment . . . go to the extent of living single thought by single thought."[27] The vampire D exemplifies this principle to a degree: a "man" of few words and emotions, he is also one who lives for the moment. In duels, D practices the art of *mushin* ("no mind"), which manipulates "no way" *as* the way, "no sword" *as* the sword. This is the samurai's discipline. The enemy cannot defeat the samurai using a sword or mere agility because the samurai has no presence, or self, for the enemy to attack. As such, there is nothing to defeat or kill, because the samurai, by virtue of his belief, is already (un)dead. If eyes are windows to the soul, then D's eyes, which are often shrouded, indicate an absence of such an essential part of his being. This mystery of presence that is absent is the Zen notion of *mushin*. Here, the self does not exist, only emptiness; "nothingness" becomes more powerful than "everything-ness."[28]

That life and death are intricate aspects of existence and must be both equally embraced is vital to an understanding of what this essay refers to as Zen Gothic. Every moment becomes a part of a natural cycle of rejuvenation and destruction, of cause and effect. Time is not so much a progressive march toward the future as it is a warping mechanism that results in either *ennui* or *déjà vu*. Such is the grandeur, the dread, and the paradox of *samsara* (the Buddhist cycle of death and rebirth). The hunter D shapes his existence in precisely this cyclic configuration: that he is always seeking new adventures suggests his never-ending quest for meaning. In fact, as part human and part vampire, his very embodiment already suggests a balanced embracement of death and life. Throughout the narrative, we see D at the point of death (such as his near-fatal battles with Reiginsei, the Snake Women of Midwich, and Count Lee), but he always overcomes his foes by either resurrecting himself or by invoking his (un)dead or vampire half. It is this blending of Eastern existential philosophy and Western images of monstrosity that engenders an Asian genre that is at once uniquely Japanese and uniquely Gothic—or Zen Gothic, as we would term it.

VAMPIRISM, MULTICULTURALISM, ENLIGHTENMENT

When Western audiences view Japanese anime characters in films like *Vampire Hunter D*, they may misunderstand these figures as merely imitating "Western features." But more than just imitations, *Vampire Hunter D* evinces how the Dracula myth can be wrested from its Western-centric parameters and be creatively deployed for multicultural purposes. This heterogeneous cult narrative enables us to recognize other ways in which the ideological intricacies (be it race, gender, class, traditions) of the Dracula cinematic myth are not isolated to Western usages and meanings only. It is in this sense that Caroline J. S. Picart has noted that *Vampire Hunter D* "reveals its tensions as a miscegenation fantasy, and shows how ambivalences reveal the struggle between conventional and progressive ideological elements in hybrid cinematic narratives of gender, race, power and technology."[29]

As a hybrid text, *Vampire Hunter D* carefully marries Eastern and Western images so that both are clearly and equally represented. For instance, in the scene when D faces the Snake Women of Midwich, Kabuki-like imagery of long, flowing black hair and pale facial features are foregrounded alongside the familiar Western vampire icon. Nuances of the Noh plays are also carefully captured in the anime through its characters' mask-like demeanors and artistically calculated, stylized movements. And although, as mentioned, the dystopic frontier of the narrative inheres metaphors of the postapocalyptic and the Gothic (Count Lee's castle is reminiscent of Usher's House), it is also at once subscribing to a Confucian principle that "the order of the universe [is] reflected [by] the moral conditions of a kingdom."[30] In other words, the world of *Vampire Hunter D* mirrors the evil nature of its ruler, Count Lee.

In Japan, hungry ghost scrolls (*gaki zoshi*) have become a popular Zen art (*zenga*). Creating and experiencing them have become a means to exorcising the demons that reside in our unconscious, which then leads to enlighten-ment (*satori*). Schodt explains that "the ultimate goal [in experiencing this art form] was not the creation of an image on paper but reinforcement of a state of mind."[31] One important feature of this Zen art is "an economy of line."[32] This aesthetic principle seems to manifest in *Vampire Hunter D* as well. By ap-propriating a minimalist style, the narrative perfects this haunting *zenga's* spe-cial effect. For example, in one of the opening sequences, despite the ap-proaching of a dark, indefinite figure from mid-shot to close-up (it turns out to be D), this spatial unfolding is not translated by greater detail to the art work, unlike conventional animation. Throughout the film at various points, D's mask-like facial features are amplified by this minimalism through elim-ination of distinct facial features. Only his eyes are visualized, and nothing else. This replicates the use of masks in Noh dramas where "less is more." Such a minimalist style at once creates a dark, haunting pathos.

If the point of Zen art is to help its artist "arrive at a statement of qui-etude . . . when the agitations on the surface of actuality have reached an equi-librium and the essential form of object emerges in an aura of timelessness,"[33] then perhaps, for viewers of *Vampire Hunter D*, the aim should be an identi-fication with the *supahiro* in his resistance against seductions (power, sexual) on various levels so that we too may come to a degree of enlightenment about our own divided nature and interpellated identities. Thereafter, we can per-haps also begin the next cycle of our journey: to seek transcendence beyond our ideological confinements. But that is another story.

NOTES

1. Fred Botting, *The Gothic* (London and New York: Routledge, 2003), 2–3.

2. David Mogen, Scott Sanders, and Joan Karpinski, eds., *Frontier Gothic: Terror and Wonder at the Frontier in American Literature* (Madison: Fairleigh Dickinson Uni-versity Press), 14–15.

3. See Morgen, Sanders, and Karpinski, *Frontier Gothic*, for essays discussing this Gothic subspecies.

4. From the Latin, *vir* [man].

5. Dracula-type vampires typically invoke one or several recognizable (i.e., mar-ketable) stereotypes that the London and Broadway stage adaptations of *Dracula* helped to engender in the 1920s. These stereotypes were then extended and univer-salized in film, appropriately by Universal in the 1930s–1940s, then by Hammer in the 1950s–1970s. Among them include clothing (cape [with/out stand-up collar], crest ring, tuxedo, black-red coloration, medallion), mannerism (Eastern-European accent, suave), physical features (tall, pale skinned, piercing eyes, dark slicked-back

hair [with/out widow's peak]) and engagements (moving into town and buying up real estate, searching for lost love)—most of which became instituted *after* Stoker's 1897 novel. See also David J. Skal, *Hollywood Gothic: The Tangled Web of Dracula* (New York: Faber and Faber, 2004); Raymond T. McNally and Radu Florescu, *In Search of Dracula: The History of Dracula and Vampires* (Boston and New York: Houghton Mifflin, 1994); and Nina Auerbach, *Our Vampires, Ourselves* (Chicago: University of Chicago Press, 1995). The more recent retelling with Columbia's *Bram Stoker's Dracula* (1992) reinvigorated the character again with what would inevitably become "new" staples: long, rather than slicked-back hair; princely, rather than countly status; a Romanian accent specifically; and we would come to know [Vlad] Dracula on a first name basis.

6. Franco Moretti, *Signs Taken for Wonders: Essays in the Sociology of Literary Forms*, trans. Susan Fisher, David Miller, and David Forgacs (London: Verso, 1983), 83–108.

7. Isolde Standish, *A New History of Japanese Cinema: A Century of Narrative Film* (New York and London: Continuum, 2005), 330. Films like Fukasaku Kinji's *Battle Royal*, Miike Takashi *Triad Society* trilogy, and many post-1960s films in Japan are described as "postmoral" (*jingi naki*) narratives, according to film historian Isolde Standish. Postmoral cinema has easily recognizable characteristics: "No one is saved and no apparent heroes exist; all are damaged individuals existing as global drifters lacking any geographical or emotional sense of connectedness. Violence and sex provide an alternative libidinal economy through which these characters negotiate their lives in alien cityscapes" (330).

8. Mari Kotani, "Techno-Gothic Japan: From Seshi Yokomizo's *The Death's Head Stranger* to Mariko Ohara's *Ephemera the Vampire*," in *Blood Read: The Vampire as Metaphor in Contemporary Culture*, eds. Joan Gordon and Veronica Hollinger (Philadelphia: University of Pennsylvania Press, 1997), 193.

9. The *dhampir* is a vampire of Gypsy folklore. Of *dhampirs*, J. Gordon Melton writes in *The Vampire Book: The Encyclopedia of the Undead* (Farmington Hills, MI: Visible Ink Press, 1999): "The product of such a union, usually a male, was called a *dhampir.* [It] had unusual powers for detecting and destroying the vampire [. . .]. Some individuals believed to be *dhampirs* supplemented their income by hiring themselves out as vampire hunters" (196). For further discussion of "dhampirs," see Elwood. B. Trigg, *Gypsy Demons & Divinities* (1973) and T. P. Vukanovic, "The Vampire," in *Vampires of the Slav*, ed. Jan L. Perkowski (Cambridge, MA: Slavica Publishers, 1976), 201–34.

10. Hideyuki Kikuchi, *Vampire Hunter D*, trans. Kevin Leahy, vol. 1 (Milwaukee: Dark Horse, 1995), 64. In *Ravenloft: A Guide to Transylvania* (Lake Geneva: TSR, 1996), Nicky Rea also notes the conflicting identity that these human-vampires experience:

> At night, [*dhampirs*] often betray their vampire heritage by their red eyes which glow after sunset and their fangs. . . . They are tragic creatures who spend their lives torn between two natures—that of a blood-thirsty creature of the night and that of an innocent who is horrified by a facet of his nature. (96)

11. James K. Folsom, "Gothicism in the Western World," in *Frontier Gothic: Terror and Wonder at the Frontier in American Literature*, eds. David Mogen, Scott Sanders, and Joanne Karpinski (Madison: Fairleigh Dickinson University Press, 1993), 36.

12. David Mogen, "Wilderness, Metamorphosis and Millennium: Gothic Apocalypse from the Puritans to the Cyborgs," in *Frontier Gothic: Terror and Wonder at the Frontier in American Literature*, 102.

13. Mogen, "Wilderness, Metamorphosis and Millennium," 103.

14. Mogen, Sanders, and Karpinski, *Frontier Gothic*, 22.

15. Cyberpunk, whose birth and popularity are marked by two important works, like William Gibson's novel *Neuromancer* (1984) and Ridley Scott's *Blade Runner* (1982), was created at around the same time as *Vampire Hunter D*. In both *Neuromancer* and *Blade Runner*, the future—a noir, Gothic state—is a 1940s dystopian nightmare where East and West have merged. Both works are also allegorical commentaries on the Reagan years.

16. Charles Shirō Inouye, "Introduction: The Familiarity of Strange Places," in *Japanese Gothic Tales* (Honolulu: University of Hawaii Press, 1996), 5.

17. Marilyn Ivy, *Discourses of the Vanishing: Modernity, Phantasm, Japan* (Chicago: University of Chicago Press, 1995), 10.

18. Mogen, "Wilderness, Metamorphosis and Millennium," 102.

19. Mark Neocleous, "Gothic Fascism," *Journal for Cultural Research* 9.2 (2005): 136. Neocleous is actually referring to Hitler's demonizing of the Jews by grafting vampirism onto Jewish identities.

20. Gregory Barrett, *Archetypes in Japanese Film: The Sociopolitical and Religious Significance of the Principal Heroes and Heroines* (London: Susquehanna University Press, 1989), 103.

21. *Vampire Hunter D* is also at heart a revenge narrative. Doris hires D to destroy Count Lee as a means to not only prevent her passage into the ranks of the undead, but to punish Count Lee for violating her flesh.

22. Henry J. Hughes, "Familiarity of the Strange: Japan's Gothic Tradition," *Criticism* 42.1 (2000): 60.

23. Frederik L. Schodt, *Manga! Manga! The World of Japanese Comics* (Tokyo: Kodansha International, 1997), 78.

24. Andrew Hock-Soon Ng, *Dimensions of the Monstrosity in Contemporary Narratives: Theory, Psychoanalysis, Postmodernism* (Basingstoke: Palgrave, 2004), 2.

25. Ng, *Dimensions of the Monstrosity*, 5.

26. Hughes, "Familiarity of the Strange," 59.

27. Yamamoto Tsunetomo, *Hagakure: The Book of the Samurai*, trans. William S. Wilson (Tokyo: Kodansha International, 2002), 68–69.

28. It is perhaps fascinating to note that one of the most well-known spaghetti Westerns, John Sturges's *Magnificent Seven* (1960), is based on the *Seven Samurai* (1954). In fact, James Coburn, who plays the character Britt, studied and adopted the Zen-like acting style of Seiji Miyaguchi. In Japanese *manga* (comics), Golgo 13, an assassin for hire, is perhaps one of the most popular heroes who exemplifies the *zen* spirit, Schodt writes, that less is more: "Golgo never smiled, and his typical response

to any query has been a grunt, written in dialogue balloon as *mu*, or stony silence, represented by five vertical dots. Golgo is the embodiment of *mushin*, the *Zen* concept of the transcended, a moral state" (79). Like Golgo, D too responds to situations with *mu*, a Zen "stony silence."

29. Caroline J. S. Picart, "The Third Shadow and Hybrid Genres: Horror, Humor, Gender and Race in Alien Resurrection," *Communication and Critical/Cultural Studies* 1.4 (2004): 18–19.

30. Stephen Prince, *The Warrior's Camera: The Cinema of Akira Kurosawa* (Princeton: Princeton University Press, 1999), 147.

31. Schodt, *Manga! Manga*, 30.

32. Schodt, *Manga! Manga*, 30.

33. Erle Ernst, *Three Japanese Plays from the Traditional Theatre* (London: Oxford University Press, 1959), 4.

Index

Abbas, Ackbar, 205, 207, 211
Abbott and Costello Meet Frankenstein
  (film), ix, 17–18
abjection, horror and, 190
addiction cycle, 58
Adjani, Isabelle, 152*f*, 154
aesthetics: of cyberpunk, 281–85; issues
  in, 263–64, 270, 275; of South Asian
  film, 233n95
African Americans: and *Blacula*, 19–36;
  and cultural revolution, 22–23, 32;
  and serial killers, 41
Ahab, Captain, 87
Aileen: Life and Death of a Serial Killer
  (film), 100
Akiko, 241–42, 270–71
alchemy, in *Dracula in Pakistan*, 188
Alfie (film), 139
Allen, Robert, 264, 276n5
ambiguity: moral, vampires and,
  137–40; *pontianak* and, 168, 170, 175
An American Werewolf in London (film),
  57
An American Werewolf in Paris (film), 57
angel of mercy, 110n23
anime: *Blood: The Last Vampire*, 242,
  245–47; *Vampire Hunter D*, 242–44,
  279–93; *Vampire Princess Miyu*, 242,
  244–45

anti-Semitism, and vampires, 127–28,
  292n19
The Ape Man (film), 17
Arata, Stephen D., 126n49
Argentina, 11
Armstrong, Hugh, 145
Armstrong, Robert, 5
Arnold, Tracy, 43
Asian film: *Dracula in Pakistan*,
  187–202; Hong Kong, 203–33; Stein
  on, 235–60; Toho Dracula Trilogy,
  261–78; *Vampire Hunter D*, 279–93
assimilation: Borg and, 77–92; *Dracula
  in Pakistan* and, 196
Asylum (film), 137
Attila the Hun, 129–30
Atwill, Lionel, 4
Auerbach, Nina, 124n24
Auslin, Michael, 268
Austria, 116–17
authenticity, moral, and Asian film,
  236–42
Azzopardi, John, 158

Baba, Shuhaimi, 167, 176
Badley, Linda, 175, 180
bad-rooh, 190, 193
Baker, Roy Ward, 136–37, 149n11, 213,
  236, 248–49

295

London, 150n12, 150n17, 276n3; *A Bite of Love* and, 220; *Death Line* and, 145; *Dracula A.D. 1972* and, 138–40; Lucendo on, 121; Whitechapel, 128, 276n3
love: in *Nosferatu the Vampyre*, 155; Romanticism on, 156, 159
Löwensohn, Elina, 52
Lucas, Henry Lee, 41–44
Lucas, Tim, 270, 273–74
Lucendo, Santiago, 115–26
Lucy: Cain on, 132; in *Nosferatu the Vampyre*, 152f, 155–56, 159; Nystrom on, 65–66, 68–70, 73–74
Lugosi, Bela, 4, 8–9, 17–18, 276n2
Luk, Jamie, 203
Lüke, Martina G., 153–64
Lung Chan, 215
Lust for a Vampire (film), 242, 267
Lynch, David, 42

M (film), 40
Macau, 204, 219
Macaulay, Charles, 20f
machines, and horror, 77, 79–80
Macias, Patrick, 266
The Magnificent Seven (film), 292n28
Mai Kwei, 213
mail-order wife, serial killer, 110n23
mak yong, 179–80, 185n29
Malay culture, *pontianak* in, 167–85
Malkovich, John, 163n17
Manners, David, 6
Mansell, Carol, 45
Marchetti, Gina, 217
Marshall, William, 20f, 23–29, 31, 33
Martin (film), 99
Marx, Karl, 206
Mary Shelley's Frankenstein (film), 102, 107
mass killers, 57
Matheson, Richard, 48, 99
Maysles, Albert, 144
Maysles, David, 144

McGann, William, 7
McGee, Vonetta, 20f
McKay, Craig, 49
McNaughton, John, 42
media, vampires and, 206
Medicine Ball Caravan (film), 142
Megibben, Artie, 55–56
Melford, George, 11
Mérimée, Prosper, 123n7
Meyer, Carla, 105
Micheaux, Oscar, 19
Miike Takashi, 291n7
military, and vampires, 246–47
Mina: Nystrom on, 63, 65–66, 68–71, 74–75; in *Sequel to Dracula*, 11
Mr. Vampire (*Goeng si sin sang*; film), 203, 207–8, 215–17, 252–53
Mr. Vampire 2 (*Goeng si ga chuk*; film), 220
Miyaguchi, Seiji, 292n28
Miyamoto Musashi, 286
modernity: and China, 209–10; counterculture and, 143–44; Deleuze on, 194; and Hong Kong, 203–33; and Japan, 268–69
Mogen, David, 283–85
Mohd, Ghouse Nasuruddin, 179–80
Moldavians, 129
Monster (film), 93–112
monstrous, xii; counterculture and, 137, 145; *Dracula in Pakistan* and, 195–96; in Japanese film, 269; *pontianak* and, 171–72; and women, 66
Monzaemon Chikamatsu, 286
Moore, Tyria, 102, 104
moral ambiguity, vampires and, 137–40
moral authenticity, and Asian film, 236–42
Moreland, Sean, 187–202
Moretti, Franco, 215, 282
Morris, Meaghan, 210
Morrison, Helen, 57
mother: *pontianak* as, 171; and serial killer, 45

About the Editors and Contributors

John Edgar Browning is the coauthor (with Caroline Joan [Kay] Picart) of *The Dracula Film, Comic Book, and Game Sourcebook* (forthcoming). Recent works also include several published and forthcoming book chapters and reviews, journal articles, and encyclopedic entries on *Dracula*, vampires, and horror in such scholarly venues as *Film & History, Studies in the Fantastic, Dead Reckonings: A Review Magazine for the Horror Field, Asian Gothic: Essays on Literature, Film and Anime* (2008), and *The Encyclopedia of the Vampire* (forthcoming). He is completing a PhD at Louisiana State University, where he also teaches courses on composition, monstrosity, and identity politics.

Caroline Joan (Kay) Picart is a scholar, critic, and author of thirteen published and forthcoming books. She has been a professor of philosophy, biology, English, and film, across the Philippines, South Korea, and various parts of the United States for twenty-one years. Recent projects include a coauthored book with John Edgar Browning, *The Dracula Film, Comic Book, and Game Sourcebook* (forthcoming); a coedited book with Cecil Greek, *Monsters In and Among Us: Towards a Gothic Criminology* (2007); a coauthored book with David Frank, *Frames of Evil: Holocaust as Horror in American Film* (2006); *From Ballroom to DanceSport: Aesthetics, Athletics and Body Culture* (2005); and *The Holocaust Film Sourcebook* (2004). Since August 2008, she has produced and hosted her own radio show, which boasts over two million monthly listeners, nationally and internationally.

—◦∾◦—

Jimmie Cain, professor of English and Writing Center director at Middle Tennessee State University, has published and presented papers on the subjects

311

of vampires, Dracula, Bram Stoker, film, gender studies, and race, in such journals as *West Georgia Review*, *Pynchon Notes*, *Balkanistica*, *Critical Studies in Television*, *Review of Contemporary Fiction*, and *Film Criticism*. His article "With the Unspeakables, *Dracula*, and Russophobia: Tourism, Racism, and Imperialism" was published in *Dracula: The Shade and the Shadow—A Critical Anthology* (Ed. Elizabeth Miller, 1998), and his most recent book was *Bram Stoker and Russophobia* (2006).

Justin Everett is assistant professor of English at the University of the Sciences in Philadelphia, where he directs the Writing Center and teaches in a sciences-based writing program. In addition to courses in first-year writing, Dr. Everett teaches advanced courses in argumentation, scientific writing, rhetoric of science, evolutionary linguistics, and science fiction. His research interests include the application of evolutionary theory to writing theory, science fiction studies, and popular culture. Along with Dr. Robert Lamm of Arkansas State University, he has written *Dynamic Argument* (2007). His most recent publications include a book chapter titled "Fan Culture and the Recentering of *Star Trek*," in *The Influence of Star Trek on Television, Film and Culture* (2008) edited by Lincoln Geraghty. He regularly reviews nonfiction for the SFRA Review for the Science Fiction Research Association.

Cecil Greek is associate professor of criminology at Florida State University, and the director of the college's online master's degree program and the summer program in Prague. His books include *Monsters In and Among Us: Towards a Gothic Criminology* (2007), *The Religious Roots of American Sociology* (1992), and *Exploring Criminal Justice* (forthcoming). He has also published numerous book chapters on the subjects of horror, crime, the Gothic, visual criminology, and serial killing, in addition to numerous articles in such journals as *Journal of Criminal Justice Education*, *Journal of Criminal Justice and Popular Culture*, *Communication and Critical/Cultural Studies*, and *Crime, Media, Culture*. His research interests focus on media coverage of crime and criminal justice and what responses such coverage produces, and he has written on antipornography crusading, the use of forfeiture penalties, and cybercrime.

Dale Hudson is a visiting assistant professor of film studies in the Department of English at Amherst College. His research focuses on cinema and new media in relation to the political economies of globalization. Dale's dissertation considers vampire films, both US- and foreign-made, as allegories of race and nation in an increasingly globalized cultural marketplace. Also, his work appears, or is forthcoming, in the journals *Screen*, *Journal of Modern Jewish*

Studies, Studies in Documentary Film, Journal of Film and Video, and the anthology *The Persistence of Whiteness: Race and Contemporary Hollywood Cinema* (2007). He is co-curator of the online exhibits "Undisclosed Recipients" (2007) and "ubuntu.kuqala" (2008) for the Finger Lakes Environmental Film Festival.

Paul R. Lehman, who earned a PhD from Lehigh University, 1976, is a university professor emeritus in the Department of English, and a former dean of the Graduate College, at the University of Central Oklahoma. His teaching experience spans a wide range of subjects including American literature, ethnic American literature, Black American literature, short stories, American fiction, contemporary themes as literature, and Chaucer. He has lectured throughout the state of Oklahoma as well as in other states across America. He has published scholarly books, scholarly and creative articles, poetry, short stories, interviews, books, and book reviews. Other recent publications are *The Development of a Black Psyche in the Works of John Oliver Killens* and *The Making of the Negro in Early American Literature*. He is active in both academic and community service. He is also listed in *Who's Who among Black Americans*, *Who's Who in American Education*, and *Who's Who among American Teachers*.

Santiago Lucendo, a doctoral graduate in art history from the Universidad Complutense de Madrid and a master's graduate of the Faculty of Fine Arts, has conducted investigational projects such as "Representaciones del Mal y la violencia en el arte y la cultura contemporánea" and "Arte y política." His dissertation, titled *El vampiro como imagen reflejo: Estereotipo del horror en la modernidad*, examines vampire stereotypes and was financed by a four-year government grant. Some of his publications include "Sobre algunos Lugares del Mal en la cultura moderna: La geografía del vampiro" in *Imágenes de la violencia* (ed. Valeriano Bozal, 2005); "Vampiros" in the collection *El Jardín Ameno* (2005); and "El Vampiro y el Poder" in *Arte y naturaleza* (November–December 2004).

Martina G. Lüke studied German, history, and education at the University of Hamburg; the University of Osnabrück, Germany; and at the University of California at Berkeley. She received her PhD at the University of Hamburg in 2005 after finishing her first and second Staatsexamen in 2000 and 2002. She is a doctoral candidate (ABD) at the University of Connecticut. Her areas of research include Romanticism, German and comparative modernism, modern history, and film.

Sean Moreland, a lecturer at the University of Ottawa, completed his PhD at the University of Ottawa in the spring of 2008, where he was also a part-time professor. His doctoral thesis is titled *Cartographies of the Abyss: Tropics of Sub-limity in Charles Brockden Brown and Edgar Allan Poe*. He has presented papers on the subjects of British horror and censorship at conferences in Canada. He has also published poetry in venues including *The Malahat Review*, *NoD Magazine*, *Bywords*, and the *Ottawa Arts Review*, and was the recipient of the 2007 John Newlove Poetry Award.

Paul Newland is an AHRC Postdoctoral Research Fellow in film at the University of Exeter (United Kingdom). He is also an associate lecturer at the University of Plymouth. His first monograph, *The Cultural Construction of London's East End: Urban Iconography, Modernity and the Spatialisation of Englishness*, was published in Amsterdam (2008). He has also published on 1970s British cinema, cinema and the city, British television and contemporary British fiction, and has forthcoming articles on Joseph Losey and Harold Pinter, Iain Sinclair, Aki Kaurismäki, and Robin Hardy's *The Wicker Man*.

Andrew Hock-Soon Ng obtained his PhD from the University of Western Australia. His research interest includes the Gothic and postcolonial literature. He is the author of *Dimensions of Monstrosity in Contemporary Narratives* (2004) and *Interrogating Interstices* (2007), and the editor of *Asian Gothic* (2008) and *The Poetics of Shadows* (forthcoming 2008). He is completing a manuscript that looks at the role of religion in English-language Malaysian literature. He teaches contemporary fiction and postcolonial writing at Monash University Malaysia.

Lisa Nystrom is working toward her PhD in literature at Deakin University in Geelong, Australia. She has concentrations in both critical and creative writing, and she first approached the topic of *Dracula* when writing her honors thesis on "Women in the Gothic Genre."

Summer Pervez teaches primarily South Asian literature and literary theory in the Department of English at the University College of the Fraser Valley. She holds a BA and MA from the University of Western Ontario and a PhD from the University of Ottawa and has previously taught courses at both institutions. Her publications include work on Salman Rushdie, Homi Bhabha, Wole Soyinka, Naguib Mahfouz, and Hanif Kureishi, among others. Her current research interests—an extension of her doctoral work—include the philosophy of Gilles Deleuze, film and film theory, British South Asian diaspora literature, as well as global terrorism.

Gary D. Rhodes, formerly an assistant professor at the University of Oklahoma Film and Video Studies Program, is lecturer of film studies at The Queen's University in Belfast, Northern Ireland. His nine books include *Lugosi: His Life in Films, on Stage, and in the Hearts of Horror Lovers* (1997); *White Zombie: Anatomy of a Horror Film* (2002); *Bela Lugosi, Dreams and Nightmares* (2007); *Horror at the Drive-In: Essays in Popular Americana* (2002); *Docufictions* (2006); and *Edgar G. Ulmer: Detour on Poverty Row* (Lexington Books, 2008). Rhodes was also writer-director of numerous documentary films, including *Fiddlin' Man* (1993), *Lugosi: Hollywood's Dracula* (1997), and *Banned in Oklahoma* (2003). He is working on a book about the origins of the US horror film.

Nicholas Schlegel is a doctoral candidate and instructor in the Department of Communication at Wayne State University, where he conducts research on horror, cult, and exploitation cinema with a global emphasis. He balances critical studies with video production work; his latest film is a documentary that focuses on the DVD distribution company Synapse Films and areas of exploitation cinema in general. His dissertation examines the "horror boom" experienced in late-Francoist and post-Francoist Spain during the late 1960s and 1970s. In Spring 2008, he conducted archival research on this topic at the Ministry of Culture in Madrid, Spain.

Wayne Stein is professor of English and assistant chair in the Department of English at the University of Central Oklahoma, where he enjoys teaching classes on kung fu films, Chinese cinematic vampires, Asian American literature, Asian ghost and vampire lore, Vietnam War cinema and fiction, and the films of Bruce Lee. He edited and cowrote *Fresh Takes* (2008), a rhetoric/reader, with Deborah Israel and Pam Washington. With James Dolph and cartoonist Cary Stringfield, he also wrote *Languaging Force X* (2007), a cyberpunk role-playing game for writers wherein some adventures containing vampires appear. His chapter "Stanley Kwan's Centre Stage (1992): Postmodern Reflections of the Mirror in the Mirror" appeared in *Docufictions* (2006), a collection by Gary D. Rhodes and John Parris Springer. He is using films like *The Good, The Bad and the Weird* (2008) and *Sukiyaki Western Django* (2008) to develop a steampunk role-playing game for composition courses, which will incorporate various vampires and "hungry ghosts" and clashes between Eastern and Western cultures during the eighteenth and nineteenth centuries.